Buying [Retail Is Stupid!]

"*Buying Retail Is Stupid!* has [...] one of [...] selling regional books."

Entrepreneur magazine

". . . for those of us who like to feel as though we're saving money every time we make a purchase, this book is just what you're looking for."
Newhall Signal

". . . an invaluable directory for serious bargain hunters."
L.A. West magazine

"If the word 'sale' sends shivers of excitement up your spine, then *Buying Retail Is Stupid!* may be just the shopping companion you've been looking for."
Valley Magazine

"I've literally saved hundreds of dollars in time, gas, and money from the information contained in this book, and I've given copies to my friends, too."
John Woodard
Hollywood Hills

"We saved about $850 on tile we needed to remodel our home."
Charles and Valerie Christian
Rancho Cucamonga

"Thank you for putting together such a great book. My son recently got married, and I can't tell you how many times we referred to your book. We used it for clothing, flowers, craft supplies, etc. It saved us so much money, as well as time."
Sharyn Robinson
Downey

"I used the coupon in the back of your book to save additional money on some decorative items I bought. I never heard of the store before, and they had the largest selection I ever saw."
Celeste Anlauf
Los Angeles

"Many is the time I've gone to furniture, food, and clothing stores recommended by your book—very helpful."
Len Lesser
Burbank

"I found a place in your book that sells flowers in single stems and bunches at unbelievable prices. Now when I entertain, my house is brightened with fresh flowers for less than the cost of one flower arrangement."
Marguerite Wise
Santa Ana

BUYING
RETAIL IS
STUPID!

Southern California

The Discount Guide to Buying Everything
at up to 80% Off Retail

TRISHA KING AND DEBORAH NEWMARK

CB

CONTEMPORARY BOOKS

A TRIBUNE COMPANY

Library of Congress Cataloging-in-Publication Data

King, Trisha.
    Buying retail is stupid! : Southern California : the discount guide
to buying everything at up to 80% off retail / Trisha King and
Deborah Newmark. — [Rev. & expanded 1997–1998 ed.]
      p.   cm.
    Previous eds. published by Newmark Management Institute.
    Includes index.
    ISBN 0-8092-3136-0
    1. Shopping—California, Southern—Guidebooks.
2. California, Southern—Guidebooks.   I. Newmark, Deborah.
II. Title.
TX336.5.C2K55   1996
380.1'45'000257949—dc20   96-19643
                                                  CIP

Cover design by Scott Rattray

Important Notice: The authors have taken great care and made all
reasonable efforts to ensure the accuracy of the information in this
book. Nevertheless, there is the chance that an error may have
occurred, or circumstances may have changed. Please check the
information with the listed businesses before visiting them and before
making purchases. Advice, tips, and strategies presented in this book
should be used as a guide and not be relied upon as a substitute for
the reader's own experience, judgment, and common sense in buying
goods and services and in making decisions. The authors, publisher,
distributors, and other entities connected with this book do not assume
any responsibility or liability in connection with the information
contained herein or the use to which it is put.

To our loved ones
for their unfailing encouragement, support, and patience.
To our readers,
who have supported us since 1983.
To the media,
who have provided us with numerous opportunities
to inform consumers about
how and where to shop smart and save money.

Acknowledgments

To produce a book of this scope, magnitude, and length requires the dedicated efforts and teamwork of many individuals. The authors thank all those who have participated in this effort and contributed to its completion.

Thanks to the following persons who, at different stages, contributed to data collection, processing, or proofreading activities: Monica Alvarez, Cynthia Citron, Ellen Erwin, Kathy Flood, Brian Lasky, Beth Lawrence, Eileen Lizer, David Newmark, Taylor Raymond, Janet Segal, and Elise Sloan.

Special thanks to Kathy Arft, who supervised the work of the part-time staff involved in the above-mentioned tasks and coordinated interactions among authors and all other participants. In this role, Kathy was the glue that held things together and the grease that kept things moving.

Much appreciated has been Steve Gussman's advice and guidance throughout the planning, design, and production stages of each edition.

We are also grateful to Norman Horowitz for his valuable insights as our unofficial media advisor since the project's inception.

Thanks to Kara Leverte, senior editor at Contemporary Books, for setting up a workable structure and whose enthusiasm and suggestions got us off to a good start. We are also indebted to Kathy Willhoite, managing editor at Contemporary Books, who worked very effectively with us during the final stages of the project. Her attention to detail and accuracy added to the quality of the book.

Many thanks to our agent, Stan Corwin, whose confidence in our vision brought the project to fruition and also for his ongoing encouragement and guidance.

Trisha King   Deborah Newmark

CONTENTS

Overview

SMART SHOPPING   1

1 Strategies for Saving Money and Time

4 DIRECTORY OF DISCOUNT MAIL-ORDER COMPANIES   359
Money-Saving Shopping Without Leaving Home

PREFACE

It's hard to believe, but it's true! With the publication of the fifth edition of *Buying Retail Is Stupid!*, we celebrate our ninth anniversary of bringing discount shopping information to economy-minded Southern Californians.

We are excited and proud to share with you our latest, completely revised smart shopping guide. In these pages, we provide access to the largest number of discount businesses in Southern California in one publication, including hundreds of new discoveries, plus many new discount mail-order companies nationwide. We describe where and how to buy everything from A to Z at up to 80% off retail—and don't forget to save even more money by using the *Buying Retail Is Stupid!* discount coupons and senior discounts available to our readers.

We continue to write our weekly bargain column for the *Los Angeles Daily News* and particularly value the education we receive while interviewing and researching new discount stores. It gives us an inside view of a large variety of businesses, industries, and products and enables us to pass on this information to the consumer public.

Also, we are very appreciative of the continued flow of letters from our readers, which adds to the richness of the book. A young woman wrote to us recently about how she purchased a wedding gown at great savings. She explained that, although this would probably be the most sentimental dress she would ever buy, she was still looking for a bargain—especially since she would wear it only once and was tight for money. After locating a discount store in our book, she writes, "I walked in with a few photos from a magazine and walked out with my wedding gown and veil. I saved $500 off the retail price, plus an additional $25 with the coupon in the back of the book." Our response to her was, "Good going—great way to start a marriage."

We trust that this fifth edition of *Buying Retail Is Stupid!* will continue to help all consumers find the right product, at the right price, with the greatest convenience.

We wish you happy shopping and happy savings!

Trisha King   Deborah Newmark

INTRODUCTION

HOW TO GET THE MOST OUT OF THIS BOOK

Welcome to *Buying Retail Is Stupid!*®—your window into the exciting world of discount shopping. The following pages should make it easier for you to use this book and get the most out of it.

Using the Book
This is not a book that you are going to read in large chunks like a novel. It is a reference book, a manual, a guide—but one that you will refer to frequently. Since everyone shops for something—daily, weekly, monthly, throughout the year—the more you use the book, the more money you will save and the easier, more efficient, and more pleasurable your shopping experience will be.

First Steps
Given the wealth of information in the book, initially you will want to familiarize yourself with the contents. We suggest you proceed as follows:

- Review the Contents. This will give you a feel for the book's totality.

- Skim Chapter 1, *Smart Shopping*, for a quick overview of some of the basic principles, strategies, and approaches to value-oriented, economy-minded shopping.

- Skim Chapter 2, *Grass Roots Bargain Outlets*, to get an overview of how to get great "buys" and avoid pitfalls when shopping for bargains at garage sales, thrift shops, resale stores, swapmeets, and flea markets.

- Read the following brief descriptions of Chapters 3, 4, and 5 to learn what's in these chapters:

  Chapter 3, *Directory of Discount Stores and Outlets*, describes each company with enough information for you to know what it has to offer—products and brands it carries, how it operates, hours and days, services offered, where it's located, the kind of discounts available. Many stores sell items you will not find in the mall and at prices that will make you smile.

  Chapter 4, *Directory of Discount Mail-Order Companies*, contains brief descriptions of several hundred companies offering the possibility of big shopping savings without leaving home—these include names, addresses, telephone numbers, products sold, and amount of discounts offered. The introduction describes the best ways to buy by mail and how to use the chapter.

Chapter 5, *Directory of Consumer Resources*, will introduce you to more than 35 publications that can serve as your personal advisor on buying any item on the market with confidence regarding price and value—including many high-ticket items such as automobiles, appliances, homes, clothing, and much more. Many of the publications are inexpensive or free—an excellent way to start your own personal "smart shoppers" reference library.

- Review briefly the indexes at the back of the book to get an idea of how to locate anything you want quickly and easily.

- Complete the *Smart Shopper's Quiz*. You'll find it fun to take and score, and will learn how smart you are or could be at "buying more for less."

Ongoing Actions
After completing the initial steps above, you'll have a good idea of the contents of the book. The following are ways to use it on an ongoing basis, at your own speed, and within your own time schedule and needs.

- Write for free and low-cost publications in Chapter 5 and start your own bargain hunter's reference library.

- Before purchasing a high-priced product, check Chapter 5 for publications that might help you become more knowledgeable. You usually can consult the publication in a public library. In some cases you may want to purchase it—if the cost is very low and/or you expect to get much use out of it.

- Reread Chapter 1 on smart shopping and bargain tips. This time make notes on the most important strategies, ideas, and tips that you will want to incorporate into your daily, weekly, monthly, or yearly shopping behavior. Keep them on 3 × 5 cards or any way that makes them easily accessible at the appropriate time. This may include reviewing them from time to time.

- Call the national headquarters of major off-price megastores and clearance centers and request a list of store locations throughout the United States. This will indicate which ones are in your local area and which ones you might be able to visit while traveling.

★ BONUS DISCOUNT COUPONS

The last section of *Buying Retail Is Stupid!* contains several hundred discount coupons. These coupons represent, for the most part, additional percentage or dollar discounts on the products sold by participating stores and outlets described in Chapter 3, *Directory of Discount Stores and Outlets*. Using these extra-bonus coupons—available exclusively to *Buying Retail Is Stupid!* purchasers—can save you a considerable amount of additional money yearly. Before making a purchase, check the index listing all companies offering these discount coupons and the store descriptions in Chapter 3. Remember to take the coupon with you when visiting the store.

♦ SENIOR DISCOUNTS

More than 125 discount stores and outlets in Chapter 3 offer special Senior Discounts. These discounts are obtained merely by showing proof of age. The specific age required is different for each store and is indicated in the description of the store in the chapter. Some of the stores accept the bonus discount coupon, described above, in addition to the Senior Discount; others do not. The store description indicates when the bonus discount is not valid with the Senior Discount.

CHECK BEFORE SHOPPING

- Things change. Always call and check with companies on availability of products and locations and hours of stores before your shopping trip. Where stores indicate additional locations, the hours are frequently different.

Concluding Thoughts
You have invested in a great money-saving tool. The more you use it, the more money and time you'll save and the more fun you will have shopping. If you have questions or make some great bargain discoveries, we'd love to hear from you.

Best wishes!

GLOSSARY OF DISCOUNT TERMS

The following are some of the terms most commonly used in connection with discount shopping.

- **Auction:** A public sale in which goods are sold to the highest bidder.
- **Auctioneer:** A person who conducts sales by means of an auction.
- **Bankrupt Stock:** When a business goes bankrupt, the stock on hand is sold in lots at lower than wholesale or manufacturer's prices in order to pay off creditors.
- **Close-out:** Usually odds and ends or last season's merchandise sold at discounted prices in order to make room for new inventory.
- **Cost:** Either the price incurred manufacturing an item or the wholesale price a business pays for items to be resold.
- **Cost Plus:** The cost of an item to the dealer plus his or her percentage of profit. When calculating cost, a dealer is likely to also include operating expenses—shipping, rent, advertising, etc.—and then add an override.
- **Coupon:** Specified discount or rebate on a form redeemable in person or by mail.
- **Department Store Outlet** (also clearance center or off-price outlet): Location in which merchandise from all company stores is brought together (either in a separate facility or in a designated area of one of their larger stores) to be sold at reduced prices. Includes items that aren't selling, seconds, slightly damaged goods, returns, floor models, previous season's merchandise, demonstration models, and mismatched goods.
- **Discontinued or Manufacturer's Close-out:** A product no longer being manufactured that is sold at a discount to make room for current goods. Quality of the merchandise is not affected.
- **Discount:** A percentage or dollar amount reduced from the manufacturer's suggested retail price.
- **Discount Business:** One that sells merchandise regularly at a percentage or dollar amount below the manufacturer's suggested retail price.
- **Discount Clearance Center** (also called outlet or off-price outlet): Special center or outlet at which products from retail chain stores are sold at discounted prices (see department store outlet above).
- **Discount Mail-Order Company:** A company that sells products at discount prices to customers who order through catalogs by mail, telephone, or fax.
- **Discount Retail Chain Store** (also called off-price store): Discount store selling direct to consumers and having multiple locations—sometimes throughout a city, but also statewide or nationally; includes general merchandise and specialty stores.

- **Flea Market and Swapmeet:** Groups of vendors in individually rented areas. Low overhead usually means lower mark-ups on new and used merchandise. Sellers will often negotiate price.

- **Floor Sample:** A model used for display in the store.

- **Freight Damage:** During shipment items can be broken, burned, chipped, marred, or otherwise affected. The merchandise may be noticeably damaged, but often it is in top condition.

- **Garage Sale:** Accumulated unwanted "stuff" people sell at very low prices in front of their homes or apartments. Sometimes excellent "buys" can be found.

- **In-season Buying:** Whereas most retailers buy merchandise months in advance (summer items are purchased in winter), discounters often purchase goods during the season (winter items are bought in winter), relieving the manufacturer of goods from canceled orders or overruns.

- **Inventory Reduction:** A big sale by a business to improve cash flow rapidly and make room for new merchandise. Also, reduced stock means that fewer worker hours will be needed to take inventory.

- **Irregular:** Merchandise with minor imperfections, often barely discernible.

- **Job Lot:** Miscellaneous goods gathered for sale as one quantity.

- **Jobber:** A person who buys or imports quantity goods from manufacturers and then sells the merchandise to dealers.

- **Liquidated Stock:** When a business is in financial trouble, its goods are sold by the lot at less than wholesale prices to convert assets into quick cash.

- **Loss Leader:** An item purposely priced low to attract customers into the store.

- **Manufacturer's Outlet:** A store containing a single manufacturer's products at discounted prices. The merchandise may include discontinued lines, unsold merchandise, overruns, irregulars, seconds, and sometimes new lines made specifically for the outlet.

- **Manufacturer's Outlet Mall:** A number of outlet stores located together.

- **Membership Club:** Warehouse store, superstore, or other business that requires a small annual membership fee (sometimes for a specific category of customers—e.g., government employees, teachers, businesses, or the public at large).

- **Megastore:** Generic term used to describe warehouse stores, superstores, and membership clubs similar in their extremely large facility size, quantity, and variety of name-brand and private-label products offered at substantially discounted prices—either within a special product category (office supplies, home building) or in a general merchandise store offering just about everything.

- **Odd Lot:** A small quantity of unsold merchandise that remains after orders have been filled at the wholesale level.

- **Overrun:** An excess of quantity over the actual amount the manufacturer wanted to produce.

- **Past-season or Last-season Goods:** Items left over from a previous season.

- **Rebate:** A refund, usually a certain dollar amount, offered from the manufacturer when you purchase one of their products.

- **Resale Store:** Generally, a store selling used clothing, but some also sell used furniture and miscellaneous items. Quality varies from store to store. Some stores will carry only certain brands; others carry anything and everything. Goods in most stores are sold on consignment. Some items may be famous brand-name products that are like new—i.e., used once or not at all.

- **Retail:** The selling of goods directly to the customer or end user generally at or close to the manufacturer's suggested price.

- **Sample:** An item used by a salesperson or manufacturer to show to prospective buyers, but not for sale itself.

- **Second:** An item with either cosmetic or functional flaws.

- **Suggested Retail Price:** The price of an item the manufacturer recommends the retailer charge the consumer.

- **Surplus or Overstock:** A quantity in excess of what is needed by a dealer or manufacturer.

- **Thrift Store:** A store in which second-hand items are resold at very low prices.

- **Wholesale Price:** The actual cost of an item to the retailer.

- **Warehouse Store:** A very large facility—50,000- to 100,000-square-foot range—housing a department-store type business selling almost every product on the market from A to Z, in a no-frills, self-service atmosphere, including name-brand and private-label items, frequently in quantity packages at discount prices.

WANTED: FEEDBACK FROM READERS

We want to hear from YOU! If you know of any great discount businesses not already included in this book, please send us their names, addresses, and telephone numbers. We'd like to include them in future editions of *Buying Retail Is Stupid!* And if you have any comments about any of the shops listed, we'd like to hear those, too. This book is for YOU. Please write to us at *Buying Retail Is Stupid!*, P.O. Box 872, Tarzana, CA 91357.

HOW TO BE INCLUDED IN THIS BOOK

Discount stores and outlets and mail-order discount companies are included in this book at the sole discretion of the authors. No fees are required or accepted. If you operate a discount store or outlet in Southern California or a discount mail-order business anywhere in the United States and wish to be included in the next edition, either write to us for a questionnaire or send us the details of your business following the format in this edition. Address correspondence to: *Buying Retail Is Stupid!*, P.O. Box 872, Tarzana, CA 91357.

LEGEND
Explanation of Symbols Used in Book

Additional Locations

Whenever any of the listed stores has from one to five other locations in Southern California, the cities, addresses, and the telephone numbers have been included following the description of the store. Where any store has six or more additional locations, only the number of locations is indicated. In this case, please consult your local telephone directory for a store located near you. Note: Store hours may vary from location to location. Check with store for hours.

Credit Card Abbreviations

AE	= American Express	MC	= MasterCard
DC	= Diners Club	OPT	= Optima
DISC	= Discover	V	= Visa

Other forms of payment are also listed if a vendor doesn't accept credit cards.

Stores Accepting Coupons

Stores that accept *Buying Retail Is Stupid!* discount coupons are designated by a star (★) placed at the end of the store name in the store directory chapter, and in the index.

Stores Offering Senior Discounts

Stores offering senior discounts are designated by a diamond (♦) in the text and index.

1

SMART SHOPPING
STRATEGIES FOR
SAVING MONEY AND TIME

SMART SHOPPING

STRATEGIES FOR SAVING MONEY AND TIME

Smart shopping enables a consumer to make wise decisions, spend less, and buy more with greater ease, convenience, and confidence in having received true value for every dollar spent. It involves formulating an approach to shopping and following it. The information in this book is designed to help all consumers become smart shoppers.

GOALS

The goals of a smart shopper include:

- **Saving money**
  Getting good "buys" by obtaining merchandise or services at the most favorable prices—below full retail.

- **Conserving time and energy**
  Locating discount opportunities close to home. Traveling only for multiple purchases, higher-ticket items, or special products.

- **Getting value for your money**
  The quality of a product must be consistent with, or even better than, what might be expected for the price you are paying. Cheaper is not a value purchase if the lower-priced "bargain" product lasts only half as long as it should or doesn't work well. Buying for value includes avoiding rip-offs by knowing what you are getting.

MISCONCEPTIONS ABOUT DISCOUNT SHOPPING

You might wonder how discounters can compete with the buying power of large retail operations such as department stores and supermarket chains. The answer involves a combination of factors: high sales volume which makes up for low profit margins, low overhead achieved by the absence of large corporate staffs and salaries, limited or no advertising, fewer personnel, less expensive locations, and no-frills offices. The buying approach of a discount operation is also different: flexible and unrestricted by established procedures, formulas, or traditions. This allows discounters to take advantage of opportunities to buy any product at any time of year. Finally, management is often closer to the operation and can keep expenses down by paying attention to detail.

3

Here are some of the truths behind misconceptions surrounding discount shopping.

Issue 1: Quantity and Location

Myth: Discount stores are few in number and are usually located in out-of-the-way, hard-to-find locations.

Truth: In larger cities such as Los Angeles, the opposite is true. There is an incredibly large number of discount entities, and they are everywhere— downtown areas, suburbs, main streets, back streets, exclusive areas, industrial parks, malls, small shopping centers, and manufacturer outlet parks.

Issue 2: Size and Type

Myth: Discount stores are generally small, "mom and pop" type operations.

Truth: On the contrary, a tremendous variety exists in the discount field including small, single-owner, one-item specialty stores; large specialty stores (of almost every kind: books, plants, clothes, food); small and large department-type stores selling everything; local and national chain stores; resale stores; manufacturer's outlets; membership warehouse companies; plus hundreds of mail-order, discount catalog businesses throughout the country.

Issue 3: Quality

Myth: Discount stores carry products of inferior quality—seconds or "knock offs" of name-brand goods.

Truth: Almost every top-quality and name-brand product can be purchased at discounts of from 20 to 80%. Some stores do carry seconds or slightly damaged goods, but these are usually marked. The buyer does, however, have to be careful of the occasional unscrupulous discounter who would attempt to pass these off as first quality.

Issue 4: Service and Atmosphere

Myth: When buying discount, you have to give up service and atmosphere.

Truth: In many of the larger operations, such as membership warehouse stores, staffs are smaller, and you'll do more waiting on yourself. But take a moment to consider: how much attention are you getting in the typical retail department store these days? The decor also will often be simple or barren. On the other hand, there are numerous discount stores where you will be waited on by the owners themselves or some dedicated employees. And many of them will be in beautiful settings where coffee, soft drinks, and snacks are served.

Issue 5: Selection

Myth: Limited selection is available when buying discount.

Truth: Almost everything produced, from A to Z, can be bought at a discount. The same is true for a considerable number of services. In large specialty stores that carry a wide selection in a single product category, you are more likely to find the size, color, and style you want than at a typical department store.

Issue 6: Convenience

Myth: To buy discount, you have to give up convenience and travel long distances to seek out stores that don't advertise.

Truth: With books such as *Buying Retail Is Stupid!* and weekly bargain columns such as the one Trisha and Deborah write for the *Daily News* in Los Angeles, the work has been done for you. They make it easy for you to find what you want at the right price. And frequently, you can find discount stores in the vicinity of your home or work. In addition, given the large number of discount mail-order companies, sometimes you don't even have to leave home to get a bargain.

Issue 7: Bargain Integrity

Myth: All merchandise marked "sale," "reduced," "regularly $250 now $62.50," "savings up to" always represent true bargains.

Truth: "Savings up to 80%" may refer to only one item in the store, with the rest at 5% or 10% off retail. "Reduced" may refer to a price excessively marked up originally and then discounted. "Regularly" may mean a price that is listed for only a brief period of time; otherwise, it's always on sale. This is not the rule but rather a practice of some less-than-honest merchants. By knowing what items are selling for at other stores, you can avoid being fooled by unscrupulous merchants.

ELEMENTS OF SMART SHOPPING

Time Is Money

Do you ever find yourself wishing that there were more hours in the day? The old adage "time is money" has never been more important. When it comes to shopping, let's review some simple ways to save time and money:

- Call ahead. After you've decided on a particular model of any given product, call the store to make certain they have it in stock. If they do, ask the clerk to put it on hold for you. The few minutes it takes to call can save you the round-trip drive to the store, including gas and wear and tear on your car as well as your psyche when you find out the item is not there.

- Check out your purchases before leaving the store. Regardless of what you are buying, look it over, plug it in, try it out. Don't wait until you get home. Returning items not only is a waste of travel time, but also includes the red tape of returning or exchanging an item.

Streamline Your Gift Giving

- Start your own "gift shop." Like millions of other Americans, every year we are faced with the problem or pleasure (depending on your point of view) of spending our hard-earned dollars on gifts for all sorts of occasions: birthdays; anniversaries; graduations; confirmations and bar mitzvahs; holidays such as Christmas and Hanukkah, Mother's, Father's, Valentine's, and Secretary's Days; going away-parties; hospital visits; and many others. Some are for the same people every year.

Many people frequently find themselves looking for a present at the last minute. Usually they feel rushed and wind up paying more than they had planned and sometimes not being especially satisfied with their choice. There is a way to deal with this situation that saves money and time and is fun, too. At any time during the year that we find a great bargain that could possibly be a gift for someone, we buy it, even though we may not have a particular person in mind at the time. In other words, we create our own "gift shop." When we need a gift for an occasion, the first place we look is in our own "shop."

Having your own gift shop is really a lot of fun. So, when we see a good buy that we can't use ourselves, we buy it anyway. You would be amazed at the great gifts to be had for $5, $10, and $20. And we almost never are rushing around at the last minute looking for a present.

- Buy greeting cards and wrapping paper at one time. Whenever you have to make a special trip to the store to buy a card or wrapping paper, including drive time, you probably are using an average of about one hour per occasion. Since you generally celebrate birthdays and anniversaries with the same friends and relatives every year, and can anticipate your needs, why not buy these items all at once? The savings in time and gas can really add up.

Take Advantage of Free Advice
In decision-making, it's important to distinguish between low-risk and high-risk decisions. In shopping, it's important to do the same for low-priced and high-priced purchases. Low-priced items do not require or merit as much consideration as high-ticket items. For these more important purchases, consult one or more resource books such as those listed in Chapter 5, *Directory of Consumer Resources*. Consult a friend who knows something about the item or check the phone book to locate a specialist. One or two calls may enable you to shop for your bargain with confidence.

Research Items
- Check your local library for the *Consumer Reports* rating of high-priced products in which you are interested.
- Check for features to look for and pitfalls to avoid in books such as the Better Business Bureau's *A to Z Buying Guide* and *The Frugal Shopper* by Ralph Nader. These books and others are described in Chapter 5.

Comparison Shop for Availability and Price
- Call retail stores to find out their prices; also consult newspaper ads.
- Check the Yellow Pages for the nearest locations of discount stores that are likely to carry the item.

- Check the Table of Contents of this book for possible sources of the item.
- Call discount stores to check on availability of items and prices. Some discount stores will not give a price on the phone; however, if you specify a price, they will usually tell you if they can beat it.

Comparison Shop for Favorable Store Policies
- Ask if the store guarantees lowest price and what proof is required to verify the offer you've received.
- Check on the return policy.
- Check on whether the item is in stock and the quantity available before going to the store.
- If the item is in short supply, ask to have it held for you.
- Compare with the prices of discount mail-order companies.

Establish Personal Relationships
- Select favorite store(s) and frequent them regularly.
- Establish a relationship with a particular salesperson and/or manager. They will level with you and give you useful information, advice, and personal attention.
- Have the store notify you when they have a special sale and when items or brands of interest to you arrive.

Plan Your Buys
- Identify discount stores that are near each other, such as a cluster of stores or an outlet mall; this way you can visit several on one trip.
- Find out the best time to buy certain items—for example, the January white sales that are mentioned in the Seasonal Shopping section that follows. Unless there is an urgent need, wait for the "best" time to buy.
- Buy only what you need—avoid buying a bargain item if you don't need it, unless it is for your own gift shop mentioned previously.

Talk Shopping
Talk smart shopping with your friends and acquaintances. At one time it was considered tasteless to mention prices or bargains, but in the '90s—called the "Bargain Hunting" decade by *USA Today*—it is the "in" thing to talk about a terrific "buy" or discount store you discovered. You'll be pleasantly surprised at how many good ideas you can get through talking with others. There's a wealth of information within yourself and your circle of friends. Something you take for granted might be unknown to someone else and vice versa. When you share an idea, a lead, or your latest bargain with someone, you'll probably get one or more back. Make "smart shopping" a habit; begin by making it a topic of conversation, and last but not least, have fun in the process.

SEASONAL SHOPPING

Retailers make their money on the wants and needs of their customers. Have you ever noticed how many different kinds of fans are for sale during hot weather? Go to the same store in the dead of winter and there is a much smaller selection, but that's the time to buy if you want bargain prices. During the sweltering summer heat, a company that specializes in air conditioning is going to be in demand and therefore, in most cases, has no problem getting full retail for an air conditioning unit.

All retailers have months when they can sell at full retail and months when they must drop their prices to make sales. Common sense tells us when certain goods are likely to go on sale. It's no surprise that Christmas cards, wrapping paper, and ribbons go on sale after Christmas and continue on sale during the month of January, but why appliances and linens go on sale during that month is not clear. Fortunately, we do not have to know the underlying reasons to take advantage of these off-season sales.

According to major retailers, shopping for in-season clothing (bathing suits in July) means you are actually buying off-season clothing because in July retailers are featuring fall clothes. We know this doesn't seem to make sense, but this is the formula for shopping in retail stores, because production schedules require retailers to buy two seasons in advance. In August stores are ordering goods for January.

A retailer must clear the shelves of goods toward the end of every season to make room for the coming season. The closer the next season approaches, the better the sale prices become on the current merchandise. You can save money by planning ahead and buying certain products off-season. Here are some things to keep in mind:

• Best buys when the weather starts to warm up: Winter clothing, winter sporting goods such as skis and ice skates, heating systems, beds, and toys. People tend to spend more time outside during warm weather, so household goods (china, linens, furniture) generally go on sale at this time.

• Best buys when the weather starts to cool down: Warm weather clothing, barbecues, bicycles, gardening tools, patio furniture, and outdoor sporting goods. At the end of the outdoor entertaining season, Labor Day sales feature barbecues and patio furniture. Wait until after the holiday to make your purchases—that is the time when prices will be rock bottom.

• After-holiday sales: Retailers usually drop their prices 50% the day after a holiday. That is the best time to pick up next year's holiday items. While retailers may have big ads in the newspaper featuring special holiday sales (Presidents' Day, Memorial Day, Valentine's Day), the "sale" prices are frequently minimal in savings and are used to entice you into the store to buy other goods at full retail.

GROCERY STORE SHOPPING

Since most of us eat every day, grocery shopping is an area where expenses or savings can add up. Here's how you can save money grocery shopping:

- Try to limit yourself to one day a week for shopping. The more times you enter the market, the more likely you are to purchase items on impulse.

- Shop from a list. This will also cut down on impulse buying.

- Watch food section newspaper ads once or twice a week. You'll save money planning your menus around specials. It's also an easy way to comparison shop.

- Coupons can save you money; however, unless you can really use a new item, stick to clipping coupons on products and brands you normally use.

- Take your calculator with you. Sometimes breaking prices down to individual units is the only way to tell which of two differently sized items is the best buy. We are led to believe that the bigger the container, the better the price, but sometimes that's not true. A small container of dishwashing liquid may run several cents an ounce higher than a larger one. But then again, it may not. Using your calculator removes the guessing.

- We all have our favorite brand names, but a lot of money can be saved by buying the store brands. The following are just a few items where the store brand is usually of similar quality but priced lower: ammonia; all-purpose, enriched, bleached flour; bleach; distilled white vinegar; granulated sugar and iodized table salt.

- There are a few places in the market to avoid. One of these places is the end-of-the-aisle product display. Manufacturers pay a premium to feature their products in these displays which are away from similar products, making price comparison difficult. They also want their products at eye-level on the shelves, so for lower prices, take a look at the top and bottom shelves. Markets, and other retailers with checkout lines, also make money on the impulse buys you make while waiting your turn in line.

Finally, recognize that supermarket scanners are not always correct. Pay attention to prices displayed on shelves and those that come up at the cash register. Prices change often, and many times the scanner has not been corrected. It's up to you, the consumer, to be observant. Some stores will even give you the item free if you've been incorrectly charged. Ask!

COUPONING

With prices continuing to go up, we suggest using coupons as another way to put extra money in your pocket. Today, in contrast to other times, we see more and more people sifting through their coupons at the grocery store. We've also been pleased to see many more men using coupons.

So what's the big deal about coupons? The big deal is saving money on food and sundry items that all families need. Some people think it's a waste of time to cut, sort, and use a coupon just to save 25¢ on a jar of mustard. Of course, 25¢ doesn't sound like a lot of money, but if you save 25¢ here and 50¢ there, it adds up. If you save a total of $12 a week using coupons, it doesn't seem like much money. But if you save $12 every week, in one year you'll have an extra $624. Saving $30 a week adds up to $1,560 in a year. That's not too bad.

Where Do You Get Coupons?
Coupons are very easy to find. Just about every newspaper in the country has glossy coupon inserts in the Sunday issue. In addition to offering cents-off, or even dollar-off coupons, these publications may contain forms you can fill out to request coupons through the mail. Most newspapers also have a special food section once a week with recipes, supermarket ads, and coupons. These special food sections usually come out on Wednesdays or Thursdays, depending on the newspaper.

Magazines geared toward women and families are another good source for coupons. *Family Circle, Good Housekeeping, Ladies Home Journal* and many other similar publications have brand-name coupons scattered throughout their pages.

Friends and family are also good resources for coupons. After going through our coupons and cutting out the ones we can use, we trade coupons with friends and relatives. This leads us to the number one rule in clipping coupons. Only clip coupons for things you normally use. Saving $1 on a $3 item that will never be eaten or used is a waste of money. One exception to the rule is clipping a coupon on an item you know someone else uses. For example, one of our sisters used a particular brand of disposable diapers and another had a favorite restaurant geared toward children. Whenever we saw a coupon for this particular brand of diapers, or for extra game tokens at the restaurant, we clipped them and gave them to our sisters.

To get more deeply involved in saving money with coupons, you can join a coupon club. Usually information about these clubs is posted on the community bulletin boards located in many local grocery stores.

What Do I Do with My Coupons?
There are many ways to file and sort coupons. Some people organize their coupons by dates, some by brand name, some by subject, and others lump them all together in a box. While we don't recommend the last method, do whatever you are comfortable with. We have found that arranging our coupons by subject works best for us.

To store your coupons, you might purchase an accordion file at a stationery store and label the sections, or buy a coupon holder through the mail that has everything needed to organize coupons to your specific needs. In addition to sections such as canned goods, dairy and deli products, snacks, frozen goods, soft drinks, and sundries, we have a section specifically for coupons that expire within the current month.

This brings us to another coupon rule. On any designated day toward the end of the month, it's a good idea to go through your coupons and pull out those that will expire in the coming month. On some coupons, it is nearly impossible to find the expiration date, while on others it is printed quite clearly. In order to make things easier, we highlight the expiration date on coupons with a florescent marker.

Shopping with Your Discount Coupons
Now that you have the coupons organized, you're ready to put them to good use. Always make a shopping list before going to the market. If you usually go to the same market, save time by making out your list in the order the products are arranged in the store. To the necessities on your list, add any items you can use that are on special at the market. You can find out what is on special by consulting the Sunday newspaper or the special food sections on Wednesdays or Thursdays. Next, go through your coupons and pull those that match items on your list. We have found it helpful to mark an asterisk next to those items on our list for which we have a discount coupon. Combining special sales with discount coupons can result in big savings.

Now that your list and coupons are ready, you're poised to hit the market. Be sure to take all coupons with you, not just the ones for items on your shopping list. You may find unadvertised specials at the store, and you'll be glad you have your coupons available. And remember, don't go grocery shopping on an empty stomach or you'll be tempted to buy unnecessary food.

Coupons and Loss Leaders
Although you aren't supposed to buy anything you don't really need, there is an exception to this rule—loss leaders. These are items sold at or below cost to entice you into the store. If your favorite grocery store is running a special loss leader and you have a coupon for the item, go for it.

This is a great way to get things for free. The supermarket we frequent doubles the face value of coupons, and we do our best to take advantage of loss leaders. Recently, a shaving gel was on special for $1.99 and we had several $1 off discount coupons for this product. Doubling the face value of the coupon meant a $2 discount, and although this market doesn't give money back when a doubled coupon exceeds the price of an item, we did walk away with several cans of shaving gel for free.

Taking advantage of loss leaders works best with sundry items. After all, a container of shaving cream or body lotion has a very long shelf life. Unless you have a big family that can eat everything before the expiration dates, you should stick to stocking up on non-perishable goods.

What About Rebates?

Many manufacturers provide rebate application blanks that you can send in along with a required proof of purchase and cash register receipt to receive cash, coupons, or gifts through the mail. There are people who have furnished their entire homes simply by saving money from rebates or gifts received from rebates. If you are interested in how to make extra money with rebates, here is some basic information:

- Proof of purchase: Any part of the packaging from box top to can label can be designated by its manufacturer as a proof of purchase; the one most commonly required is the bar code—the rectangle of black vertical lines on a package used by cashiers to scan prices.

- Organizing proofs of purchase: The best way to organize proofs of purchase is alphabetically by brand name. Because there is no brand name on the bar code, it helps to cut the brand name off the package of the product and staple it to the bar code before filing.

- Cash register receipts: Keep your cash register receipts accessible, as they will most likely be required in addition to the proof of purchase and rebate form.

Using coupons is a great way to add extra dollars to your savings account, child's college education fund, next year's vacation, or whatever it is you never seem to have enough money for. In the long run, the few hours a month that it takes to clip, sort, and utilize coupons pays off. Rebates can add considerably to your savings too, if you are willing to take the time required to pursue the process.

SHOPPING FOR CLOTHING

Clothing can take a chunk out of the individual or family budget. Since few of us can afford to buy an entirely new set of clothes every season, building a wardrobe of basics and staying away from fads are good strategies for saving money. To ensure that you will have the necessary clothes for all occasions, make a list of what constitutes a minimum, basic wardrobe for you. Consider the types of clothing, quantity of each, quality, and fabric as well as colors and seasonal wear. Obviously, this list will differ for each person according to work, lifestyle, personal taste, and income.

When shopping with your basic list in hand, you will be less likely to buy something you don't need or won't wear often or at prices you can't afford. You'll be able to scan the newspaper ads and use *Buying Retail Is Stupid!* with greater focus to get the best buys on your entire basic wardrobe. Once you have completed your basic wardrobe, ask yourself the following questions before making each new purchase:

• Will it go with anything else in my closet?
• Will I actually wear it more than once?
• Will it wear well?
• Will it resist soilage?
• Is it washable, or does it need special maintenance or dry cleaning?
• Is it within my planned price range for this type of item?

When you shop for clothes, make sure you are not only saving money, but also buying well-made items. If a shirt falls apart the first time you put it through a wash cycle, you have wasted your money. Here's a checklist to consult when purchasing clothing:

• Tug gently on the seam and zipper areas to make sure they've been completely sewn.
• All seams should be flat and even with no puckering.
• Stitching should be even, the smaller the better.
• Shoulders and armholes of jackets should be wrinkle-free.
• Jacket lapels should spring back into shape when you crumple them.
• Zippers should zip, lie flat, and be sewn in straight.
• Buttons should fit easily.
• Try on skirts or pants, and make sure you can sit comfortably in them.

It takes only a minute or two to go over a garment while you're at the store, and it sure beats finding out there's something wrong with your new outfit five minutes before leaving for work. Remember, with clothing, a little planning can save you a lot of money!

Shoes
When you buy shoes, make sure they are comfortable at the time of purchase. If the idea that they'll stretch out a bit and then they'll be perfect crosses your mind, go up a half size. Unless they are made of extremely soft leather, shoes should be comfortable right at the start. Also, buy your shoes toward the end of the day when your feet will be a bit larger. Many of us, especially women, are wearing our shoes too small. If you haven't had your feet measured since high school, we recommend you have it done the next time you shop for shoes.

Clothing Rentals
Renting clothing is an idea that doesn't commonly occur to most people, but if you need an article of clothing for a special event that you will wear only once or twice, rentals might be the most

cost-effective solution. Not only will you save money, but also you may be able to use the expense as a tax deduction, depending on the nature of the event.

For years, men have been renting tuxedos for special occasions. Recently, women have started to do the same thing. These rentals include cocktail dresses, evening gowns and suits, mother-of-the-bride dresses, and even bridal gowns. You can rent a dress that will knock the socks off everyone, and no one needs to know that it's a rental unless you want to share the secret. It's an affordable way to wear a "be-seen-in-only-once dress" that would normally cost hundreds of dollars only to gather dust in the back of your closet. For rental stores, check your Yellow Pages.

SHOPPING AT MANUFACTURER OUTLETS

Manufacturer outlet malls are popping up all over the country, and bargain-seeking consumers are flocking to them in increasing numbers. Also referred to by terms such as "factory" or "brand-name," "designer" or "company" outlets or stores, they are becoming the wave of the future. As of 1994, more than 400 such outlets are estimated to be in operation—an increase of about 40% since 1990. They are now located in almost all 50 states.

A manufacturer or factory outlet is a retail store established and operated by a manufacturer to offer its products directly to the public at below-retail prices. A manufacturer outlet mall is a collection of such stores in one location. Many stores carry first-quality, current-season merchandise offering shoppers great values. Other merchandise offered in outlet stores at reduced prices may include overruns, non-selling, last season, returns, and seconds. As the trend accelerates, more and more major brand manufacturers are locating in these outlet centers.

These malls have become very popular because they offer dollar-stretching bargains, and when their already-discounted products go on sale, they offer super bargains. Further, with so many major outlets in one place, consumers can satisfy many of their needs in one convenient shopping excursion and have fun in the process. Increasing numbers of restaurants and recreational amenities give the malls a very relaxed, pleasant, fun-type atmosphere. Since manufacturer outlet malls are located throughout the country, and frequently in vacation areas, consumers can combine bargain shopping with a vacation, sometimes saving enough money to pay for part of their vacation. A wide variety of products is available, including most major brands, at discounts of from 10 to 80% off retail.

Here are some tips to make sure you get the most out of shopping at manufacturer outlet malls:

- Plan ahead. If you know you'll be visiting a manufacturer outlet mall, call or write for a brochure or any other information they have available. Familiarize yourself with the individual stores and their products. Ask if they have any special discount coupons for groups such as tours, senior citizens, auto club members, and others.
- Make a shopping list along with a budget, and do your best to stick to both.
- Wear comfortable shoes because you'll probably have a lot of ground to cover.
- Wear a fanny pack instead of a handbag to keep your hands free for carrying packages.
- If you plan to buy clothing, wear a leotard and tights to save the time and trouble involved in removing and replacing your clothing over and over.
- Make a tour of all the stores in the outlet mall before you buy anything. In a small notebook, jot down stores and items with prices that interest you. Look over your notes prior to returning to stores to buy. A bit of time between looking and actual purchasing may quell "bargain mania" and save you money.
- When buying for others, make sure you have the current size of each person on your list.
- Examine items to make sure all are in top-quality condition. Returns, if accepted at all, are a time-consuming inconvenience.
- Check on return policies before you buy.
- Allow enough shopping time so that you are not rushed.
- If you are going to spend a day shopping at a manufacturer outlet mall, maximize the visit. Make a list of all the presents you expect to be giving during the next 12 months—birthdays, births, anniversaries, graduations, and so on—and shop for those too. Think of the money, time, and energy you can save.

Yes, there are great bargains available at manufacturer outlet malls; however, not everything available for sale is a super bargain. Here are some pitfalls to keep in mind. At a manufacturer outlet mall located in Southern California, a crystal store had second-quality items "on sale" at 33% off retail. A 33% discount on first-quality crystal is a decent discount, but on second-quality merchandise the discount should be a minimum of 50% off retail. In another instance, a famous shoe manufacturer's outlet store had a pair of shoes priced at $26. The regular retail price on this pair of flats was $28. If you have to drive any distance, a two-dollar saving obviously is not worth it.

Be aware of the range of prices on the merchandise in a manufacturer's outlet store. The fact that one item in a store is a great deal doesn't mean everything is priced accordingly. In a store filled with decorator items, we found deep discounts on linens but discovered something entirely different on bathroom items such as tissue holders and wastepaper baskets. The prices at the outlet store were higher than prices for the same items found in a national chain that regularly discounts household goods 20% off retail.

Shopping at factory outlet malls can be a lot of fun and save you lots of money, especially if you make use of the information in this chapter. Finally, if at all possible, visit these malls during the week and arrive as early as possible. From our experience, the crowds on Fridays, Saturdays, and Sundays are frequently as heavy as some of the busiest shopping days of the year, including the few days prior to Christmas and the day after Thanksgiving.

Remember: Before visiting a mall, consumers are urged to call and request one of their detailed informational brochures. This will let you know exactly what they have and the best way to get there.

SHOPPING AT MEGASTORES, RETAIL CHAINS, AND CLEARANCE CENTERS

Megastores

Megastore is the generic term used to encompass warehouse stores, superstores, and membership clubs similar in their extremely large facility size (some in the 50,000- to 100,000-square-feet range), and quantity and variety of private-label and brand-name products offered at substantially discounted prices—either within a specialty category (office supplies, home building materials) or in a general merchandise store offering everything. As a direct result of consumers wanting more bang for their bucks and retailers desiring to reduce overheads and achieve economies of scale and high-volume sales, more and more of these giant stores are opening featuring almost every kind of product on the market.

Warehouse Stores

For the most part, warehouse stores are general merchandise stores that buy in mass quantities and usually feature many different name-brand products as well as lesser-known products and some private-label items made for them by small manufacturers. Unlike special category stores, your selection of an item may be limited (for example, two or three toothpastes from which to choose rather than 10 or 15 brands). Many goods are packaged in very large sizes and/or quantities. Instead of a package of 4 rolls of toilet paper, a warehouse store might have packages of 24 rolls. This is great for a big family, but not if you're single or there are just two of you. Nevertheless, even two dozen rolls of paper will eventually be used. One alternative is to split the purchase with another person or family. Also, taking turns shopping for each other for these regularly used items cuts down on the number of shopping trips and saves time, gasoline, and energy.

The same is true of food items. Either package size is much larger or you have to buy more than one of an item—instead of one can of soup, you often have to buy a six-pack. Most warehouse stores also offer the same goods as regular retail stores in the most popular and common sizes and packages. No, you don't have to buy 12 ski parkas at a time, but you might have to buy socks or video tapes by the dozen.

Most warehouse stores carry a large number of core brands and goods—their staple items. These are almost always in stock. Other items represent one-time, special purchases—including goods brought in just for holiday seasons. They normally don't restock these goods—a rule of thumb is, if you need it, buy it now; don't procrastinate because it may be gone by the time you make up your mind. Also, if you are in doubt whether this is a staple or special item, ask a clerk.

Superstores
Superstores are similar to warehouse stores in many respects but usually specialize in one category of product such as books, auto parts, office supplies, and computers. They often have much more ambiance than warehouse stores and may be located in more upscale areas. Along with discount prices, superstores offer a larger selection of individual products—instead of carrying three or four brands of an item, you may have 10 or 20 from which to choose.

Membership Clubs
Membership club is a general term for stores that have certain criteria to become a member. Upon meeting the criteria and filing an application, you are issued a membership card. Sometimes the criterion is simply payment of a small annual fee or might be belonging to a certain consumer category (for example, government employees, teachers, business owners). You are required to show the card in order to purchase at the store and receive special member discounts. Many, but not all, megastores are membership clubs.

Most megastores, such as Price/Costco, CompUSA, and Staples, have locations throughout the United States (sometimes hundreds of stores). By calling the telephone number of the national headquarters (often an 800 number), you can request a list of all their stores—thus, you can locate ones in your local area and others you might want to visit while traveling.

Off-Price Retail Chain Stores
Off-price chains sell brand-name and private-label products always at

discounted prices and have multiple locations on a national, state, or citywide level. They include special product stores such as beauty supplies, clothing, and jewelry, and also general merchandise stores. While both specialty and general merchandise stores carry goods from a variety of manufacturers and designers, specialty stores carry a larger variety of brand names per item. Discounts run to 50% and more. New products arrive daily and weekly, so it pays to drop in often. The store has the flexibility to take advantage of one-time, great "buys" from manufacturers. The same items are not necessarily restocked. If you see something you like at a good price, it pays to buy it then; it may not be there on your next visit. Be prepared to wade through much mediocre stuff before you strike gold. Expect a no-frills atmosphere and service approach. Return policies are usually quite liberal, but check on them before you buy. Since there are hundreds of these stores nationally, telephone the national headquarters for a list of their locations. You should also check your local Yellow Pages for any particular one.

RETURN STRATEGIES

Have you ever bought something and decided to return it because you changed your mind, someone at home didn't like it, or it didn't fit or work exactly as you thought it would? Perhaps you decided it had been too expensive, or the next day or week you saw it advertised for much less than you paid. If so, join the club. Millions of dollars of merchandise is returned every year for many reasons, including "buyer's remorse."

Save yourself some headaches by knowing the return policy of the businesses you buy from. Remember, they vary greatly. Some of the differences are:

• Time limit: 7 days to 6 months

• Conditions: Full refund, to in-store credit only, to no refunds or exchanges

• Customer satisfaction: Satisfaction guaranteed—no questions asked, to must show damage or malfunction

• Receipt: Absolutely necessary, to not necessary or credit card slip acceptable

Here are suggestions for dealing with returns effectively:

• Return policies are usually posted or can be found in the small print of your receipt. If this isn't the case, ask about the return policy. Wherever possible, get it in writing. Salespeople and managers change. You don't want to be faced with, "Who told you that? That's not our policy."

• Keep receipts, and file each by date so that it will be easy to locate one when needed.

• If you've purchased an item with a warranty, complete and return warranty cards immediately after purchase. If you put it aside to complete later, you may never get to it and probably won't be able to find it when you need it. Staple your sales receipt to the warranty card you keep. File all warranty cards in one place.

- When returning something that is somewhat outside the store policy, don't take no for an answer from the first salesperson you talk to. Ask to talk to the manager. In today's competitive market with the emphasis on customer service, they will frequently go along with your request.

- Another option is to call the customer service department of the manufacturer. Many have 800 numbers. The company will often accept the return even when the store won't.

Finally, all other things being equal, shop more often at the discount stores that have the most flexible return policies.

REMINDERS FOR THE SMART SHOPPER

Learn all you can about the high-priced products you wish to buy—features, models, and brands. This information can be obtained from consumer guides (see Chapter 5, *Directory of Consumer Resources*), sales representatives, and people you know who have purchased the item. Consider the various places from which you could possibly buy the item. Compare availability, price, reputation, convenience, and company policies. Don't forget to consider using money-saving coupons, off-season buying, and renting rather than purchasing if the situation warrants it.

Challenge yourself to find or create the best deal you can. Shopping will soon seem like a game with all the fun of competing skillfully and the rewards of saving money, conserving time and energy, and getting more value for your dollar.

And don't forget to use your *Buying Retail Is Stupid!* coupons for extra discounts.

2

GRASS ROOTS
BARGAIN OUTLETS
GARAGE SALES, THRIFT SHOPS, RESALE STORES, SWAPMEETS, FLEA MARKETS

GRASS ROOTS BARGAIN OUTLETS

Economic conditions of the late '80s and early '90s have energized a multitude of grass roots, money-saving opportunities for the bargain-seeking consumer. Among the most popular are garage sales, swapmeets, flea markets, thrift shops, and resale stores. Swapmeets offer mostly new goods, some used—flea markets about 50/50 new and used. The buyer is attracted by the generally low prices and also the possibility of finding a terrific "buy." For the seller, it is a way to clear out the clutter, make some money, and participate in recycling rather than just contributing to the city dump. We call them grass roots because, for the most part, the merchandise sold is provided by private individuals—you and me, from our own homes and possessions. Also, prices are uniquely flexible and open to negotiation.

Shopping at swapmeets, flea markets, and garage sales can be a real treasure hunt. Sometimes you can find incredible buys, such as a necklace of Victorian glass beads bought for $6 and, after appraisal, found to be valued at $300; a beautiful walnut fruit bowl purchased for 50¢ turned out to be worth several hundred dollars. Several times, we've been impressed with a unique or interesting piece of furniture in someone's home only to be told, "Oh, I found it at a garage sale—you should have seen it before I got it cleaned up!" Some special items to look for at these sales include art and paintings, antique jewelry, costume jewelry, oriental rugs, baby and children's clothing and furniture, appliances, dishes, silver, glassware and crystal, pottery and vases, collectibles, and sporting gear. Thrift shops and resale stores offer the same possibility for great buys in clothing.

GARAGE SALES

Garage sales have become big business in recent years, generating millions of dollars in income. Many people are turning their front lawns and driveways into virtual showrooms of castoffs and hand-me-downs. Some have created a garage sale business and hold regular weekly or monthly sales. For others, it's a one-shot deal or perhaps once or twice annually, like spring cleaning.

Shopping at Garage Sales:
• The earlier you arrive, the better. You'll skip the brunt of the crowds, have greater choice, and frequently get better prices from owners eager to take some cash in early.

• Don't be afraid to negotiate price.

• If you feel an item is overpriced, give the seller reasons.

• Once the owner seems firm about an article you really want, don't hem and haw too long or someone will buy the bargain out from under you.

• If you are not totally sold on an item, make a final offer and then be willing to walk. Frequently, you'll get it at your price.

• Ask questions. The more you know, the better you'll be able to spot bargains.

• Be prepared for rejection. Sellers are not all equally flexible. If it's something you want, but only at your own price, come back another time, if convenient; the longer the item is there, the more likely the price will come down.

• Don't be penny wise and dollar foolish. If it's being sold at a bargain price and you really want it, don't get into an ego battle with the seller and lose out on the purchase for a few dollars.

Having Your Own Garage Sale
Making money on a continuing basis with garage sales takes an eye for value and knowing how to repair things. Repeat garage sellers collect merchandise over several weeks, generally at other yard sales and swapmeets, sometimes buying a seller's entire lot in preparation for their own sale. They bring home the items, clean them up or repair them, then double or triple the value at resale. Whether you are holding a one-time cleanup or going into the garage sale business, certain strategies can increase your likelihood of success.

Why Have a Garage Sale?
You might do it because you have too many possessions, a lot of clutter, and not enough storage space, or maybe you're tired of holding on to things you never use; perhaps you just need a little cash, or you might think it will be a good family project—educational for the kids. A garage sale can be a great way to mix fun and profit. Once you've held one, you are likely to find it an interesting and profitable experience.

Choosing What to Sell
Involve all members of the family. Without consulting with the others, each person makes a list of things to sell by answering the following questions:

- What things of my own do I know I want to get rid of?
- What are some things in the house that I don't like?
- What are some things that nobody seems to use?
- What are some things that I haven't used or worn in more than a year?
- What are some things that I question whether to keep?

After making the above lists, have each one go through the house looking for anything else that might be added to the list. Have one family member combine all the lists, eliminating duplication. Hold a meeting to review the combined list as follows:

- Quickly check off each item for which there is no disagreement.
- Discuss the remaining items and seek a consensus.
- Decide on a final sale list.
- Include everything you want to get rid of. Don't assume no one will want to buy an item.

Pricing—How Much to Charge
What to charge depends on your main purpose. Is the amount of profit important, or are you mainly looking to get rid of clutter and simplify your life? Some people price things higher assuming shoppers want to haggle and won't feel anything is a bargain unless they can knock the price down; however, absolutely not wanting to put anything back in their house, others will price on the low side. You may want to set up tables on which all the items are one price—for example:, $1, $2, or $5. Mark prices on everything. In pricing clothing, mail-order catalogs might help you remember what you originally paid for things. The condition of each item should influence the price. Asking too much for items that are hardly usable will make you look foolish and will send the potential customer away quickly.

Length of Sale
The length of the sale depends on how many items you have to sell. Typically a garage sale will run from one to three days. If you have lots of merchandise, a two- or three-day sale gives you ample time to sell most of your goods. Word-of-mouth can increase your clientele substantially after the first day. You can expect to be visited by professional shoppers such as antique dealers and others who regularly scour the newspapers for weekend sales and plan their shopping itineraries accordingly. You will also have amateurs, browsers, and people who were driving by, noticed your sign, and stopped impulsively. At the end of each day, mark down any items you want to move faster. With one-day sales, you will do this in the afternoon. Near the end of the

day of a one-day sale or on the last day of a longer sale, all prices should be slashed to give-away levels. Sometimes you will simply ask people to make you an offer.

Advertising—Letting People Know About the Sale
Probably the easiest and cheapest advertising is simple word-of-mouth. Talk it up as much as possible. Send a postcard to your friends and tell them to mention it to others. Post index cards, signs, and posters wherever you can—local laundromat, grocery store, school bulletin boards.

The most effective form of advertising is found in the classified section of the newspaper. These little ads are read religiously by bargain hunters everywhere. One small, well-worded ad is worth a thousand well-placed signs. It's a good idea to list special items such as furniture—a draw for antique dealers—and yard equipment, bicycles, and children's items.

You should begin your ad with an attention-grabbing phrase. Then list some of the most appealing items. Be sure to include your address and easy-to-follow directions. Here's an example:

> World's Best GARAGE SALE! Riding tractor mower, antique bedroom suite of bird's eye maple, cast iron stove, plus original oil paintings, fur coat and other period clothes. Many additional wonderful items. Sat. & Sun. June 4 & 5 from 10 a.m. to 4 p.m. Follow Exeter Drive West, turn right on Glenhaven, then left on Glenoit to 2517.

Run your classified ad two or three days in advance of the sale and during the sale. Newspapers often have a staff person who can help you write the ad. Take advantage of it.

Preparing Your Sale
- Get a permit. The need for a permit varies among communities and types of yard sales. Check with your city or town clerk to learn which ordinances apply to you.
- Use signs. Stake out signs on a pole planted in your lawn. String balloons to attract attention and direct shoppers to your sale.
- Locate for accessibility. Locate the sale in an area that is easily accessible and has safe parking. If weather permits, roping off your driveway increases your display space and saves wear and tear on your lawn. If you live in a condominium or apartment, see if you can use the complex recreation room or yard area.

• Get ready early. If you're planning to start at 9 a.m., be ready at 7 a.m. Dealers of antiques and secondhand goods may visit sales the night before or first thing in the morning; regular shoppers also come early. You may want to include in your advertisement "no early birds."

Organize for Convenience and Efficiency

• Have plenty of small bills and change. A small adding machine will come in handy and help keep your sales straight. Set up a head table convenient for your customers and where you can keep an eye on the entire sale. Never leave the sale unattended. Keep your change in a box and your adding machine, paper, pencils, tags, and sacks all at the head table.

• Place sale items in aisle-like rows so everything is easily accessible. Leave plenty of walking room to minimize accidents and breakage. Hang clothes on a rack or line for easy access, and provide a mirror for people trying on hats and outerwear. Keep string and rope on hand to help in packing furniture and bicycles into car trunks. Providing old grocery bags will keep shoppers from standing around juggling items.

• Have enough help. There should be at least two people working the sale at all times—one to field questions, another to handle cash exchanges. It also helps to wear an apron with pockets to hold bills and change.

• Keep your house locked. Don't assume that some people won't take advantage of an unlocked front or side door.

• Plan what to do with unsold items. Donate leftover goods to places such as charity thrift shops, homeless shelters, soup kitchens, churches, or the Salvation Army.

Joint Sales

A one-home yard sale may work fine if you live in the city or on a main street. But in the suburbs and rural towns, multi-family or neighborhood sales offer a better draw. People don't want to venture out into the country for one sale. A neighborhood sale attracts people because they can shop at half a dozen places in one group.

Whether in the city or suburbs, if you have gathered a fair amount of goods, but not enough to make a sale worthwhile, check with a neighbor or friend and see if you can conduct a joint sale. There are many advantages besides the companionship and the sharing of ideas. You can split the cost of advertising, and have help on pricing and moving of goods, plus you'll have two people for more word-of-mouth advertising. Separate inventories for double sales can easily be kept straight by color-coding the price tags or marks with corresponding items on the inventory sheet.

RESALE STORES

Resale stores are another fun way to save money, and they are starting to appear everywhere. Resale stores generally take in clothes on consignment from individuals and keep a percentage of the sale price for themselves. Even though these stores deal mostly in used clothes, some garments have been worn only once or sometimes not at all. Most of their clothes are high-end, unlike thrift stores, which deal with low-end, donated used clothes.

If you've never been in a resale store, you are in for a treat. It's a great way to get expensive clothing at rock-bottom prices. Resale stores usually specialize in clothing from medium-priced department stores or very high-end department stores and boutiques. For example, you can pick up a Jones New York skirt for $12 instead of $50 retail, or a cocktail dress for $195 made of French lace by Carolina Herrera that originally retailed for over $2,500. Most resale stores are for women, but stores geared strictly for children and men are growing in number. We are also starting to see more resale stores filled with goods for the entire family.

Most clothing in resale stores is second-hand, but you'll also find brand-new merchandise with tags still attached. We picked up a gorgeous wool suit in royal blue, with the $300 Nordstrom tags still attached, for $95. Many resale stores also carry manufacturer samples, overruns, and last season's clothing from retail stores.

Shopping resale for children's clothing is a fabulous way to save money. Kids outgrow their clothes long before they wear them out. The best buys for children are play clothes and party clothes. A frilly girl's party dress that was probably worn for only one occasion is a much better buy at $18 than $80.

How to Shop in a Resale Store

- Usually, the better organized the store is, the better the merchandise.
- Almost always, clothes for sale have been laundered or dry cleaned, but ask anyway.
- Pay special attention to cuffs, collars, pockets, armpits, and crotches for stains and wear and tear.
- Make sure the garment has all necessary parts—buttons, working zippers, etc.
- If the item is made of a natural fabric such as wool, look it over to make sure there are no moth holes.
- When you find a resale store that carries brands you prefer, ask the owner or manager to give you a call when items of interest arrive.

• Since new merchandise is always coming in, find stores conveniently located so that you can stop by periodically.

You can find a variety of resale stores for men, women, and children in your local Yellow Pages.

THRIFT STORES

Saving money and doing a good deed go hand in hand when you shop at thrift stores. Most thrift shops are affiliated with a charitable organization and are staffed by volunteers. Whether you're buying or donating, it's all for a worthy cause.

Unlike resale stores, which usually deal exclusively in apparel, thrift stores will have, in addition to clothing, all manner of other merchandise—housewares, books, toys, and anything that people want to clean out of their cluttered garages, attics, and closets. You never know what you will encounter at a thrift store. Most of the merchandise is visibly used, but sifting through everything from clothing to housewares can be rewarding. One of our best "finds" at a retirement home thrift shop was a huge fruit bowl made of bird's eye walnut for 50¢. Sometimes you will be lucky enough to find clothing that has been worn only once or not at all—possibly even a high-end, expensive item.

Even though everything is wonderfully priced, be sure to examine the items closely to make sure that, no matter how low the cost, you don't end up with something that you will regret purchasing at any price.

SWAPMEETS AND FLEA MARKETS

Flea markets and swapmeets are groups of vendors in individually rented booths, under one roof or in one large area. We use the terms interchangeably here. Flea markets are like one big yard sale where you can find new and recycled items alike, at bargain-basement prices. Since overhead is quite low, prices usually are too; best of all, you will be dealing directly with the "store owner," and haggling is part of the experience. The following dialogue is not uncommon at these events: "How much is this? Twenty-five dollars. That's too much. How much will you give for it? Twelve dollars. It's yours."

Vendors are frequently local people selling their own hand-crafted products. Others are dealers specializing in perhaps antiques and collectibles or in recycled, brand-name merchandise; in addition to the regular semi-professionals, you have the occasional and one-time customers and vendors. Prices for merchandise range from a few dollars to hundreds, and stories abound regarding incredible bargains and an occasional rip-off because someone overvalued an item—from the ridiculous to the sublime, one might say.

Flea markets are enjoying an ever-increasing popularity and have turned into big business. There are thousands of them covering just about every state in the U.S. They exist in and around urban areas and in rural, countryside locations. Some have only a handful of vendors, while others have hundreds. Outdoor markets are held at drive-in theatres, country fairgrounds, sports venues, vacant lots, and other locations. Indoor swapmeets, many several levels high and with air conditioning, are insurance against bad weather and are more likely to function throughout the year.

Most flea markets offer a tremendous variety of merchandise ranging from valuable antiques to backyard junk—almost everything and anything can be found at these events. Recent trends include selling new merchandise. Some swapmeets specialize in one category of product— e.g., computers, skiing equipment.

By adding restaurants, entertainment, music, games, and play areas, many flea markets have created a down-home, country, amusement-park-type atmosphere, where the whole family can enjoy a day together.

The following tips can help you get the most out of a flea market visit, whether as a buyer or seller.

Buying at Flea Markets

- Come prepared. Make a list of the things you are looking to buy. Know the approximate value of the items you are considering for purchase. Don't assume that everything you see is a bargain. Smart shopping principles apply here as elsewhere. Be wary of fakes when shopping for "brand-name" items. Some imitations can fool even a seasoned shopper.

- Know when to bargain. Bargaining can be as important as the shopping when it comes to walking away with a good deal. Don't automatically assume that the first price you hear is final, even if it is written on a price tag. Part of the trick is in knowing the real value of the item. Even if something is already priced low, you might be able to get it for less. Always offer a lower price, especially if you are buying more than one item. Vendors are interested in moving their goods. Know what you want to pay, and walk away if you can't get that price. Come back later and you might be able to get your price then. However, don't be foolishly stubborn—don't go overboard on insisting on your price. If you really want something badly and the price is a good one, don't walk away in the hopes of saving a few dollars later—the article might not be there when you get back.

- Carry lots of cash. Many merchants offer better deals when they see the color of your money.

• Dress for comfort and convenience. Wear comfortable shoes, and use a backpack or fanny pack to keep your hands free. A collapsible luggage cart with wheels may also help make your day easier—especially if you make several purchases.

Selling at Flea Markets

• Selecting markets. Visit several markets—if possible, for a whole day. Observe what's going on and take notes. How is attendance? What seems to be the busiest part of the day? What booths seem to be attracting the most customers? What's the atmosphere like? Do the people seem to be enjoying themselves—visitors and vendors? Interview some vendors and managers. Tell them your goals and ask if they believe them to be realistic. What are some of the advantages and disadvantages of selling at this market? Is anyone selling successfully the type of items you intend to sell? What are the rules and regulations and costs? What kind of support is provided by management? Talk to some of the customers. Ask what they like or dislike about this market. And finally, you must decide if this is a market in which you would enjoy participating and have a good chance to be successful.

• What to sell at the market. Make a list of things you have at home that you would like to get rid of. Eliminate from the list those items in which you think there would be little or no interest—no point in burdening yourself with low-probability items. If uncertain, have a friend check your list. Brainstorm other potential items that you can obtain or make. Estimate your potential profit. Is your goal fun or profit, or both?

• How to display your goods. Whatever you sell, whether junk or new articles, should be in the best possible condition. Clean up merchandise before displaying at the show. Arrange items in a way that makes everything easily accessible to the shopper.

• How much to charge for items. Decide what your bottom-line price is for each item. Prepare price tags and attach them to each item before the event. One rule of thumb is to start with a price somewhere between what you think an item is worth and what you think you can get. Know the selling points of each item, and be prepared to state them to the potential buyer when justifying the price. For example, a small flashlight key ring which sells for $4 can be used to open your front door at night when it's difficult to see, but also when finding a seat in a movie theatre after the lights are out or looking for a lost item under your seat after the film is over—and how about looking in your mouth when your gums feel slightly irritated. Four dollars is beginning to sound like quite a bargain, wouldn't you say?

- Decision time. Review all your notes and observations. Consider your potential costs and profit. Go over your goals again. All things considered, is this something you still want to do?

COMMON ASPECTS OF GRASS ROOTS OUTLETS

Grass roots bargain outlets are very accessible and growing in number. They are in our front yards, just down the block, or almost anywhere you look. They are the most "down home" example of the free market system and have several aspects in common:

- You can participate as a buyer or a seller and can profit in either role.

- You can engage in them occasionally as an amateur or regularly, taking a more business-like approach.

- You can negotiate the price for which you are willing to buy or sell.

- They provide a terrific recycling program—"one person's trash is another person's treasure!"

- They give you the opportunity to clear out your excess possessions for fun, profit, or charity.

- You can obtain something you want for much less than buying it new.

- Being aware of the value of the item helps you to bargain intelligently.

- Checking the condition of your prospective purchase prevents buyer's remorse.

3

DIRECTORY OF
DISCOUNT STORES
AND OUTLETS
WHERE TO FIND GIANT $$$
SAVINGS IN YOUR LOCAL AREA

DIRECTORY OF DISCOUNT STORES AND OUTLETS

In this chapter we provide you with access to hundreds of discount stores and outlets of every type, shape, kind, and variety imaginable—from the Rose Bowl Flea Market with its hundreds of different vendors to the small Mom and Pop shop in your neighborhood—and everything in between. You'll find almost every product from A to Z (antiques to zippers)—and also an incredible variety of generic and name-brand items. You can locate them by product category in the Table of Contents or by company name in the Index. We describe the stores in enough detail to give you a good feel for what they offer—products, services, atmosphere, price range, discounts, credit cards, brand names, and more; also, we tell you where they are located and how to contact them. Before going to a store, call to verify store hours and address, to make sure it is still in business, and to check that what you want is in stock. "See Also" at the end of a particular product category indicates what other companies in the chapter carry the item. Refer to the Index of Discount Stores and Outlets for the page numbers of these stores.

★ BONUS DISCOUNT COUPONS

Several hundred stores offer bonus discount coupons representing, for the most part, additional percentage or dollar discounts off their already discounted prices. Using these extra bonus coupons—available exclusively to *Buying Retail Is Stupid!* purchasers—can save you a considerable amount of extra money yearly. Clip them from the back of the book and take them with you to the store for additional savings. A ★ next to its name indicates that the store offers a discount coupon, and the amount is indicated in the description.

◆ SENIOR DISCOUNTS

More than 100 discount stores and outlets in this chapter offer special Senior Discounts. These discounts are obtained merely by showing proof of age. The specific age required and amount of discount offered are different for each store and are indicated in the description of the store below. Some of the stores accept the bonus discount coupon, described above, in addition to the Senior Discount; others do not. The store description indicates when the bonus discount is not valid in addition to the Senior Discount.

The Antique House ★
1428 Foothill Blvd.
La Canada, CA 91011
818/790-1119

Hours: Tues-Sun: 10-6
Credit Cards: DISC, MC, V

You know you're shopping in the right place when you see other antique dealers buying merchandise for their own stores. The Antique House is appropriately housed in a historical building constructed in 1880. The store is filled with lovely, turn-of-the-century furniture made of mahogany, country pine, walnut, and American oak, as well as European and American period pieces. Prices run at least 20 to 40% less than you can expect at most antique stores. You can spend hours looking over quality antique furniture, art, sterling, cut glass, primitives, glassware, trunks, quilts, books, jewelry, china, lighting, clocks, mirrors, and more. Don't overlook the bargain table, where prices are dropped another 50% off their already discounted prices. With much of their inventory on consignment, they are open to buying one piece or an entire estate. They offer a flexible layaway plan, as well as worldwide delivery and shipping services. If you use your *Buying Retail Is Stupid!* coupon, you'll receive a $25 gift certificate with a minimum purchase of $100. You can use the gift certificate as a gift or on a future purchase.

Antique Way ★
11729 Santa Monica Blvd.
West Los Angeles, CA 90025
310/477-3971

Hours: Mon-Sat: 10:30-6 Sun: 12-6
Credit Cards: AE, MC, V

"We don't have crazy decorator prices—just down-to-earth, realistic selling prices," says Antique Way owners Bernard Fischer and Richard Litt. They search the world for beautiful and unusual European and American antique furniture and offer a selection of Nouveau, Mission, Deco, Victorian, oak, pine, walnut, and mahogany furniture at 20% less than other dealers. They also have a nice selection of arts and crafts. Keep an eye open in mid-June and December for sales featuring an additional 15 to 50% off their entire inventory. These are sales not to be missed. Your *Buying Retail Is Stupid!* coupon is worth an additional 10% off nonsale items only.

Collector's Eye
21435 Sherman Way
Canoga Park, CA 91303
818/347-9343

Hours: Mon-Sat: 10-5:30
Credit Cards: AE, DISC, MC, V

This is definitely one of our favorites. Walking into the Collector's Eye is like walking through a rainbow and finding the pot of gold. All of their elegantly displayed vintage jewelry is arranged by colors and/or style. You might find an antique vanity draped in pearl brooches, bracelets, earrings, chokers, necklaces, rings, and ropes. Another display might consist of 75 various styles in shades of blue or, perhaps, sterling silver. The antique jewelry, real and costume, is from the early 1800s up through the early 1960s, and all is at 50 to 70% below retail. You can literally spend hours browsing through this oasis of jewelry acquired from estate sales, swapmeets, and retirement homes. The Collector's Eye offers jewelry repair, and a layaway plan is also available. A definite stop when in the San Fernando Valley!

Estate Home Furnishings ★
1901 Holser Walk, Suite 300
Oxnard, CA 93030
805/983-2211, 800/273-9390

Hours: Wed-Sun: 9:30-5:30
Credit Cards: MC, V

Why pay retail when you can take advantage of outstanding values and quality merchandise at Estate Home Furnishings? Browsers and buyers alike will be delighted roaming through 17,000 square feet of mementos and memories. Whether you are looking for furniture, collectibles, glassware, fine and costume antique jewelry, paintings, sterling silver, clothing, china, lamps, or pianos, Estate Home Furnishings has it all. They are also noted for their large collection of antique dolls. With three estates arriving weekly, their selection of merchandise is always changing. So, if you're in the mood for a drive, it would be well worth your while to head up to Estate Home Furnishings. They offer great terms, too. Your *Buying Retail Is Stupid!* coupon is good for an extra 10% discount on any item not already marked down.

Memory Lanes Antique Mall
20740 S. Figueroa Blvd.
Carson, CA 90745
310/538-4130, 800/585-9878

Hours: Mon-Sat: 10-6 Sun: 12-8
Credit Cards: DISC, MC, V

Shop among 200 antique and collectible dealers under one roof and save 10 to 50%. Many offer special discounts, as well as free coffee and tea. There are additional savings during the following holidays: Presidents' Day, Memorial Day, Fourth of July, Labor Day, October Fest, and pre-Christmas.

Penny Pinchers
4265 Valley Fair St.
Simi Valley, CA 93063
805/527-0056

Hours: Mon-Sat: 10-5 Sun: 11-5
Credit Cards: DISC, MC, V

There are 72 individual collectible dealers in this 17,000-square-foot antique mall. The prices are so good here that you may see antique dealers from the more expensive parts of Southern California. Penny Pinchers has been in business since 1966 featuring furniture, porcelain, pottery, linens, paintings, lamps, figurines, rugs, jewelry, and just about anything else normally found in an antique store. There is a central sales register, and you can take advantage of their 30-day layaway plan. Special sales are held in July and December. Plenty of parking is available, and there are two refreshment areas.

72 vendors at one location

Prince of Wales
1316 Montana Ave.
Santa Monica, CA 90403
310/458-1566

Hours: Mon-Sat: 10-6 Sun: 12-5
Credit Cards: MC, V

If you are looking for antique furniture at a great price, look no further than Prince of Wales. You will find antique and reproduction furniture at 20 to 50% below retail. For larger savings, check their yearly Winter Sale (January-February) and Summer Sale (July-August). They import directly from Wales to give you the lowest available prices.

Uniquities—The Consignment House

634 N. Robertson Blvd.
West Hollywood, CA 90069
310/289-7770

Hours: Mon-Sat: 10-6
Credit Cards: AE, MC, V

Merchandise moves so quickly at Uniquities, you may find yourself making it a weekly stop. Savings are 35 to 70% on some of the finest quality antiques and estate household items. Their stock usually consists of furniture, accessories, artwork, china, crystal, and silver. From time to time, you might find Waterford and Baccarat crystal, Lenox china, Gorham silver, and Henredon furniture.

See Also: (refer to index)
> Burbank Monthly Antique Market
> Outdoor Antique and Collectible Market
> Ray Ferra's Iron & Antique Accents

> Start your own gift shop by making purchases year-round when you find exceptional bargains.

APPLIANCES

MAJOR & SMALL APPLIANCES

Asmara Overseas Shippers
5568 Sepulveda Blvd.
Culver City, CA 90230
310/398-0080

Hours: Mon-Fri: 9-6 Sat: 10-6
Credit Cards: MC, V

Going overseas? If you are, you should consider stopping into Asmara Overseas Shippers to make sure you have the right kind of electrical plug for your hair dryer, or the correct A/C adaptor for your camcorder's rechargeable battery-pack. If you're taking your phone with you, Asmara can sell you the right adaptor or adaptors for the countries you will be visiting. Asmara specializes in 220-volt export products such as PAL-SECAM TVs, VCRs, dishwashers, microwaves, food processors, juicers, coffeemakers, camcorders, and travel converters. With the exchange rates the way they are, you can save 50% of the cost you would pay overseas! So buy it here and take it with you. They carry such brand names as Sony, Panasonic, Frigidaire, Dirt Devil, and Toshiba, and many more. To place an order by phone, call 310/398-0080.

Barrett's Appliances
2723 Lincoln Blvd.
Santa Monica, CA 90405
310/392-4108

Hours: Mon-Fri: 8-6 Sat: 8-5
Credit Cards: MC, V

Since 1946, Barrett's has been offering low-price guarantees on every major appliance for your kitchen and laundry room. Buying their inventory as part of a national buying group, they are able to pass on the huge volume discounts they receive. Brand names include Maytag, Amana, Whirlpool, Westinghouse, G.E., Frigidaire, KitchenAid, and Viking, and many more. Their award-winning service department and friendly salespeople have one thing in mind—making sure their customers are satisfied! While credit cards are accepted, you'll receive an additional 2% discount paying by cash or check. They also offer 0% financing (OAC). Another reason to shop here is their low-price policy. If within 30 days of purchase you see the same item advertised for less

40

by any appliance dealer, Barrett's will gladly refund you the difference upon presentation of the ad. As a thank-you to their customers, private sales are held twice a year. They pride themselves in being involved with their local community activities.

Bay City Appliances ★
8151 Beverly Blvd.
Los Angeles, CA 90048
213/651-2800

Hours: Mon-Fri: 8:30-6 Sat: 9-5:30 Sun: 10-5
Credit Cards: DISC, MC, V

This is not your usual whitegoods store. Bay City carries major appliances, televisions, and housewares at discounts of 20 to 50%. They also have plumbing fixtures and custom kitchen cabinets. They have six experienced salespeople to help you, and there is parking in back of the store. This store is a favorite for those who want to find everything under one roof. When you use your *Buying Retail Is Stupid!* coupon, you'll receive free delivery and installation with purchase ($40 to $100 value).

Additional Location:
Santa Monica–1302 Santa Monica Blvd., 310/393-3771

Carlson's T.V. & Appliances ★
1342 Fifth St.
Santa Monica, CA 90401
310/393-0131

Hours: Mon-Sat: 9-6 Sun: 11-4
Credit Cards: AE, MC, V

Carlson's carries a large stock of brand-name televisions and appliances at just 10% above cost. They claim prices are lower, on an overall basis, than their best-known competitors. On display are more than 100 refrigerators, 20 freezers, 40 washers, 20 air conditioners, 30 ranges, and 20 dishwashers. You'll find Westinghouse, Frigidaire, Hot Point, RCA, General Electric, Mitsubishi, Gibson, Maytag, and others. In the same location since the late 1930s, they're proud of their reputation "built on service." Fast delivery is also available. If you use your *Buying Retail Is Stupid!* coupon, you'll save an additional $10! Deals don't get any better than this.

Caston's T.V. & Appliance ★
23736 Lyons Ave.
Newhall, CA 91321
805/259-1466, 818/362-2610

Hours: Mon-Thur, Sat: 9-6 Fri: 9-8 Sun: 11-4
Credit Cards: All Major
♦ **Senior Discount:** 5% **Age:** 65

There will be no hassles when you purchase a stove, big-screen television, microwave oven, or any other major appliance from Caston's T.V. & Appliance. Their 7,000-square-foot store displays only brand-name merchandise: Sony, RCA, Mitsubishi, General Electric, Maytag, Caloric, Hotpoint, and more. All deliveries are done in their own trucks, and they personally service their electronics. Ask about their parking-lot, tent, and Christmas-in-July sales. Once you purchase something from them, you'll be on the invitation list for their private sales. By the way, they have a guaranteed best-price policy and will give you an Akira 35mm camera #TC-002 with your first purchase and the *Buying Retail Is Stupid!* coupon.

Fator's Appliances & Plumbing/Baker & Wells
9030 Wilshire Blvd.
Beverly Hills, CA 90211
310/273-9415

Hours: Mon-Fri: 9-6 Sat: 9-5
Credit Cards: MC, V

If you know where to shop, you definitely don't have to wait for sales on current-line, major appliances. Family owned and operated since the 1950s, Fator's offers major appliances for the home at discounted prices. In fact, their everyday prices on brand-name appliances even beat those of well-known mass merchandisers. Knowledgeable salespeople are always happy to give useful information and to point customers in the right direction. They also have microwaves and gas barbecues. If you're going to install your new dishwasher yourself, you'll be relieved to know they carry a complete line of plumbing materials.

Additional Location:
Chatsworth–Baker & Wells, 9640 Topanga Canyon Blvd., 818/700-0606

Friedman's Microwave & Appliance
5515 Stearns St.
Long Beach, CA 90815
310/598-7756

Hours: Mon-Sat: 10-6 Sun: 12-4
Credit Cards: AE, DISC, MC, V

There are more than 100 microwaves on display, so if you can't find what you want, it hasn't been invented yet. In addition to microwave ovens, Friedman's carries residential and commercial-grade appliances, including built-ins. Their merchandise is offered at discounted prices with a low-price guarantee.

Additional Locations:
Encino–17312-A Ventura Blvd., 818/501-0794
San Diego–4646 Convoy St., #103, 619/292-5444

H & M Appliances ★
18510 Sherman Way
Reseda, CA 91335
818/705-2240

Hours: Mon-Sat: 9-6 Sun: 10-6
Credit Cards: AE, DISC, MC, V
♦ **Senior Discount:** 10% **Age:** 65

Those looking for a refrigerator, stove, washer, dryer, or other major appliance can save 30 to 50% off the retail price at H & M Appliances. The store purchases models from companies going out of business and offers these savings to its customers. All new merchandise comes with the manufacturer's warranty. The store also carries used merchandise such as refrigerators starting at $125 and a washer and dryer set for $299. All used merchandise comes with a 90-day warranty. Don't forget: your *Buying Retail Is Stupid!* coupon will save you an additional 10% on appliances and 50% off on a service call.

> Research high-priced products in publications such as *Consumer Reports* before purchasing.

Home Service & Sales Company
17242 Beach Blvd.
Huntington Beach, CA 92647
714/847-3537

Hours: Mon-Fri: 8:30-5:30 Sat: 8:30-5
Credit Cards: DISC, MC, V

If you've been tossing around the idea of getting a new refrigerator, head on over to Home Service & Sales Company where you can save 10 to 40% on major appliances. Name brands include Amana, Magic Chef, Caloric, Tappan, Frigidaire, Jenn Air, Whirlpool, Maytag, General Electric, and KitchenAid. You'll save the most on factory seconds and freight-damaged goods (all come with a full factory guarantee) from G.E., Frigidaire, and Amana.

Reid's Discount Appliance Warehouse
2709 E. Main St.
Ventura, CA 93003
805/648-5381

Hours: Mon-Sat: 8-6 Sun: 11-5
Credit Cards: MC, V

It seems as though when one major appliance goes on the blink, the rest soon follow. If you find yourself needing new major appliances, Reid's Discount Appliance Warehouse has a huge selection (20,00 square feet of showroom and warehouse space) priced 10 to 20% below retail. They carry all major brands such as General Electric, Maytag, Roper, KitchenAid, Magic Chef, Hotpoint, Sub-Zero, and Whirlpool. You'll save even more on close-outs and floor models, and during special sales. Installation, as well as same-day or next-day delivery, is also available.

Vinotemp International
17631 S. Susana Rd.
Rancho Dominguez, CA 90221
310/886-3332

Hours: Mon-Fri: 8:30-5 Sat: 9:30-3
Credit Cards: All Major

If you have a wine collection or are thinking about creating one, then you want to see the folks at Vinotemp International. They manufacture the Vinotemp wine cellar used by wine lovers all over the world. Manager Alvin Patrick says, "Compare first, then come see us. We will not be undersold." Whether you want your wine cellar built-in or free standing, Vinotemp can help you store from 24 bottles to literally thousands. The lockers are available in all sorts of styles, including some that fit into the category of fine furniture. In addition to wine storage, they sell cedar-lined fur vaults (for 8-10 furs), as well as a combination wine and fur vault with two independently cooled compartments, and customized cigar vaults. If you'd like, they will visit your home and give you an estimate on which storage device is best for you. You'll save 20% or more off the retail price.

Warehouse Discount Center ★
30621 Canwood St.
Agoura, CA 91301
800/334-4932, 805/497-0733, 818/991-8846

Hours: Mon-Fri: 9-8 Sat: 9-6 Sun: 10-5
Credit Cards: DISC, MC, V

Warehouse Discount Center has one of the largest display showrooms (33,000 square feet) in Southern California. They carry almost every major appliance, in-home electronics, and kitchen and bath plumbing needs. You'll find brand names such as G.E., RCA, Wolf, Maytag, Kohler, Whirlpool, Magic Chef, Viking, Kenwood, and many more on items such as microwave ovens, ranges, conventional ovens, washers, dryers, dishwashers, freezers, bathtubs, toilets, and jacuzzis. Their policy is to meet or beat competitors' prices. They also have a small section in the store that has freight-damaged (scratched or dented) goods with additional savings of 20 to 50%. Make sure to get on their mailing list for notification of private sales held in May and November. Don't forget to use your *Buying Retail Is Stupid!* coupon for an extra 5% discount. Call the Oxnard store for its hours.

Additional Locations:
Oxnard–1701 E. Ventura Blvd., 805/278-0388
Santa Barbara–3917 State St., 805/692-2477

SEWING MACHINES & VACUUMS

Higham's Vacuum and Sewing Center ★
3789 Van Buren Blvd.
Riverside, CA 92503
909/354-5323, 800/499-5323

Hours: Mon-Sat: 9:30-6
Credit Cards: All Major
♦ **Senior Discount:** 10% **Age:** 60

Since 1975, Higham's Vacuum and Sewing Center family-owned business has maintained its most important goal—to educate customers. Once you know about all the products available, you can intelligently satisfy your needs without regrets. To back up this policy, they offer free one-hour lessons for life on any sewing machine, and a 100% exchange policy on selected models during the first year. Not only is Higham's service excellent, but also the prices are 30 to 50% off retail, with a guarantee to beat any advertised price on such brand names as Royal, Hoover, Eureka, Kirby, Pfaff, Singer, Viking, Brother, and New Home, and many more. Higham's also has selected models of used sewing machines and vacuums. Your *Buying Retail Is Stupid!* coupon gives you an additional 10% discount off notions and supplies (sale items excluded and not valid with senior discount). Make sure to find out about their parking-lot and warehouse sales for even greater savings.

Orange Appliance & Vacuum ★

12845 Chapman Ave.
Garden Grove, CA 92640
714/750-3151

Hours: Mon-Fri: 10-6 Sat: 10-4
Credit Cards: All Major
♦ **Senior Discount:** 5% **Age:** 65

As an authorized factory service center for more than 30 manufacturers, Orange Appliance & Vacuum is able to extend discounts of 20 to 50% off retail on vacuum cleaners and small household appliances. Brand names include Bissell, Black & Decker, Dirt Devil, Eureka, Krups, Royal, Remington, Braun, Sharp, and many others. They're so sure their prices are the lowest on vacuum cleaners they guarantee to beat any advertised price. For added savings on your purchase, you'll receive an additional 5% discount by using your *Buying Retail Is Stupid!* coupon. And, if your purchase happens to be a vacuum cleaner, you'll also receive a free year's supply of bags and belts.

Rainbow Vacuum Center ★

634 E. Colorado Blvd.
Glendale, CA 91205
818/247-1944

Hours: Tues-Fri: 10-6 Sat: 10-4
Credit Cards: AE, DISC, MC, V
♦ **Senior Discount:** 10% **Age:** 65

The last time you were on a nuclear submarine, did you happen to notice how clean and dust free it was? The Rainbow Vacuum is purchased by the U.S. Navy for the super clean environment that must be maintained in their subs. Doctors recommend the same product for their allergy patients needing their homes to be dust free. If you'd like to see the Rainbow Vacuum in action, they offer free in-home demonstrations. They'll beat anybody's price on brand names such as Hoover, Eureka, Electrolux, Panasonic, Royal, and rebuilt Kirbys. Warranty and repair work is done right on the premises. Trade-ins are accepted. You can use your *Buying Retail Is Stupid!* coupon for a 10% discount (not valid with senior citizen discount).

U.S. Sew-N-Vac ★
21430 Sherman Way
Canoga Park, CA 91303
818/348-6014

Hours: Mon-Sat: 9-6
Credit Cards: AE, DISC, MC, V
♦ **Senior Discount:** 10% **Age:** 65

Why not check out U.S. Sew-N-Vac the next time you need a sewing
machine, vacuum cleaner, or typewriter? You can save 10 to 40% off
retail. They specialize in Royal, Eureka, Panasonic, Sharp, and Hoover
vacuums and are an authorized Riccar dealer. In addition to sales, they
offer same-day repair service on sewing machines and vacuums with free
pick-up and delivery. Trade-ins are accepted and financing is available.
Take along your *Buying Retail Is Stupid!* coupon for an extra 10%
discount.

Vacuum & Sewing Center ★
21360 Devonshire Blvd.
Chatsworth, CA 91311
818/993-1973

Hours: Mon-Sat: 9-6
Credit Cards: MC, V

New, rebuilt, and used vacuum cleaners by Hoover, Eureka, and Royal,
and sewing machines by Singer are some of the products found at the
Vacuum & Sewing Center. You can select from more than 100 different
vacuum cleaners and 10 different models of sewing machines in stock.
They guarantee their service and merchandise for one full year. With
friendly salespeople and a skilled technician on the premises, you can't
go wrong. Savings start at about 20% below retail, and for super savings,
take in your *Buying Retail Is Stupid!* coupon for an extra 20% discount.

REPAIRS

Appliance Servicenter ★
7129 Balboa Blvd.
Van Nuys, CA 91406
818/989-1709

Hours: Mon-Fri: 8-5:30 Sat: 8-3
Credit Cards: All Major
♦ **Senior Discount:** 5% **Age:** 62

Repair your own microwave and appliances and save money. Appliance

Servicenter has one of the largest selections of parts. Their staff offers free technical advice. If you're not a do-it-yourselfer, they offer in-house repairs on all electronic and major appliances. Take in your *Buying Retail Is Stupid!* coupon and you'll save an extra 10% off your purchase.

USED APPLIANCES

Appliance Recycling Factory
3851 Pyrite St.
Riverside, CA 92509
909/681-5300

Hours: 7 Days a Week: 8-7
Credit Cards: All Major

Washers, dryers, refrigerators, stoves, freezers, or dishwashers, this is truly an appliance recycling factory with a huge showroom and 5,000 square feet of factory. Save at least 50% off what the same item would cost brand new! There are always at least 800 reconditioned units for sale and at least 3,000 units on hand. (Reconditioned means they replace all worn parts.) If you see a unit not yet reconditioned, you can "stake your claim," and it will be moved up to the front of the line for reconditioning. Included in the sale price is a 90-day warranty, and you can purchase their service warranty for six months or one year ($35 every six months), which includes parts and labor service in home. If the unit can't be fixed, you'll receive a replacement. Also, if your service agreement is renewed every year, the price stays the same as the original contract price. There is usually something on special; if they are overstocked on some items, those units can be on special for 30% below what they charge normally. They will also paint the appliances for you should you desire a different color.

See Also: (refer to index)
  H & M Appliances
  Sears Outlet Store

ART DEALERS

Decor Art Gallery ★
12149 Ventura Blvd.
Studio City, CA 91604
818/755-0755

Hours: Tues-Sat: 10:30-6:30 Sun: 12-5
Credit Cards: AE, DISC, MC, V

You know you've come to the right place when you hear customers looking at ready-to-hang art and saying, "Is this price for the print only?" With prices marked 30 to 50% below retail, Decor Art Gallery is an inexpensive alternate to genuine art. Large commercial accounts allow them to pass on volume pricing to the public. Owner Lynne Crandall loves her work and dealing with customers. If you're looking for something not already framed, she'll help you focus on your theme from among catalogs featuring over 10,000 prints. If you don't happen to care for the glossy look of reproductions, you might be interested in a process called "canvas transfer." The glossy overlay is removed and the print is adhered to canvas. Brush strokes are added to the picture to make it look more like an original. You can even have your own photographs or small prints canvas transferred. Make sure to get on the mailing list for notification of special sales, exhibitions, and benefits. Your *Buying Retail Is Stupid!* coupon is good for an extra 10% discount on items not previously marked down.

Edward Weston Fine Arts
19355 Business Center Dr.
Northridge, CA 91324
818/885-1044

Hours: Mon-Fri: 8-5:30
Credit Cards: AE, DISC, MC, V

This is a showroom (10,000 square feet) of wholesale art that generally deals with gallery owners. If you're an art connoisseur, this is your kind of place. They have posters, limited edition graphics, original oils and sculptures, pottery, photography, Southwestern art, and artifacts all at 50 to 70% off retail prices. You can find Picasso, Miro, Dali, Chagall, Bragg, Bert Stern, George Barris, and hundreds of other artists here. Ann Weston is the National Sales Manager. If your schedule during the week doesn't fit into their posted hours, call to arrange an evening or Saturday appointment.

UCLA/Armand Hammer Art Rental and Sales Gallery
10899 Wilshire Blvd.
Los Angeles, CA 90024
310/443-7012

Hours: Tues-Sat: 11-4 Sun: 12-4
Credit Cards: AE, MC, V

Turn your home or office into a showplace for contemporary art by renting it from the UCLA/Hammer Art Rental and Sales Gallery. To rent, you must be a member of UCLA/Armand Hammer Museum of Art and Cultural Center. Membership for a year starts at $45. Works currently on display at the gallery, as well as those from previous exhibits, are available to rent for $35 to $190 for three months. Some artists who have exhibited at the gallery are Joe Goode, Ed Moses, Lita Albuquerque, and Woods Davy. If you're interested in purchasing your rental, a portion of the fee can be applied to the purchase price. You also can utilize a corporate consulting service which will evaluate your space, present works for approval, and arrange for installation at a fee of $100 (also good toward the purchase/rental of any piece).

FRAMES & FRAMING SERVICES

Allan Jeffries' Framing ★
8301 W. 3rd St.
Los Angeles, CA 90048
213/655-1296

Hours: Mon-Sat: 10-6
Credit Cards: MC, V
♦ **Senior Discount:** 10% **Age:** 65

In business since 1984, Allan Jeffries' Framing provides professional custom framing and has ready-made frames as well. This is a great place to shop for special frames to adorn your desk or credenza. With their wide variety in brass, silver, porcelain, and marble, they have the largest selection of picture frames in Los Angeles. Their trained staff will help you design a framing layout that will fit perfectly in any room of your home. You will regularly save 10 to 20% on custom framing, and you will save an additional 10% when you present your *Buying Retail Is Stupid!* discount coupon.

Additional Location:
Santa Monica–2602 Santa Monica Blvd., 310/453-1512

Discount Frames ★
12811 Victory Blvd.
North Hollywood, CA 91606
818/763-6868

Hours: Mon-Sat: 9:30-5:30
Credit Cards: MC, V

This is the solution you've been searching for if you need your paintings reframed to match your new decor. Discount Frames has one of the biggest selections of frames in Los Angeles, and you can take advantage of the tremendous savings they offer on every size, color, style, and shape. They also provide excellent custom framing. Your *Buying Retail Is Stupid!* coupon will save you an extra 10%.

Additional Location:
Woodland Hills–22713 Ventura Blvd., 818/224-3500

Framex
4054 Laurel Canyon Blvd.
Studio City, CA 91604
818/509-0700

Hours: Mon-Sat: 10-6
Credit Cards: MC, V

Why take photographs if they're only going to end up in a box under your bed? Get some enlargements made and take them over to Framex, where you can save 20 to 60% off retail on custom framing. They can literally frame or box anything, and they also have some great discount prices on decorative mirrors (ready-made, or cut and framed to your specifications). Lots of framing shops subcontract work, but not here. All work is done on the premises using the latest equipment. With lower prices than so-called discount chains, you can be sure your pictures, not you, are getting framed.

Grey Goose Custom Framing ★
111 N. La Brea Ave.
Los Angeles, CA 90036
213/525-1611

Hours: Mon-Fri: 9-6 Sat: 10-6 Sun: 11-5
Credit Cards: AE, MC, V
♦ **Senior Discount:** 12% **Age:** 65

Everything you want in custom framing at competitive prices can be found at the Grey Goose. A metal frame measuring 24″ x 36″, including dry mounting and glass, runs $39.50 and is available in 62 different colors. Shoppers will generally save 50% on what others charge for metal frames. Check out all their other varieties of frames, too. If you have any framing questions, you can call 800/213-FRAME (3726). You can use your *Buying Retail Is Stupid!* coupon for an additional 10% discount (not valid with senior citizen discount).

Additional Locations:
Los Angeles–615 N. La Cienega, 310/652-0273
Los Angeles–1170 S. La Brea, 213/525-1611

On The Wall Frames ★
1100 Olympic Dr., #102
Corona, CA 91719
909/340-3426

Hours: Tues-Sat: 9:30-6
Credit Cards: DISC, MC, V
♦ **Senior Discount:** 10% **Age:** 60

Since 1978, On The Wall Frames has provided custom picture framing and matting at prices 25% below retail. They manufacture three profiles of high-quality oak moulding for the budget buyer and have more than 3,000 corner moulding samples to choose from. They do beautiful work and their staff is very experienced at choosing suitable frames, colors, and matting. In addition, they have a huge selection of ready-made matted and framed artwork at spectacular savings. On The Wall Frames has an additional location in Santa Ana, but hours differ, so call first. Use your *Buying Retail Is Stupid!* coupon and you'll save an extra 15% (not valid on sale or discounted items).

Additional Locations:
Santa Ana–1916 East McFadden Ave., 714/543-9811

U-Frame-It, Inc. ★
13630 Sherman Way
Van Nuys, CA 91405
818/781-4500

Hours: Mon-Fri: 10-7 Sat-Sun: 11-5
Credit Cards: All Major

U-Frame-It, a family-owned business, gives you the opportunity to frame your own pictures. After purchasing your materials, you can assemble your pictures on their large tables, with the use of their paper towels, glass cleaner, and tools. Their staff will happily give any advice on framing. If you don't have the time to do-it-yourself, they can frame your pictures at approximately 35% below retail prices. Custom framing is also available in one hour. The *Buying Retail Is Stupid!* coupon saves you an extra 25% off do-it-yourself materials.

ARTS & CRAFTS

ART SUPPLIES

Art Supply Warehouse ★
6672 Westminster Blvd.
Westminster, CA 92683
714/891-3626

Hours: Mon-Fri: 9:30-6 Sat: 10-5 Sun: 11-4
Credit Cards: AE, DISC, MC, V

The Art Supply Warehouse has been committed to bringing the best possible combination of savings, selection, and service on art supplies since 1977. They have more than 12,000 square feet of merchandise for students, fine artists, designers, illustrators, draftspersons, and hobbyists at savings of 10 to 50% off retail. An additional 10% savings is offered with your *Buying Retail Is Stupid!* coupon (valid only on nonsale items).

Michael's Art Supply Inc.
1518 N. Highland Ave.
Hollywood, CA 90028
213/466-3944

Hours: Mon-Fri: 8:30-7 Sat: 10-6 Sun:11-5
Credit Cards: AE, MC, V

Since 1972, Michael's Art Supply has been the one-stop art store for artists of all types. Here you will find supplies for artists, drafters, and graphic designers at regular savings of 10 to 60%. Michael's also stocks a large inventory of brushes, canvases, paints, and fine pens. Name brands include Liquitec, Winson Newton, Letraset, Parker, Waterman, Mont Blanc, Grum Bacher, and more. In addition to their low-price guarantee, Michael's has bi-monthly sales in which everything in the store is 40% off. Stop by and check them out or give them a call. Michael's ships nationwide.

Additional Location:
Long Beach–2137 Bellflower Blvd., 310/498-1504

BEADS, RHINESTONES, ETC.

Bohemian Crystal
812 S. Maple
Los Angeles, CA 90014
213/627-9554

Hours: Mon-Sat: 9-5
Credit Cards: AE, DISC, MC, V

Bohemian Crystal has one of the largest selections of beads, rhinestones, pearls, metal parts, trimmings, apparel embroidery, appliqués, and all the accessories needed to make custom jewelry. Crystal accessories and chandeliers are also available. At Bohemian Crystal you can save 10 to 40% off retail prices, and they always have monthly specials. They have been in business since 1944 and occupy 7,000 square feet of property. You can purchase quality items made of Bohemian crystal from Czechoslovakia or Austria. Whether you're buying a set of crystal stemware for yourself or a crystal ball for your favorite fortune teller, you can't go wrong shopping here for price and selection.

Klein's Bead Box ★
309 N. Kings Rd.
Los Angeles, CA 90048
213/651-3595

Hours: Mon-Tues, Thur-Fri: 10-6 Wed: 10-7 Sat: 10-4 Sun: 11-5
Credit Cards: AE, DISC, MC, V

Put together your own designs with merchandise from Klein's Bead Box, in business since 1959. You can be as creative as you want with beads, Swarovski crystals, rhinestones, glass sew-on jewels, pearls, sequins, and appliqués. They also carry a large selection of sterling findings, semiprecious beads, and fresh water pearls. A professional skater we know from Orange County tells us that Klein's is the only place that carries what she needs for her costumes. Make earrings and necklaces or spice up that basic black dress hanging in the back of your closet! You'll also find a large selection of buttons—many from France and Italy. The helpful staff at Klein's will give you free advice about jewelry and clothing design, as well as show you how to make jewelry. Take your *Buying Retail Is Stupid!* coupon with you for an additional 10% discount.

Nebraska Bead Co. ★
2952 Nebraska Ave.
Santa Monica, CA 90404
310/828-2878

Hours: By Appointment Only, Mon-Fri: 10-5:30
Credit Cards: Cash or Checks Only

Nebraska Bead Co. manufactures costume jewelry right on the premises, and you can save up to 75% off retail prices found in many of your favorite department stores. For example, a pair of gorgeous matte gold pearl earrings, about three inches in length, would cost you $22 to $24 at the mall. You can get them here for $6. Earrings that retail for $50 at high-end department stores run $15. Nebraska Bead Co. has been selling nationwide to hundreds of department stores and boutiques for more than 10 years. The inventory in their small showroom consists of last season's goods, overruns, and samples. The prices usually run at or below wholesale. For do-it-yourselfers there is a room filled with millions of items no longer used in production. There are floor-to-ceiling bins of findings (jump rings, clasps, earring wires, etc.), beads in all kinds of materials from all over the world, crystals, cameos, charms, jewels, buttons, and more. One entire wall is full of stampings. For extra savings, take in your *Buying Retail Is Stupid!* coupon for a 10% discount.

CRAFT & FLORAL SUPPLIES

Bev's Crafts & Lace ★
7620 Tampa Ave.
Reseda, CA 91335
818/881-2257

Hours: Mon, Wed, Fri: 9:30-8 Tues, Thur, Sat: 9:30-6 Sun: 11-5
Credit Cards: DISC, MC, V

Are you envious of creative friends who decorate their homes with handmade seasonal items? If you want to try your hand at crafts, you can get started with supplies at discount prices. Create your own items or borrow some ideas from the samples all over the store. You'll find lots of beads, rhinestones, studs, Christmas boutique supplies, dried and silk flowers, and just about any item you need for creating holiday and special-occasion centerpieces. For both sewing and crafts, an entire room of the store is devoted to lace and trims. Depending on the time of year, 725 to 1,000 colors and varieties of flat and ruffled lace are available at rock-bottom prices. On display throughout the store are items of wearable art so beautifully decorated you might think they were made by a professional artist, but don't let that intimidate you. The staff is very helpful; they can assist you in getting started on your own work of art. Your *Buying Retail Is Stupid!* coupon will give you an extra 10% discount.

Crystal's Laces & Gifts ★
18215 Parthenia St.
Northridge, CA 91325
818/701-0168

Hours: Mon-Fri: 9-6 Tues: 9-8 Sat: 10-5
Credit Cards: MC, V
♦ **Senior Discount:** 10% **Age:** 65

Wall decorations can add a lot of warmth to your home, especially with your own personal touch. You can get ready-made items here at about 25% below retail, but you'll save even more if you provide the labor. Crystal's is a large boutique filled with everything needed for crafts and floral arrangements (no needlework). Every Tuesday, Thursday, and Friday they have a free craft-making class. There is a huge 99¢ sale every Thanksgiving weekend where most items are sold at cost or below. In October, they hold a "bring your own bag" sale where you'll save an additional 15% off on anything and everything you can fit into your bag. You can bring any size bag you want. October 1st is the beginning of the winter season, and Crystal's turns into a Christmas store. Layaway is also available. Remember to take in your *Buying Retail Is Stupid!* coupon and you'll save an extra 40% off your purchase of $25 or more (not valid with senior citizen discount).

Ferguson's Marine Specialties ★
617 N. Fries Ave.
Wilmington, CA 90744
213/775-1696

Hours: Mon-Fri: 8-4:30 Sat: 8-3
Credit Cards: Cash or Checks Only

Shells, shells, and more shells—several million in over 500 varieties—is what you'll find at Ferguson's Marine Specialties. Whether you collect seashells or use them in arts and crafts projects, you'll find them in every shape, size, and color at discounted prices. They also have nets, ropes, and net floats guaranteed to add realism to a room or party with a nautical theme. The next time you're in the area take in your *Buying Retail Is Stupid!* coupon for a 10% discount and a free carved cowrie shell.

General Wax Wholesale Outlet Store ★
6863 Beck Ave.
North Hollywood, CA 91605
818/765-6357

Hours: Mon-Fri: 9-5 Sat: 9-2
Credit Cards: MC, V

The best deals around town on candles are found at General Wax Wholesale Outlet Store where, in addition to traditional candles, you'll find plenty of unusual ones as well. They come in all shapes and sizes, and many look too good to burn. For you romantics out there, they even have scented candles made to float in your bath or hot tub. They also carry 24″ tapers, usually used for flower arrangements or in a candelabra, that automatically go out after burning down about eight inches or so. The best buys of all are in the "Close-Out Room," and store manager Scott Messick makes certain he keeps it well stocked with a good variety of candles. Discounts run 20 to 50% off their own products and 15% off candles brought in from other vendors. By the way, if you're handy with crafts, you may want to make candles either for yourself or to give away as gifts. They carry everything needed for the do-it-yourselfer including molds, scents, wicks, dyes, four kinds of paraffin, beeswax, and, of course, instruction booklets. For extra savings, don't forget to take in your *Buying Retail Is Stupid!* coupon for a 10% discount.

Grason's Art Crafts and Floral Supplies
31149 Via Colinas, No. 601
Westlake Village, CA 91362
818/707-6008

Hours: Mon-Tues: 9-8 Wed-Fri: 9-6 Sat: 10-5:30
Credit Cards: MC, V
♦ **Senior Discount:** 10% **Age:** 65

Do you get a sense of satisfaction when you complete an arts and crafts project? Whether you are a novice or an old hand at do-it-yourself creativity, you'll find just what you need for almost any project at Grason's priced 10 to 50% off retail. Brides-to-be on a budget will find supplies for party favors, decorations, bridal veils, headdresses, centerpieces, and even umbrellas for bridesmaids. If you'd like to start an arts or crafts hobby but have no idea where to begin, call Grason's for a schedule of classes. Students in these classes can buy their supplies (if not already included in the price of the class) at an additional 10% discount off their regularly low prices.

Additional Location:
Canoga Park–7945 Canoga Ave., 818/888-5029

Kids' Art Space ★
12532 Riverside Dr.
North Hollywood, CA 91607
818/752-9767, 800/8-FUN ART (838-6278)

Hours: Tues-Fri: 10:30-5:30 Sat-Sun: 10:30-5
Credit Cards: MC, V
♦ **Senior Discount:** 10% **Age:** 65

If you'd like to get your children involved in a wholesome activity and at the same time have someone else clean up the mess, then this is your kind of place. You'll find approximately 3,000 white, ready-to-paint plaster and ceramic items at 20% off retail, plus all necessary paints and brushes. Owners Al and Vicky Abrams go one step further. Included in the price of any plaster or ceramic piece is studio space, paints, brushes, and a smock. There is also no charge for the time you spend working on the project. You will find project pieces such as statues, cookie jars, plaques, animals, and fantasy characters. Parents can join in the fun or relax watching cable TV or reading periodicals and newspapers. Keep Kids' Art Space in mind for children's and adult birthday parties. Free popcorn, coffee, and tea are also provided. Don't forget to use your *Buying Retail Is Stupid!* coupon for a 10% discount (not valid with senior citizen discount or birthday parties).

Pottery and Floral World ★
3350 San Fernando Rd.
Los Angeles, CA 90065
213/254-5281

Hours: 7 Days a Week: 8-6
Credit Cards: AE, MC, V
♦ **Senior Discount:** 10% **Age:** 55

Pottery and Floral World has one of the largest (4,000 square feet) home decor selections of pots, pottery, dried and silk flowers, and all the accessories that go along with them. Baskets, wrought-iron products, and living plants can also be found here. They are both a factory outlet and a direct importer, so you can expect discounts of 20 to 50% off retail prices found elsewhere. Close-outs occur weekly, so you always find a changing inventory. If you're looking for seasonal decorations, they carry a complete line. You'll get an additional 10% off your purchase price when you use your *Buying Retail Is Stupid!* discount coupon (not valid with senior citizen discount).

Robertson's ★
18217 Parthenia Ave.
Northridge, CA 91325
818/701-0168, 800/272-3898 (Orders Only)

Hours: Mon, Wed-Fri: 9-6 Tues: 9-8 Sat: 10-5
Credit Cards: MC, V
♦ **Senior Discount:** 10% **Age:** 60

Robertson's is a wholesaler to craft stores all over the country. If you belong to Price/Costco or Sam's Club, or have a resale number, you can shop in their warehouse. Prices are at least 50% off retail. There is a minimum $50 first order and $10 on future purchases. There is so much to see that you may lose track of time. This 10,000-square-foot warehouse is full of wedding supplies (headpieces, centerpieces, favors, trimmings), ceramics, paper mache figures ready to be decorated, T-shirts, styrofoam, ribbon (wired, painted, lace, and satin) and items in any seasonal theme you can imagine. The Christmas items alone fill two long aisles. The bins all have prices clearly marked, and some offer multiple discounts. If you don't belong to any of the membership stores mentioned above or have a resale number, once a year they open the warehouse to the public. It happens on Thanksgiving weekend during their annual "99¢ Sale." Layaway is available, and your *Buying Retail Is Stupid!* coupon is worth an additional 10% discount (not redeemable during special sales or with senior citizen discount).

Second Nature ★

1206-10 W. Burbank Blvd.

Burbank, CA 91506

818/567-0101

Hours: First Saturday of every month: 10-5
Credit Cards: DISC, MC, V
♦ **Senior Discount:** 10% **Age:** 65

Dress up your home or office with custom artificial florals, trees, and plants from Second Nature's manufacturer showroom floor sample sale. The showroom is open to the public only the first Saturday of every month. So mark your calendars and stop by their sale featuring savings of 30 to 70% off retail. All samples are high-quality, one-of-a-kind floral arrangements or 5- to 50-foot trees designed on natural wood. Remember your *Buying Retail Is Stupid!* coupon and you'll save an extra 15% off your purchase of $25 or more (not valid with custom orders or senior citizen discount).

FABRICS & NOTIONS

A-1 Foam & Fabrics ★

1812 S. Main St.

Santa Ana, CA 92707

714/835-1181, 800/995-8515

Hours: Mon-Fri: 8-5 Sat: 8:30-5
Credit Cards: DISC, MC, V

A-1 Foam & Fabrics is a one-stop upholstery store for your home, auto, boat, restaurant, hotel, and airplane needs. Their 35,000-square-foot warehouse has fabric, vinyls, adhesives, foam, canvas, binding, cording, tools, and more. They also carry carpets for autos, boats, and vans. Their prices are 50 to 60% off retail and feature name brands such as 3M, Bolaflex, Velcro, Bostitch, and Prefixx. You'll be glad to know that you can save an extra 10% with your *Buying Retail Is Stupid!* coupon.

Big Y Yardage Outlet
440 S. Main St.
Orange, CA 92668
714/978-3970

Hours: Mon: 9:30-9 Tues-Fri: 9:30-6 Sat: 9:30-5:30
Credit Cards: AE, MC, V

After you've decorated your house with new furniture, stop by Big Y Yardage Outlet for do-it-yourself assistance in making new draperies, bedspreads, valances, tablecloths, cushions, pillows, and more. You'll find a large assortment of decorator drapery and upholstery fabrics, along with a sales force knowledgeable about the right fabric to use for your needs. For those of us who are not so creative, Big Y Yardage Outlet also offers made-to-order services on the items mentioned above. Mini-blinds and Roman shades can be ordered here, too. You'll save at least 25 to 50% off the retail price, and remnants are offered at just 50¢ a yard. Big Y has been beautifying homes in the Orange County area since 1964.

CFOS Factory Outlet ★
19345 Victory Blvd. (Loehmann's Plaza)
Reseda, CA 91335
818/758-9026

Hours: Mon-Wed: 9-6 Thur-Fri: 10-9 Sat: 9-6 Sun: 11-6
Credit Cards: AE, DISC, MC, V

If you are one of the fortunate and talented people who can make your own clothing, CFOS (California Fabric Outlet Store) has discounted fabrics with an unusual source. All of the fabrics are from a leading Southern California designer whose clothes are featured in medium- to high-end department stores. After a line of clothing has been completed, the remaining fabric (and other necessary items such as zippers, trims, and buttons) is shipped to CFOS. The fabrics, which consist mainly of rayons in prints and solids, start at about 30% off retail. Much of the fabric is from Europe, so you are apt to see patterns and designs unavailable in local sewing stores. If you wear clothes from this well-known designer, you will probably recognize the name as soon as you walk into the store. Most fabrics are on large rolls lining the walls in color-coordinated sections. Occasionally you'll see two rolls of the same fabric, but if you take a closer look, one might be a dress weight and the other a sheer. There's always a table of remnants for $1.99 and $2.99 a yard. The remnants average three to five yards with retail values up to $20 a yard. They bring out a new assortment several times a week. Trims and unusual buttons are also available at prices at least 50% below retail. Your *Buying Retail Is Stupid!* coupon is worth an extra 10% discount off any fabrics in the store.

Additional Location:
Torrance–24422 Hawthorne Blvd. (Walteria Plaza), 310/375-3681

D/M Yardage Outlet ★
16510 Hawthorne Blvd.
Lawndale, CA 90260
213/772-0301

Hours: Mon-Sat: 9:30-6
Credit Cards: DISC, MC, V
♦ **Senior Discount:** 10% **Age:** 55

Any day of the week you can save up to 70% off retail prices at D/M Yardage Outlet on thousands of in-stock fabrics, plus discounts on their special-order fabrics, too. D/M will custom make your draperies and your bedspreads, if you like. They have a beautiful selection of upholstery and drapery fabrics, ready-made draperies, and even discounted mini-blinds. Take in your *Buying Retail Is Stupid!* coupon for an extra 20% discount on in-stock fabrics (not valid with senior citizen discount).

Dawn's Discount Lace/Ruban Et Fleur ★
8655 S. Sepulveda Blvd.
Los Angeles, CA 90045
310/641-3466

Hours: Mon-Sat: 10-6 Sun: 12-5
Credit Cards: MC, V

Buy direct from the importers of European ribbons and accessories and save 20 to 40%. Dawn distinguishes her business from other craft stores by offering unique items such as new and antique French ribbon, velvet fruits, old berries, foliage, and much more. Bring in your *Buying Retail Is Stupid!* coupon for an additional 10% off your purchase of $25 or more.

Designer Fabric Showcase ★
10199 Hole Ave.
Riverside, CA 92503
909/354-6684

Hours: Mon-Thur: 10-5:30 Fri: 10-4 Sun: 12-4
Credit Cards: MC, V

Designer Fabric Showcase is the place to get some spectacular savings on decorative fabrics for the home. They have at least 1,000 bolts of first-quality fabric to choose from. Their fabrics are all kept on rollers, enabling you to actually pull out the fabric for a total visual concept rather than having only a little square to look at. If you don't want to do the job yourself, you can order custom draperies, bedspreads, and upholstery work. With savings at 50% below manufacturer's list and 25% less for labor, you can't go wrong. You can use your *Buying Retail Is Stupid!* coupon for a 10% discount on nonsale items only.

Fabric Barn
3111 E. Anaheim St.
Long Beach, CA 90804
310/498-0285, 800/544-9374

Hours: Mon-Sat: 9-5 Sun: 10-4
Credit Cards: Cash or Checks Only

"Disneyland For Ladies" is what the Fabric Barn is known as. They are one of the largest ribbon, lace, and trim stores with wholesale prices in Southern California. Their manufacturers design products that you won't see anywhere else. You'll find walls of polyester ribbon in 96 colors as well as specialty ribbons such as French Ambre, gold metallics, and organzas. They also have thousands of ruffled laces in 18 colors per style, name-brand fabrics, tapestries, silk and dried flowers, and craft items at prices that can't be beat. When in the neighborhood attend one of their two free craft demonstrations per month. All this and downright fantastic service too!

Fabric Gallery ★
405 N. Robertson Blvd.
Los Angeles, CA 90048
310/271-7815, 800/322-7457

Hours: Mon-Fri: 9-5 Sat: 10-4 Sun: 12-4
Credit Cards: AE, MC, V

Shop at Fabric Gallery and save 50% off retail on designer fabrics. They carry more than 1,000 rolls of fabrics ranging from silks and chenilles to woven tapestries and damasks. All fabrics are purchased directly from mill sources worldwide, and there is no middleman. Fabric Gallery ships nationwide and guarantees the best price on any competitor's item. Use your *Buying Retail Is Stupid!* coupon and receive an additional 10% discount when you purchase $100 or more.

Foam Mart ★
628 N. Victory Blvd.
Burbank, CA 91502
818/848-FOAM (848-3626)

Hours: Mon-Sat: 9-6
Credit Cards: AE, MC, V
♦ **Senior Discount:** 10% **Age:** 65

If you're in the market for foam, look no further. Foam Mart has the largest selection around for replacing foam in your sofa and chair cushions. Prices are about 10 to 20% off retail, but what makes this a super deal is that they'll install the foam for free if you bring in the cushions. In addition to foam, there are several other departments in this 8,000-square-foot store. Italian tapestries are about 50% off retail, and most of the other fabrics found here are 40% off retail. You'll also find polyester pillow forms in all sizes, furniture, and marine vinyls in solids and prints, canvas in all widths and colors, burlap, felt, and simulated furs. Foam Mart, in business since 1964 and a supplier to the film, special effects, and recording industries, will give you an additional 10% discount when you take in your *Buying Retail Is Stupid!* coupon. Discount applies on nonsale items only and is not valid with senior citizen discount.

Golden Fleece Designs Inc. ★

441 S. Victory Blvd.
Burbank, CA 91502
818/848-7724

Hours: Mon-Fri: 8-5
Credit Cards: AE, MC, V
♦ **Senior Discount:** 5% **Age:** 70

Canvas, canvas, and more canvas. Anything made from canvas can be found here. Canopies, flags, duffle bags, boat covers, sailboat accessories, nautical gift items, marine hardware, and hats. They will also custom make any canvas item to suit your needs. You can purchase industrial canvas by the yard and you can also silkscreen and embroider on any item. If you remember to use your *Buying Retail Is Stupid!* coupon, you can sail off with an additional 15% discount.

Kagan Trim Center

750 Towne Ave.
Los Angeles, CA 90021
213/627-9655

Hours: Mon-Fri: 8-4:30
Credit Cards: Cash or Checks Only

People who do their own sewing or tailoring will find this store to be truly amazing. If you can imagine it, Kagan Trim Center has it. Apparel construction and fashion products is the proper description of the merchandise they carry. Translated, that means you'll find items such as beads, laces, pearls, ribbon, appliques, tassels, webbing, netting, fringe, ruffling, and anything else you need. You have the convenience of finding everything you need under one roof, and because they are wholesalers (since 1945), you can count on exceptional savings. Please note, they sell their merchandise only in full rolls or boxes, no cut yardage and no samples.

Lincoln Fabrics ★

1600 Lincoln Blvd.
Venice, CA 90291
310/396-5724

Hours: Tues-Fri: 10-6 Sat: 10-5:30
Credit Cards: AE, DISC, MC, V
♦ **Senior Discount:** 20% **Age:** 65

This family business has been at one location since 1955. Their warehouse—so big it covers an entire block—contains more than a million yards of fabric. Lincoln Fabrics has drapery fabrics and hardware, hall runners, and upholstery fabrics. And you'll be paying at or below wholesale prices! They also carry art and marine canvas, cottons, linens, silks, foam rubber, vinyl, leather, natural burlap, and more. You get good service along with a massive selection of merchandise. It's no wonder they've been around for so many years! Take in your *Buying Retail Is Stupid!* coupon for extra savings of 20% (not valid with senior citizen discount).

Michael Levine, Inc. ★

920 S. Maple
Los Angeles, CA 90015
213/622-6259

Hours: Mon-Fri: 9-5:30 Sat: 9-4:30 Sun: 11-4
Credit Cards: AE, MC, V

Michael Levine has been in business since 1969; the store occupies more than 55,000 square feet near 9th and Maple, in the heart of LA's garment district. Everything you need in fabrics can be found here—a complete bridal department, upholstery products, and drapery goods as well as fun furs, piece goods, and other apparel necessities. Everything is priced at 20 to 50% below retail. Actually, there are two stores. The address above is where they house thousands of items for general apparel, and right across the street is everything needed for draperies and reupholstering. Parking is validated for one hour with a $15 purchase. Take in your *Buying Retail Is Stupid!* coupon for an extra 10% discount.

Off the Bolt ★

6812 De Soto Blvd.
Canoga Park, CA 91303
818/999-0441

Hours: Mon-Fri: 9-6 Sat: 10-5
Credit Cards: MC, V

All major mills are represented here. Off the Bolt has about 75,000 yards of fabric for your selection. This is a wonderful place to browse through, and you can save about 50% off retail prices. Their selection of decorative fabrics is perfect for drapery and upholstery projects. The salespeople here are most perceptive of your needs. Take in your *Buying Retail Is Stupid!* coupon and you'll receive a 14-16" pillow form, free with any $10 minimum purchase.

Additional Location:
Oxnard–1741 Ventura Blvd., 805/981-4975

Oriental Silk Co.
8377 Beverly Blvd.
Los Angeles, CA 90048
213/651-2323

Hours: Mon-Sat: 9-6
Credit Cards: MC, V
♦ **Senior Discount:** 10% **Age:** 65

The Oriental Silk Co. has exceptional buys on elegant silks, linens, and wools. You will discover a large selection of different colors and patterns in this 2,600-square-foot store. They import their own products in large quantities and pass the savings on to their customers. You will not only save about 25% off what you'd pay in a fabric store at the mall, but also have a lot more to choose from. Call Ken every now and then to make sure you don't miss out on anything. He'll tell you about his current stock or let you know when his next fabulous shipment will be arriving.

Stern's Discount Drapery Center ★
13861 Ventura Blvd.
Sherman Oaks, CA 91423
818/789-3838

Hours: Mon-Sat: 9:30-5
Credit Cards: MC, V
♦ **Senior Discount:** 10% **Age:** 65

Stern's Discount Drapery Center is a leading wholesaler and retailer (since 1952) of drapery and upholstery fabrics. You will save 40 to 50% off retail and even more on unclaimed items. Custom-made draperies are available, but the savings aren't quite as much as they are on fabrics or unclaimed orders. Look for their special close-out selection of fabrics for more savings (up to 70% below retail). Don't forget to use your *Buying Retail Is Stupid!* coupon for an additional 10% discount (not valid with senior citizen discount).

AUTOMOBILE NEEDS

ALARMS, STEREOS & TELEPHONES

Ahead Stereo
7426 Beverly Blvd.
Los Angeles, CA 90036
213/931-8873

Hours: Mon-Fri: 11-7 Sat: 11-6
Credit Cards: AE, DISC, MC, V
♦ **Senior Discount:** 15% **Age:** 65

Here are discount prices for home and car stereos and cellular phones, with personalized service, in a store that stocks everything. Their inventory includes names such as Pioneer, Paradigm, Marantz, Nakamichi, NHT, and lots more. "We dare you to beat our prices," they say. You'll appreciate the full service provided by the sales staff. Installation is also available. All of this, and they guarantee the best price, too.

Alan Graham Motoring Accessories ★
8618 Lindley Ave.
Northridge, CA 91325
818/993-8622

Hours: Mon-Sat: 9-6
Credit Cards: AE, MC, V

Buy direct from the manufacturer and save 10 to 35% on sheepskin seatcovers and auto accessories. Since 1977, Alan Graham Motoring Accessories has been servicing satisfied customers on their domestic and imported automobiles and meeting their budgets with quality goods. Not only can you get sheepskin items, but also you receive discounts on auto accessories such as a lifetime warranty on a car alarm or window tinting. When purchasing an alarm, bring in your *Buying Retail Is Stupid!* coupon for a free steering wheel lock valued at $69.

Additional Location:
Encino–17412 Ventura Blvd., 818/783-8161

Pacific Audio & Alarm ★
2370 E. Orangethorpe Ave.
Anaheim, CA 92806
714/992-5595

Hours: Mon-Sat: 8-7 Sun: 10-6
Credit Cards: All Major

If you're unhappy with the stock audio system in your car, you can replace it at Pacific Audio & Alarm. They have 4,000 square feet filled with brands such as Sony, Kenwood, Alpine, Viper, Rockford Fosgate, MTX, Infinity, Clifford, and many others. Whether you need a stereo, new speakers, an alarm, or accessories, you'll find it here at about 30% below retail. For more savings, mark your calendar for their annual sidewalk sale, usually held the first weekend in December. They offer a lifetime warranty on all installations, plus an extra 20% discount on installation labor with your *Buying Retail Is Stupid!* coupon.

Sounds Good Stereo ★
6405 Independence Ave.
Woodland Hills, CA 91367
818/999-4523

Hours: Mon-Fri: 8:30-6
Credit Cards: AE, DISC, MC, V

This discount store offers you a selection of stereo systems, cellular telephones, and automobile alarms for your car or truck. You'll find their merchandise priced at about 30 to 40% off retail. Since 1978, Sounds Good Stereo has been featuring low prices and high quality with such names as Alpine, Rockford, JBL, Fosgate, Concord, and more. They're equipped for repairs and are very proud of their professional, award-winning installation department. If you purchase equipment from Sounds Good Stereo, your *Buying Retail Is Stupid!* coupon is good for 50% off their regular installation price of $55 an hour. Sounds good to us.

See Also: (refer to index)
   All Systems Go
   Speaker City

BATTERIES

Battery Specialist/Powerline
21303 Sherman Way
Canoga Park, CA 91303
818/884-2288, 800/234-2444

Hours: Mon-Fri: 9-6 Sat: 9-4
Credit Cards: All Major
♦ **Senior Discount:** 15% **Age:** 65

Battery Specialist/Powerline is a nationwide distributor of batteries and battery-related products. As distributors to the electronic, industrial, commercial, medical, recreational, and automotive industries, they are able to offer discount prices to the public. So whether you need a new battery for your car, truck, motorcycle, or golf cart, make sure to give them a call first.

Additional Location:
Simi Valley—4268 Los Angeles Ave., 805/527-2288

Lynwood Battery Mfg. Co., Inc.
4504 E. Washington Blvd.
Los Angeles, CA 90040
213/263-8866

Hours: Tues-Fri: 7-3:30
Credit Cards: Cash or Checks Only
♦ **Senior Discount:** 5% **Age:** 60

Just as the name implies, the Lynwood Battery Co. manufactures their own batteries. They've been selling their merchandise to the trucking industry and marine dealers in California, Arizona, and Colorado since the 1930s. Even though they use only the highest-quality materials, you can buy your battery at 20 to 50% above cost! That should give you a charge.

Selco Battery Co. ★
2220 E. Foothill Blvd.
Pasadena, CA 91107
818/577-6713

Hours: Mon-Fri: 8-5:30 Sat: 9-1
Credit Cards: MC, V

For discounts of 10 to 30% on automotive, commercial, and special application batteries, contact Selco Battery Co. Selco stocks a wide selection of new and reconditioned batteries and will install your battery in minutes. Use your *Buying Retail Is Stupid!* coupon to save an extra 10% off your purchase.

INSURANCE

Survival Insurance
6301 Sunset Blvd., #104
Hollywood, CA 90028
800/441-5533

Hours: Mon-Sat: 9-9
Credit Cards: DISC, MC, V

Survival Insurance says they'll save you 15 to 20% on auto insurance if you give them a call—even if you drive an exotic car or have a few tickets. If you need an SR-22, they can usually offer same-day service. Remember, in California you have to have insurance on your car—it's the law! So in order to survive, you may want to call Survival Insurance.

Additional Locations:
Orange County–6731 Westminster Blvd., Suite 120, 714/934-1400
Sherman Oaks–14396 Ventura Blvd., Suite 200, 818/382-7100
Upland–345 S. Mountain Ave., 909/931-3000
West Los Angeles–11819 Wilshire Blvd., Suite 201, 310/231-5770

PARTS & ACCESSORIES

ABC Auto Parts Distributing
20339 Nordhoff St.
Chatsworth, CA 91311
818/773-4222

Hours: Mon-Sat: 8-5 Sun: 9-4
Credit Cards: DISC, MC, V

ABC Auto Parts sells all brake parts, shock absorbers, clutches, brake drums, disc rotors, power steering components, machine drums, and fly wheels. Name brands include, among others, Bendix, TRW, KYB, and Wagner. Started in 1968, this family operation is reputed to be the most knowledgeable in the business. They have the largest inventory in the San Fernando Valley and offer their customers savings of 30 to 50% off retail prices.

APA Industries
10505 San Fernando Rd.
Pacoima, CA 91331
818/834-8473

Hours: Mon-Fri: 6:30-5:30
Credit Cards: AE, DISC, MC, V

Instead of going into debt buying a new car, why not fix up your existing vehicle? APA Industries is a nationwide distributor of auto accessories that come with or without logos. By skipping the middle man, you can usually save 50% below retail on all kinds of goodies needed to spruce up the interior and exterior of both domestic and foreign cars. Plus, you save the cost of installation labor when you do the job yourself. Interior kits go from basic plastic to those made of various exotic woods. Other interior items include armrest and door panels, console covers, dashboard skins that adhere to an existing dash for a factory-fresh appearance, steering wheels, and just about anything else for car interiors. Custom covers for cars, light trucks, vans, station wagons, and even limos are available in six fabrics. The covers can also be made with special pockets for hood ornaments and mirrors. Although APA Industries sells to the public directly out of their warehouse, they don't really have a storefront. Most items (and APA has much more than we've covered here) are ordered from APA's 50-page catalog. You can request a catalog by writing to the address above and enclosing $5 (refundable with first purchase).

Auto Parts Club
2320 E. Orangethorpe
Anaheim, CA 92806
714/449-7800

Hours: Mon-Fri: 8-8 Sat-Sun: 9-5
Credit Cards: DISC, MC, V

You'll find 27,000 square feet filled with top-quality, name-brand domestic and imported auto parts and accessories and auto shop equipment at Auto Parts Club. Savings are 20 to 60% off retail with guaranteed best prices. Become a member for $10 a year and receive shelf prices. If you decide not to join, you'll pay an additional 10% on posted prices.

Additional Location:
Redondo Beach–2500 Marine Ave., 310/644-0822

Bavarian Auto Parts ★
4838 Lankershim Blvd.
North Hollywood, CA 91601
818/766-1927

Hours: Mon-Fri: 8-6
Credit Cards: Cash or Checks Only

As the name implies, Bavarian Auto Parts sells goods strictly for BMW and Mercedes automobiles. Depending on the item you need, discounts run 30 to 70% off retail on name-brand parts. If you don't quite know what's wrong with your car, their knowledgeable staff can steer you in the right direction. In fact, they are so customer oriented that you can page them if you need something in a hurry when the company is closed. Now, that's service! You'll also receive an additional 5% discount with your *Buying Retail Is Stupid!* coupon.

Bob's Auto Supply
1539 W. Manchester Ave.
Los Angeles, CA 90047
213/759-1155

Hours: Mon-Fri: 8-6 Sat: 8-5
Credit Cards: MC, V

Instead of running all over town, do-it-yourselfers can find everything they need at Bob's Auto Supply. Savings run 30 to 50% on all auto parts and machine shop services. They carry quality AC-Delco parts as well as brake drums and can provide engine repair and parts—foreign and domestic. Complete engines are also available for sale.

Jasmak Auto Parts & Accessories ★
1435 S. La Cienega Blvd.
Los Angeles, CA 90035
310/659-8441

Hours: Mon-Sat: 8-6
Credit Cards: MC, V

Auto parts and accessories can become quite expensive if you own a British, German, or Japanese import. Jasmak Auto Parts & Accessories carries all kinds of motor parts and motoring accessories at 20 to 50% off retail. Just a few of the brand names stocked are Febi, Hella, Bosch, Jurid, G & K, Knecht, Graf, Lucas, Ballo, Repco, Boge, Kaiser, and Lemforder. They guarantee to meet or beat anyone else's price, and if they don't have a part, they'll get it for you in a hurry! In addition to all necessary mechanical parts, they carry accessories such as body kits, fender trims, car emblems, and car covers. So, whether you need a new fuel injection system or a gold-plated accessory kit, Jasmak is the place to go. Don't forget to use your *Buying Retail Is Stupid!* coupon for an extra 15% discount.

Pacific Body Parts ★
8695 Venice Blvd.
Los Angeles, CA 90034
310/839-1140, 310/844-0231, 800/826-7741

Hours: Mon-Fri: 7-7 Sat: 7-3
Credit Cards: AE, MC, OPT, V

Here's a place for automobile parts, mechanical and electronic work, collision repairs, paint jobs, towing, and car rentals. Pacific Body Parts is a company that is truly committed to service and low prices. Savings are up to 50% on all services and parts for imported and domestic cars. If you're a teacher or on the police force, you pay only 10% above cost.

Others can save an additional 10% with their *Buying Retail Is Stupid!* coupon. What a great way to help make your paychecks go further. So if there is any kind of work you need on your car—and we mean anything—give Pacific Body Parts a call. Services vary with location. Call 800/826-7741 for information on which location meets your needs.

Additional Locations:
Culver City–10401 Washington Blvd., 310/839-5406
Culver City–10429 Washington Blvd., 310/839-5443, 310/839-0965
Los Angeles–5310 W. Century Blvd., 310/839-1152

Sonny's Radiator Exchange ★
34996 Yucaipa Blvd.
Yucaipa, CA 92399
909/790-1991, 800/551-3388

Hours: Mon-Fri: 8:30-5 Sat: 8:30-1
Credit Cards: MC, V

This warehouse distributor stocks more than 3,000 radiators. They discount additional items such as headers, air conditioner condensers, shock absorbers, transmission oil coolers, mufflers, and fan clutches. They also sell freon. Some of the brand names they carry are K.Y.B., Modine, Blackstone, Mando, Stuart, and Daniels. Prices quoted are cash prices. You'll receive a 10% discount when you purchase a radiator and a free tube of Permatex Sealant by using your *Buying Retail Is Stupid!* coupon.

Surplus City Jeep Parts
11796 Sheldon St.
Sun Valley, CA 91352
818/767-3666

Hours: Mon-Fri: 9-6 Sat: 9-5
Credit Cards: MC, V

Whether your jeep is new or used, this is the place to go for all your jeep needs. Expect to find their prices 20 to 30% below dealer prices. Your vehicle may be all terrain, but you won't need to go over hill and dale to find good prices—just stop here.

Valley Radiator ★
14408 Oxnard St.
Van Nuys, CA 90401
818/782-8231, 800/564-5855

Hours: Mon-Fri: 8-5 Sat: 9-1
Credit Cards: AE, MC, V

People who enjoy working under the hood should know about Valley Radiator. When it comes time to replace your radiator, you can buy new and used radiators directly from the source. They are so sure of their low prices you are encouraged to call them last. They carry name-brand goods for American, European, and Japanese cars. Your *Buying Retail Is Stupid!* coupon is good for an additional 10% discount off the price they quote on new radiators only.

See Also: (refer to index)
      Alan Graham Motoring Accessories
      Autocessories Wholesale

Used Parts

Ecology Auto Wrecking
13780 E. Imperial Hwy.
Santa Fe Springs, CA 90670
310/921-9974, 714/994-0703

Hours: 7 Days a Week: 7-5
Credit Cards: MC, V

After paying a $1 entrance fee to Ecology Auto Wrecking, you can look through their lot of more than 1,000 used cars and remove the part you need to repair your car. You pay only for the items you remove. Savings can range up to 80% off new parts. If you find you're spending a lot of time here, ask them about their frequent-buyer card, which offers 50% off your purchase after spending $500. Don't want to fix up your junk car? They will pay you cash for it and tow it away.

Additional Locations:
8 other stores throughout Southern California

Marv's U.S.A. Auto Dismantling
11021 Tuxford St.
Sun Valley, CA 91352
818/767-6615, 213/875-2781

Hours: Mon-Fri: 8-5
Credit Cards: DISC, MC, V

Marv's U.S.A. Auto Dismantling carries more than 45,000 item numbers in their computerized used parts inventory. All their parts (domestic only) are cleaned and tested and carry a six-month guarantee. They have experienced countermen to help you find the part you need. You can save 50 to 65% off the cost of new parts when you buy from Marv's. Why spend more on new parts when Marv's costs less and are guaranteed?

U-Pick Parts
11409 Penrose St.
Sun Valley, CA 91352
818/767-1211, 800/422-3536

Hours: 7 Days a Week: 8-5
Credit Cards: Cash Only

Bring your own tools and have a field day removing parts from used American-made cars and trucks at U-Pick Parts. They have 13 acres of used-car parts available for purchase. Prices are $22.95 for items such as a hood, fender, bumper, or windshield; hubcaps and speakers are $1; radios and jacks are $5. Check prices on the lot. Cars are mounted for removal of parts from underneath. Fork lifts also are available to assist you with heavy items such as engines. Used cars on the lot go up to 1990 models. Admission to the car lot costs $1, and you must be 18 years or older. There is also a used foreign-car parts lot next door.

Additional Location:
Los Angeles–8103 S. Alameda St., 213/583-1094, 800/526-0913

REPAIRS
Body & Engine Work

Associated Auto Body ★
11803 Sherman Way
N. Hollywood, CA 91605
818/764-5884

Hours: Mon-Fri: 8-5 Sat: 9-12
Credit Cards: MC, V

Associated Auto Body mainly does contract work for insurance companies, combining high quality with thoroughness and consistency. Luckily, they also welcome the individual customer and offer a discount on the labor charges. Serving the public in this area since 1969, they do complete frame work, auto body repair, and repainting. Price and time estimates are given in advance. The job usually gets done in the promised time, but if it doesn't, they will let you know. Not only will you find the people accommodating and friendly, but also their work is guaranteed. You'll save an additional 5% on labor charges by using your *Buying Retail Is Stupid!* coupon.

Carb Care USA ★
965 N. Batavia, #D
Orange, CA 92667
714/532-CARB (532-2272)

Hours: Mon-Sat: 8-5
Credit Cards: Cash or Checks Only

Carb Care USA is a small company of professional rebuilders of domestic and import carburetors offering large savings of 30 to 40%. You'll also receive a six-month or six-thousand-mile warranty as well as same-day service, and they speak Spanish. On top of this, you can get an additional $20 off with your *Buying Retail Is Stupid!* coupon.

Franco's Engine Rebuilders
4989 N. Huntington Dr.
Los Angeles, CA 90032
213/225-4129

Hours: Mon-Sat: 8-6 Sun: 8-4
Credit Cards: Cash Only

A professional engineer supervises the remanufacturing of the engines, and you also get factory-direct, wholesale prices. Franco's services domestic and foreign engines, plus they have a large inventory of engines and a complete line of auto parts. They offer a good warranty and have been in business since 1973.

See Also: (refer to index)
Autocessories Wholesale
Pacific Body Parts

Glass Replacement

All Star Glass ★
1136 E. Willow
Long Beach, CA 90806
800/659-9429

Hours: Mon-Fri: 8-5 Sat: 8-12
Credit Cards: All Major

All Star Glass specializes in windshield replacement for autos. Free mobile service is provided, which means they will do the work at your home at no extra charge. If you need an estimate, All Star Glass will give you one on the phone. They provide written guarantees and have qualified technicians/installers maintaining factory standards. Some of their locations also provide glass replacement for your home. All Star Glass services all of Southern California from Ventura to San Diego.

Your *Buying Retail Is Stupid!* coupon is good for an extra 10% discount on windshields, and a 5% discount on other parts.

Additional Locations:
21 other shops throughout Southern California–call 800/225-4185.

SALES, LEASING & RENTALS

Auto Insider Service, Inc.
818/994-8999, 800/446-7433
Hours: Mon-Fri: 6-5 Sat: 7-3

Auto Insider Service is billed as the number one auto buying program in the United States. The dealers in their program are approved to offer special discount pricing to their referrals. These prearranged discount prices are guaranteed in writing, assuring customers of honest savings without negotiating. This is a "one-price, no-hassle" car-buying program. There is no fee to the customer for this referral service.

Mickey's Auto Sales & Leasing
5554 Reseda Blvd., Suite 211
Tarzana, CA 91356
818/996-9601, 800/322-AUTO (322-2886)
Hours: By Appointment Only, Mon-Fri: 9-5:30
Credit Cards: Cash or Cashier's Checks Only

Since 1957, Mickey's Auto Sales & Leasing has helped thousands of people save time and money on the purchase and lease of new vehicles. This licensed and bonded dealer, through its computerized dealer network, researches hundreds of dealers to find your new vehicle, in your choice of color and equipment, at the lowest price possible. They handle all makes and models, foreign and domestic, including vans and trucks. Trade-ins are welcomed. Low-cost financing and leasing are available, or they'll work with your credit union or bank. Substantial discounts are offered on after-market items such as alarms and telephones. Mickey's charges no service fee! Decide on the make, model, color, and options you want, and call for an appointment. At your meeting, you'll find out how easy it is to get your next car without the hassling and haggling usually associated with purchasing or leasing a new vehicle.

National Auto Leasing & Sales, Inc.
23011 Moulton Parkway, Suite I-11
Laguna Hills, CA 92653
714/770-7441

Hours: Mon-Fri: 9-6:30
Credit Cards: Cashier's Checks

National Auto Leasing & Sales has serviced Southern Californians for more than a decade. They have sold and leased thousands of cars and trucks to customers at enormous savings. They sell all makes and models, domestic or foreign. Their volume allows them to purchase new vehicles at the lowest prices, and because they operate on a low fixed fee, the savings are remarkable. You can save hundreds of dollars depending on the make or model. They take trade-ins and provide financing and leasing. Leases can be tailored to the buyer's specifications, and they offer the lowest-cost "bumper-to-bumper" extended warranty available anywhere. Cashier's checks are preferred, but bank drafts are accepted.

TIRES

Autocessories Wholesale
8801 N. Sepulveda Blvd.
Van Nuys, CA 91343
818/894-4045

Hours: Mon-Fri: 8-6 Sat: 9-5 Sun: 10-3
Credit Cards: All Major

Since 1971, Autocessories Wholesale has been offering tires, wheels, and accessories with savings from 20 to 60% off retail. They also have a full-service repair shop offering competitive prices. Most important to them is to make sure their customers are satisfied.

Bob Mirman's Westcoast Tire and Brake ★
2239 Pontius Ave.
West Los Angeles, CA 90064
310/477-7057

Hours: Mon-Fri: 7:30-5:30 Sat: 7:30-5 Sun: 9-3
Credit Cards: MC, V

If your tires are looking a little bald, then head on over to Bob Mirman's. He'll meet or beat any advertised price in town. To remove any doubt, current ads from their discount competitors are posted for do-it-yourself price comparisons. There are 14 lines of brand-name tires in stock, and special orders are no problem. Other services include alignment, brakes, struts or shocks, air conditioning and heating, radiators, batteries, tune-ups, transmission work, and more. Vehicle inspection and a written report are always free. Mirman's also provides a waiting room complete with cable TV and refreshments. *Buying Retail Is Stupid!* customers will save at least an extra $10 on a set of four tires, and your *Buying Retail Is Stupid!* coupon is good for a 10% discount on labor.

Bob's Tire Town
2478-2484 W. Washington Blvd.
Los Angeles, CA 90018
213/731-6389

Hours: Mon-Fri: 7:30-5:30 Sat: 7:30-3:30
Credit Cards: AE, MC, V

Bob's Tire Town offers B. F. Goodrich, Pirelli, Uniroyal, Michelin, and Solar Shocks at 10 to 20% above cost. They also offer brake repair, alignment, and front-end work at significant savings. There are great buys on custom wheels for those of you with real hot "rides."

Valley Discount Tire Service
7139 Canoga Ave.
Canoga Park, CA 91303
818/340-3200

Hours: Mon-Fri: 8-5:30 Sat: 8-2
Credit Cards: MC, V

It's nice to know about a tire store that not only offers terrific prices, but has great service, too. They carry Michelin, Goodyear, and Remington tires at excellent prices and will service you quickly with a smile. Brake and alignment services are also available.

> A good source for auto parts is an auto dismantler who offers working parts that are guaranteed, usually for a minimum of 60 days.

COSMETICS, FRAGRANCES & SUPPLIES

Ball Beauty Supplies

416 N. Fairfax Ave.
Los Angeles, CA 90036
213/655-2330

Hours: Mon-Sat: 8:30-5:30
Credit Cards: AE, MC, V

Ball Beauty Supplies carries everything for your hair and manicuring needs, and you'll save 30 to 50% off retail by shopping there. They've been serving the public for over 35 years and know what their customers like. You'll find everything from hair coloring to curling irons. Excuse the pun, but you'll have a ball shopping at Ball Beauty Supplies.

Jilmond Perfumes & Cosmetics Company ★

222 E. 9th St.
Los Angeles, CA 90015
213/688-7881

Hours: Mon-Fri: 10-5 Sat: 11-5
Credit Cards: All Major
♦ **Senior Discount:** 10% **Age:** 60

You can get your own or your loved one's favorite perfume or cologne at Jilmond, discounted 20 to 60% below retail. Current brands are always in stock, as well as those no longer stocked in department stores. Take in your *Buying Retail Is Stupid!* coupon and they'll give you another 10% off (not valid with senior citizen discount). If your purchase comes to $60 or more, they'll throw in a free, 3.4-ounce bottle of Rodeo Drive. Call Beverly Hills store for its hours.

Additional Location:
Beverly Hills–Perfume Center, 371 N. Camden Dr., 310/278-8883

Lora Beauty Center ★

18737 Ventura Blvd.
Tarzana, CA 91356
818/705-4030

Hours: Mon-Sat: 10-6
Credit Cards: DISC, MC, V
♦ **Senior Discount:** 20% **Age:** 60

Looking for the best prices in town on Lancome products? Noga Douek, the owner of Lora Beauty Center, guarantees to beat anyone's price on Lancome products and fragrances. In addition to Lancome, they carry a complete line of beauty supplies and professional hair-care products. You'll also find name-brand fragrances such as Halston, Fendi, Chanel, Polo, and many others. You'll save 10 to 50% off retail shopping here, plus another 10% when you remember to use your *Buying Retail Is Stupid!* discount coupon (not valid with senior citizen discount).

Perfume City ★

12215 Ventura Blvd., No. 204 (Times Square Center)
Studio City, CA 91604
818/763-1875, 800/997-3738

Hours: Tues-Fri: 11-7 Sat: 10-6
Credit Cards: All Major

Whether you're looking for men's or women's fragrances, Perfume City has hundreds of scents at 10 to 60% off retail. Brand names include Bijan, Byblos, Kenzo, Opium, Red, Sung, Escada, Iceberg, and lots more. They also carry scents no longer carried by many retailers, plus a nice selection of miniatures. This neatly organized boutique is always on the lookout for super buys to pass on to their satisfied customers. Gift wrapping is free, and if you're buying for several people, they will put removable stickers on each package so you'll know what's what when you get home. Your *Buying Retail Is Stupid!* coupon will save you an additional $2 when your purchase totals $20 or more.

Perfumes West for Less

2099 Westwood Blvd.
West Los Angeles, CA 90025
310/470-8556

Hours: Mon-Sat: 10-6 Sun: 11-4
Credit Cards: AE, MC, V

Since department stores rarely discount their perfumes and colognes, places such as Perfumes West for Less can be very beneficial to your wallet. They carry hundreds of name-brand scents for men and women at prices 10 to 70% below retail. If your department store no longer carries your favorite brand, chances are you'll find it here for less than you're used to paying.

Prestige Fragrance & Cosmetics

100 Citadel Dr. (Citadel Outlet Connection)
Los Angeles, CA 90040
213/887-1135

Hours: Mon-Sat: 10-8 Sun: 10-6
Credit Cards: MC, V

Most of your favorite names in cosmetics and fragrances can be found at up to 70% off retail at Prestige Fragrance & Cosmetics. They are a factory-direct outlet, so make it a point to check out their prices, service, and quality. Additional health and beauty aids and gift items can also be found here.

Additional Locations:
Barstow–2586 Mercantile Way, 619/253-3503
Ontario–3700 E. Inland Empire Blvd., 714/994-5881
Oxnard–2000 Outlet Center Dr., 805/485-6686
San Ysidro–4498 Camino de la Plaza, 619/428-4400

Tarzana Beauty Supply ★

18456 Clark St.
Tarzana, CA 91356
818/881-1444

Hours: Mon-Sat: 9-6
Credit Cards: All Major
♦ **Senior Discount:** 10% **Age:** 65

Tarzana Beauty Supply is a full-service beauty salon and supply house with discount prices. All popular brand names—Matrix, Mastey, Goldwell, KMS, Sebastion, Aveda, Murad, M.D. Formulation, and many others—are offered at about the same prices as those found at swapmeets (at least 25% lower than regular retailers). The major difference is the very deep selection of brands and sizes, as well as the beauty accessories usually found in high-end department stores at 20 to 50% below retail. You'll also find name-brand skin-care, make-up, and nail products, and a nice selection of designer fragrances for men and women. All this and they offer makeovers, facials, and hairstyling, too. Don't forget to use your *Buying Retail Is Stupid!* coupon for an extra 10% discount (not valid with senior citizen discount).

Wilshire Beauty Supply Co.
5401 Wilshire Blvd.
Los Angeles, CA 90036
213/937-2000

Hours: Mon-Fri: 9-8 Sat: 9-6 Sun: 11-5
Credit Cards: MC, V

Your hair really is your crowning glory. You can have on an unbelievable outfit, but if your hair isn't together, forget it. At Wilshire Beauty Supply Co. you can purchase all the hair products you need for 20% above cost. Their prices are marked for the pros in the beauty business, and the public can buy at the same prices. If you'd like to try a new product, someone there will be happy to recommend something suitable for your type of hair. You will also find a selection of cosmetics and nail products. They have a monthly catalog for professional cosmetologists, as well as seminars and educational classes.

Additional Locations:
Arleta–8915 Woodman Ave., 818/891-5745
Beverly Hills–153 S. Beverly Dr., 310/276-0627
Simi Valley–2311-G Tapo St., 805/526-2281
West Los Angeles–10863 W. Pico Blvd., 310/475-3531

WIGS

Hair 4 Men ★
17743 Sherman Way
Reseda, CA 91335
818/705-9603, 800/818-HAIR (818-4247)

Hours: By Appointment Only, Tues-Fri: 10-5 Sat: 9:30-2
Credit Cards: Cash or Checks Only

Since 1948, Jack Swede has been manufacturing custom men's hairpieces and offering services such as hair adding, styling, perming, coloring, cutting, cleaning, and shampooing at 20% off retail prices. Take in your *Buying Retail Is Stupid!* coupon and you'll save an additional 20%. Satisfaction is guaranteed or they will replace the product. Ask when their twice-a-year, two-for-one sales occur.

Shaky Wigs of Hollywood ★
6364 Hollywood Blvd.
Hollywood, CA 90028
213/461-8481

Hours: Mon-Sat: 10-7 Sun: 1-5
Credit Cards: AE, MC, V

If you are looking for that perfect wig, hair accessory, or even hairspray, go straight to Shaky Wigs of Hollywood. We flipped our wigs when we saw more than 100 wigs to choose from! Don't be shy! Go ahead and try on any number of their wide selection of wigs at a discount of 10 to 20% off retail. By the way, this store isn't just for women. Men will find wigs and toupees made from 100% human hair. Other services offered are braiding and weaving. If you remember to use your *Buying Retail Is Stupid!* coupon, you'll receive an extra 15% discount.

Wilshire Wigs, Inc.
13213 Saticoy St.
North Hollywood, CA 91605
818/764-0200, 800/927-0874

Hours: Mon-Fri: 9-5:30 Sat: 9-4
Credit Cards: All Major

Men and women alike will find whatever they need in wigs and hairpieces (synthetic and human hair) at Wilshire Wigs priced 40 to 70% off retail. They have 6,000 square feet filled with 800 models with brand names such as Eva Gabor, On-Rite, Revlon, Alan Thomas, Tony of Beverly Hills, Adolfo, and Rene of Paris, and many others. You can buy ready-made items or have something customized just for you. If you're new at this, the staff can help you find the right style and color. They also have wigs made just for children. For saving even more money, take a friend or two with you because when you buy four or more wigs, you get an additional $5 discount off each wig.

Compare contents of generic and famous brands; often there is little difference, except in the price.

NEW & USED

Book Mart U.S.A.
12152 Victory Blvd.
North Hollywood, CA 91606
818/980-2241

Hours: Tues-Sat: 10-5:30
Credit Cards: Cash or Checks Only

You've been playing the game all your life. Now learn "How to Win at Bingo." This is probably the only store that carries this manual of current Bingo games. Along with this book, you can get complete Bingo game supplies. Offering paperback books only, Book Mart stocks more than 10,000 separate titles at 20 to 50% off the publisher's printed price. They also specialize in hard-to-find, first printings and out-of-print paperbacks for collectors.

Bookstar
3005 El Camino Real (Tustin Marketplace)
Tustin, CA 92680
714/731-2302

Hours: 7 Days a Week: 9-11
Credit Cards: All Major

Books, books, and more books! Bookstar is one of the largest suppliers of books offering discounts on any book featured on the *New York Times* bestsellers list. Best-selling paperbacks are discounted 20%, and best-selling hardbacks are discounted 30%. All other hardbacks are discounted 20% off retail. Although everything else is sold at regular retail, you'll always find super buys on their bargain tables.

Additional Locations:

12 other stores throughout Southern California

Dutton's Books ★
5146 Laurel Canyon Blvd.
North Hollywood, CA 91607
818/769-3866

Hours: Mon-Fri: 9:30-9 Sat: 9:30-6 Sun: 10-6
Credit Cards: AE, MC, V

You'll find a huge stock of new, used, and rare books at Dutton's Books. With more than half a million books in stock, this is a book lover's paradise! They also carry publishers' overstock, including research and scholarly books on nearly every subject, at tremendous discount prices. Your *Buying Retail Is Stupid!* coupon will save you an extra 10%. To top it all, they have free gift wrapping.

Additional Locations:
Burbank–3806 W. Magnolia, 818/840-8003
Los Angeles–5th & Flower (Arco Plaza), 213/683-1199

Encyclopedias Bought & Sold
14071 Windsor Pl.
Santa Ana, CA 92705
714/838-3643, 310/821-6888

Hours: Daily by Appointment Only: 10-10
Credit Cards: All Major

E-N-C-Y-C-L-O-P-E-D-I-A—remember when you knew you could spell when you sang Encyclopedia? Well, Kathleen Italiane has been singing this song since 1964. She has one of the largest and most varied collections of encyclopedias in the western U.S. dating from the late 1800s to current editions. Her collection includes Brittanica, Americana (rated number one by the American Library Association for adults and upper-age students), Colliers, orld Book, New Book of Knowledge (for ages 7 to 14 and rated number one by the American Teacher's Association), Compton's, and Academic American, and she sells them at a savings of 10 to 75% on used sets and 30 to 60% on new sets. Brittanica's Great Books and classical literature books are also available.

Super Crown Books
391 State College Blvd.
Brea, CA 92621
714/529-4161

Hours: Mon-Sat: 10-9 Sun: 11-5
Credit Cards: AE, DISC, MC, V

You save 10 to 50% off retail on current books, magazines, and books on tape at Super Crown and Crown Books, and they have convenient locations all over Southern California. If you're a book browser, you'll be glad to know that every store has a section filled with books—usually hardbacks—with even deeper discounts. All Crown Books (33 locations) have a great selection, but for mega selection, be sure to pay a visit to one of the much larger Super Crowns (27 locations). The Super Crowns also have places to sit. Store hours vary by location.

Additional Locations:
59 other stores throughout Southern California—call 714/379-3900.

USED BOOKS

A & M Book Cellars ★
19801 Vanowen St.
Canoga Park, CA 91306
818/716-6259

Hours: Mon-Wed, Fri: 11-7 Thurs, Sat: 10-5 Sun: 1-5
Credit Cards: Cash, Checks, or Trade-ins Only
♦ **Senior Discount:** 10% **Age:** 60

A & M Book Cellars sells recycled books, and after you see their prices, you'll wonder why you ever purchased brand-new books. Paperbacks—which make up 85% of the inventory—sell for about 50% off the publisher's price. Further, when you pay cash and your purchase adds up to $10, you'll get an additional paperback free. This family-owned and operated business is divided into much the same subjects as retail bookstores. For super low prices head toward the back of the store to the bargain room where inventory consists mainly of books that are either very worn, slow movers, or overstock of a particular book. As a used book dealer, A & M Book Cellars always welcomes trade-ins. Every January and July they have a sale where all books (bargain room not included) are half off their regular prices. Your *Buying Retail Is Stupid!* coupon is good for a 10% discount for regular customers. New customers receive a 10% discount plus a free paperback book of their choice. Call them for their winter hours.

Acres of Books
240 Long Beach Blvd.
Long Beach, CA 90802
310/437-6980

Hours: Tues-Sat: 9:15-5
Credit Cards: Cash or Checks Only

Acres of Books, in business since 1934, has an overwhelming selection of books. With 13,000 square feet of floor space and 750,000 books, it's about the largest store of its kind. In fact, it's so big there are maps strategically placed around the store to help their customers find their way around. Acres of Books attracts bookworms from all over Southern

California. Head on down to Long Beach if you are searching for a particular book no longer in print. If you love books, you'll find a visit a real treat, and they get new shipments every day.

Affordable Books & Collectibles ★
10324-B Sepulveda Blvd.
Mission Hills, CA 91345
818/365-1190

Hours: Mon-Fri: 11-6 Sat: 10-6 Sun: 11-3
Credit Cards: Cash or Checks Only

Curl up with a good book from Affordable Books & Collectibles. The store sells mostly used books with prices starting at 25¢ for paperbacks and 50¢ for hardcovers; some new books offer savings up to 50% off retail. They take paperbacks in for trade and purchase hardcover books that meet their current needs. The store also has a book search service if you are trying to find a special book. Take along your *Buying Retail Is Stupid!* coupon and save an additional 20% off your purchase of books only.

Bodhi Tree Bookstore
8585 Melrose Ave.
West Hollywood, CA 90069
310/659-1733

Hours: 7 Days a Week: 11-11
Credit Cards: MC, V

There are actually two stores at this address. If you are interested in homeopathic remedy, herbs, and all metaphysical subject matter, Bodhi Tree Bookstore sells new books at retail prices and offers discount specials every month. Bargain prices on the same type of books are found next door at the Bodhi Tree Used Book Branch. They buy and sell, and it's a fun place to browse, especially if you are philosophically undernourished.

The Book Baron ★
1236 S. Magnolia Ave.
Anaheim, CA 92804
714/527-7022

Hours: Mon-Tues, Thurs, Sat: 9:30-6 Wed: 9:30-8 Fri: 9:30-7 Sun: 9:30-5
Credit Cards: All Major

You can truly get lost among the 500,000 used, rare, and collectible books, magazines, and comics at The Book Baron. Prices start at $1 and go up to $10,000, with special sales in February and October. There's even a free children's library to encourage young readers. With your *Buying Retail Is Stupid!* coupon, you'll receive an additional 10% savings.

Book City ★
6627 Hollywood Blvd.
Hollywood, CA 90028
213/466-2525

Hours: Mon-Sat: 9-9 Sun: 10-8
Credit Cards: MC, V

This truly is a city of books—literally thousands and thousands of them. You can save 20 to 50% on your purchases, and in addition, Book City has one of Southern California's largest selections of used books. If you have a little time to spare, just browse through the book stacks and find reading treasures for as little as 49¢. As if their prices aren't low enough, your *Buying Retail Is Stupid!* coupon will save you an extra 10%. And if you are a movie or music buff, then you must visit their separate collectibles store right next door where you can find photos, magazines, autographs, and the like, dating back to 1900!

Additional Location:
Burbank–308 N. San Fernando Blvd., 818/848-4417

The Bookaneer
6755 Tampa Ave.
Reseda, CA 91335
818/881-6808

Hours: Tues-Sat: 10-6
Credit Cards: Cash or Checks Only

Genuine bookworms will have a hard time leaving this used bookstore. Opened in 1974 by Jim and Shirley, The Bookaneer has over 150,000 titles in their collection of paperbacks, hardbacks, comic books, biographies, mysteries, science fiction, romance, western, nonfiction, and children's books. They buy, sell, and trade 500 books a day, so the stock is always changing. Though not the largest used bookstore in the area, it is definitely the friendliest. Jim's sense of humor seems to rub off on his customers.

Additional Location:
Thousand Oaks–3186 E. Thousand Oaks Blvd., 805/379-9667

Bookman ★
840 N. Tustin Ave.
Orange, CA 92667
714/538-0166, 800/538-0166

Hours: Mon-Fri: 10-8 Sat: 10-6 Sun: 12-5
Credit Cards: All Major

We love when we've read a good book and paid only $1 for it. At Bookman you can pick up lots of $1 books in their bargain basement, as well as choose from their stock of more than 200,000 used books at savings of 30 to 50% off retail. They also specialize in rare out-of-print books. Remember, with your *Buying Retail Is Stupid!* coupon, you'll save an extra 10% off your purchase.

Booksville
2626 Honolulu Ave.
Montrose, CA 91020
818/248-9149

Hours: Mon, Tues, Thurs-Sat: 9:30-7
Credit Cards: Cash or Checks Only

The proprietress of this charming bookstore is Shirley McCormick. You'll be able to find special buys in used books for every member of the family. Start your search here for treasures at bargain prices. They are closed on Sundays and Wednesdays.

Cosmopolitan Book Shop
7017 Melrose Ave.
Los Angeles, CA 90038
213/938-7119

Hours: 7 Days a Week: 11:30-6
Credit Cards: Cash or Checks Only

Nothing is new at Eli Goodman's Cosmopolitan Book Shop, which has been in business since 1958. There is, however, for those who enjoy rummaging through used, out-of-print, and antiquarian books, the possibility of finding the rare, the unusual, and the different. Also included in the 2,200 square feet of space are paperbacks, select copies of magazines, and LPs of every description. Top prices are offered for whole collections, or they'll make acceptable trades. A customer can expect to save as much as 50% on books in print, and it's even possible to buy a book for as little as 50¢.

Green Ginger Bookshop ★
21710 Sherman Way
Canoga Park, CA 91303
818/713-1601

Hours: Mon-Sat: 11-7
Credit Cards: MC, V

If curling up with a good book is your favorite form of relaxing, then Green Ginger Bookshop is your kind of store. There are at least 80,000 used books priced at least 50% below original retail prices. Subjects include an extensive selection of photography, cooking, art, and Americana books. There's also a good selection of technical manuals, and unlike many used bookstores, Green Ginger doesn't devote much space to romance novels. The store is well stocked and neatly organized. So, whether you're a student looking for required reading material, or an avid reader looking for recently published hardbacks with dust covers, Green Ginger is the place to go. For a walk down memory lane, you'll also find about 5,000 used LPs (mostly classical, jazz, and show tunes) starting at $1. Your *Buying Retail Is Stupid!* coupon is good for a 10% discount. Free parking is available in back of the store.

Recyclepedia ★
3006 Lincoln Blvd.
Santa Monica, CA 90405
310/392-6917

Hours: Mon-Sat: 12-7
Credit Cards: Cash or Checks Only

We love the name of this store! Recyclepedia offers used books with savings of 30 to 80% off retail. Their wide range of subjects features sci-fi and fiction, film, art, philosophy, sports, and much more. They also offer collectible books. The *Buying Retail Is Stupid!* coupon will save you an additional 10%.

Sam's Book City ★
5245 Lankershim Blvd.
North Hollywood, CA 91601
818/985-6911

Hours: Mon-Fri: 10-7 Sat: 10-6 Sun: 11-5
Credit Cards: DISC, MC, V

There are more than 50,000 used books here, and you can save at least 50% off in-print prices! They have thousands of paperbacks at 50% off cover price (some exceptions). Their books are arranged in more than 200 categories. They not only accept cash, checks, and credit cards, but they've been known to haggle on occasion as well. You will find all of this in a quiet, relaxed atmosphere that encourages browsing. There are discount racks located in front of the store where paperbacks are sold for as little as 25¢. For additional savings of 10%, don't forget to use your *Buying Retail Is Stupid!* coupon.

AIR CONDITIONING & HEATING

Air Conditioning Exchange ★
6900 San Fernando Rd.
Glendale, CA 91201
818/845-8544, 213/849-2495

Hours: Mon-Sat: 8:30-5
Credit Cards: DISC, MC, V
♦ **Senior Discount:** 10% **Age:** 55

You can find everything you need for central heating and air conditioning equipment at Air Conditioning Exchange. Whether you are installing a complete system or fixing an old one, you will find prices at 50 to 60% less than retail. Their showroom has extensive displays designed especially to be unintimidating to do-it-yourselfers, and they will go out of their way to make you feel comfortable doing this kind of work. Not only do they carry major brand names such as Carrier, York, Day & Night, Tempstar, Heil, and Coleman Rheem, but they also stock supplies and parts in their 10,000-square-foot warehouse. They also fabricate custom sheet metal for adapting existing units to new equipment. For super bargains, don't forget to ask if they have any factory close-outs or items that are scratched or dented. This family-owned and operated business has been serving the community since 1974 with great prices and customer service. You'll receive an additional 10% discount on equipment, plus a free tape measure when you use your *Buying Retail Is Stupid!* coupon (not valid with senior citizen discount).

Home Comfort Center ★
18419 Vanowen St.
Reseda, CA 91335
818/345-9557

Hours: Mon-Fri: 8-6 Sat: 10-4
Credit Cards: AE, MC, V
♦ **Senior Discount:** 10% **Age:** 65

If you're the handywoman or handyman in your household, you will definitely want to head over to Home Comfort Center, a place geared toward home owners. They carry everything you'll need for do-it-yourself heating and air conditioning at savings of 50 to 60% off retail prices. Whether you're doing repair work or installing an entire system, you'll find everything at Home Comfort Center. Experts on their staff will help you every step of the way, and it's all free. You'll find extra comfort saving an additional 5% on equipment when you use your *Buying Retail Is Stupid!* coupon (not valid with senior citizen discount).

Nutone Products Distributor
14670 Firestone Blvd., #410
La Mirada, CA 90638
310/921-8933, 800/368-8663
Hours: Mon-Fri: 8-5 Sat-Sun: By Appointment Only
Credit Cards: MC, V

These people are the factory distributors for all the Nutone products. You'll save 30 to 35% off the retail price on heaters, exhaust fans, paddle fans, intercoms, door bells, bath cabinets, food centers, central vacuum systems, ironing centers, and more. Prices are gladly quoted over the phone. They have been in business since 1971, and they offer shipping on all items.

BRICKS, BLOCKS & FENCING

Elliott Precision Block Co.
157 N. Rancho Ave.
San Bernardino, CA 92410
909/885-6581
Hours: Mon-Fri: 7-5 Sat: 7-Noon
Credit Cards: MC, V

Elliott Precision Block Co. has been around since 1946 offering first-quality materials for the do-it-yourselfer at factory direct prices. Their customers are generally professional contractors needing materials for projects such as building walls, fences, and courtyards. They carry blocks, brick, cement, pavers, sand, steel, and everything needed to build a fireplace from scratch. If you know exactly what you need, they will be happy to quote you prices over the phone.

Fence Factory
29414 Roadside Dr.
Agoura, CA 91301
818/889-2240, 805/497-9233
Hours: Mon-Fri: 8-5 Sat: 9-3
Credit Cards: MC, V

Save 10 to 50% below retail on wood fences, ornamental iron fences, chain link fences, fittings, gates, poultry wire, electric gate motors, and more at the Fence Factory. They have a superb staff to install everything for you, or provide the do-it-yourselfer with all necessary materials. Custom work is available, too.

Additional Locations:
Goleta–60 S. Kellogg, 805/965-2817
Saticoy–1601 Los Angeles St., 805/485-8831
Santa Maria–2709 Santa Maria Way, 805/928-5848

CABINETS, CLOSETS & COUNTERTOPS

The Closet Warehouse
3113 La Cienega Blvd., Unit B
Los Angeles, CA 90016
310/837-0417

Hours: Mon-Fri: 9-5 Sat: 9-4
Credit Cards: AE, MC, V
♦ **Senior Discount:** 5% **Age:** 65

The Closet Warehouse is a company that specializes in systems made to organize everything from bedroom closets to garages, with discounts that start at 20% off retail. The most economical system they carry is made for the do-it-yourselfer. It's called ventilator shelving, and it's made of epoxy or vinyl coated wire. You can take in your closet measurements, and they'll help you figure out which of the many available units are most applicable to your needs, at a cost of 20 to 30% below retail. The Closet Warehouse doesn't have a fancy showroom because they are actually a factory. They also design and manufacture dream closets at 20 to 30% below retail. The systems come in all kinds of configurations, and they offer free in-home consultations with absolutely no obligation to buy. After your closets have been designed, you can either install the units yourself or have them do it. Cost for delivery and installation is $25 per section.

The Kitchen Store ★
6322 W. Slauson
Culver City, CA 90230
310/572-7515

Hours: Mon-Sat: 8:30-5:30 Sun: 9:30-3
Credit Cards: AE, DISC, MC, V

The Kitchen Store (previously called Panel-It Discount Stores) specializes in pre-finished kitchen cabinets at discounted prices. Their 6,000-square-foot showroom is devoted to kitchen displays. Instead of trying to imagine how a sample cabinet door is going to translate into an entire kitchen, you can pretty much stand in a completed kitchen. With their computerized design system, you'll be able to "see" your new kitchen layout in several angles and door styles. All you have to do is take in the measurements of your kitchen. In addition, they also carry bathroom vanities, countertops, glass tub enclosures, doors, and windows. They have a well-trained, professional sales staff to help you. Whether you're a professional contractor or do-it-yourself homeowner, everyone receives the same discounted prices and special customer service. Take in your *Buying Retail Is Stupid!* coupon for extra savings of 5%.

The Kitchen Warehouse ★
2093 W. Washington Blvd.
Los Angeles, CA 90018
213/734-1696

Hours: Mon-Sat: 9-5
Credit Cards: DISC, MC, V

The Kitchen Warehouse has cabinets of all qualities and price ranges, from ultra contemporary to old-world traditional, priced 10 to 60% below retail. There are 40 kitchen and cabinet displays in their showroom, making selection much easier than seeing just cabinet door samples. When you visit the store, make certain to take your room measurements with you. An expert designer will help you create a beautiful room, one that maximizes storage space and work flow, and one that you will be proud of. Computer imaging is available for a fee and by appointment only. They also have cabinets for all rooms, storage systems, entertainment centers, wall units, and wall beds. Save another 5% by using your *Buying Retail Is Stupid!* discount coupon (nonsale items only).

Marble Products of Fullerton ★
112 W. Commonwealth, Bldg. A
Fullerton, CA 92632
714/738-4384

Hours: Mon-Fri: 10-5
Credit Cards: Cash or Checks Only
♦ **Senior Discount:** 10% **Age:** 55

Vanity tops for bathrooms, shower panes, walls, window sills, and table tops can be found here, and Marble Products of Fullerton promises to be 10% lower than anyone in Orange County, including large warehouse stores. They manufacture their own products, so they are able to make anything of any size or color. Don't leave your *Buying Retail Is Stupid!* coupon at home or you'll miss out on an additional 5% discount.

Pride Enterprises, Inc.

7326 Fulton Ave.
North Hollywood, CA 91605
815/983-0992

Hours: Mon-Fri: 7-5
Credit Cards: Cash or Checks Only

Order custom kitchen and bathroom countertops direct from the manufacturer and save up to 50% off retail prices. Pride Enterprises, Inc. manufactures laminated plastic and formica countertops to your specifications. Products can be picked up at their plant or installed by one of their skilled employees. Countertops can be made for your house, apartment, or commercial building. A large selection of decorative laminates in a variety of colors is on display in their showroom. Pride takes pride in their work and in serving you.

See Also: (refer to index)
   Froch's Woodcraft Shop, Inc.
   Rich Door and Window

CERAMIC & STONE TILE

American International Stone and Tile

112 N. Catalina Ave.
Redondo Beach, CA 90277
310/937-5830

Hours: Mon-Fri: 8:30-5:30 Sat: 9-2
Credit Cards: MC, V

It's nice to know in this day and age, when people are changing careers so often, that the staff at American International Stone and Tile have more than 40 years' experience in the building supply industry. Their 20,000-square-foot consumer-friendly showroom features ceramic tile and natural stone—that is, slate, sandstone, limestone, marble, granite, and parquet wood flooring. Their guaranteed lowest price on stocked items is an incentive to visit the store. Even better, they will match the price if you find an item for less elsewhere.

California Wholesale Tile
1656 S. State College Blvd.
Anaheim, CA 92806
714/937-0591

Hours: Mon-Fri: 7:30-5 Sat: 8-4:30
Credit Cards: MC, V

Whether you're looking for bathroom, kitchen, entryway, or patio tiles, California Wholesale Tile is the place to shop. You'll find quarry tile, terra cotta tile, pool tile, hand painted tile, small mosaic tile, and Italian decorative floor and wall tile at one of the largest ceramic tile showrooms in Orange County. They have more than 6,000 square feet of showroom filled with great buys. Also, they have another location in the same area of Anaheim called Tile Importers. So if one store doesn't carry exactly what you have in mind, it's a short distance to another showroom.

Additional Location:
Anaheim–Tile Importers, 1320 S. State College Blvd., 714/533-9800

D'Mundo Tile
77725 Enfield Ln., #170
Palm Desert, CA 92211
619/360-0097

Hours: Mon-Fri: 7-5
Credit Cards: DISC, MC, V

D'Mundo Tile imports most of their tile from Italy, Spain, Brazil, and Mexico, and they also have a few American-made lines. They specialize in rustics perfect for Southwest decor. In business since 1984, D'Mundo Tile has a 6,000-square-foot warehouse filled with tile, furniture, and pottery priced 40 to 60% off retail. In stock are more than 40 styles of pavers and nearly 100 patterns in handpainted Talavera tiles. Custom work is available (you may bump into landscapers and interior designers when shopping here), and they'll send you a free brochure filled with tile and furniture for sale to get your creative juices flowing.

Discount Tile Center
8627 Venice Blvd.
Los Angeles, CA 90034
310/202-1915

Hours: Mon-Fri: 8-5:30 Sat: 9-5
Credit Cards: MC, V

This is a great wholesale, factory-direct center for ceramic tiles of all kinds. Discount Tile Center has imports from all over the world. In addition to decorative and terra cotta tile, they carry granite, marble, slate, and limestone. Everything is usually in stock or can be obtained in just a few days. They also carry handpainted sinks. You'll save at least 30 to 50% off retail prices all the time, and they also feature special sales during the year, in which you could be paying less than wholesale!

Monterey Ceramic Tile & Marble

3130 N. Del Mar Ave.
Rosemead, CA 91770
818/288-8693, 800/700-8694

Hours: Mon-Sat: 7-5 Sun: 10-2
Credit Cards: MC, V

Monterey Ceramic Tile & Marble has a 2,500-square-foot showroom situated in the heart of San Gabriel Valley, showcasing a thorough line of ceramic tiles, mosaics, marble, granite, limestone, and several other related stones. Their tiles and stones derive from Europe, the Mediterranean, and the Pacific Rim. They also sell tools, adhesives, and many other related tile and stone products for maintenance and cleaning. With more than 50 years' experience in the tile and stone industry, Monterey Ceramic Tile & Marble has seasoned relationships within the industry to sell at 25 to 50% below retail. Call to inquire about their blow-out sales featuring savings of up to 80%.

New Metro Tile Company ★

5477 Alhambra Ave.
Los Angeles, CA 90032
213/221-1144

Hours: Mon-Fri: 7-5 Sat: 8-2:30
Credit Cards: MC, V
♦ **Senior Discount:** 5% **Age:** 55

This store handles imported and domestic tiles of all major brands such as H & R Johnson, Huntington/Pacific, American Olean, and many more. This is a real do-it-yourselfers' headquarters. You can save 20 to 50% on your purchases, and they have extra special prices on discontinued items and seconds. When you buy their tile, you can leave a deposit, and they will lend you tools to complete the job. Take in your *Buying Retail Is Stupid!* coupon for a 5% discount (not valid with senior citizen discount).

Tile, Marble & Granite Warehouse ★
7114 Reseda Blvd.
Reseda, CA 91335
818/881-1056

Hours: Mon-Fri: 8-6 Sat: 9-5
Credit Cards: MC, V

You'll find miles of tiles at this business based entirely on great service! If you've looked everywhere for just the right color and design to no avail, head on over to Tile, Marble & Granite Warehouse. They have such a deep selection that making up your mind will be the tough part. (You'll know exactly what we mean when you see the multitude of colors and designs in just bathroom tiles and trims.) And their prices are still 30% below most discount tile stores. Owner Jeff Joss imports most of the tile himself and passes the savings on to you. You'll be pleased with the selection of tile, marble, and granite for your floors, walls, counters, kitchen, bathrooms, pool, or spa. They offer marble and granite slab as well. They have in-house designers and all the supplies needed for installation. Not only do they offer free professional advice, but they also provide free use of tools. If doing the job yourself doesn't sound like such a great idea, ask about their installation services. They will meet or beat any validated price, and if you take in your *Buying Retail Is Stupid!* coupon, they'll give you an additional 10% discount. Now, that's a deal carved in stone!

Additional Locations:
Glendale–1264 S. Central Ave. (N. of Los Feliz), 818/240-7555
San Diego–6330 Miramar Rd., 619/457-1352
West Los Angeles–11043 W. Pico Blvd., 310/575-3059

Tileclub ★
6945 Reseda Blvd.
Reseda, CA 91335
818/345-2276

Hours: Mon-Fri: 9-7 Sat: 9-5 Sun: 10-4
Credit Cards: MC, V

Tileclub caters to the homeowner. They have a large inventory, and there is no more than a five-to-seven-day wait on nonstock items. You will find ceramic tile and related products for counters, walls, and floors. Their staff will teach you how to install ceramic tile, and they have rental equipment and a tile cutting service too. Savings run 20 to 50% off retail, and you can save more at their January clearance sale. Whatever you do, don't forget to take along your *Buying Retail Is Stupid!* coupon for an additional 10% discount!

Additional Locations:
7 other stores throughout Southern California–call 800/700-8453.

DOORS, WINDOWS & MIRRORS

A-1 Shower Door Co. ★
2019 Richey St.
Santa Ana, CA 92705
714/258-3005

Hours: Mon-Fri: 9-6 Sat: 10-2
Credit Cards: DISC, MC, V
♦ **Senior Discount:** 10% **Age:** 65

A-1 Shower Door Co. has the largest stock of standard-size tub and shower enclosures in Orange County. Their showroom has more than 35 framed, frameless, and trackless doors and features brands such as Aluminax, American, Tub Master, and more. They will even fabricate custom-size enclosures. A-1 will install anywhere in Orange County, or you can pick it up and do it yourself. Use your *Buying Retail Is Stupid!* coupon and you'll save an extra 10% off on will-call orders (not valid with senior citizen discount).

All Valley Shower Door Co. ★
14665 Arminta St.
Van Nuys, CA 91402
818/782-7477.

Hours: Mon-Fri: 8-5 Sat: 8-1
Credit Cards: Cash or Checks Only
♦ **Senior Discount:** 5% **Age:** 60

Marilyn Singer is the manager of this establishment that offers standard and custom shower enclosures, mirrors, wardrobe doors, and anything in glass at discounted prices. Because All Valley Shower Door Co. is a distributor for American Shower Door, you'll save lots of money over specialty boutiques. You can either do the installation yourself or use one of their journeyman installers. Take in your *Buying Retail Is Stupid!* coupon for an extra 5% discount.

Mastercraft Door & Window Center
9136 De Soto Ave.
Chatsworth, CA 91311
818/407-8900

Hours: Mon-Fri: 8:30-5 Sat: 10-4
Credit Cards: MC, V

Mastercraft Door & Window Center is a full-line door and window store. Their 2,000-square-foot showroom is complete with today's newest models, along with hardware and molding samples. Savings range from 25 to 40% off retail prices on entry and closet doors, swing and sliding

French doors, skylights, and aluminum, vinyl, and wood windows. In addition to the lines they manufacture themselves, they carry brand names such as Milgard, Cobb, Fleetwood, Weathershield, Velux, Simpson, Marvin, and many more. Since Mastercraft Door & Window Center is a licensed general contractor, installations are no problem. They also offer free in-home estimates. Ask when their parking-lot and one-day sales occur for greater savings. Call West Los Angeles store for hours.

Additional Location:
West Los Angeles–2215 S. Sepulveda Blvd., 310/268-9118

Rich Door and Window ★
17453 Clark Ave.
Bellflower, CA 90706
310/866-4090

Hours: Mon-Fri: 9-5 Sat: 10-2
Credit Cards: MC, V

Doors and more doors and more doors are what you will find here. Since 1990, Rich Door and Window has been offering 20 to 57% off on wood and metal doors, aluminum and vinyl windows, and premanufactured cabinets. Their two showrooms feature kitchens, windows, doors, moulding, weatherstripping, and hardware. Ask about their once-a-month home improvement sales. Your *Buying Retail Is Stupid!* coupon will save you an additional 10% off your purchase of $100 or more.

Rion Sash and Door Co. ★
7166 Firestone Blvd.
Downey, CA 90241
310/928-2511, 213/773-3397

Hours: Mon-Fri: 7:30-4:30 Sat: 8-3
Credit Cards: MC, V

With more than 40 years' experience serving the contractor's trade and homeowners, Rion Sash and Door Co. knows the importance of offering professional workmanship at low prices. You'll save 20 to 40% off doors, windows, and mouldings, as well as free in-house estimates. They have a showroom and wood mill on site and offer an additional 5% savings when you bring in your *Buying Retail Is Stupid!* coupon.

Rolleze, Inc. ★
13581 Desmond
Pacoima, CA 91331
818/899-9561

Hours: Mon-Thur: 7-4 Fri: 7-3:30
Credit Cards: Cash or Checks Only

Buy direct from the manufacturer and save 25% on residential windows and patio doors. Since 1967, Rolleze has been custom manufacturing windows and screen doors and selling them direct to the homeowner or contractor. With your *Buying Retail Is Stupid!* coupon, you'll save an extra 5% on any order.

FLOOR COVERINGS

Able Carpets
8854 W. Pico Blvd.
Los Angeles, CA 90035
310/859-1522

Hours: Mon-Fri: 9-5:30 Sat-Sun: By Appointment Only
Credit Cards: DC, DISC, MC, V

All major brands of carpets are discounted for you at Able Carpets, in business here since 1959; quotes are cheerfully given. You can carry out your carpet purchases, or they will deliver. They have expert installation service, plus a good selection of vinyl and mini-blinds to complement your decor. In addition to the huge stock of full rolls, there are always good remnants to check out.

A•P•T Carpet Co.
8910 Washington Blvd.
Culver City, CA 90232
310/836-1313

Hours: Mon-Fri: 8-5 Sat: 8:30-2
Credit Cards: Cash or Checks Only

When it gets to the point where your old carpet is beyond help, A•P•T Carpet Co. has just what you need. As a major supplier to property management companies, they are able to offer volume pricing to the public. In addition to the many rolls of carpet in stock, they have linoleum and remnants, and expert installation is available. Make the time to look here before you make your next carpet purchase. If you already know what you want, give them a call to make sure it's available before making the drive.

Carpet Bazaar Factory Outlet

9216 De Soto Ave.
Chatsworth, CA 91311
818/998-4085

Hours: Mon-Fri: 9-6 Sat: 10-5
Credit Cards: MC, V

With more than 15,000 square yards of carpet in stock and hundreds of styles and colors to choose from, in a showroom-warehouse of 17,000 square feet, the Carpet Bazaar Factory Outlet is a place you should shop before making a decision. Special prices on mill close-outs and slightly irregulars are below their everyday low prices. Their truckload buying power saves you money. They offer volume discounts, and prompt installations are available. Name brands include Shaw, Gulistan, Alladin, and others.

Carpet Collection ★

8126 Van Nuys Blvd.
Van Nuys, CA 91402
818/994-1555

Hours: Mon-Sat: 10-5
Credit Cards: Cash or Checks Only
♦ **Senior Discount:** 5% **Age:** 65

In business since 1925, Carpet Collection carries a large inventory of floor coverings—carpets, vinyl, tile, and linoleum—and also window coverings. According to the owners, any carpet a customer on any budget might want is available. As a wholesaler, they will beat any legitimate price. Service is emphasized, and immediate installation is available. They carry a large selection of name brands such as Philadelphia, Salem, Royalty, El Dorado, Catalina, Armstrong, Horizon, and more. Their 3,500-square-foot showroom is housed in a 14,000-square-foot warehouse. The public is welcome, and special low discounts are offered to contractors and interior decorators. You can save an additional 5% off your purchase price when you use your *Buying Retail Is Stupid!* coupon (not valid with senior citizen discount). The Northridge store has different hours, so call before you visit.

Additional Locations:
North Hollywood–12126 Sherman Way, 818/982-4554
Northridge–19520 Nordhoff Pl., 818/993-1977

Carpet Land Mills

6951 Reseda Blvd.
Reseda, CA 91335
818/609-0339

Hours: Mon-Fri: 10-8 Sat: 10-6
Credit Cards: MC, V

In their 1,500 square feet of showroom, there are more than 100 mills represented and more than 2,000 samples from which to choose. They also carry hardwood, vinyl, and tile flooring, and vertical blinds and mini-blinds. Prices are at about 5% above cost, and phone quotes are welcomed. Among the name brands carried are Stainmaster and Weardated carpets. They offer immediate delivery. Don't forget to ask about their 18-month replacement guarantee.

Carpet Manor ★

18314 Sherman Way
Reseda, CA 91335
818/344-2277, 800/286-2860

Hours: Mon-Fri: 9-6 Sat: 10-5 Sun: By Appointment Only
Credit Cards: MC, V

In business since 1953, Carpet Manor offers a wide selection of carpets, remnants, wood and vinyl flooring, and window coverings. Prices are up to 70% off retail, and they guarantee best price. They carry all major brands in their 5,000-square-foot warehouse and offer prompt delivery and service, as well as free advice to ambitious customers who want to do it themselves. They'll roll out the carpet for an additional 5% discount if you use your *Buying Retail Is Stupid!* coupon!

Carpet Market Outlet

5900 Kester Ave.
Van Nuys, CA 91411
818/989-0940

Hours: Mon-Sat: 9-5:30
Credit Cards: MC, V

The Carpet Market Outlet is a discount outlet for most major brands of carpeting and linoleum. They carry only major brands such as Anso V, Stainmaster, and DuPont Certified. Joe Zeldin says he has the guaranteed best price anywhere. Spanish-speaking customers should ask for Enrique Cisneros.

The Carpet Store ★
17831 Clark Ave.
Bellflower, CA 90706
310/804-2621

Hours: Mon-Fri: 8-5 Sat: 9-5
Credit Cards: AE, OPT
♦ **Senior Discount:** 10% **Age:** 60

The Carpet Store is committed to offering its customers the highest-quality carpet at the lowest possible cost. They also make that promise on vinyl, hardwood floors, and window dressings. Brand names you'll find are Diamond, Mannington, Shaw, Queen, Stainmaster, and many more. With your *Buying Retail Is Stupid!* coupon, you'll save an extra 10% off your purchase (not valid with senior citizen discount).

Culver Carpet Center
4026 S. Sepulveda Blvd.
Culver City, CA 90230
310/398-2458

Hours: Mon-Fri: 8:30-6 Sat: 8:30-5
Credit Cards: MC, V

Culver Carpet Center is a large discount carpet and vinyl warehouse, one of LA's largest volume dealers. You can save 25 to 60% off retail on first-quality, name-brand rolls and remnants of carpets. You'll also find a complete line of custom wood flooring, linoleum, and a fine vinyl selection. These experts can install everything they sell. In business since 1952, they offer selection, service, and big savings.

Decorator Warehouse
612 S. La Brea Ave.
Los Angeles, CA 90036
213/938-5264

Hours: Mon-Fri: 9-5 Sat: 9-3
Credit Cards: MC, V

Enjoy savings of 10% above cost on carpets, wood floors, and linoleum from Decorator Warehouse. Savings on window treatments such as mini-blinds, verticals, duettes, silhouettes, and wood blinds are up to 75% off retail. In fact, they say they have the lowest prices in Los Angeles and will even quote prices over the phone. Give them a try and see for yourself.

Floor Covering Unlimited ★
8480 W. 3rd St.
Los Angeles, CA 90048
213/651-5290, 800/334-4434

Hours: Mon-Fri: 8-5:30
Credit Cards: AE, DISC, MC, V

Whatever you want to put on the floor, including the floor itself, Floor Covering Unlimited has it and at wholesale prices. Custom hardwood floors, vinyl and ceramic tile, mini-blinds and vertical blinds, and draperies are available in an almost limitless array of choices. They have been in business since 1972 and give free estimates. There's always a pile of carpet doormats and remnants for $1 to $2. Your *Buying Retail Is Stupid!* coupon is good for $10 off any minimum purchase of $250.

G & S Carpet Mills
3205 Pomona Blvd.
Pomona, CA 91768
909/468-5600

Hours: Mon-Fri: 8-5 Sat: 9-1
Credit Cards: All Major
♦ **Senior Discount:** 5% **Age:** 62

The dog chewed your carpet; Aunt Rose spilled cranberry juice on your carpet; the kids are grown up and there are holes in your carpet—it's time to finally get new carpets. G & S Carpet Mills offers factory-direct prices on their carpets—generally 25% off retail.

Lester Carpet Co., Inc. ★
7811-7815 Beverly Blvd.
Los Angeles, CA 90036
213/934-7282

Hours: Mon-Sat: 8-5
Credit Cards: MC, V

If you want to cover your floors or windows, Lester Carpet Co. guarantees the lowest price! They have been in business since 1954; with that kind of experience and more than 13,000 square feet of warehouse, they know how to buy in volume and pass the savings on to you. You can carpet your home with name brands such as Tuftex, Armstrong, Hollytex, Tarkett, and Queen. Other items carried are linoleum sheets, tiles, and wood flooring. Custom work is available as well. For more savings, your *Buying Retail Is Stupid!* coupon is good for an extra 10% discount.

Linoleum City
5657 Santa Monica Blvd.
Hollywood, CA 90038
213/469-0063, 213/463-1729

Hours: Mon-Thur: 8:30-5:30 Fri: 8:30-7 Sat: 9-5
Credit Cards: DISC, MC, V

Since 1948, Linoleum City has been serving the needs of LA's shoppers
for floor coverings. They have a combination warehouse and showroom
in Hollywood of more than 15,000 square feet. Claiming to have the
largest selection of vinyls, linoleum, and carpeting in the city, Linoleum
City offers brand names such as Armstrong, Mannington, Tarkett,
Congoleum, and Hartco, as well as many others. In addition to the
thousands of rolls of vinyl floor covering in stock, they have cork and
wood flooring, commercial and residential tiles, rolls of carpets, and
hundreds of carpet samples. Their sales staff is very knowledgeable, and
installation is available through independent contractors.

Melrose Discount Carpet ★
7951 Melrose Ave.
Los Angeles, CA 90046
213/653-4653, 310/275-3601

Hours: Mon: 9-7 Tues-Fri: 9-5
Credit Cards: AE, MC, V
♦ **Senior Discount:** 15% **Age:** 70

If you're going to replace your carpeting, here's the place for you. Family-
owned and operated since 1965, Melrose Discount Carpet carries carpet,
sheet vinyl, ceramic tiles, marble and hardwood flooring, and area rugs. You
can even buy blinds for your windows. Savings run 50% over most places,
and they have remnants, close-outs, and Class A seconds for sale. They are
located one block west of Fairfax, and parking is on the street only. You will
save an extra 10% on in-stock merchandise when you present your *Buying
Retail Is Stupid!* coupon (not valid with senior citizen discount).

Royal Discount Carpets
529 N. Fairfax St.
Los Angeles, CA 90036
213/655-4343

Hours: Mon-Sat: 9-4
Credit Cards: Cash or Checks Only
♦ **Senior Discount:** 10% **Age:** 65

This shop is stuffed with wonderful buys on carpeting, area rugs, and vinyl
flooring. Most of the merchandise is priced at 10% over cost. If you're looking

for carpeting, then this shop is a must, because the prices are really hard to beat. Go on over and check out what Royal Discount Carpets has to offer.

HARDWARE & PAINT

A.A. Baker's Hardware & Paint ★
3925 San Fernando Rd.
Glendale, CA 91204
818/242-7467

Hours: Mon-Fri: 7:30-6 Sat: 7:30-5 Sun: 9-4
Credit Cards: AE, DISC, MC, V
♦ **Senior Discount:** 10% **Age:** 60

Baker's is an institution in Glendale, having been there since 1915. They are a full-service hardware, paint, and lighting store. Discounts on lighting goods run at about 40% off retail. When it comes to hardware, the more you buy, the more you save. For example, if you buy half a box of bolts, you'll automatically receive a 30% discount at the register, and if you buy a whole box, your automatic discount is 40%. Baker's always has monthly specials, and you can't beat the customer attention provided by long-standing employees. Your *Buying Retail Is Stupid!* coupon, with a $50 minimum purchase, is good for an extra 10% discount (not valid with senior citizen discount).

Catalina Paint Factory
7107 Radford Ave.
North Hollywood, CA 91605
818/765-2629

Hours: Mon-Fri: 7-5 Sat: 7:30-2:30
Credit Cards: DISC, MC, V

For a change of color to your house, you can buy direct from the paint manufacturer, Catalina Paint Factory, and save up to 33%. They have more than 2,000 colors to choose from. This family-run business is rated number one in customer service. Ask about their free, expert technical advice.

Additional Location:
Northridge–18924 Roscoe Blvd., 818/772-8888

Nor-Mar Sales Co., Inc.
20835 Nordhoff St.
Chatsworth, CA 91311
818/700-8804

Hours: Mon-Fri: 7-5
Credit Cards: MC, V

After 20 years of selling only to the building trade, Nor-Mar Sales is now open to the public. Don't be overwhelmed when you see their 20,000 items of every type of builders' hardware and plumbing fixtures (faucets, sinks, toilets, bath accessories), along with earthquake latches and cabinet knobs. Their factory-trained sales personnel are ready to spend time helping you make a selection and educate you about all the options available. Prices on most items are 40% off retail. Not bad, and you get wonderful service too! Call the West Los Angeles store for hours.

Additional Location:
West Los Angeles–2215 S. Sepulveda Blvd., 310/312-1537

Par Paint Company ★
1801 W. Sunset Blvd.
Los Angeles, CA 90026
213/413-4950

Hours: Mon-Fri: 7:30-5 Sat: 7:30-2:30
Credit Cards: MC, V
♦ **Senior Discount:** 5% **Age:** 62

Talk about guys that know paint? Par Paint Company has been in business since 1949 selling paints, lacquers, varnishes, compliance coatings, automotive paints, industrial paints, and supplies at wholesale prices. They represent 3M, Sunbelt, Guardsmen, Purdy, Pittsburgh, Spectrum, Krylon, Zynolite, Nason, and Ellis. They also have rollers, spray cans, covers, brushes, and all acoustical supplies. Whatever you need in this department, they've got, and their prices are 20% below retail. You will save an additional 5% when you use your *Buying Retail Is Stupid!* coupon (not valid with senior citizen discount).

Post Tools
3838 Santa Fe Ave.
Vernon, CA 90058
213/588-1255

Hours: Mon-Sat: 8-5
Credit Cards: AE, DISC, MC, V

Previously known as Santa Fe Tool & Supply, this is the undisputed leader in discount prices for tools. They say they have no competition because they will beat all prices. What's more, they guarantee everything they sell. What do they sell? TOOLS—power tools, hand tools, air tools, auto tools, and shop tools—including such names as Skil, Hitachi, Makita, and the rest. They also sell work gloves and work brushes too. Ask to be put on their mailing list so you can hear about special sales. Any day you visit Post Tools you'll save 30 to 50% off the retail prices. They've been in business since 1975.

Additional Locations:
17 other stores throughout Southern California–call 800/767-8669.

Scotch Paints Factory Store
555 W. 189th St.
Gardena, CA 90248
310/329-1259, 800/404-2878

Hours: Mon-Fri: 7-5 Sat: 8-12
Credit Cards: All Major
♦ **Senior Discount:** 10% **Age:** 65

In business since 1951, Scotch Paints Factory Store is the place to go when you know what you want and are eager to get up to 50% off retail. The paints you purchase here are manufactured on the premises and are the same ones they sell to million-dollar construction companies, cities, counties, and school districts. There are 32 exterior and interior stock colors, as well as thousands of custom colors from which to choose. Color matching is offered at no extra charge. You'll also find everything in equipment and supplies needed for house painting. Dealing mainly to professionals over the years, Scotch Paints Factory Store personnel offer expert advice free for the asking. For those of you who aren't very handy with a paint brush, the service-oriented staff can recommend reliable painting contractors.

PLUMBING & ELECTRICAL

McNally Electric
10792 Los Alamitos Blvd.
Los Alamitos, CA 90720
310/598-9438, 714/761-0692

Hours: Mon-Sat: 9-5
Credit Cards: DISC, MC, V

Whatever your lighting needs, McNally Electric can satisfy them. Table and floor lamps, fluorescents, incandescents, low voltage, track or recessed lighting, indoor or outdoor, you'll find them here at 20 to 50% savings. Whether your needs are commercial, residential, or office, their trained sales personnel will help you with your purchase. They also carry all the "stuff" that goes behind the light fixture, such as switches, breakers, and fuses. If you have a favorite lamp that needs repair, take it in. We can't begin to list all of the brand names they carry, but some are Tivoli, Fredrick Ranond, Hilite, Nutone, Plantation, Melissa, Angelo, Dinico, and Halo Lighting.

Save-Mor Plumbing Supplies
3361 Hamner Ave.
Norco, CA 91760
909/735-4655

Hours: Mon-Sat: 8-5:30
Credit Cards: DISC, MC, V
♦ **Senior Discount:** 10% Off Labor **Age:** 55

At Save-Mor Plumbing Supplies, every employee can take do-it-yourselfers by the hand and help them with their projects. These projects can range from installing a garbage disposal to plumbing an entire house. While their showroom is only 900 square feet, their inventory of supplies and equipment takes up 2-1/2 acres! Prices run about 20 to 40% below prices at hardware chain stores. They have three plumbers who make calls at far less than most, since they are the material suppliers. Another plus for shopping here is that their personnel appear to be genuinely pleased to serve you.

See Also: (refer to index)
        Fator's Appliances & Plumbing
        Nor-Mar Sales Co., Inc.
        Warehouse Discount Center

SERVICES

End Result
818/784-1572

Hours: 7 Days a Week: 9-9

Do you need some work done on or in your home? End Result has been referring people to trustworthy tradespeople—with down to earth prices—since 1979. Whether you need a roofing contractor, electrician, painter, plumber, carpenter, mason, general contractor, or handyman, End Result will refer you to someone thoroughly screened and reliable. They have nearly 10,000 satisfied customers, including some of the biggest names in Hollywood. There is no charge for this service.

Additional Locations:
Orange County Referral Service–714/546-6008
Santa Barbara Referral Service–805/964-5001

Haz Equipment Rentals
8642 Garden Grove Blvd.
Garden Grove, CA 92644
714/638-3640

Hours: Mon-Sat: 8-6 Sun: 8-4
Credit Cards: AE, MC, V

Since 1969, Haz Equipment Rentals has been here to help. Whatever you need to rent, they have it all: Ryder and Ford trucks, Bosch tools, Briggs & Stratton small garden engines, JVC stereos and karaoke machines, IBM typewriters, Milwaukee chainsaws, Pro Cut tile saws, Samsonite chairs, Landa pressure washers, and more. Savings are 20% off retail, with lower rates for repeat customers.

Hiawatha Homes ★
16700 Bollinger Dr.
Pacific Palisades, CA 90272-1148
310/454-4809

Hours: By Appointment Only
Credit Cards: Cash or Checks Only
♦ **Senior Discount:** 5% **Age:** 65

Looking to save money on building your own home? The first thing you should do is place an order with Hiawatha Homes. Seven books filled with more than 1,000 designs for single-family homes will cost you a total of $23. After you decide on the home of your dreams, order a set of four working drawings and two outline specifications, at a cost ranging from $95 to $600. Some of these plans could easily cost $3,000 to $10,000 prepared by a designer or architect as a custom plan, and yet the quality would be no better than the plans you can buy from Hiawatha Homes. Their plans, for small cottages to homes with more than 4,000 square feet, meet California and Uniform building codes. Save time and money on building your next home, and build in an additional 15% discount using your *Buying Retail Is Stupid!* coupon. Remember, the coupon works with the plans, not the house.

Stripper Wallpaper Service ★
818/789-7949, 800/500-0117

Hours: 7 Days a Week: 8-6
Credit Cards: Cash or Checks Only
♦ **Senior Discount:** 10% **Age:** 62

If you want a new look in your home but don't have the time to remove your wallpaper, give Stripper Wallpaper Service a call. They specialize in wallpaper removal only. No one will try to sell you anything else. They will make your walls spic-and-span clean by removing the paper and any glue for a smooth surface, and scrubbing the walls. Now you're ready to make your house beautiful with new wallpaper. Prices to remove paper are $8 per single roll for a vacant room, $10 per single roll if they have to move furniture, and $12 for high ceiling work. These are about 20 to 30% lower than other wallpaper strippers. They promise on-time performance, prompt return of telephone calls, and a bonded, trained staff to do the work. In addition to servicing most of the Los Angeles area, they reach parts of Orange County. Call their 800 number for information. If you pay by cash, they also offer an extra 10% discount with your *Buying Retail Is Stupid!* coupon.

WALL & WINDOW TREATMENTS
Wallpaper

MH Designs ★
19328 Londelius St.
Northridge, CA 91324
818/366-1721

Hours: Mon-Sat: 10-5
Credit Cards: AE, DISC, MC, V

You'll find plenty of your favorite brands in wall coverings at MH Designs. Wallpaper, mostly consisting of overruns and discontinued lines, is priced at 20 to 80% below retail. Pay attention to the cards attached to each bin. If the card indicates the wallpaper is "in-stock," it means more is available. Cards that are marked "overrun or close-out" mean you should buy an extra roll or two because the wallpaper is no longer being manufactured. If you don't see anything to your liking in the bins, you can place special orders from at least 900 books with a selection of traditional to masculine themed wallpapers. Discounts run 20 to 60% off book prices. In addition to wallpaper, MH Designs carries window coverings and carpeting with discounts starting at 20% below retail. An additional 10% savings is offered with your *Buying Retail Is Stupid!* coupon (valid only on nonsale items).

Obalek Tile & Wallpaper
2301 S. Hill St.
Los Angeles, CA 90007
213/748-4664

Hours: Mon-Fri: 8-6 Sat: 9-5
Credit Cards: MC, V

If you want to find great discount prices on a huge stock of tiles from around the world, visit Obalek Tile & Wallpaper. They have approximately 500,000 square feet of ceramic and vinyl tiles in stock. The savings found here are fantastic. For example, tiles that retail for $1.79 to $1.89 at other stores cost as little as 59¢ to $1.29 per tile. In addition to tile, they have carpeting and 250,000 rolls of wallpaper. They carry all the tools necessary to do-it-yourself, and their professional staff will be glad to instruct you on the how-to. General manager Bill Cochran and his staff are extremely helpful. By the way, Obalek always has special close-outs.

Wallpaper Bin
17139 Ventura Blvd.
Encino, CA 91316
818/788-1291

Hours: Mon-Sat: 10-6
Credit Cards: MC, V

If you're looking for high-quality decorator and famous-maker wallcovering, how would you like to save up to 80% off original book prices! That's exactly what you can save on items in stock at Wallpaper Bin, the very best resource for quality, in-stock wallpaper. They carry brands such as Mirage Light Reflectives, Palisades Classics, Marburg Dimensionals, Waverly, Schumacher, Imperial, John Wilman, Bolta, and Sanitas, and many more. You'll be able to make your selection from a variety of vinyls, mylars, textures, handprints, strings, grass cloths, and more. Most all of these absolutely marvelous buys are discontinued collections from factory and mill inventories. Lest you think they have leftovers that nobody else wanted, Wallpaper Bin places their order three to six months before production is stopped. This assures them of having a fine variety of popular patterns. To be on the safe side, when you buy wallpaper here, pick up an extra roll or two, because when it's gone, it's gone for good. For super savings, take a peek at the Clearance Corner where you may find bagged lots of two double rolls (four rolls of paper) for $10, or three double rolls for $20.

Additional Location:
Ventura–4255 E. Main St., 805/642-6422

Wallpaper City
1320 Lincoln Blvd.
Santa Monica, CA 90401
310/393-9422

Hours: Mon-Fri: 8:30-5:30 Sat: 9-5
Credit Cards: MC, V

There are more than 1,000 rolls of different wallpaper in stock at any one time, and 1,000 wallpaper books to order from, and you can save 20 to 50% on your selection. Their large stock of wallpaper can be matched to shades and drapery treatments. Fabric can also be ordered to match your designer paper from companies such as Schumacher, Waverly, Brewster, and Imperial. At Wallpaper City, you can purchase vinyls, grass cloths, custom bedding, pillows, and window coverings, all at big savings.

Window Treatments

Aero Shade

8404 W. 3rd St.
Los Angeles, CA 90048
213/655-2411

Hours: Mon-Fri: 8:30-5
Credit Cards: MC, V

In business since 1950, Aero Shade has everything for windows, including motorized window coverings. If you're looking for pleated or laminated shades, shutters, or Levolor or vertical blinds, they have a complete stock and quick service. Custom drapers are also available. You're buying factory direct at Aero Shade and can save 20 to 50%. Some of the styles available are custom, decorative, and simple. They'll provide new rollers or put the new cloth on your old rollers. You can also have your fabrics laminated.

Blue Chip Drapery, Inc.

2139 Stoner Ave.
Los Angeles, CA 90025
310/477-2421

Hours: Mon-Sat: 9-5:30
Credit Cards: DISC, MC, V

You will usually save 50% or more on draperies and blinds at Blue Chip Drapery. This company is California's largest discount drapery manufacturer, with seven window covering showrooms throughout greater Los Angeles and Orange counties. There are 120 sizes of ready-to-hang draperies in a great variety of textures and colors, always available at factory-direct prices in each showroom. All ready-mades (standard, elegant, luxury, and close-out lines) are sold on a satisfaction-guaranteed basis, allowing a 10-day exchange or refund. When you order custom draperies from their huge stock of discounted decorator fabrics, there is no labor charge added to most selections. Major brands of mini-blinds, verticals (same-day service), and other window treatments are also discounted.

Additional Locations:
6 other stores in Southern California–call 310/477-2421.

Brite and Shine, Inc. ★
7625 Hayvenhurst Ave., #4
Van Nuys, CA 91406
818/782-5326

Hours: Mon-Fri: 8:30-4:30
Credit Cards: MC, V
♦ **Senior Discount:** 5% **Age:** 60

Brite and Shine offers name-brand window coverings with bottom-line lowest prices. They carry such brand names as Levolor, Graber, Louverdrape, Hunter Douglas, Del Mar, Kirsch, and Verosol. A six-foot sliding glass door can be covered with vertical blinds for as little as $78.50, including a valance. Brite and Shine offers fast delivery and lifetime warranties on all their merchandise. They specialize in mini-blind cleaning using ultrasound. In fact, you'll get an extra 10% discount off the cleaning of five or more mini-blinds with your *Buying Retail Is Stupid!* coupon. With prices up to 70% below retail, you'd be "brite" to shop here.

Discount Blinds, Shades & Shutters
16147 Roscoe Blvd.
North Hills, CA 91343
818/891-6060

Hours: Mon-Fri: 9-6 Sat: 10-6
Credit Cards: All Major

Since 1975, this family-owned-and-operated business has been offering guaranteed lowest prices on window coverings and treatments, blinds and shades, draperies, and shutters. They give quick, courteous, free phone quotes, and have an attractive showroom displaying all major name brands. A manufacturer's warranty is available on all their products.

Interior Motives
8362 W. 3rd St.
Los Angeles, CA 90048
213/658-6017

Hours: By Appointment Only
Credit Cards: MC, V

Interior Motives is really a window covering specialist, but they also offer 20 to 50% discounts on carpets, custom bedding, and upholstery in name-brand fabrics. You'll find an extensive selection of mini-blinds, vertical blinds, woven blinds, shutters, Levolors, Roman shades, pleated shades, and custom draperies. In business since 1979, they offer free estimates and also have a home shopping service.

Melrose Draperies ★
7748 Santa Monica Blvd.
Los Angeles, CA 90046
213/653-1601

Hours: Mon-Fri: 8:30-5
Credit Cards: AE, DISC, MC, V
♦ **Senior Discount:** 10% **Age:** 55

These folks have been in business since 1962 manufacturing, selling, and installing window coverings. Want your bedspread to match your bedroom drapes? Look no further! Want to see how the fabrics will look in your home? They'll bring out samples to your home. Draperies, bedspreads, window shades, at true discount prices. Savings run about 30% below department store prices, and you'll save an additional 10% with your *Buying Retail Is Stupid!* coupon (not valid with senior citizen discount).

Star Draperies Mfg. ★
5900 Van Nuys Blvd.
Van Nuys, CA 91401
818/787-7841, 213/463-1574, 800/541-7827

Hours: Mon-Sat: 9-5:30
Credit Cards: DISC, MC, V
♦ **Senior Discount:** 5% **Age:** 65

Star will come to your home, measure your windows, and give you a free estimate. When your order has been completed, their pro will handle the installation. Vertical blinds are their specialty, and they make mini-blinds, pleated shades, and wood blinds. Draperies are also custom-made. Look forward to factory-direct prices, with savings as much as 60 to 70% off retail prices. They have been in business since 1974 serving the counties of Los Angeles, Orange, and Ventura. Don't forget to use your *Buying Retail Is Stupid!* coupon for an extra 10% discount. Now, that's a deal!

Superior Window Coverings ★
10701 Chandler Blvd.
North Hollywood, CA 91601
818/762-6685

Hours: By Appointment Only, Mon-Sat: 9-5
Credit Cards: MC, V

Wholesale prices on draperies, vertical blinds, mini-blinds, pleated shades, wood blinds, shutters, draperies, Roman shades, balloon shades, cloud shades, and cornice boxes are found in Superior Window Coverings' factory showroom. In addition to being a manufacturer of their own lines since 1979, they carry a large variety of brand names such as Hunter Douglas, Waverly, Barrow, and many more. Bring in your *Buying Retail Is Stupid!* coupon to get an extra 10% discount! The store in Woodland Hills is open only on weekends from 10 a.m. to 6 p.m.

Additional Location:
Woodland Hills–6701 Variel Ave., Unit O-38, 818/888-1550

See Also: (refer to index)
   Bedroom & Window Creations

For major tasks, use licensed contractors, check with your state board to make sure they are in good standing, ask to see finished work, request referrals, and check with them. An ounce of prevention . . .

ACTIVE WEAR

Blue Moon

608 Main St.
Ventura, CA 93001
805/643-2553

Hours: Mon-Sat: 10-6 Sun: 12-5
Credit Cards: AE, MC, V

Blue Moon carries a wide variety of women's and junior clothing at great prices, usually wholesale or below. You will also find a wide range of accessories available to complete your outfit. Blue Moon carries sizes from 1 to 16, and occasionally they carry larger sizes. They have lots of free parking, three dressing rooms, and a very relaxed atmosphere. This is a great place to buy swimwear. Bikinis and one-piece suits are $13.99 all summer long.

Canyon Beachwear's Swimwear Outlet ★

2772 Artesia Blvd.
Redondo Beach, CA 90278
310/793-2599

Hours: Mon-Sat: 10-6 Sun: 10-5
Credit Cards: MC, V

Canyon Beachwear's Swimwear Outlet has the largest year-round selection of ladies' designer swimwear and accessories by leading manufacturers at savings up to 70% off retail. They specialize in bikinis, one-piece, and mix-and-match sizes. Brand names include Gottex, La Blanca, Mossimo, Anne Cole, Baja Blue, and more. Even greater savings can be found at their end-of-season clearance sale. Canyon Beachwear focuses on service, style, and selection and ships nationwide. With your *Buying Retail Is Stupid!* coupon, you'll save an extra 10% off your purchase of $50 or more.

Shelly's Discount Aerobic & Dance Wear ★
2089 Westwood Blvd.
Westwood, CA 90025
310/475-1400

Hours: Mon-Sat: 10-6 Sun: 11-4
Credit Cards: AE, MC, V

You'll save from 30 to 70% on leotards, tights, and active wear that are perfect for dancing and those strenuous aerobic workouts. Shelly Seeman has them in all sizes and styles and colors—even for mothers-to-be and children. She has special sales all the time, as well as a parking-lot sale once a month. Brand names include Rachelle, Softouch, Marika, and Cathy George, to name a few. You'll find a complete selection of costumes and accessories, dance shoes, and dancewear in this well-stocked 3,000-square-foot store. Dressing rooms and parking are available. Call the Tarzana store for hours. Your *Buying Retail Is Stupid!* coupon will save you an extra 20% on nonsale items only.

Additional Location:
Tarzana–Apparel Warehouse, 6010 Yolanda St., 818/344-3224

BRIDAL & FORMAL

$9.99 Store
6633 Fallbrook Ave. (Fallbrook Mall)
West Hills, CA 91307
818/703-8592

Hours: Mon-Fri: 10-9 Sat: 10-8 Sun: 11-7
Credit Cards: AE, DISC, MC, V

There are bargains, super bargains, and finally, the beyond-belief bargains also known as, "What? Are they crazy? How can they stay in business with these kinds of prices?" Well, welcome to the $9.99 Store. We're talking bridesmaid, mother-of-the-bride, prom, and cocktail dresses that originally retailed for as much as $350 all priced at $9.99! Now and then you might see a beaded number in the $500 range priced at, you guessed it, $9.99. The dresses carry the same labels found in most bridal stores across the country. You can easily buy 10 dresses for the retail price of one. In fact, just the buttons or rhinestone accents on some dresses retail for more than $9.99! At these prices, if you see a formal you like but need a cocktail dress, cutting off the extra length is definitely an option. Sizes generally run 4 to 18, but it's not unusual to find larger sizes up to 40. Also, instead of searching used clothing stores for a little girl's dress-up games, or perhaps drag costumes for Halloween, you can always find something here that's brand new and maybe even less expensive. All sales are final—no returns or exchanges.

Anna Queen ★
8761-8763 Garden Grove Blvd.
Garden Grove, CA 92664
714/537-9326

Hours: Mon, Wed-Fri: 12:30-8 Sat-Sun: 11-5
Credit Cards: Cash or Checks Only

Since 1989, Anna Queen has been renting and selling everything for the bride and groom at savings of 50% off retail. She carries sizes 4 through 44 in bridal gowns, bridesmaid dresses, flowergirl dresses, and tuxedos. If you don't see what you're looking for, she can special-order your dress at 20% off retail. Want to match your bridal shoes to your dress? She sells shoes for $19.89, which includes dying. Receive an additional 5% off a purchase of $300 or more with your *Buying Retail Is Stupid!* coupon.

Deja Vu Bridal Boutique ★
Venice, CA 90291

310/821-8460

Hours: By Appointment Only
Credit Cards: Cash or Checks Only

Relax in the privacy of Deja Vu Bridal Boutique while listening to soft music, sipping a glass of sherry, and viewing their designer bridal gowns. They accept clients only by appointment and give individual attention to each person. You won't be disappointed at the 50 to 60% you'll save on new and once-worn designer bridal gowns, headpieces, and slips by Diamond, Golena, Jim Helm, Bob Mackie, and more, in sizes 2 through 14. Prices for gowns range from $350 to $1,500 (normally selling for $500 to $3,000). Selected gowns are accepted for resale on consignment, making your old dream gown a new dream gown for another bride. Save an additional 10% off your headpiece with the *Buying Retail Is Stupid!* coupon.

Dressed Up!
6000 Reseda Blvd.
Tarzana, CA 91356

818/708-7238

Hours: Mon-Sat: 10-5:30 Sun: 11-4:30
Credit Cards: All Major

Dressed Up! is a fantastic boutique located in the "Alley in the Valley." The merchandise, consisting of labels rarely found discounted in high-end department stores until the end of a season, reflects owner Michael Weintraub's wonderful sense of style. The clothing styles run from casual elegance to ball gowns, and if you have a special occasion coming up, you can't beat the selection of evening dresses and suits. All of the first-quality clothing is current and is priced 20 to 80% off retail. If you have something particular in mind, the first-class staff will do their best to fill special orders, including bridesmaid and prom dresses. Dressed Up! has many high-end brand names that can't be named here, so pay them a visit. You won't be disappointed.

Jessica McClintock Company Store
18577 Main St.
Huntington Beach, CA 92626

714/841-7124

Hours: Mon-Wed, Sat: 10-6 Thur-Fri: 10-9 Sun: 11-6
Credit Cards: AE, MC, V

It's so nice to find outlets that provide deep discounts on expensive brand names most of us can't afford. This store has the feminine and flattering styles of Jessica McClintock priced 40 to 60% below department and specialty store prices. The Jessica McClintock Company Store also carries Gunne Sax and Scott McClintock. Their stock is bursting at the seams with bridal gowns and bridesmaid, mother-of-the-bride, and flowergirl dresses. In addition, you'll find plenty of special-occasion dresses suitable for proms, cocktail parties, graduations, and bat mitzvahs, along with women's daywear and infant and toddler clothes. Call the Montclair store for hours.

Additional Location:
Montclair–5458 Moreno St., 909/985-2770

Price-Less Bridals
6633 Fallbrook Ave., Suite 204
West Hills, CA 91307
818/340-6514

Hours: Mon-Fri: 10-9 Sat: 10-8 Sun: 11-7
Credit Cards: AE, DISC, MC, V

Price-Less Bridals has new wedding gowns priced 50 to 80% below retail, sometimes more! They've always had unbelievable prices here, but after remodeling, the look of the store isn't the only thing that's changed since the last edition. Now most wedding gowns—more than 2,000 in sizes 2 to 44—are priced at $399.99. How about a traditional gown by Dimitrios—Chantilly lace covered in clear sequins, illusion neckline, and strands of pearls draped across an open back—for $399.99 instead of $1,300? You can skip the fitting, special order, and months waiting for your dress because, as always, gowns are ready for purchase right off the rack. Only well-known companies and designers are represented. Most labels have been removed, but the excellent staff can tell you the maker. You'll also find gowns with blue tags for $699.99. These are usually high-end gowns such as a $2,600 Eve of Milady in Dupioni silk. The $199 and $99 racks remain with deals such as a $1,350 Bianchi for $99. This dress had yards of beaded French lace that wholesales at $110 per yard! Pink-tagged dresses that can be reordered are discounted 15%, as are any special orders from a full line of bridal gowns. Headpieces—with or without veils, from simple to elegant—are $99. All sales are final—no returns or exchanges.

See Also: (refer to index)
> Damone

Bridal Services

Forever Treasured ★
10049 Rubio Ave.
Granada Hills, CA 91343
818/360-9943

Hours: Mon-Fri: 9-7 Sat: 10-3
Credit Cards: Cash or Checks Only

You can't prevent your wedding gown from yellowing and becoming brittle just by putting it in a pretty box. Specializing in the cleaning and preservation of wedding gowns at 40% less than most other places charge, Forever Treasured carefully handles wedding gowns as though they were rare museum artifacts. In fact, only museum-quality archival supplies are used here. Owners Lynda and David Valenti understand the emotional value placed on wedding gowns. Rather than the same harsh chemicals utilized in the dry cleaning industry, only environmentally safe products are used on delicate fabrics and laces (new or heirloom), sequins, pearls, beads, and the like. After the gentle cleaning process, the gowns are enclosed in tissues and boxes. Forever Treasured offers their services nationwide. Your *Buying Retail Is Stupid!* coupon is redeemable for a 25% discount on any cleaning, pressing, or preservation service.

Wedding Dreams Library
20969 Ventura Blvd.
Woodland Hills, CA 91364
818/587-3440

Hours: Tues-Wed, Fri-Sat: 10-4 Thur: 10-8
Credit Cards: Free Service

We love the word *free*—and that's just what the Wedding Dreams Library referral service is. Since 1987, Wedding Dreams Library has helped thousands of couples make their wedding preparations a breeze. How many people remember their wedding preparations being fun and easy? Stop by their store and see videos, displays, and portfolios representing businesses that handle every aspect of weddings—invitations, cakes, caterers, deejays, and much more. There are more than 65 businesses in one location for you to choose from. If you can't visit their store, you can call the library as often as you like—and remember, there is never a fee.

FAMILY APPAREL

Bugle Boy Factory Store
355 E. Easy St.
Simi Valley, CA 93063
805/581-1907

Hours: Mon-Sat: 9-7 Sun: 11-6
Credit Cards: All Major

The clothing—for boys, young men, men, and women—at Bugle Boy Factory Store is all first-quality merchandise currently found in most medium-priced department stores. For the most part, everything is priced 20 to 40% off retail. Lucky for us, this outlet (there are 146 across the country) is located at Bugle Boy's main distribution center, resulting in the best selection of Bugle Boy products. The store is well organized, goods are neatly displayed, and they have very efficient salespeople. Although there is a small area of women's clothing, most of the merchandise is devoted to boys and men. Sizes run 4 to 7 for boys, 8 to 20 for young men, and men's sizes run 32 to 44 and medium to XX-large. Women's sizes run 4 to 18 and also small, medium, and large. They have an open return policy, which means if you keep your receipt, you'll receive a full refund. If you have no receipt you can make an exchange. They have special sales during the year, so get on their mailing list for advance notification.

Burlington Coat Factory Warehouse
7777 Edinger Ave. (Huntington Beach Mall)
Huntington Beach, CA 92647
714/379-6077

Hours: Mon-Fri: 10-9 Sat: 10-7 Sun: 11-6
Credit Cards: AE, DISC, MC, V

Burlington Coat Factory Warehouse carries far more than just coats. You'll find clothing for the entire family—babies, children, women, and men. In addition, they carry linens and accessories for the home. Some of the brand names you'll see are Jones New York, Guess?, Avanti, Liz Claiborne, Pipp, Childcraft, PePe, Fieldcrest, and Wamsutta. Although the majority of their inventory consists of first-quality merchandise, they do have some factory seconds. These huge stores offer discounts of 20 to 50% off retail, and twice a year they have warehouse sales featuring even deeper discounts.

Additional Locations:
Arcadia–1201 S. Baldwin Ave., 818/447-8784
Torrance–395 Del Amo Fashion Center, 310/370-9090
San Marcos–1617 Capalina Rd., 619/471-5437
West Hills–22835 Victory Blvd., 818/340-2494

California Jeans ★
1228 Obispo Ave.
Long Beach, CA 90804
310/494-1300

Hours: 7 Days a Week: 11-7
Credit Cards: MC, V

California Jeans always has low prices on Levi, Lee, and Wrangler jeans, jackets, shirts, coveralls, and overalls. Prices for jeans range from $16 to $42. You'll also find great buys on other men's, children's, and women's wear. Free alterations are available on all items bought from California Jeans. For extra savings, take in your *Buying Retail Is Stupid!* coupon. You'll save 5% if your purchase is more than $50, and 10% if your purchase is more than $100.

Additional Location:
Cudahy–7910 Atlantic Ave., Suite L, 213/562-1503 (closed Tuesdays)

Jet Apparel Outlet ★
1700 Sunflower Ave.
Costa Mesa, CA 92626
714/979-8801

Hours: Wed-Sat: 10-7 Sun: 11-6
Credit Cards: MC, V

We can't mention brand names, but you'll recognize the men's, women's (missy and large sizes), and children's clothing at Jet Apparel Outlet because they carry the same labels found in your favorite specialty stores. Opened in 1990, this factory outlet has more than 25,000 units in stock all the time. New merchandise is brought in every week, and 80% of their goods is first-quality overruns and cancellations. The balance of their clothing is irregulars and slightly damaged, with the average price of $10. Get on the mailing list for their special "Midnight Madness" sales held twice a year. You'll save an additional 10% (excluding sale merchandise) with your *Buying Retail Is Stupid!* coupon with any $10 minimum purchase.

Nordstrom Rack
901 South Coast Dr.
Costa Mesa, CA 92626
714/751-5901

Hours: Mon-Fri: 9:30-9 Sat: 9:30-7 Sun: 10-6
Credit Cards: MC, Nordstrom, V

Nordstrom Rack offers savings on quality brand names and designer merchandise for the entire family. Most prices are 30 to 70% below retail.

In addition to the merchandise from Nordstrom full-line stores, the Rack offers specially purchased, end-of-season apparel and accessories, as well as merchandise developed specifically for the Rack division.

Additional Locations:
Chino–5537 Philadelphia St., 909/591-0551
San Diego–824 Camino del Rio, 619/296-0143
Woodland Hills–21490 Victory Blvd., 818/884-6770

Real Cheap Sports
36 W. Santa Clara
Ventura, CA 93001
805/648-3803

Hours: Mon-Wed, Fri-Sat: 10-6 Thurs: 10-8 Sun: 11-5
Credit Cards: AE, MC, V

This is the outlet for Patagonia outdoor clothing. Prices start at about 30% below retail. The merchandise consists of discontinued items from the previous season and overruns and seconds from the current season. The seconds are clearly marked, and the flaws are always cosmetic, never functional ones. There are always at least a half-dozen items on special at low, low prices, and the sale items change every two weeks. In addition to ski pants, parkas, sweats, polo shirts, long underwear, and other wearables, you'll find various types of outdoor equipment such as sleeping bags and backpacks.

Ross Dress for Less
4315 Pacific Coast Hwy.
Torrance, CA 95050
310/373-0784

Hours: Mon-Sat: 9:30-9 Sun: 11-7
Credit Cards: All Major
♦ **Senior Discount:** 10%* **Age:** 55

Ross Dress for Less is the perfect place to go if you want to outfit the entire family with quality merchandise at savings of 20 to 60% off retail. They attempt to accommodate everyone—infants, children, men, and women, who will find clothing in petite to plus sizes. You can satisfy many needs at Ross stores including shoes, hosiery, handbags, gifts, home accessories, and popular name-brand fragrances. Since their price tags note the Ross price compared with the suggested retail price, you will enjoy knowing just how much you are saving. You won't lose out on any of the amenities that you find at major department stores because Ross offers exchanges, cash refunds, and private dressing rooms. *Senior citizen discount is available on Tuesdays only.

Additional Locations:
More than 75 stores throughout Southern California–call 800/945-7677.

Susie's Factory Direct
17140 Bear Valley Rd.
Victorville, CA 92392
619/951-5572

Hours: Mon-Fri: 10-9 Sat: 10-7 Sun: 11-6
Credit Cards: DISC, MC, V

You probably won't believe this, but everything is $5 at Susie's Factory Direct. They carry garments for infants, toddlers, girls, boys, women—junior, missy, plus sizes—and men. It's amazing that you can buy clothing in today's marketplace for $5, but seeing is believing.

Additional Locations:
18 other stores throughout Southern California

FASHION ACCESSORIES

Antelope ★
12212 Ventura Blvd.
Studio City, CA 91604
818/980-4299

Hours: Mon-Sat: 9:30-6:30
Credit Cards: AE, DISC, MC, V
♦ **Senior Discount:** 10% **Age:** 65

Antelope carries leather goods, especially 24K gold-plated evening bags. With about 2,000 bags on display, even the most finicky shoppers are bound to be satisfied. If there is only one remaining of a certain style bag, it's usually sold at cost. They also carry briefcases, attaché cases, organizers, wallets, luggage, and overnighters. On most items you'll pay 20 to 50% off retail. In business since the early 1970s, they know how to make their customers happy—by standing behind their merchandise for one year. Whether the stitching starts to unravel or the hardware falls off, Antelope will fix it or replace it within one year of purchase. They also repair leather clothing and accessories. Some of the brand names they carry are Viva, Pinky, Fellini, Marco Ricci, and Samsonite. You can use your *Buying Retail Is Stupid!* coupon for a 10% discount (not valid with senior citizen discount).

Bag Lady
31954 San Luis Rey
Cathedral City, CA 92234
619/323-5062

Hours: Mon-Sat: 9:30-5 Sun: 11-4 (Closed July 4 through Labor Day)
Credit Cards: AE, DISC, MC, V

Claiming to have the largest selection in the entire Cochella Valley, Bag

Lady has women's handbags, leather jackets, leather accessories, and fashion jewelry at great savings of 20 to 50% off retail. Since they carry at least 4,000 handbags, it would be nearly impossible to walk out without finding the one for you. You will always find a great selection, complete with buys on the bargain table. By the way, Bag Lady is closed from July 4 through Labor Day.

Additional Location:
Palm Springs–187 S. Palm Canyon Dr., 619/325-7000

Le Club Handbag Co. ★
2772 W. Artesia Blvd.
Redondo Beach, CA 90278
310/214-8080

Hours: Tue-Sat: 10-6
Credit Cards: MC, V

At Le Club Handbag, you can buy most popular brands of handbags that are carried by major department stores—for example, Frenchy, Perlina, Bally, and Dooney & Bourke. They are also a factory outlet for Jack McDonnell hats. In addition, they carry accessories, gloves, hats, Cazal sunglasses, costume jewelry, watches, and small leather goods. Their prices average 25 to 80% off department store prices. You can save even more during their semiannual sales. If you don't see what you're looking for, ask owner Bill Reich, and he'll help you out! Special ordering from their catalogs is no problem. For example, all products made by Bally, including men's shoes and belts, can be special-ordered at 25% below retail. As an added service, they will fax customers pictures of whatever it is they are interested in buying. Take in your *Buying Retail Is Stupid!* coupon for an extra 10% discount redeemable on anything except Dooney & Bourke products.

Marlene Gaines Handbags ★
6000 Reseda Blvd.
Tarzana, CA 91356
818/344-0442

Hours: Mon-Sat: 10-5:30
Credit Cards: MC, V

As the name implies, Marlene Gaines Handbags specializes in handbags. You'll find buys at 30 to 50% off the retail prices department stores charge. They carry brand names such as Cem, Sharif, and Ellen Tracy. The quality handbags are all leather, and they have sales in June and December, with prices discounted even more. You'll find Marlene has an unbelievable selection, including white handbags year-round. There are more than 2,000 bags, including great knock-offs, and each style comes in several colors. They also carry wallets, small gift items under $20, and one-of-a-kind jewelry, making this store a worthwhile shopping venture. Take in your *Buying Retail Is Stupid!* coupon for an extra 10% discount on any nonsale item.

Simon ★

173 Santa Monica Pl.
Santa Monica, CA 90401
310/260-1230

Hours: Mon-Thur: 11-8 Fri: 11-9 Sat: 10-9 Sun: 12-7
Credit Cards: All Major

Simon has one of the largest selections of leather items in the Southern California area—3,000 items, which is a lot. You can find handbags, backpacks, wallets, luggage, portfolios, and much more at savings of 10 to 70% off retail. Anne Klein, Sharif, Montana, Nine West, and Guess? are just a few of the brands they carry, and they have recently added their own Simon label. Don't forget your *Buying Retail Is Stupid!* coupon for an additional 10% discount.

Additional Location:
Los Angeles–7562 Melrose Ave., 213/658-7330

INFANTS' & CHILDREN'S APPAREL

David's Children's Wear

712 S. Los Angeles St.
Los Angeles, CA 90014
213/683-1622

Hours: Mon-Sat: 9:30-6 Sun: 11-5
Credit Cards: AE, DISC, MC, V

David's Children's Wear has been offering great savings on children's clothing since 1940. Sizes start with infants and go to size 16 for girls, size 20 for boys. The basement is dedicated to a fantastic selection of boys' wear. With 5,000 square feet of clothing at savings of 20 to 50% off retail, this place is a must for mothers with young children.

For Kids Only ★

18332 Ventura Blvd.
Tarzana, CA 91356
818/708-9543

Hours: Mon-Sat: 10-6 Sun: 12-6
Credit Cards: AE, DISC, MC, V

How often do you say, "I can't believe how quickly the baby is growing"? Well, For Kids Only is the place to keep taking your baby until he reaches size 20! You'll find fine European and American clothing and shoes priced 30 to 60% lower than upscale department stores charge. Dresses that can retail for more than $200 are less than $100 here. They also have a terrific selection of dressy clothes—suits, slacks, ties, and more—for boys. Since For Kids Only always keeps the most up-to-date fashions in stock (new merchandise arrives weekly), your young ones will be the best-dressed children in your neighborhood. Your *Buying Retail Is Stupid!* coupon is good for a 10% discount (redeemable on nonsale items only).

Additional Location:
Los Angeles–746 N. Fairfax, 213/650-4885

Jazzy's World ★

624 E. Main St.
Alhambra, CA 91801
818/457-6763

Hours: Mon-Thurs: 10:30-6 Fri: 10:30-7 Sat: 11-6
Credit Cards: All Major
♦ **Senior Discount:** 10% **Age:** 65

You will get the best-quality merchandise at great prices at Jazzy's World. They sell brand names such as Sideout, Guess?, Sweet Potatoes, Patsy Aiken, Lambs & Ivy, Medela, and many more at 30 to 80% off retail. Jazzy's World carries children's clothing, furniture, strollers, car seats, toys, bedding, and other items. They also have seasonal sales in which everything is offered below cost to make room for new inventory. With their personal service, layaway plans, easy credit, and guaranteed best prices, Jazzy's World is the complete children's store. Take in your *Buying Retail Is Stupid!* coupon and save an extra 10% off your purchase of $50 or more (not valid with senior citizen discount).

Kids Outlet ★
5170 Kanan Rd.
Agoura, CA 91301
818/991-8730

Hours: Mon-Sat: 10-6 Sun: 11-5
Credit Cards: MC, V

Anyone who buys clothing and accessories for babies and children can save 40 to 50% off retail, sometimes even more, by shopping at Kids Outlet. The store is filled with about 100 brands of the latest fashions from local and Eastern manufacturers that sell mainly to high-end department stores. The inventory is always changing, and most of it is simply irresistible. Styles from casual to dressy run from size 0 to 14 for girls and 0 to 7 for boys. Whatever you do, don't overlook the clearance rack. We couldn't pass up a floral-print dress in polished cotton, with pink satin bordering the hem and collar. Suitable for church on Sunday or special occasions, this dress was $79 retail; Kids Outlet originally sold it for $30, and we found it on the clearance rack for $12, an 85% discount. How we love bargain shopping! Although the Newbury Park store carries many of the same brands, you'll find that the inventory leans toward basic, good-quality clothing, with most prices in the $4 to $10 price range. Purchases can be returned for store credit or exchanges only. You'll save an extra 10% with your *Buying Retail Is Stupid!* coupon.

Additional Location:
Newbury Park–2349 Michael Dr., 805/376-2489

Mudpies . . . A Children's Store ★
19353 Soledad Canyon Rd.
Canyon Country, CA 91351
805/252-4767

Hours: Mon-Sat: 10-5
Credit Cards: MC, V

If children's clothing is a major expense in your family, Mudpies . . . A Children's Store may bring you some needed financial relief. The store offers manufacturer close-outs and overruns on children's clothing found in boutiques and in discount and high-end department stores. For example, a little girl's dress in a bright cotton print was $9.98. The same dress in specialty boutiques featuring only this particular label retails for $25. Discounts on new merchandise run 10 to 60% off retail. Owners Kathie Weitzman and Marcia Bowren are constantly price-shopping to make sure their goods are lower than sale prices at discount chains. They take this philosophy one step further on car seats. As a community service, they sell car seat close-outs at $5 over cost (the invoice is posted so you can verify). In addition to new merchandise, about one-third of Mudpies is devoted to resale items—children's and maternity clothes, furniture, etc.—that are sold on consignment. If you put your name on their wish list they'll call you as soon as the item or brand becomes available. Your *Buying Retail Is Stupid!* coupon is good for a 10% discount on new merchandise only.

See Me Now ★
15605 Graham St.
Huntington Beach, CA 92649
714/379-3744

Hours: Mon-Fri: 9-5 Sat: 9-12
Credit Cards: Cash or Checks Only

This is a factory outlet filled with first-quality overruns priced at or under $15. You'll find the hottest styles in either 100% cotton or stretch clothing made of a cotton/lycra blend. Children's sizes run 2 to 14, with the largest selection devoted to little girls. They have leggings, tops, shorts, dresses, and stretch pants at 20 to 50% below retail prices. Don't forget your *Buying Retail Is Stupid!* coupon for savings of an extra 10%.

SFO Kids ★
1439 W. Olive St.
Burbank, CA 91506
818/840-0571

Hours: Mon-Tues: 11-6 Wed-Sat: 11-7 Sun: 12-5
Credit Cards: MC, V

SFO Kids has brightly colored, in-season clothing for children priced 30 to 70% below retail. Owners Jim and Tanya Norrington decided to open SFO Kids when Jim discovered how much Tanya was spending on clothing in boutiques and department stores for their own children. As a result, their stores offer discounted prices (30 to 60% off retail) on first-quality clothing made primarily of 100% cotton. Sizes run from infants up to size 14 for girls, and infants up to size 20 for boys. Make sure to get on their mailing list for notification of special sales held in January and July. There is no layaway plan, but they will hold items for one day. Your *Buying Retail Is Stupid!* coupon will save you an extra 15% on nonsale items only.

LARGE SIZES FOR WOMEN

The Big, The Bad & The Beautiful ★
19225 Ventura Blvd.
Tarzana, CA 91356
818/345-3593

Hours: Tues-Sat: 10-7 Sun-Mon: 12-5
Credit Cards: AE, MC, V
♦ **Senior Discount:** 10% **Age:** 65

Wouldn't it be great to have clothing that looks fantastic no matter how much your weight fluctuates? This store has contemporary clothing at discount prices for women wearing up to a size 60 (to 600 pounds). Owner Marsha Alexander's motto is, "Dare to be beautiful." Marsha opened The Big, The Bad & The Beautiful because she was tired of going into department stores and ending up with three or four outfits she hated because she was stuck buying what fit, not what she wanted. Sound familiar? Much of the clothing is really one-size-fits-all. For example, on one visit to the store, four women, ranging in size from 4 to 32, tried on the same French-lace jacket. It looked terrific an all of them, with a minor adjustment to the shoulder pads. To maximize shoppers' wardrobes, most of the merchandise is made to be mixed and matched or reversed. One of the most popular items is comfortable pants that fit. You'll find clothing for every occasion from casual to dressy, including bathing suits and lots of sexy lingerie for big, bad, beautiful women. Brand names such as Dumas, Wild Rose, and Jazz have recently been added to the inventory. Don't forget to take your *Buying Retail Is Stupid!* coupon for an additional 10% discount. Note: A second location will open soon in Thousand Oaks. Call the Tarzana store for information.

Extra Touch
12178 Ventura Blvd.
Studio City, CA 91604
818/508-1662

Hours: Mon-Sat: 10-6 Sun: 12-5
Credit Cards: AE, MC, OPT, V

When it comes to women's clothing, oversized and fashionable are usually mutually exclusive. Not so at Extra Touch. Owner Ester Nemes offers high-fashion garments in sizes 14W to 32W at discounts running 20 to 30% off retail on current merchandise and higher on end-of-season goods. The theme here is year-round dressing in high-fashion, classic styles made to be flattering on full-figured women. Special-occasion and mother-of-the-bride dresses in large sizes can be pretty boring, but not here. An entire wall of this elegant boutique is devoted to drop-dead gorgeous outfits in pastels, jewel tones, and black. Because sizes vary so much among designers, all clothing is arranged by style, not size. Alterations are done on the premises.

See Also: (refer to index)
Anna Queen
Bailey's Backstreet
Damone
Ladies Apparel
My Secret Place
Ross Dress for Less
Rotey's Boutique

LEATHER GARMENTS & FURS

David Appel–The Fur Shop ★
287 S. Robertson Blvd.
Beverly Hills, CA 90211
310/659-1113

Hours: Tues-Fri: 10-5:30 Sat: 10-4
Credit Cards: AE, OPT
♦ **Senior Discount:** 10% **Age:** 65

Buy direct from the manufacturer and receive savings of 40% off retail prices on fur coats, jackets, vests, wraps, slings, and hats. David Appel–The Fur Shop is a third-generation furrier offering complete fur services: repairs, remodeling, storage, cleaning, custom-made furs, and a large inventory of new furs. Storage is available for $35 a year. Your coat can be taken in and out at no extra charge and will be brushed and steamed before it is returned to you. The *Buying Retail Is Stupid!* coupon offers you two years of storage and cleaning free with any purchase (not valid with senior citizen discount).

Leonore's Fur Outlet ★
223 S. Beverly Dr., Suite 200
Beverly Hills, CA 90212
310/278-4001

Hours: Mon-Sat: 9:30-5:30 Sun: By Appointment Only
Credit Cards: AE, DC, MC, V

This is the place for fine furs, new and pre-owned. The family has been in the fur business since 1927 and has fine fur salons throughout the country. They carry the same merchandise found in most high-end department stores. Name brands include Christian Dior, Bill Blass, and Oscar de la Renta offered at 30 to 50% off retail. You'll find sable, lynx, mink, and other varieties of fur in every design imaginable. The store is small but carries at least 300 fur garments at all times. When you purchase a fur at Leonore's, you'll receive a furrier cover as well as your name or initials monogrammed in the lining. If you can't decide between sable or chinchilla, you can experiment by renting a fur from Leonore's. In addition to selling and renting, Leonore's buys new and nearly new furs. Services include cleaning, repairing, and remodeling furs. There is metered parking on the street and free parking across the street in the Beverly Hills multilevel parking structure. Don't forget your *Buying Retail Is Stupid!* coupon good for an extra 5% discount.

Wilson's Suede & Leather Outlet Store
3117 W. Magnolia Blvd.
Burbank, CA 91502
818/841-7789
Hours: Mon-Sat: 10-6 Sun: 11-6
Credit Cards: All Major

Have you wanted a leather coat for quite a while but haven't found anything reasonably priced? This outlet has all kinds of leather garments at up to 90% off original retail prices. There are lots of jackets, skirts, tops, and accessories consolidated from Wilson's stores all over the country. Some of the buys we've seen were $25 gloves for $4.99, first-quality leather suede skirts in several colors for $5, and full-length men's coats for $99.99 instead of $450. In fact, the highest price tag you'll find in this store is $99.99. The front of the store has racks and tables of first-quality clearance items. The rest of the store consists of seconds, returns, and damaged merchandise. All sales are final (no refunds or exchanges), so go over your purchases with a fine-tooth comb before leaving the store.

LINGERIE

Amore Creations
647 S. Los Angeles St.
Los Angeles, CA 90014
213/624-8048
Hours: Mon-Sat: 10-5:30
Credit Cards: AE, MC, V

Everyone loves lingerie! Especially when you can buy all those gorgeous creations (bras, girdles, panties, G-strings, and teddies) at 40 to 75% off retail prices. They have 5,000 square feet of lingerie and are always getting new things. Amore Creations stocks the standard lines from most of the major manufacturers such as Playtex, Bali, and many others. Sometimes they're able to buy an entire discontinued line, which means more savings for their customers. As an extra touch, they'll always let you know if what you are buying is a regular item or one that has been discontinued. They're open Sundays during the holiday season.

Chic Lingerie Outlet ★
693 High Lane
Redondo Beach, CA 90236
310/372-9352

Hours: Mon-Fri: 7:30-3:30
Credit Cards: Cash or Checks Only

This is a factory outlet where you will find savings from 40 to 50% on sleepwear, lingerie, and loungewear. Their merchandise is the same as that found in specialty and department stores. Any flaws are clearly marked on the garments. Don't hesitate to try on anything you like from a selection of 15,000 garments. They've been in business for 50 years, saving people a lot of money on their "unmentionable" products! Don't forget to take in your *Buying Retail Is Stupid!* coupon for a 10% discount.

Additional Location:
Los Angeles–3435 S. Broadway, 213/233-7121

Creative Woman
1530 S. Myrtle Ave.
Monrovia, CA 91016
818/358-6216

Hours: Mon-Fri: 10-7 Sat: 10-6 Sun: 12-5:30
Credit Cards: AE, DISC, MC, V

Located off the Myrtle Avenue exit from the 210 Freeway, this store is run by the very personable Ed and Bonnie Kaufman. They carry lingerie in all sizes, garter belts, stockings, corsets, and feathers. Feathers? They even have a department with sexy costumes. Corsets range in sizes from 32A to 52DDD, and backless strapless bras come in sizes from 32A to 48DD. They also have custom-fitted bras in sizes 26BB to 52HH. Now, that's a selection! Savings run about 10 to 20% off retail, and they always have monthly specials with additional savings. Alterations are done on the premises.

J. Whitt Intimates ★
6701 Variel Ave., #B-50
Woodland Hills, CA 91301
818/888-1663

Hours: Sat-Sun: 10-6
Credit Cards: All Major

Ladies' intimate apparel now can be bought directly from the manufacturer at savings of 20 to 70% off retail. J. Whitt sells camisoles, chemises, boxers, panties, tank tops, pajamas, gowns, robes, bodysuits, catsuits, and much more, all in 100% cotton. Bring in your *Buying Retail Is Stupid!* coupon to receive an additional 5% off any purchase.

Lingerie for Less
2245 S. Sepulveda Blvd.
West Los Angeles, CA 90064
310/477-8605

Hours: Mon-Sat: 10-8 Sun: 11-6
Credit Cards: All Major

Lingerie for Less offers luxurious lingerie at discounts of 20 to 65% off retail. Although we have been asked to omit brand names, they carry the same merchandise found in most major middle-of-the-road to high-end department stores. Each store caters to the area it is in, so if you don't find something you like at one store, chances are you'll find something to your liking at another location. You can choose styles ranging from simple and conservative to slinky and exotic. They have everything from bras and panties to sexy peignoir sets. If you're into silk, you'll like the prices on silk lingerie for men and women.

Additional Locations:
20 other stores throughout Southern California

Playmates ★
6438 Hollywood Blvd.
Hollywood, CA 90028
213/464-7636

Hours: Mon-Fri: 10-8 Sat: 10-7:30 Sun: 12-6
Credit Cards: All Major

If sexy is what you want, from saint to sinner, Playmates has it. As the world's largest lingerie store, Playmates carries Pat Fields, Dreamgirl, XTC, Deviations, Versatile, Lip Service, and Ziganne—provocative fashions at 25% below retail. They feature lingerie to die for, club clothes that will make people notice, and exotic stripper dance outfits. Bring your *Buying Retail Is Stupid!* coupon to save an extra 15% off your purchase of $25 or more.

MATERNITY CLOTHES

Baby Makes Three Discount Maternity Fashions
1979 N. Tustin
Orange, CA 92665
714/974-5742

Hours: Mon-Fri: 10:30-5 Sat: 10-5 Sun: Call for Hours
Credit Cards: Cash or Checks Only

Shop at Baby Makes Three and save at least 20% on maternity clothes.
They carry office wear, professional outfits, bras, bathing suits, and
casual clothes for the mommy-to-be. Greatest discounts can be found on
their denim items. You will quickly realize the quality of their
merchandise even though all labels have been cut out. Sales occur
frequently, so be sure to call and ask for dates.

Dan Howard's Maternity Factory ★
22817 Hawthorne Blvd.
Torrance, CA 90505
310/375-2640

Hours: Mon, Thur: 10-9 Tues-Wed, Fri-Sat: 10-6 Sun: 12-5
Credit Cards: All Major

Everything an expectant mother needs in the way of apparel is available
through this factory outlet which designs and manufactures their own
maternity clothing. There's always a wide selection from sportswear to
evening wear, in sizes 4 to 20, at 25% off retail. Professional women will
be pleased with the attire they carry suitable for the office. Lingerie and
pantyhose are also available. Dan Howard's Maternity Factory has been
producing stylish and quality maternity clothes since the 1940s. Your
Buying Retail Is Stupid! coupon is good for a 10% discount. Discount
coupon is not redeemable on lingerie or sale items.

Additional Locations:
Cerritos–11326-1/2 South St., 310/402-1953
La Mesa–5500 Grossmont Center Dr., 619/698-8278
Montclair–5027 S. Plaza Lane, 909/626-6516
Santa Ana–3930 Bristol St., 714/557-4342
Woodland Hills–20929 Ventura Blvd., 818/887-6317

Mom's the Word ★

1008-1/2 Fair Oaks Ave.
South Pasadena, CA 91030
818/441-9692

Hours: Mon-Fri: 10:30-7 Sat: 10-6 Sun: 12-5
Credit Cards: AE, DISC, MC, V

Mom's the Word has a fabulous selection of discounted clothing (15 to 60% off retail) from top designers for every occasion. They carry current styles and are able to offer low prices by purchasing their goods during the season. (Most retailers place their orders with manufacturers two seasons ahead.) We've been asked not to name names, but everything is extremely tasteful and well made, with lots of attention to detail. Shipments arrive weekly, so the inventory is always changing. The store carries cruise wear and swimsuits, as well as dressy outfits year-round. And speaking of dressy outfits, they also rent formal and evening wear. If you aren't very far along, they'll lend you a pillow so you get an idea of how the outfit will look in the future. They have outfits made specifically for nursing, and nursing bras run from sizes 34B to 40E. Children are welcome, and there are plenty of toys to keep them occupied. Get on their mailing list for notification of special sales held twice a year. You'll receive an additional 10% discount if you take in your *Buying Retail Is Stupid!* coupon.

MEN'S APPAREL & ACCESSORIES

Academy Award Clothes, Inc.

821 S. Los Angeles St.
Los Angeles, CA 90014
213/622-9125

Hours: Mon-Sat: 9-5:30
Credit Cards: All Major

In business since 1950, Academy Award Clothes offers a fine selection of men's clothing and accessories at discounted prices. They stock thousands of men's suits, sport coats, slacks, formal wear, and haberdashery, with most designer names available. The majority of their inventory is devoted to clothing made in the U.S. As you enter through the front door you will be assigned a salesman to assist you in your selection. Parking is validated with a $100 purchase.

Alandales
8775 Beverly Blvd.
West Hollywood, CA 90048
310/838-8100

Hours: Tues-Fri: 10-7 Sat: 10-6
Credit Cards: AE, MC, V

Bargains come in all price ranges! Alandales carries high-end goods for men at low prices in an "attitude-free" environment. Because Alandales deals directly with the same fabric mills and manufacturers used by many high-end design houses, consumers can save about 35 to 50% off retail (suits start at $595). In this 6,000-square-foot store men will find clothing and accessories appropriate for executive boardrooms to baseball games. Unusual to men's stores, the focus here is on a man's total image. Alandales has the ability to literally dress a man from head (four hair stations) to toe (lots of socks, but no shoes). There is also a tailor shop on the premises. Special sales are held every January and July, so make certain to be added to their mailing list. By the way, they log clothing information about each customer into their computer system; the loved one in your life can shop for you and come home with all the right sizes and colors.

Compagnia Della Moda Inc.
31192 La Baya Dr., #F
Westlake Village, CA 91362
818/706-8177

Hours: Mon-Fri: 9-5 Sat: 10-4
Credit Cards: MC, V

Now you can look as though you've just stepped out of GQ, dressed in classically styled, Italian men's clothing of the highest quality, without paying Beverly Hills' men's store prices. A local television host said, "This is LA's best-kept secret!" He is absolutely right. You'll find 4,000 square feet consisting of suits, sport coats, slacks, shirts, ties, and sometimes formal wear priced 50 to 60% below intrinsic value. Most of the garments are made of wool, silk, or cotton, and you can forget about finding any polyester. Believe me, if you want to wear the very best, and we do mean the very best, it's well worth a trip to Westlake Village. Please note: Even at savings of 50 to 60%, this clothing is *not* inexpensive.

Eagleson's Outlet
1700 Ventura Blvd., Suite B
Oxnard, CA 93030
805/981-9472

Hours: Mon-Wed, Sat: 10-6 Thurs-Fri: 10-9 Sun: 12-5
Credit Cards: All Major

You can really spend a lot of money in specialty stores for tall or large men, but now there's an alternative. The Eagleson's retail chain has opened several outlet stores where you can save 20 to 50% off original store prices. The outlets are stocked with merchandise from their 29 retail stores and are set up like nice men's stores. Many people think that Eagleson's caters only to sizable gentlemen, but that's not true. They also carry a good selection of clothing for tall and lanky body styles. You'll find items such as warm-up suits and sweaters sized extra large, extra tall, and extra large tall. Other sizes run 1X to 8X for casual knit shirts; 16 to 22 for dress shirts; casual and dress slacks run 34-long to 64-regular; belts start at 38 and sometimes go up to size 64. Even the ties here are extra-long. You'll also find a nice selection of suits and sport coats. Service is terrific, and they offer alterations. Most outlets shun returns, but as long as you have your receipt, you can return purchases for a refund.

Additional Locations:
Fullerton–1345 S. Harbor Blvd., 714/871-1195
El Cajon–700 N. Johnson Ave., 619/440-7225
Huntington Beach–7700 Edinger Ave., 714/848-9988
Northridge–19480 Nordhoff St., 818/773-8822
Riverside–10113 Hole Ave., 909/351-0404

Funky & Damnear New
123 S. First St.
La Puente, CA 91744
818/330-0303

Hours: Wed-Sat: 10-6 Sun: 12-5
Credit Cards: MC, V

Their specialty is "remanufactured," repaired, and new Levi's. The "remanufactured" Levi's run 98¢ to $25. What's great about this place is that you don't have to worry about how the pants you buy will fit after you wash them. Why won't they shrink? All new Levi's at Funky & Damnear New are laundered and high-heat-dried to remove all shrinkage. And if you have a backlog of old Levi's, trade them in for Funky Bucks, which can be spent on any merchandise in the store.

Harris & Frank Warehouse Outlet
7306 Coldwater Canyon
North Hollywood, CA 91605
818/764-4872

Hours: Mon-Fri: 9-5:30 Sat: 9-5 Sun: 11-4
Credit Cards: All Major

This large outlet store gives you the best buys on Harris & Frank clothing. Merchandise is brought in from their five stores, so you'll find quality men's clothing and accessories. Brand names include Jaymar, Petrocelli, and many others. Discounts of 40% off retail are guaranteed at this outlet and often go up as high as 70%.

Larchmont Shirts ★
107 N. Larchmont Blvd.
Los Angeles, CA 90004
213/962-8010

Hours: Mon-Fri: 9:30-6 Sun: 12-5 (Closed Saturdays)
Credit Cards: MC, V
♦ **Senior Discount:** 5% **Age:** 65

Larchmont Shirts offers 25 to 40% off retail prices on men's and boys' clothing. You'll find brand names such as Christian Dior, Gant, Perry Ellis, Pierre Cardin, and Givenchy, and many more. They pride themselves on individual attention to all their customers and will special-order big and tall sizes. Remember to take in your *Buying Retail Is Stupid!* coupon and you'll save an extra 5% off your purchase of $100 or more (not valid with senior citizen discount).

Max Levine & Son
845 S. Los Angeles St.
Los Angeles, CA 90014
213/622-2446

Hours: Mon-Sat: 9-5
Credit Cards: All Major

Max Levine & Son has been around since 1936, evolving into a discount operation selling men's clothes. They always carry between 6,000 and 8,000 suits and slacks here. They also carry sport coats, formal wear, belts, ties, and other fashion accessories. Designer names such as Perry Ellis and Christian Dior are available in shorts, regulars, longs, and extra longs, from sizes 35 to 50. The savings are generally 40% below retail department stores. Get on their mailing list for notification of special sales.

Men's Fashion Depot

3730 Sports Arena Blvd.

San Diego, CA 92110

619/222-9570

Hours: Mon-Fri: 9:30-9 Sat: 9:30-6 Sun: 11:30-5
Credit Cards: DISC, MC, V

You won't find any brand names here because they rip out the labels. What you will find are discounts of up to 50% off retail on men's suits, sport coats, slacks, shirts, ties, warm-up suits, and even tuxedos. With 6,500 square feet of clothing, you're bound to find something to your liking. Sizes range from 34 X-short to 60 long, and suits are $69 to $249.

Roger Stuart Clothes, Inc.

729 S. Los Angeles St.

Los Angeles, CA 90014

213/627-9661

Hours: Mon-Sat: 9-5:30
Credit Cards: All Major

When it comes to price and selection, it's hard to beat Roger Stuart Clothes. They carry brand names such as Cricketeer, Geoffrey Beene, Chaps by Ralph Lauren, Harve Bernard, and many others. Prices are usually 25 to 65% below retail, so you could pay from $219 to $359 for an Italian-made, 100% wool suit that could retail for $1,295 in better department stores and boutiques. They have over 6,000 square feet of men's clothing (10,000 suits) and 12 dressing rooms, so you can be sure of the fit. Alteration is not a service they provide, but they'll recommend a nearby tailor so you can get your purchases altered the same day. They also carry slacks (super 100s, 110s, and 120s), sport coats, dress and sport shirts, tuxedos, overcoats and rain coats, ties, and other accessories. Men, unless unusually large or small, will be able to find a good fit here. They carry almost every size (36–56 regular, 38–56 long, 42–56 extra long, 36–46 short, 35–42 extra short), including shirts up to size 19-1/2″ neck, 37″ sleeve. Customer files are computerized, so gifts and accessories can be matched up with previous purchases. There is a huge sale every year; it's worth getting on the mailing list.

Roseman's Menswear ★
2211 E. Olympic Blvd.
Los Angeles, CA 90021
213/622-6266

Hours: Mon-Sat: 10-6 Sun: 11-5
Credit Cards: All Major

Roseman's Menswear is a men's clothing wholesaler that offers quality men's wear at prices from 40 to 80% below retail. In business since 1974, Roseman's emphasizes fashion. They carry names such as Chaps by Ralph Lauren, Nino Cerruti, Pierre Cardin, Bill Blass, Krizia, Yves St. Laurent, and many more. Their 15,000-square-foot location offers suits, sport coats, dress and sport slacks, dress and sport shirts, sweaters, ties, and Italian shoes. There are 10 dressing rooms, and their private parking lot provides plenty of free parking. In-house tailoring is also available. You'll want to get on their mailing list for advance notice of their warehouse sales. For first-time customers only, the *Buying Retail Is Stupid!* coupon is redeemable for an extra 10% discount (not valid on sale items or during warehouse sales).

MEN'S & WOMEN'S APPAREL

Cooper & Kramer, Inc. ★
1401 Santee St.
Los Angeles, CA 90015
213/747-5816

Hours: Mon-Fri: 9-4:30 Sat: 9-4
Credit Cards: MC, V

Whether you're looking for career apparel or something a little more on the casual side, Cooper & Kramer will fit the bill. With thousands of American and Italian suits in their 8,000-square-foot warehouse, you're bound to find plenty of new additions to your wardrobe. Clothing for men runs 30 to 50% off retail, and women's clothing is discounted 30 to 60%. They also have a men's shoe department featuring popular American brands at 30% off retail. Savings run higher during special sales held four times a year. We can't name names, but if you're curious give them a call and they'll fill you in. They've been in business since 1932. Save an additional 10% on nonsale items only, with your *Buying Retail Is Stupid!* coupon.

Designer Labels for Less
4734 Admiralty Way
Marina del Rey, CA 90291
310/827-5115

Hours: Mon-Sat: 10-6 Sun: 12-5
Credit Cards: DISC, MC, V

One of our favorite places to purchase famous-maker clothing at 40 to 80% off retail is at Designer Labels for Less. In fact, during one of their blow-out sales, we bought a Carole Little silk dress for $10. Other brand names you'll find are Christian Dior, Jones New York, Saint Germain, and more. Men's clothing and accessories are carried in 10 of their stores—including the store listed above—with brand names such as Polo, Chaps by Ralph Lauren, Louis Raphael, and others. Store hours vary by location.

Additional Locations:
19 other stores throughout Southern California–call 800/367-3274.

Piller's of Eagle Rock ★
1800 Colorado Blvd.
Los Angeles, CA 90041
213/257-8166

Hours: Fri-Sat: 10-5:30 Sun: 12-5
Credit Cards: AE, DISC, MC, V (No Checks)
♦ **Senior Discount:** 10% **Age:** 65

Would you like to find a good deal on men's or women's clothing? How about 50% off the retail price of nationally advertised brands just for a start? During the year, they have sales with prices up to 90% off retail. No hole-in-the-wall, Piller's of Eagle Rock has nearly 25,000 square feet of merchandise on display. Dressing rooms are provided, so you can be sure of the fit. In the shoe department you'll find about 25,000 pairs of brand names such as Bruno Magli and Geoffrey Beene and many more. Piller's has been in business since 1949, so you know you can depend on them. Remember to use your *Buying Retail Is Stupid!* coupon for an extra 10% discount (not valid with senior citizen discount).

Piller's Outlet Store
1421 Marcelina Ave.
Torrance, CA 90501
310/212-5152

Hours: Thurs-Sat: 10-5:30 Sun: 12-5
Credit Cards: AE, DISC, MC, V

This is one store you should put on your list for men's and women's clothing. Piller's Outlet Store specializes in liquidation and close-out goods featuring brands found in middle- to high-end department stores. Savings run 50 to 90% off original retail prices. Brands and selection vary from visit to visit. Women can usually find sportswear to evening wear, as well as shoes (sizes 4 to 13), purses, belts, and fashion jewelry. Men can choose from suits, sportswear, and shoes, and you'll also find a selection of children's clothes and shoes.

Sacks SFO Inc.
2101 E. Broadway
Long Beach, CA 90803
310/987-0099

Hours: Mon-Wed, Sat-Sun: 11-7 Thurs-Fri: 11-8
Credit Cards: MC, V

You can save a bundle of money, all the time, on men's and women's fashionable and trendy clothing. Save 40 to 70% on great ready-to-wear items, with a special emphasis on natural fibers. Much of this store's merchandise is designer clothing. Sacks SFO also has leather jackets, pants, and fashion accessories such as jewelry, belts, and ties. For your convenience, they have private dressing rooms. Get on their mailing list for sales notices. If you'd like, they'll even coordinate your wardrobe for you. David Sacks goes out of his way to make certain he has the nicest salespeople in all Sacks SFO stores.

Additional Locations:
6 other stores throughout Southern California

Stuart Felman's (Hong Kong) Custom Tailors ★
9429 Brighton Way
Beverly Hills, CA 90210
310/858-7177, 800/698-SUIT (698-7848)

Hours: Tues-Sat: 10-5
Credit Cards: AE, MC, OPT, V
♦ **Senior Discount:** 5% **Age:** 62

Since 1966, Stuart Felman has been making custom suits, sport jackets, slacks, and shirts for men and women. Best of all, his prices are 70% off retail. Even though you'll save a great deal of money, they don't skimp on workmanship. In fact, they guarantee a perfect fit every time. Remember to take in your *Buying Retail Is Stupid!* coupon to receive a free custom-made shirt with each suit.

RENTALS

A Nite On The Town ★
1631 Sunflower Ave., Suite C-35
Costa Mesa, CA 92704
714/557-9088

Hours: Mon-Fri: 11-7 Sat: 10-6
Credit Cards: AE, DISC, MC, V

Why spend lots of money on a dress to impress when you can rent it at a fraction of the retail purchase price? Smart women rent the latest in designer cocktail, formal, and bridal dresses at A Nite On The Town. Rental fees start at $39, and the dress is custom-fitted to you. There's a selection of more than 1,500 dresses that are perfect for parties, galas, proms, weddings, pageants, cruises, and reunions. Sizes are available in 2 through 44 with complete accessories (shoes, earrings, etc.) for rent. Refer five customers and you'll receive a $50 gift certificate. A Night On The Town also sells these fantastic dresses, but you might want to wait for their twice-a-year sales to save 50 to 75% off retail. The Costa Mesa store is located in South Coast Plaza Village next to Planet Hollywood, and the San Diego store is in the Costa Verde Center across from UTC. Take along your *Buying Retail Is Stupid!* coupon when renting a dress and receive an additional 10% savings.

Additional Location:
San Diego–8650 Genesee Ave., Suite 222, 619/457-1233

One Night Affair Gown Rentals ★
2370 Westwood Blvd., Suite H
Los Angeles, CA 90064
310/474-7808

Hours: By Appointment Only, Tues-Fri: 11-7 Sat: 10-6
Credit Cards: MC, V

Happily, women now have places such as One Night Affair where they can rent expensive designer evening, pageant, and bridal gowns, cocktail dresses, mother-of-the-bride and bridesmaid dresses, and all necessary accessories, except shoes, for a fraction of the retail purchase price. If you went to 10 malls, you wouldn't come close to finding the selection housed here. They have 900 styles of evening wear in sizes 2 to 30. The garments retail for $300 to $3,000, but rental rates run $45 to $150. Wedding wear and accessories are also available. A future bride might very well find the dress of her dreams at One Night Affair. All bridal gowns (500 styles) are current and run $100 to $495 ($800 to $12,000 retail). Sizes run 2 to 30 in most gowns, but high-end designers go up to size 18. Veil rentals are $25 to $95. Each bridal gown is in the store for 12 months and is retired after being rented five times. For the best selection, go in six to eight months before your wedding date to choose a gown. They also have 50 styles of bridesmaid dresses in several colors that rent for $45 to $95. Alterations are done on the premises at very reasonable rates. A fully refundable deposit is required on all rentals, usually three times the rental price. Because privacy and one-on-one service are so important, hours are by appointment only. Your *Buying Retail Is Stupid!* coupon is good for a 5% discount.

Additional Location:
Westminster–16575 Magnolia St., 714/375-2200

Penelope of California

1500 E. Katella Ave.
Orange, CA 92667
714/532-2360

Hours: Wed-Fri: 11-6 Sat: 12-5
Credit Cards: AE, DISC, MC, V

This rental and resale bridal salon had its beginnings as a Fashion Design Studio in 1980. Owner Penny Griebel, a fashion designer with 30 years' experience in the garment industry, tries to appeal to the average buyer— someone who would normally spend approximately $600 for a wedding gown—with the opportunity to rent a gown for around $195. It has become "chic" for today's bride to rent her gown! P.S.: Evening wear for all occasions can be rented, and expert alterations are available.

Tightwad

2002 N. Tustin Ave.
Orange, CA 92665
714/921-8852

Hours: Mon-Fri: 10-6 Sat: 10-5 Sun: 11-4
Credit Cards: MC, V

As you walk through the doors of Tightwad, you will probably think that all the glitzy and glamorous clothes are new. But look again, as they are extremely selective in what they choose for consignment. Their specialty is the sale and rental of resale competition ballroom, Latin, country, swing, and other dance wear, as well as designer women's clothing, jewelry, and accessories. Savings range from 50 to 80% off retail on labels such as Ann Taylor, Liz Claiborne, Adrienne Vittadini, Diane Fries, St. Johns Knits, and more. They also carry new ballroom, western, and jazz dance shoes and costumes for rent. For extra savings, visit their sale on the third Saturday of every month.

See Also: (refer to index)
Anna Queen
Leonore's Fur Outlet
Mom's the Word

RESALE STORES
Infants' & Children's

Baby Deja-Vu ★
8311 W. 3rd St.
Los Angeles, CA 90048
213/653-2181

Hours: Mon-Sat: 10-6
Credit Cards: AE, DISC, MC, V

Baby Deja-Vu is new to the resale/consignment industry. They feature maternity and newborn to size 6 children's clothing, at 50% and more off retail. Your children will love their choice of Baby Gap, Baby Guess?, OshKosh, and more. Moms will love their Motherhood, Pea In The Pod, and Mother's Work maternity clothes. Happily, you'll also save on bassinets, strollers, toys, books, car seats, walkers, swings, baby carriers, and changing tables. Nostela products for skin protection are offered at 10% below retail. Items in good condition are accepted on consignment without an appointment. Don't forget to take in your *Buying Retail Is Stupid!* coupon for an extra 10% discount.

Baby on a Budget ★
2697 Orange-Olive Rd.
Orange, CA 92665
714/282-0622

Hours: Mon: 11:30-6:30 Tues-Sat: 11-5
Credit Cards: Cash or Checks Only

Since 1989, Baby on a Budget has been offering children's consignment clothing, furniture, accessories, and toys for 50 to 80% below retail. You can find name-brand merchandise such as Little Tikes, OshKosh, Gap, Gymboree, Graco, Simmons, Carters, Aprica, Childcraft, and Fisher Price (specializing in pre-1989 Little People sets). They buy new merchandise every day, accepting only top-of-the-line items. They offer a 50%-off rack for those seeking an even bigger bargain. Save an additional 5% off a purchase of $10 or more with your *Buying Retail Is Stupid!* coupon.

Everything for Kids
24407 Hawthorne Blvd.
Torrance, CA 90505
310/373-4863

Hours: Mon-Sat: 10-5
Credit Cards: Cash or Checks Only

Located near the Palos Verdes area, this store gets a lot of look-like-new clothing and furniture for babies all the way up to teenagers. All of the items in the store are sold on consignment. This results in customers paying a fraction of the original price, plus there are always items that have been reduced another 25 to 50% off the original store prices. There are dressing rooms and a play area for the kids. You'll find many top name brands here, and friendly service is always available. Mark the 1st and the 15th of every month on your calendars for their special markdown sales. If you have some items you'd like to put on consignment, call Bea Severin to set up an appointment.

Little Orphan Overalls
1938 E. Colorado Blvd.
Pasadena, CA 91107
818/793-5990

Hours: Tues-Sat: 10-5
Credit Cards: Cash or Checks Only

With kids outgrowing their clothes so quickly, we can't understand why parents don't buy all their children's play clothes at resale stores. Little Orphan Overalls has plenty to offer parents. Brand names include OshKosh, Sara Kent, Rare Edition, Polly Flinders, Sassoon, Levi, and more. When available, you can also get good buys on nursery furniture, walkers, and strollers. Put your name on a list for favorite brands, and they'll call you when the merchandise comes in. To keep things on the move, there's a 50%-off sale rack featuring "new" items every Saturday.

Once Upon a Child
8945 Tampa Ave.
Northridge, CA 91324
818/882-7777

Hours: Mon-Fri: 10-7 Sat: 10-6 Sun: 11-5
Credit Cards: AE, DISC, MC, V

Once Upon a Child offers 40 to 70% off department-store prices on baby and children's items. They carry brand-name apparel, toys, cribs, strollers, changing tables, books, and games. Brands include OshKosh, Century,

Gymboree, Simons, Million Dollar Baby, and much more. You can also get cash for gently used and new items for babies and children.

Additional Location:
La Crescenta–2607 Foothill Blvd., 818/248-9996

Something for Baby
1359 N. Hill Ave.
Pasadena, CA 91104
818/791-3314

Hours: Mon-Sat: 11-6
Credit Cards: DISC, MC, V

Something for Baby is a resale/consignment children's store. They buy good-quality used clothing such as OshKosh, Gap, Gymboree, Esprit, and many other names; their sizes are newborn to 4, and their prices range from $2 to $15. They also carry baby equipment such as cribs, bassinets, and strollers. Inventory on consignment usually means good quality. Their prices are 50 to 75% below retail, so you can shop for baby and still have a little left over to spend on yourself. Check out the monthly tag sales where items are reduced another 50%.

Twerp's Resale Shop for Children
5060 Eagle Rock Blvd.
Los Angeles, CA 90041
213/256-7608

Hours: Tues-Sat: 11-6
Credit Cards: DISC

At Twerp's Resale Shop your children can play and color in a special area while you shop for their clothes. This store overflows with friendly service and a wonderful choice of name-brand newborn through teen gently used clothes. They also have accessories such as car seats, cribs, strollers, highchairs, walkers, and hand-crafted gifts. Prices are generally one-third of retail if the item was purchased new. There is always a special bargain section featuring an additional 10 to 50% off. Consignments are accepted by appointment only and pay 40 to 60%, depending on the item.

Wearagains For Kids ★
15061 Edwards St.
Huntington Beach, CA 92647
714/898-3400

Hours: Mon-Fri: 10:30-6 Sat: 10:30-5
Credit Cards: DISC, MC, V

At Wearagains For Kids you can find new, and nearly new, name-brand products, for example: clothing—OshKosh, Gymboree, and Gap; toys—Little Tikes, Fisher Price, and Playskool; furniture—Cosco, Century, and Combi. Children's sizes available are 0 through 14. There is also a selection of maternity clothes. Along with their everyday savings of 35 to 70% below retail, bargain and clearance racks offer color-tagged items for half price. With your *Buying Retail Is Stupid!* coupon, you will receive an additional 10% off any purchase over $10.

See Also: (refer to index)
        Mudpies . . . A Children's Store

Family Resale Stores

Back On The Rack ★
21506 Sherman Way
Canoga Park, CA 91303
818/704-8303

Hours: Mon-Fri: 10:30-6:30 Sat: 10:30-5 Sun: 1-5
Credit Cards: MC, V

Here's a resale store for the entire family that has been growing by leaps and bounds. They have had to move into larger quarters three times since they opened their doors in 1984. Their specialty is children's used clothing that is like new, as well as infants', ladies', maternity, and men's clothing. In fact, they've recently added a large selection of used Levi's for men. They also carry shoes, baby furniture, and toys. So, when you want Guess?, Levi, OshKosh, Esprit, Liz Claiborne, or even Evan Picone brand clothing, your best bet is Back On The Rack for 50 to 80% discounts, compared with buying the same clothing new. They buy clothing that is up-to-date and in excellent condition, by appointment only. You can also bring in your *Buying Retail Is Stupid!* coupon for a 10% discount.

It's A Wrap!
3315 W. Magnolia Blvd.
Burbank, CA 91505
818/567-7366

Hours: Mon-Sat: 11-6 Sun: 11-4
Credit Cards: DISC, MC, V

O.K., admit it—you're a television and movie addict and you love the clothes your favorite stars wear. Now you can purchase them at It's A Wrap!, a movie and television clothing outlet. After a movie is made or a television series is canceled, the major motion picture studios send the wardrobes here for sale. Most clothing is worn, but some is new. Prices are 50 to 90% off clothing for men, women, and children with recognizable labels.

Janet Lee Shop
2012 N. Tustin Ave.
Orange, CA 92665
714/283-1702

Hours: Tues-Fri: 10-6 Sat: 10-5
Credit Cards: DISC, MC, V

Before consignment shops were "in," Janet Lee was already extending savings to the entire family. Since 1974, women's, men's and children's fashions as well as shoes, accessories, and household items have been selling at 20 to 50% off retail prices. The list is endless as to the brand names you'll find: Jones New York, St. John, Carole Little, Evan Picone, Esprit, Guess?, Levi, Dockers, After Six, Perry Ellis, and many more. Every 30 days everything in the store is marked down. So, bring the entire family to Janet Lee Shop and save a bundle.

Men's & Women's Resale Stores

Armani Wells ★
12404 Ventura Blvd.
Studio City, CA 91604
818/985-5899

Hours: Mon-Sat: 10-6 Sun: 11-5
Credit Cards: AE, MC, V

Although few and far between, men's resale stores offer recycled and sometimes brand-new items at affordable prices. Armani Wells is a resale store for men with everything from casual to formal wear. The inventory comes mainly from private parties and film studios. As with any store that carries recycled merchandise, the selection and sizes always vary. It's not uncommon to find $1,000 Armani sport coats for $145, or famous-maker suits for $115 to $250, instead of $300 to $3,000 retail. If you have a particular favorite brand name, add your name to their request book and they'll give you a call when they receive that brand in your size. The store also carries new suits at deeply discounted prices. Your *Buying Retail Is Stupid!* coupon is good for a 10% discount.

Bailey's ★
109 E. Union St.
Pasadena, CA 91103
818/449-0201

Hours: Tues-Sat: 11-5
Credit Cards: All Major
♦ **Senior Discount:** 10% **Age:** 65

If you'd like designer names, but without the pricey price tags, Bailey's is going to become your favorite place to shop. The first thing you'll notice about Bailey's is the expensive boutique look of the store. Well, looks can be deceiving. Inside you'll find great prices on men's suits, sport coats, dress and casual shirts, sweaters, shoes, and accessories at one-third of the original retail price. Some of the labels are Valentino, Armani, Hugo Boss, Brioni, Donna Karan, Ralph Lauren, and Calvin Klein, and there are many more. Bailey's also carries brand-new items that are close-outs from expensive manufacturers. Take in your *Buying Retail Is Stupid!* coupon and you'll receive an additional 10% discount (not valid with senior citizen discount).

Gentlemen's Exchange
24066 Neece Ave.
Torrance, CA 90505
310/375-4148

Hours: Tues-Sat: 11-5
Credit Cards: Cash or Checks Only

Let Patricia Benson, owner of Gentlemen's Exchange, dress you in her gently worn suits, sportswear, shoes, and accessories. The labels you'll find include Nino Cerruti, Nordstrom, Daniel Hechter, Christian Dior, and Boss. Half-off sales are held six times a year. She also takes men's clothing on consignment, by appointment only. In business since 1985, Gentlemen's Exchange will save you about 70% off retail prices.

Monopoly ★
8421 W. 3rd St.
Los Angeles, CA 90048
213/655-0704

Hours: Mon-Wed, Fri: 11-6 Thur: 11-7 Sat: 1-6
Credit Cards: All Major
♦ **Senior Discount:** 20% **Age:** 60

Have a wardrobe expert help put your closet together with women's and men's fashions and shoes from Monopoly. A personal shopper will advise you on the best styles and save you 75 to 80% on closeouts from Versace, Chanel, Georgio Armani, Mario Valentino, and many more. All items are first quality, and their inventory is continually being restocked with designer fashions from Italy and France. Be sure to ask about their yearly sale where you can save on their already discounted prices. Take in your *Buying Retail Is Stupid!* coupon and you'll save an extra 15% off your purchase of $150 or more.

Off Melrose ★
4255 Campus #C-195
Irvine, CA 92714
714/509-1232

Hours: Mon-Sat: 11-7 Sun: 12-5
Credit Cards: AE, DISC, MC, V

What do you do with your used surf, skate, and snowboard apparel? Take them to Off Melrose, where they will pay you from $2 to $10, depending on the item and its condition. They accept only major brand names such as No Fear, Black Fly, Quicksilver, Fuct, Rip Curl, Burton Free, Gotcha, Mossimo, and Levi's. The merchandise they sell, as well as buy, includes sweaters, T-shirts, jackets, board shorts, pants, and hats. Off Melrose is also noted for their large stock of patches. *Your Buying Retail Is Stupid!* coupon will save you an extra 15% off your purchase.

Additional Locations:
Glendora–103 W. Alosta Blvd., 818/857-0900
Rancho Cucamonga–9400 Baseline Rd., 909/948-9264
Upland–2190 W. Foothill Blvd., 909/931-7701

Once Is Not Enough
2721 East Coast Hwy.
Corona del Mar, CA 92625
714/673-9468

Hours: Mon-Thur: 10-6 Fri: 10-5 Sat: 10-4
Credit Cards: DISC, MC, V

Men can now have Armani, Celini, Ferrini, Ralph Lauren, and Calvin Klein clothes at a fraction of the retail cost from Once Is Not Enough consignment store. Just like the finer department stores, they will help put your wardrobe together and take care of any alterations. Women, too, can find top designer clothing from St. John Knits, Platinum, Joan Voss, and Jones New York. Mark your calendars for their Martin Luther King Day sale, which runs two weeks and offers an additional 50% off.

Patsy's Clothes Closet—Palm Springs
4121 E. Palm Canyon Dr.
Palm Springs, CA 92264
619/324-8825

Hours: Wed-Sat: 11-5 Sun: 12-5
Credit Cards: MC, V

If you think shopping in a resale store is like shopping in a thrift store, think again. Patsy's is one of the best when it comes to resale clothing for men and women. You don't have to worry about the condition of the garments because only clothing in fine condition is accepted on consignment. This neatly organized store is filled with high-quality, gently worn (if ever) clothing fresh from the dry cleaners. You'll find a large selection of clothing with labels such as Escada, Ralph Lauren/Polo, Carole Little, Armani, and many others.

Recycled Rags
2731 E. Coast Hwy.
Corona del Mar, CA 92625
714/675-5553

Hours: Mon-Sat: 10-6 Sun: 12-5
Credit Cards: AE, MC, V

While taking in the ocean views and salty air during a leisurely cruise down Pacific Coast Highway, you might want to stretch your legs and save money at the same time. Established in 1969, Recycled Rags was one of the first resale stores to specialize in recycled designer clothing. Men and women will find everything from tuxedos and evening gowns to sports wear and sweaters, from some of the world's best-dressed people. In addition to clothing of all sorts, you'll find plenty of fashion accessories that include costume jewelry and a large assortment of hats. On the last Sunday of every month, Recycled Rags has a parking-lot sale in which goods that have been in the store for more than 30 days are reduced to one-sixth of original retail prices. Special Sunday hours for the parking-lot sales only are 9 a.m. to 4 p.m.

Serendipity Boutique ★
31107 Rancho Viejo Rd., #3-B
San Juan Capistrano, CA 92675
714/493-5031

Hours: Mon-Sat: 11-6
Credit Cards: AE, DISC, MC, V

Seems as though women's resale stores are the norm; well, here's both a men's and women's resale store carrying famous brands such as Armani and Polo for men, and St. John, Donna Karan, Chanel, Ellen Tracy, and Montana for women. Savings are up to 75% off retail on women's dresses, blazers, blouses, pants, sweaters, shoes, jewelry, handbags, and accessories, and for men: suits, blazers, pants, shirts, ties, and shoes. Bring in your *Buying Retail Is Stupid!* coupon for an additional 25% off—that will make any purchase at Serendipity a super bargain.

Studio Wardrobe/Reel Clothes ★
12132 Ventura Blvd.
Studio City, CA 91604
818/508-7762

Hours: Mon-Sat: 10-6 Sun: 12-5
Credit Cards: MC, V

The next time you have out-of-town guests you can take them to Studio Wardrobe/Reel Clothes, where they can buy items from movies, television shows and mini-series, and commercials. This high-energy store buys and sells clothing, accessories, and props from more than 500 independent production companies and most major studios. The owners are happy to give customers a tour of the store, pointing out outfits that were worn in all kinds of shows and by what stars. Outfits, such as a robe worn by Jessica Lang in *Rob Roy*, or John Travolta's Donna Karan pin-stripe suit from *Get Shorty*, aren't discounted all that much because they're collectibles. The super deals are on items worn by those other than the principal actors, such as dress shirts for $35 instead of $135 retail, many never worn. This store was recommended by a professional costume designer and costumer who shops here not only for the movies she's working on, but also for herself. Remember to use your *Buying Retail Is Stupid!* coupon for an extra 5% discount.

Women's Resale Stores

The AdDress Boutique, Inc. ★
1116 Wilshire Blvd.
Santa Monica, CA 90403
310/394-1406

Hours: Mon-Sat: 10-6 Sun: 12-5
Credit Cards: AE, MC, V

The AdDress Boutique, considered to be one of the most elegant women's resale shops in Southern California, features after-five clothing for those special occasions. Some of the accoutrements found here may have been previously worn by one of your favorite Hollywood stars. In addition to resale, they have new designer clothing. Styles from casual to cocktail run in sizes 2 to 18. You won't be disappointed by the selection, savings, service, or hospitality. Available to first-time customers only, the *Buying Retail Is Stupid!* coupon is good for a 10% discount.

Bailey's Backstreet ★
93 E. Union Alley (Old Town Pasadena)
Pasadena, CA 91103
818/449-4104

Hours: Tues-Sat: 11-5
Credit Cards: All Major
♦ **Senior Discount:** 10% **Age:** 55

Bailey's Backstreet, in Old Pasadena, is an elegant boutique with crystal chandeliers and antiques. At first glance, you'd never consider this could be a resale store with gently worn and new designer clothing. They carry sizes from 2 to 26, as well as a large selection of sizes 1X to 3X, which is a rare find. Most women's resale stores offer a more limited size range, especially in larger sizes. The resale clothing is usually one-third of original retail on brand names such as Nicole Miller, Donna Karan, Ellen Tracy, Criscione, Adrienne Vittadini, Escada, and Forgotten Woman, and many more. For even bigger discounts, prices are dropped after a garment has been in the store for two months. With help from the fashion and service-oriented staff, it's possible to leave Bailey's Backstreet with a new wardrobe and appropriate accessories for less than the retail price of a new designer dress. For more savings, use your *Buying Retail Is Stupid!* coupon for an extra 10% discount (not valid with senior citizen discount).

Born 2 Shoppe ★
18822 Beach Blvd., #108
Huntington Beach, CA 92646
714/962-2962

Hours: Mon-Fri: 11-6 Sat: 11-5 Sun: 12-4
Credit Cards: All Major

The *Orange County Register* voted Born 2 Shoppe one of the top three consignment stores in 1994 and 1995. They offer women's clothes in sizes 4 to 16. Their well-kept, organized, clean store is located on two floors. Name brands such as Ellen Tracy, Jones New York, Carol Anderson, Esprit, Gap, Carol Little, and Ralph Lauren are available for 30 to 75% below retail. The last Saturday of every month there is a sale, and the layaway plan makes payment easy. Remember to take in your *Buying Retail Is Stupid!* coupon and save an extra 20% off nonsale purchases of $10 or more.

Cherie's Secrets
12526 Ventura Blvd.
Studio City, CA 91604
818/508-1628

Hours: Mon-Sat: 10-6
Credit Cards: AE, MC, V

Cherie's Secrets shop should not be kept a secret. It is an upscale women's resale store that carries current, in-season designer clothing and accessories at tremendous savings. Some of the labels you'll find here are Chanel, Escada, Ungaro, Armani, and Donna Karan, along with many others. Her salespeople are very friendly, and they enjoy helping their customers put together complete outfits along with that "just right" piece of jewelry or hat. You won't have to wait around for a dressing room, since they have five. Cherie's also carries new clothing at discounted prices.

Clothes Heaven
110 E. Union St. (Old Town Pasadena)
Pasadena, CA 91103
818/440-0929

Hours: Tues-Sat: 11:30-5
Credit Cards: AE, DISC, MC, V

Owner Larayne Brannon says, "Clothes Heaven is where good clothes go when they're passed on." They have been serving their long-term clientele since 1983 with a store filled primarily with gently worn designer clothing. Some of the garments, with store tags still intact, have never been worn. Their women's designer clothing and accessories have been passed on from some great closets—from Los Angeles to New York. Their labels include Anne Klein II, St. John, Valentino, Ungaro, Armani, Calvin Klein, Escada, Chanel, DKNY, Carole Little, Ellen Tracy, and many other well-known designer names. You can save about 67% off the original purchase price shopping here. For major dollar savings, head for the Sale Room in back of the store. They are experts in making customers feel special, as well as helping to coordinate their wardrobe. It's been said that Clothes Heaven is a dangerous place, because shopping there can become an addiction (price wise, designer wise, and service wise). Their hours can sometimes vary, so make sure to call before jumping in the car.

Dress Up

2043 Westcliff Dr., #102
Newport Beach, CA 92660
714/631-8290

Hours: Mon-Wed, Fri: 12-6 Thurs: 12-7 Sat: 10-5 Sun: 1-5
Credit Cards: DISC, MC, V

Dress Up is well established (since 1979), and is well known in Newport Beach. They take in only better merchandise and do many buyouts from other shops (brand-new goods at greatly discounted prices). The store is neatly organized by size, including a selection of petite and full-figured clothing. Dress Up caters to professional women with name brands such as Anne Klein, Carole Little, and Paul Stanley. You can accessorize your new outfits with Dress Up's fine and costume jewelry. They also have a small area of the store devoted to vintage clothing. The second weekend of every month they have an 80%-off sale on already low-priced goods (this is on selected merchandise).

Forever Young ★

13900 Ventura Blvd.
Sherman Oaks, CA 91423
818/990-4743

Hours: Mon-Thurs: 8-5:30 Fri-Sat: 8-6
Credit Cards: AE, DISC, MC, V

We "regular" folks can enjoy well-made, new, and slightly worn designer clothing for a fraction of the original retail prices at Forever Young, a resale store for women. They have casual, formal, and bridal wear, plus furs and leather garments. The inventory, half sold on consignment and half owned outright, is gathered mainly from private parties in Los Angeles and New York. Brand names include Chanel, DKNY, Betsy Johnson, St. John, Mondi, Giorgio Armani, and just about every other designer available in today's marketplace. They do their best to carry sizes petite to 16, but most clothing runs in sizes 8 to 12. There is also a section where all goods are marked down another 50% off the last sale price. Forever Young has such a good selection of high-quality clothing that, oftentimes, women who take their garments in for consignment end up buying other articles of clothing at the same time. Your *Buying Retail Is Stupid!* coupon is good for $35 worth of free merchandise with any $100 purchase.

The Great Name ★
311 Wilshire Blvd.
Santa Monica, CA 90401
310/395-2217
Hours: Mon-Sat: 11-6
Credit Cards: AE, MC, V

In 1975, the five Frost sisters had a great idea: they opened The Great Name and have been stocking it ever since with new and barely used designer clothing and accessories for women. You can save up to 70% off retail prices on such labels as Yves St. Laurent, Missoni, Calvin Klein, Armani, Chanel, Donna Karan, Escada, Romeo Gigli, and many more. You'll love the natural fabrics (silks, woolens, and cottons) that are featured, and you'll find clothes ranging from casual to formal in sizes 2 to 14, and sometimes larger. This is a bright, cheerful shop with private dressing rooms and a helpful staff. Speaking of helpful, your *Buying Retail Is Stupid!* coupon will help you save an extra 10%.

Jean's Stars' Apparel/Past Perfect ★
12616 Ventura Blvd.
Studio City, CA 91606
818/760-8872, 789-3710
Hours: Mon-Wed, Fri-Sat: 10-6 Thur: 10-8
Credit Cards: All Major

This is one of the nicest resale boutiques we've seen. The store is extremely neat with everything organized by size and style. Nothing is crammed on to unruly racks. Shopping here is like shopping in a very expensive boutique. And, unlike in expensive boutiques, the very professional staff offers lots of sincere service. According to owner Janet, the store was started in 1958 and stocks only the finest designer fashions previously owned by wealthy women. Prices are 60 to 90% below original cost. You'll find women's wear from dressy to casual (with a selection of shoes, handbags, and fashion jewelry) from Anne Klein, Carolina Herrera, Ralph Lauren, Armani, Donna Karan, and more. Some of these items are less than a couple of months old. Women have actually flown across the country just to buy clothes from Jean's. Why? The savings are astronomical. You might find a $4,000 Chanel suit tagged at $350, a $1,600 Escada suit priced at $140, and a pair of $300 shoes priced as low as $20! Is the picture a little clearer now? Jean's Stars'

Apparel/Past Perfect caters to every whim and fantasy with exclusive attire for every occasion; sizes range from 3 to 14, all at affordable prices. A 45-day layaway plan is available. While shopping you can enjoy cheese, crackers, and beverages. Jean's Stars' Apparel/Past Perfect invites you to come in and indulge yourself. Get on the mailing list for information about super sales held three times a year. Whatever you do, don't forget your *Buying Retail Is Stupid!* coupon for an extra 10% discount.

June Travolta's Rosebud ★
3024 De La Vina
Santa Barbara, CA 93105
805/682-4820
Hours: Tues-Sat: 11-4
Credit Cards: MC, V

Resale shopping is a great way to get expensive brand names at a fraction of original retail prices. June Travolta (yes, she's related) has a wonderful resale boutique for women, called Rosebud. Only the best-of-the-best, in top-quality condition, is accepted on consignment, and regardless of the time of year, you'll always find clothing suitable for all seasons. Name brands include Armani, Scassi, Chanel, Escada, Donna Karan, Ungaro, and many other top designer names. It's hard to believe, but women also bring her clothing they've never worn with the retail tags still attached. Brand-new items sell for about one-third of retail. In addition to clothing (casual, office, and formal wear), June has shoes, handbags, scarves, and costume jewelry. Wardrobe consulting is available, as well as an extra 10% discount when you present your *Buying Retail Is Stupid!* coupon (nonsale items only).

My Secret Place ★
18862 Beach Blvd., #116
Huntington Beach, CA 92646
714/963-4743
Hours: Tues-Fri: 11:30-6:30 Sat: 11:30-4
Credit Cards: All Major

Since 1988, My Secret Place has been offering 30 to 75% off sizes 14 and up on gently used women's fashions. They carry more than 3,000 business and dressy items featuring name brands such as Jones New York, Ellen Tracy, Sharon Anthony, Spencer Alexis, Carole Little II, Outlander, and many more. Come shop for their great prices and enjoy their many gifts and collectibles in their "Attic." Your *Buying Retail Is Stupid!* coupon can save you an additional 20% off nonsale merchandise with a $10 minimum purchase.

"New II You" Boutique ★
4292 Katella Ave.
Los Alamitos, CA 90720
310/596-1231

Hours: Tues-Fri: 11-6 Sat: 10-4
Credit Cards: DISC, MC, V
♦ **Senior Discount:** 15% **Age:** 60

At "New II You" Boutique, you can find upscale women's new and gently used fashions for 50 to 75% off retail. They carry clothing brand names such as Guess?, DKNY, and Escada. You can also find Coach and Dooney & Bourke purses, and Amalei and Stuart Weiztman shoes. "New II You" is the best-kept secret in Orange County, offering you ample parking and friendly service. By using your *Buying Retail Is Stupid!* coupon, you can save 10% on a purchase of $25 or more (not valid with senior citizen discount).

P.J. London ★
11661 San Vicente Blvd.
Los Angeles, CA 90049
310/826-4649

Hours: Mon-Sat: 10:30-6 Sun: 12-5
Credit Cards: AE, MC, V

This is the place to go to purchase top designer clothing on a bargain-basement budget. All their merchandise has barely been worn and is in perfect condition. They carry resale clothes by the top names in the world—Chanel, Donna Karan, Vittadini, and more. Sizes range from 4 to 14, and they feature four sales a year in order to clear out all items that have been around for more than 90 days. These sales cut the prices by more than 50%, and on the final day, all items are $5 and $10. So it's possible to buy a $1,500 dress for $10! In addition, you can find furs, jewelry, and accessories. Don't forget to bring in your *Buying Retail Is Stupid!* coupon for a 10% discount.

Patsy's Clothes Closet
1525 N. Main St.
Santa Ana, CA 92701
714/542-0189

Hours: Wed-Fri: 10-6 Sat: 10-4
Credit Cards: MC, V

Like designer clothing but can't stand the prices? Patsy's Clothes Closet is the place for you. How about an Albert Nipon dress for as little as $40, or a two-piece Carole Little silk for $45. Half of Patsy's stock consists of designer samples; the remainder is slightly used, gently worn resales. In the center of the store is a large case of sample and vintage jewelry, from costume to the real thing, and all at good discounts. They also carry a huge selection of hats and belts. In the same location since 1972, Patsy's Clothes Closet is housed in what used to be the first maternity hospital in Orange County (built in 1904). There are seven merchandise-filled rooms to explore and six dressing rooms. Should you need a bit of a rest, hot coffee is always available.

Additional Location:
Palm Springs–4121 E. Palm Canyon Dr., 619/324-8825

Pretty Woman ★
336 Poinsettia
Corona del Mar, CA 92625
714/673-8551

Hours: Tues-Sat: 11-6 Last Sunday of Month: 10-4
Credit Cards: MC, V

Shop in an old-fashioned atmosphere, where you will receive not only personalized service, but great prices as well. Pretty Woman carries used name-brand and designer women's fashions, sizes 2 to 14, at 75% below retail. They also hold special sales with additional savings—Winter Sale every February and a Summer Sale every November. Use your *Buying Retail Is Stupid!* coupon to receive an additional 10% off any $25 purchase.

Regeneration ★
5036 Katella Ave.
Los Alamitos, CA 90720
310/431-3727

Hours: Tues-Sat: 11-6 Sun: 9-12
Credit Cards: AE, DISC, MC, V

How would you like to save 50 to 90% off retail on women's clothing? Regeneration, a consignment boutique, carries gently worn clothing with well-known brand and designer names in sizes 4 through 20. Larger sizes are sometimes available. You'll also find shoes, hats, jewelry, belts, and other fashion accessories. Call about special sales when everything is an additional 50% off. The *Buying Retail Is Stupid!* coupon will save you an extra 10%.

The Rose Closet

9037 Adams Ave.
Huntington Beach, CA 92646
714/962-4377

Hours: Tues-Thur: 11-5 Fri-Sat: 11-6
Credit Cards: DISC, MC, V

The Rose Closet is unique, since it's one of the few consignment stores that cater only to large sizes (14 to 32). Happily, you'll find new and slightly used evening, career, and sports wear and wedding gowns with brand names such as Eight West, Venezia, Jones New York, Hunters Run, London Fog, and Sharon Anthony at savings of 50 to 75% off retail. Shoes, jewelry, hats, and accessories are also available. There's a no-return policy—so make sure you're pleased with your purchase.

Second Time Around ★

298 E. 17th St., Suite B
Costa Mesa, CA 92627
714/642-4700

Hours: Mon-Fri: 11-6 Sat: 10-6 Sun: 12-4
Credit Cards: AE, MC, V

In business since 1964, Second Time Around is a resale store that deals in consignments. They accept like-new garments, shoes, purses, and jewelry. Sizes in clothing range from 5 to 20. There are savings of 60 to 75% on names such as Picone, Anne Klein, Dior, and more. All items are carefully inspected before being accepted for sale. Take in your *Buying Retail Is Stupid!* coupon for an additional 20% discount.

Silent Partners

99 E. Union St.
Pasadena, CA 91103
818/793-6877

Hours: Tues-Fri: 11-5 Sat: 11-4
Credit Cards: AE, MC, V

Alyce Doney's Silent Partners is just what the name implies. If you want to dress professionally but really can't afford the usual price tags for St. John, David Hayes, or Chanel, then here's where Silent Partners can help you. They have clothes for every occasion, from casual to ball gowns; they also carry shoes, purses, and accessories. Here's even better news—

Alyce's daughter has a store in Claremont, Silent Partners East. The prices are usually about 33% of original retail. They also carry new clothes from eight different boutiques that are discounted. Open since 1981, Silent Partners has built a trusting relationship with customers and consignees as well.

Additional Location:
Claremont–346 Yale Ave. (at 4th), 909/624-0696

Twice The Style ★
369 E. 17th St., #1
Costa Mesa, CA 92627
714/642-1844

Hours: Mon-Fri: 10-6 Sat: 10-5
Credit Cards: AE, DISC, MC, V

"Up-to-date styles at old fashioned prices" is Sandy Miller's motto at Twice The Style consignment boutique, in business since 1990. Her loyal clientele raves about the quality-made, well-designed clothing found here. The last Saturday of every month you'll save even more at her clearance sale. Take in your *Buying Retail Is Stupid!* coupon and you'll save an extra 10% off your purchase (nonsale items only).

See Also: (refer to index)
        Tightwad

SHOES
Family

Dave's Shoe Outlet
2800 W. Pico Blvd.
Los Angeles, CA 90006
213/737-7614

Hours: Tues-Sat: 10-5
Credit Cards: All Major

Since 1966, Dave's Shoe Outlet has been selling shoes at discounts of 50% or more below retail. This is a self-service shoe store; the 2,500-square-foot store carries brands such as Sacha, Bruno Magli, Evan Picone, Florsheim, Paloma, and more. Dave's also carries new women's shoes in sizes up to 13, as well as some reconditioned shoes and boots.

Foot Mart Sports ★

8575 Knott Ave.
Buena Park, CA 90620
714/827-8540

Hours: Mon-Fri: 9-9 Sat: 9-8 Sun: 9-7
Credit Cards: AE, DISC, MC, V

If you find yourself spending lots of money for all those feet in your household, this is surely the place you'll want to go. They carry all the major brands: Reebok, Nike, Adidas, Puma, New Balance, Avia, and British Knight—all at savings of 30% or more below retail. Their 12,000-square-foot warehouse has all sorts of sports shoes for infants, children, women, and men. In addition, they handle specialty shoes for soccer, basketball, and running. Free shuttle service is offered from many Orange County hotels to the store. Don't forget to bring along your *Buying Retail Is Stupid!* coupon for an extra 5% discount.

Additional Locations:
Anaheim–Sport City U.S.A., 923 Euclid Blvd., 714/772-6921
Huntington Park–7020 Pacific Blvd., 213/583-9926

Footlocker Outlet

115 Lincoln Blvd.
Venice, CA 90291
310/450-8178

Hours: Mon-Fri: 10-9 Sat: 10-7 Sun: 10-6
Credit Cards: AE, DISC, MC, V

When it's time to buy new tennies for the entire family, you can save big bucks by shopping at one of three Footlocker Outlets. They're stocked with your favorite brands from the 80 Footlocker retail stores, and all shoes are first quality. When a shoe can no longer be ordered (the manufacturer stops making a particular style), or the company has over-purchased a line, they end up at the outlet stores. In addition to shoe sizes for every member of the family—infant to size 12 for women and 18 for men—they carry plenty of clothing. All goods are discounted 20 to 50% off the original retail prices. By the way, they don't carry any merchandise that has been returned to their retail stores.

Additional Locations:
Los Angeles–1840 W. Manchester Blvd., 213/971-1935
Manhattan Beach–1775 Artesia Blvd., 310/376-7277

Sammy's Sports
453 N. Beverly Dr.
Beverly Hills, CA 90210
310/246-0376

Hours: Mon-Sat: 10-7
Credit Cards: AE, DISC, MC, V

Are you searching for the right athletic shoe for every member of your family? Sammy's Sports has brand names such as Nike, New Balance, Adidas, Converse, Reebok, Fila, Puma, and more. While you're there, check out their athletic clothing and team outfitters department for men, women, and children. Prices are discounted 15 to 20% off retail on shoes, and 20 to 30% on in-line skates and other sporting goods. You can park for two hours free of charge at the municipal parking lot across the street.

Shoe City
11971 Brookhurst Ave.
Garden Grove, CA 92640
714/638-2303

Hours: Mon-Fri: 10-9 Sat-Sun: 10-7
Credit Cards: AE, DISC, MC, V

Known as the supermarket of athletic shoes, Shoe City is one of the largest independent chain stores in California. The stores feature a variety of styles including Reebok, Nike, LA Gear, Puma, British Knights, and many more at savings of 35 to 75% off retail. With savings like that, you can take the entire family and buy shoes for everyone. Stores are located in Los Angeles, Orange, and Riverside counties.

Additional Locations:
19 other stores throughout Southern California

Shoeteria ★
13324 San Antonio Dr.
Norwalk, CA 90650
310/864-4422

Hours: Mon-Fri: 9-9 Sat: 9-7 Sun: 10-5
Credit Cards: AE, DISC, MC, V

Since 1957, Shoeteria has always guaranteed lowest prices but won't discount their excellent service. This enormous store (8,000 square feet) has about 40,000 pairs of dress, casual, athletic, western, and work shoes, sandals, and the latest-style "grunge fashion" shoes for men, women, and children. Brand names include Florsheim, Naturalizer, Hush Puppies, Nike, Reebok, Tony Lama, Wolverine Boots, New Balance, and Nunn

Bush. Shoeteria's motto, "Where hard-to-find shoe sizes aren't hard to find," is achieved by focusing on extra-large and extra-wide shoes: men's sizes 5 through 17 AA to EEEEE and women's sizes 4 through 12 AAA to EEE. The *Buying Retail Is Stupid!* coupon offers an additional 15% off.

Men's & Women's Shoes

Maya Shoes ★
6523 Hollywood Blvd.
Hollywood, CA 90028
213/962-9467

Hours: 7 Days a Week: 10:30-7:30
Credit Cards: AE, DISC, MC, V
♦ **Senior Discount:** 5% **Age:** 65

You can save as much as 70% on casual, dressy, and athletic shoes for men and women. They import most of their merchandise from countries such as Italy, Spain, and Brazil. Their buyers are in Europe five or six times a year purchasing the newest styles in dressy and casual shoes and boots. Your *Buying Retail Is Stupid!* coupon is good for a 5% discount.

Sneaker Warehouse ★
16736 Ventura Blvd.
Encino, CA 91436
818/995-8999

Hours: Mon-Sat: 10-7 Sun: 11-5
Credit Cards: MC, V

Sneaker Warehouse has famous-maker athletic shoes for men and women, priced at least 20 to 40% off retail. Savings run even higher (40 to 75% off retail) on manufacturer close-outs. Runners will find a special selection of shoes and service. Name brands include Nike, Reebok, Avia, New Balance, Brooks, Etonic, Soccony, Keds, Boks, Rockport, Adidas, Asics, and just about any other brand favored by serious and not-so-serious athletes. In addition to shoes, Sneaker Warehouse has great buys on a variety of sports clothing, and they have a good selection of socks where you'll save the most by buying in multiples. By the way, you can do a good deed and save money at the same time. When you buy a new pair of shoes here, Sneaker Warehouse will give you a $5 trade-in for a pair of old athletic shoes, no matter what shape they're in. The trade-ins are donated to charity. Make sure to use your *Buying Retail Is Stupid!* coupon for an extra 5% discount.

Top to Top ★
2621 Wilshire Blvd.
Santa Monica, CA 90403
310/829-7030

Hours: Mon-Fri: 10-8 Sat: 10-7 Sun: 11-6
Credit Cards: MC, V

Here's a place you may want to try for current athletic shoes and clothing. You can expect a wide variety of styles for your entire family with a discount of 20 to 30% off retail. Nike, New Balance, Reebok, Adidas, Asics, and even Keds are just a few of the many brand names represented at Top to Top. Be sure to get your name on their mailing list, so you will be notified of their annual sale in which discounts run an additional 30 to 60%. These salespeople know about shoes and the proper fit, so you're in good hands. If you take in an old pair of tennies, you'll receive a $5 discount on a new pair, and your old ones will be donated to charity. Use your *Buying Retail Is Stupid!* coupon when you make a purchase and you'll receive a free pair of socks.

Additional Location:
Marina del Rey–4724-1/4 Admiralty Way, 310/821-6111

Women's Shoes

Chic Wide Shoes
10746 Washington Blvd.
Culver City, CA 90230
310/836-2568

Hours: Mon-Thur, Sat: 10-6 Fri: 10-8 Sun: 11-5
Credit Cards: MC, DISC, V

When was the last time you were personally waited on by a shoe salesperson and were able to save money at the same time? That's the policy at Chic Wide Shoes, where a salesperson will measure your feet, assist you with any questions, and handle special orders. Chic has the world's largest selection of wide-width shoes, with selected items at 20% off. At their semiannual sales, they offer up to 70% off end-of-season merchandise. You'll recognize brand names such as Hush Puppies, Soft Spots, Selby, Magdesians, Clinic, and many more. They also have a "best price guarantee" on new selections such as shoes by Easy Espirit. Get on their mailing list for personal notifications of big sale events. Store hours vary at each location.

Additional Locations:
Cypress–10035 Valley View St., 714/821-5111
La Mesa–5500 Grossmont Center Dr., 619/589-2550
Tarzana–18768 Ventura Blvd., 818/708-0855
Torrance–22150-C Hawthorne Blvd., 310/214-4824

Henry's Shoe Experience ★
9454 E. Telegraph Rd.
Downey, CA 90240
310/904-8134

Hours: Mon-Fri: 10-8 Sat: 10-6 Sun: 11-5
Credit Cards: All Major

Shoe freaks: here's a shoe store you can visit once a week and probably find something different each time. Henry's Shoe Experience carries women's shoes that are close-outs, special buys, factory-damaged, and refinished. Each week a new supply of shoes hits the store. Prices are $16.99 a pair, or two for $30. Purchase these shoes on Saturday and Sunday and pay only $12.99 a pair, or two for $24. They lower their prices on the weekend to make room for mid-week shipments. They also carry current fashion shoes always priced at $20 a pair. Brand names you'll recognize are 9 West, Calico, Bandolino, Enzo, and many more. The *Buying Retail Is Stupid!* coupon will save you an additional 10%. Prices might vary slightly at the store in Hawaiian Gardens.

Additional Location:
Hawaiian Gardens–12013 E. Carson, 310/924-8551

Ladies Shoes Plus
4148 Woodruff
Lakewood, CA 90713
310/497-1997

Hours: Mon-Sat: 10-6 Sun: 11-5
Credit Cards: MC, V

This no-nonsense store has women's shoes in sizes 4B to 12W priced 30 to 70% off retail. Brand names change constantly. You might find Hush Puppies, Cobbies, Life Stride, Naturalizer, Auditions, Joyce, Selby, and Calico. If you happen to wear narrow sizes, you are definitely in luck; they buy close-outs, and there are always tons of narrow sizes. Of course, they have regular sizes too, and there are always at least 3,500 pairs of shoes in stock.

Samples Only ★
19401 Victory Blvd.
Reseda, CA 91335
818/881-8621

Hours: Mon-Sat: 10-7 Sun: 12-5
Credit Cards: MC, V

The selection of famous brand-name, designer shoes is fabulous at Samples Only. Prices on brand names such as Bruno Magli, Stuart Weitzman, Cole Haan, Charles Jourdan, and Thierry Mugler run at 40 to 50% below high-end department store prices. Sizes range from 4B to 7-1/2B in high-fashion, evening, casual, and walking shoes. The best selection is in sizes 5-1/2 to 7. All shoes are first-quality samples, so if you see something you like, buy it—it probably won't be there on your next visit. When shoes arrive for the new season, the shoes from the previous season are dropped another 40%. They often have unadvertised specials, such as all prices discounted an extra 20% for the day. Because every manufacturer uses only one size for its samples, each brand is available in one size only. In addition to shoes, they carry sample handbags from the same shoe manufacturers. You'll save an additional 10% with your *Buying Retail Is Stupid!* coupon (not valid on sale items or other discount or promotional offers).

Shoe Explosion ★
2249 Sepulveda Blvd.
Los Angeles, CA 90064
310/478-2728, 800/775-1277

Hours: Mon-Sat: 10-7 Sun: 11-6
Credit Cards: All Major

If you've been searching for a store with a good selection of name-brand women's shoes at discount prices, head on over to Shoe Explosion. They carry many of the same shoes currently featured in malls and department stores from more than 40 vendors in sizes 5 to 10. Prices run 20 to 50% off retail, sometimes more. Three times a year Shoe Explosion sends out a mailer to regular customers with specials available only to those on their mailing list. Specials in the past have included a free belt with purchase, and another featured an extra $5 off each pair of shoes, so make sure you get signed up! Some stores carry men's shoes, also at discounted prices. All stores will accept your *Buying Retail Is Stupid!* coupon for an extra 10% discount.

Additional Locations:
Hollywood—Sacks SFO, 652 N. La Brea, 213/939-3993
Laguna Beach—254 Beach St., 714/497-5997
Woodland Hills—21516 Victory Blvd., 818/992-0567

Wild Pair Outlet

1731 Wilshire Blvd.
Santa Monica, CA 90403
310/828-9557

Hours: Mon-Fri: 10-9 Sat: 10-6 Sun: 12-6
Credit Cards: AE, DISC, MC, V

This is the outlet for Wild Pair women's shoe stores. Prices are 30 to 75% lower than retail, ranging from $19 to $129. Check out their clearance sales in January and June when you can purchase shoes for $5 to $19. Now, when was the last time you purchased a pair of leather shoes for $5? Sizes range from 5 to 10. You'll also find other brand names such as Andrea Moda, Chinese Laundry, Bronx, Poppies, Doc Martens, Reflex, and many more. Handbags and jewelry are available at discount prices, too.

Work Shoes

Industrial Shoe Warehouse ★

5176 Santa Monica Blvd.
Los Angeles, CA 90029
213/663-3981

Hours: Mon-Sat: 10-7 Sun: 10-5:30
Credit Cards: MC, V

Open for business since 1910, Industrial Shoe Warehouse is an enormous store filled with work shoes for men and women. The majority of stock is first quality, with seconds clearly marked. Savings generally start at 20% below retail, and when they get a good price on overruns, or receive extra discounts on a volume buy, they pass the savings on to customers. Men's sizes run 3 to 13, and work shoes made specifically for women come in sizes 5 to 11. Some of the brand names you'll find are Skechers, Carolina Gold, Caterpillar, Frye, and Wolverine. Fans of Dr. Martens can get some terrific discounts on current lines, overruns, and close-outs. They also carry current lines and close-outs of such famous-maker athletic shoes as Nike, Fila, Converse, Vans, and others. The staff is very customer oriented, and some employees are bilingual (English and Spanish). There is also an employee discount program for companies with more than 10 employees. Don't forget to take in your *Buying Retail Is Stupid!* coupon for an extra 5% discount.

Wally's Discount Workshoes and Boots ★
10330 Hole Ave., #6
Riverside, CA 92505
909/351-0505

Hours: Mon-Fri: 10-8 Sat: 10-6 Sun: 11-5
Credit Cards: MC, V

"As someone once said," quotes Dave Holy, owner of Wally's Discount Workshoes and Boots for men and women, "everyone deserves two things in life, a good pair of shoes and a good bed, because we spend so much time in both of them." Terri, his wife, and Dave have been operating the store since 1987, making sure every customer who buys a pair of work shoes or boots gets a good fit. With Dave's experience in the shoe industry since 1946, you can be sure he carries through on his promise. The selection of steel-toed shoes and boots for both men and women is one of the largest in Southern California. They specialize in sizes 5 through 17 and widths D through EEEE, with prices 20 to 50% off retail. Brand names featured are Wolverine, Chippewa, Rocky, Thorogood, Softspots, Nursemates, Lake Of The Woods, and many more. Save an additional 5% on nonsale items only with your *Buying Retail Is Stupid!* coupon.

Work Boot Warehouse ★
21608 Sherman Way
Canoga Park, CA 91303
818/703-8498, 800/974-BOOT (974-2668)

Hours: Mon-Fri: 9:30-7 Sat: 9-6 Sun: 11-5
Credit Cards: All Major

Work Boot Warehouse has more than 7,000 pairs of shoes in stock for just about any line of work or sport. Prices run approximately 10 to 45% off retail on brand names such as Wolverine (including steel-toed tennis shoes), Hi-Tech, Carolina, Gorilla, Chippewa, Dr. Martens, and many others. There are always close-outs with even lower prices located in front of the store. You'll save $10 on a pair of boots by using your *Buying Retail Is Stupid!* coupon. The coupon is not redeemable for boots on sale or rubber boots.

Additional Location:
North Hollywood–5760 Lankershim Blvd., 818/753-8747

UNIFORMS

Glamour Uniform Shop ★
4951 W. Sunset Blvd.
Hollywood, CA 90027
213/666-2122

Hours: Mon-Fri: 10-6 Sat: 10-5
Credit Cards: AE, DISC, MC, V

Whether you're buying a uniform just for yourself or for all your employees, you can save 20 to 50% here. You'll find uniforms for nurses, doctors, waitresses, beauticians, barbers, and chefs. The uniforms come in white and colors, and in sizes 3 to 56. Glamour Uniform will even give you a greater discount on group orders. Duty shoes are available in white or colors, sizes 4 to 12. Save an additional 10% when you use your *Buying Retail Is Stupid!* coupon. The Los Angeles store is called Owl Uniform.

Additional Location:
Los Angeles–Owl Uniform, 984 W. Vernon, 213/233-1830

Sam Cook Uniforms
2727 S. Flower St.
Los Angeles, CA 90007
213/748-4800

Hours: Mon-Fri: 9-5 Sat: 9-1
Credit Cards: MC, V

Uniforms of all kind—police, waiters, chefs, security guards, mailmen, food servers—and many different varieties of industrial garb are available here. More than 3,000 individual items are in their inventory, including such brand names as Dickies, Rocky, and Thoro-Good. You'll find a good selection of shoes, blazers, shirts, and sportswear. Here's a place to go to get dressed for work or leisure. In business since 1911, Sam Cook Uniforms lets you save 15 to 30% off retail.

School Uniform Co. ★
6168 Sepulveda Blvd.
Van Nuys, CA 91411
818/994-1197

Hours: Tues-Sat: 9:30-4:30*
Credit Cards: DISC, MC, V

If your children happen to attend schools that have adopted voluntary or mandatory uniform policies, you'll be happy to learn about School Uniform Co. With several children of their own, the owners started this business with cash-strapped parents in mind. This is a great place to buy generic school uniforms for boys and girls in sizes 4 to 20, plus husky and full sizes. Although the labels read differently, the merchandise comes from the same manufacturers used by specialty boutiques selling uniforms. All clothing—oxford shirts, blouses, slacks, shorts, jumpers, skirts, sweaters, and more in various styles and colors—is first quality. Prices run about 50% less than specialty stores and 15 to 25% below discount department stores. There is also a resale department. If you'd rather shop from home, call them for a mail-order brochure. Prices are the same as in-store prices. Shipping is $2.50 prepaid, and if necessary they arrange and pay for return shipping. School Uniform Co. also sells to schools, and they receive 5% of total sales. Your *Buying Retail Is Stupid!* coupon is good for an extra 5% discount (not valid with other discount offers). *Hours are extended during July and September.

Uniforms Depot
18552 Sherman Way
Reseda, CA 91335
818/343-7554
Hours: Tues-Fri: 9:30-5 Sat: 11-2
Credit Cards: AE, DISC, MC, V

If you're in need of uniforms and you haven't shopped here, you've missed a good deal! Uniforms Depot carries one of the largest selections in the area. Whether you want coveralls, shop smocks, lab wear, nurses uniforms, tuxedo shirts, shoes, or aprons, they have it. In addition, you'll find leather accessories, work duty shoes, and some police gear. They custom-designed the original uniforms for Charlie Browns and Bobbie McGees, and some for Disneyland, so they know what they are doing! Their regular prices are 10 to 30% below other stores, with additional discounts on specials saving you even more money. They've been around since 1948, at their current location since January of 1981.

WESTERN APPAREL

Boot Hill ★
19553 Parthenia St., Suite A1
Northridge, CA 91324
818/772-2668, 800/266-8445
Hours: Mon-Tues, Thurs-Fri: 11-6 Wed: 10-9 Sat: 10-5 Sun: 12:30-5
Credit Cards: AE, DISC, MC, V

Grab your partner and do-si-do on over to Boot Hill where they dress men and women from head to toe for a good, old-fashioned square dance.

They carry plenty of western wear, too. Their large store has a tremendous selection of such brands as H.B.C. Western Wear, Tony Lama, Mesquite, Coast Shoes, Western Collections, 1849 (Boot Hill's original designs), and others. Be the one to stand out in the crowd with a custom-designed, one-of-a-kind dress or two-piece outfit! Check out their accessories and petticoats, too! Their prices are 20 to 50% off retail, and you can use your *Buying Retail Is Stupid!* coupon to save an additional 5%. For your convenience, a layaway plan is also available.

Carol's Country Corner ★
818/347-1207

Hours: By Appointment Only
Credit Cards: All Major

Swing your partner and two-step down to Carol's Country Corner for the best in western and square dance apparel. They offer customized western clothes at 10 to 30% off retail prices. Carol can design a custom piece made especially for you. For year-round unadvertised specials and additional discounts for all callers and groups, give Carol's Country Corner a twirl. Custom clothing is available by appointment only. Appointment hours are 11 a.m. to 4 p.m. daily. Don't forget that your *Buying Retail Is Stupid!* coupon is good for an extra 10% discount.

Frontier Shop ★
11419 W. Jefferson Blvd.
Culver City, CA 90230
310/397-7793

Hours: Mon-Fri: 9:30-6 Sat: 9:30-4:30
Credit Cards: All Major
♦ **Senior Discount:** 15% **Age:** 65

In the heart of screenland (Culver City), and family owned and operated since 1954, Frontier Shop has been offering western wear such as boots, hats, jewelry, belts, and clothing at 20% and more off retail. They feature brand names such as Tony Lama, Justin, Stetson, Wrangler, Panhandle Slim, Dingo, Colorado Saddlery, Scully Australian Outback, and so many others that we haven't enough space to mention them all. The selection doesn't end with apparel and accessories. You can also deck out your horse with everything from bits, bridles, reins, and saddles, to cleaners, conditioners, horse shoes, and nails. Save an additional 10% with your *Buying Retail Is Stupid!* coupon (not valid with senior citizen discount).

Howard & Phil's Western Wear Outlet Store ★
21716 Sherman Way
Canoga Park, CA 91303
818/992-6808

Hours: Mon-Sat: 10-6 Sun: 11-5
Credit Cards: All Major

Anyone hankering for a new pair of cowboy boots should mosey on over to Howard & Phil's Western Wear Outlet Store, where discounts run 20 to 70% below prices at their retail stores. The outlet is fed by 54 Howard & Phil's Western Wear stores. Most of the inventory consists of excess merchandise, manufacturer overruns, and canceled orders. You'll recognize popular brand names such as Chisholm, Panhandle Slim, Nocona, Dingo, Roper, Wrangler, Stetson, Lucchese, Resistol, and all others normally found in their retail stores. Men and women will find clothing, boots, jewelry, and accessories. You'll wrangle in an extra 10% discount if you remember your *Buying Retail Is Stupid!* coupon.

Kowboyz ★
8050 Beverly Blvd.
Los Angeles, CA 90048
213/653-6444

Hours: 7 Days a Week: 11-6
Credit Cards: AE, DISC, MC, V

There are more than 2,000 pairs of used cowboy boots for men, women, and kids at Kowboyz. Now, that's a lot of boots to choose from! They have small, wide, and extra-large sizes, many in exotic skins such as ostrich, lizard, and alligator, as well as leathers in good to like-new condition, and vintage and hand-made custom boots. Prices start at $25 a pair and average around $80. That's about one-third the price off retail if purchased new. You'll find Tony Lama, Nocona, Justin, Acme, Lucchese, Mercedes, John Leddy, Frye, Cowtown, and many more. Leather coats are also available. Save an additional 10% with your *Buying Retail Is Stupid!* coupon.

Paris Go
2000 Outlet Center Dr., #200
Oxnard, CA 93030
805/278-0134

Hours: Mon-Sat: 10-8 Sun: 11-6
Credit Cards: All Major

Looking for western wear, boots, shirts, and the accessories that go with them? Paris Go has it all. Justin, Tony Lama, Frye, Lucchese, Nocona, and Larry Mahan are just a few of the brands they carry. Their doors opened in 1975 with prices 20 to 65% below retail. The store recently reopened at the Oxnard Factory Outlet mall.

WOMEN'S APPAREL

7th Avenue West
71-842 Highway 111
Rancho Mirage, CA 92270
619/340-6555

Hours: Mon-Sat: 9:30-5 Sun: 11-4
Credit Cards: AE, DISC, MC, V

Their concept is simple. They've been selling current New York designer fashions at 20 to 50% below department and specialty store prices since 1981. All merchandise is first quality, with new shipments arriving daily. Brand names vary from visit to visit. The biggest selection is devoted to color-matched and coordinated outfits and sportswear. Their motto is "We've redesigned designer prices."

Backdoor Boutique
14331 Chambers Rd.
Tustin, CA 92680
714/544-9360

Hours: Thurs-Fri: 12-4 Sat: 10-4
Credit Cards: MC, V

If you are into natural fabrics, this factory outlet is a good source for sportswear and separates. Most clothing is made of 100% cotton, and they also have items made of rayon. They carry a variety of dresses, jackets, tops, and bottoms in sizes 6 to 24. We know their hours are limited, but at savings of 40 to 80%, we can't complain. Sometimes leftover fabric and notions are for sale, too. Savings run higher on monthly specials.

Clothes Minded
219 Palos Verdes Blvd.
Redondo Beach, CA 90277
310/373-7865

Hours: 7 Days a Week: 10-10
Credit Cards: All Major

On your next visit to Redondo Beach, a stop at Clothes Minded should be on your list. Women's clothing from designers such as PJLA, Kenar, Chazz, Bila,

JJ, and Sarah Arizona is sold here for $15 per item. You will find first-quality, name-brand long and short dresses, skirts, sweaters, silk jogging suits, pants, shirts, jackets, and much more. Twice a week each store receives new merchandise.

Additional Locations:
Belmont Shore–5259 E. 2nd St., 310/439-2523
Beverly Hills–338 N. Beverly Dr., 310/275-5808
La Jolla–7880 Girard Ave., 619/454-3700
Laguna Beach–252 Forest Ave., 714/376-2015

The Clothing Factory
6831 Tampa Ave.
Reseda, CA 91335
818/609-7219

Hours: Mon-Fri: 8-6 Sat: 10-5
Credit Cards: MC, V

With the exception of just a few weeks a year, Southern Californians are blessed with year-round moderate temperatures. The Clothing Factory has casual women's clothing perfect for our climate at rock-bottom prices. This small store is a genuine factory outlet. They sell their goods to middle-to-high-end department stores and to the public without name-brand labels. The prices are low because there are no middlemen. In fact, the store takes up the front part of the warehouse, and you shop to the sound of sewing machines. Most of the clothing is made of a cotton/poly blend knit and is designed to be mixed and matched (at least 25 solid colors and several prints). You'll find four styles of skirts in two lengths, walking shorts, duster jackets, leggings, pants, dresses, and several styles of long, short, and sleeveless tops.

The Collection
4237 Campus Dr., #B-155
Irvine, CA 92715
714/854-4452

Hours: Mon-Sat: 10-7
Credit Cards: DISC, MC, V

The Collection carries first-quality women's sportswear, dresses, and accessories at savings of 50 to 80% below retail. They feature top-brand women's wear carried by Nordstrom, Bullocks, and Saks Fifth Avenue. They also offer great customer service and the personal care of a boutique. Don't forget to ask about their once-a-year sidewalk sale. Call their Palm Springs store before visiting—hours vary by season.

Additional Location:
Palm Springs–192 S. Palm Canyon, 619/320-4844

Contempo Casuals Outlet

1505 S. Riverside Ave.
Rialto, CA 92376
909/877-5654

Hours: Mon-Thurs: 11-7 Fri: 10-8 Sat: 10-7 Sun: 11-6
Credit Cards: AE, DISC, MC, V

Here's a place where you could probably walk out with an entire wardrobe and spend only $50. Contempo Casuals Outlet, which is also an outlet for Wet Seal stores, has everything you need in junior fashions priced 25 to 80% below original store prices. All jewelry is about 50% off retail. The outlet stores have been open since the early 1980s.

Additional Location:
Huntington Beach–18557 Main St., 714/841-0869

Cotton U.S.A. Outlet

22559 Ventura Blvd.
Woodland Hills, CA 91364
818/225-8725

Hours: Mon-Sat: 10-6
Credit Cards: MC, V

It's hard to beat cotton clothing for comfort and durability. Cotton U.S.A. Outlet has deep discounts on all kinds of clothing made of 100% cotton, grown in the United States. Cotton U.S.A. Outlet, a true manufacturer's outlet, carries overstock from their local factory. Most of the inventory is devoted to casual women's clothing in light-, medium-, and heavy-weight cottons. All clothing is preshrunk, and best of all, most of the clothing is ready to wear with little or no ironing necessary. Sizes for women run X-small to X-large. Most styles are oversized in both length and width. Normally closed on Sundays, the store is open two Sundays a month during the summer. Call for dates and hours.

Damone

1349 S. Main St.
Los Angeles, CA 90015
213/747-0355

Hours: By Appointment Only, Mon-Fri: 10-5 Sat: 10-3
Credit Cards: All Major

The discovery of Damone will be a delight for women wearing sizes 4 to 24. Their focus is on special and social occasion dresses, suits, and gowns featuring name brands such as Albert Nipon, Oleg Cassini, Karen Lawrence, and more with savings from 20 to 70% off. Service is a must at Damone, and that's what you'll get—a personal call about any sale and one-on-one wardrobe consultation. There is a one-time membership fee of $25. With the savings you'll be getting, it's worth the fee.

The Great Gatsby ★
14437 Ventura Blvd., Sherman Oaks Town Center
Sherman Oaks, CA 91403
818/789-7701

Hours: Mon-Sat: 10-6
Credit Cards: AE, MC, V

Want that fashionable European look? Then, you should stop by The Great Gatsby where you can find better women's fashions from such places as France, Belgium, and Italy. Most of their chic looks are done in 100% fine cotton. They also have unique accessories, belts, earrings, and bracelets. Even with fluctuations in the dollar, you'll save 20 to 40% off retail. Use your *Buying Retail Is Stupid!* coupon and save an additional 10% on your purchase.

Harper's Ladies Wholesale Clothing ★
8588 W. Washington Blvd.
Culver City, CA 90230
310/839-8507

Hours: Mon-Thurs, Sat: 10-6 Fri: 10-7
Credit Cards: DISC, MC, V

Because the prices are so low here (you can save 50 to 70%), we can't mention any brand names. In sizes 2 to 20, women will find dresses, suits, pants, tops, sweaters, knits, jackets, coats, and more. For super bargains, watch for Harper's special sales held at the end of each season. Women with good fashion sense have been completely outfitting themselves at Harper's since 1967. For extra savings, remember to use your *Buying Retail Is Stupid!* coupon for a 10% discount.

Ladies Apparel
840 S. Los Angeles St.
Los Angeles, CA 90014
213/627-6861

Hours: Mon-Sat: 9-5
Credit Cards: MC, V

If your eyes say "yes" but your checkbook says "no" to drop-dead gorgeous outfits from department stores, Ladies Apparel might be a good compromise. They carry the latest in high-fashion, current clothing at lower prices than most department store sales. Ladies Apparel has been around since the early 1960s, providing women with the same famous-maker suits, dresses, coats, and sportswear carried by high-end department stores. Prices usually run about 40% below retail, and there are always specials offering even greater discounts. In addition to terrific prices, the staff will help you put together ensembles that will not only look fabulous, but also stretch your wardrobe. This huge store is filled with casual to dressy garments in sizes to 24. And don't be timid about asking the energetic owner, Jules, for daily specials. Shipments arrive daily, and they also have a 30-, 60-, or 90-day layaway plan.

Lila's
31930 San Luis Rey
Cathedral City, CA 92234
619/325-7383

Hours: Mon-Sat: 9:30-5 Sun: 11-4 (Closed During the Summer)
Credit Cards: DISC, MC, V

Yes, even in Palm Springs you can find some good bargains on women's clothing. Lila's is a charming store that discounts their merchandise 15 to 20% off retail. Savings run even higher during their annual and seasonal sales. You can always find something glamorous to wear at Lila's. If you're feeling generous, you can buy a surprise for someone special from their many unusual gift items located throughout the store. Lila's also offers sensational gift wrapping. By the way, Lila's is closed during the summer.

Linda Bertozzi ★
6430 Variel Ave., Suite 104
Woodland Hills, CA 91367
818/704-5505

Hours: Mon-Fri: 10-4:30
Credit Cards: MC, V
♦ **Senior Discount:** 10% **Age:** 55

If you like the Linda Bertozzi line of clothing, head over to Woodland Hills where you'll find their factory outlet filled with overruns and canceled orders. Normally carried in high-end department stores and boutiques, items at the outlet run at least 50% below retail. The clothing—usually made up of wools, linens, silks, and rayons in missy to larger sizes—is designed to be mixed and matched. Much of the clothing is one-size-fits-all. You'll save even more when you use your *Buying Retail Is Stupid!* coupon for an extra 10% discount (not valid with senior citizen discount).

Loehmann's Clearance Center
6220 W. 3rd St.
Los Angeles, CA 90036
213/933-5675

Hours: Mon-Sat: 10-9 Sun: 11-6
Credit Cards: DISC, MC, V

Professional shoppers have been shopping at Loehmann's since the 1930s for dresses, blouses, skirts, slacks, suits, evening wear, coats, jackets, and fashion accessories. The address featured above is the clearance center for 81 Loehmann's stores across the country. Savings on new arrivals at Loehmann's Clearance Center start 25% below the lowest-ticketed price and eventually drop to 70% off. Regarding the regular Loehmann's stores, they guarantee savings of 30 to 60% below department store prices. Whenever you need something extra special to wear, Loehmann's Back Room is the first place you should visit. This is where they keep their finer designer clothing for day and evening wear. (There is no Back Room at the Clearance Center.) You'll be pleased to know that Loehmann's not only is a great place to shop, but they also appreciate their customers.

Additional Locations:
8 other stores throughout Southern California–call 310/659-0674.

Loveland Cotton Connection ★
505 State St.
Santa Barbara, CA 93101
805/568-1108

Hours: 7 Days a Week: 11-5:30*
Credit Cards: All Major
Loveland Cotton Connection has clothing for women discounted 25 to 40% below retail. Their inventory is great for Southern California weather and is also good for travelers because heavy and lightweight clothing is carried year-round. Manufactured of 100%, preshrunk, grown-in-the-U.S.A. cotton, the clothing is usually found in medium-to-high-end department stores. Sizes run small to X-large in dresses, short sets, and tank tops. Short- and long-sleeved tops, as well as skirts and pants, come in several styles. They carry fashion accessories such as scarves, costume jewelry, and straw hats perfect for packing (about $32 for hats retailing up to $200). Tie-dye clothing reminiscent of the 1960s and a small selection for men are also available. You'll save an additional 20% with your *Buying Retail Is Stupid!* coupon. *Hours listed above are winter hours, October through May. Summer hours, June through September, are 10 a.m. to 6 p.m.

Max Studio Factory Outlet
3100 New York Dr.
Pasadena, CA 91107
213/721-2200

Hours: Mon-Fri: 10-6 Sat: 10-4
Credit Cards: AE, MC, V

Any woman who wears clothing from Max Studio can save loads of money by shopping at one of three outlets in Southern California. Discounts usually run 20 to 60% below retail. The clothing—sizes 2 to 14—caters to fashion-forward women who appreciate comfortable clothing with clean lines and special attention to detail. Most of the merchandise consists of in-season wear with the Max Studio label. Any items with labels removed are overruns from clothing stores and boutiques that read like a Who's Who list of expensive retailers (they also manufacture clothing for retailers). When available, seconds are clearly marked. Located at corporate headquarters, the Pasadena outlet is the only store that sells samples. New merchandise arrives twice a month. Make certain to get on the mailing list for their annual one-day sale for preferred customers when outlets are closed to the public. All stores, with the exception of the Pasadena factory outlet, are located in outlet malls.

Additional Locations:
Cabazon–48400 Seminole Dr., #4302, 909/922-0077
City of Commerce–5675 E. Telegraph Rd., 213/721-2200
Oxnard–2220 Gonzalez Rd., 805/988-2912

Ms. Fashions ★
3877 Pacific Coast Hwy.
Torrance, CA 90505
310/373-4622

Hours: Mon-Sat: 10:30-6
Credit Cards: AE, MC, V
♦ **Senior Discount:** 10% **Age:** 60

If you're looking for variety, Ms. Fashions is the place to shop! This store offers a surprising 50 to 70% discount below retail on women's and junior clothing sizes 2 to 20. You'll find separates, sportswear, dresses, and pant suits in casual to evening styles. Most of the clothing is made from natural fibers. Their inventory is constantly changing, so you always have a huge selection. They also carry earrings, belts, hats, and unique costume jewelry. While there, get on the mailing list for their quarterly newsletter. Ms. Fashions is truly a one-stop fashion outlet for ladies. Best of all, you can use your *Buying Retail Is Stupid!* coupon to save an additional 20% when you shop here! The coupon is not valid with the senior citizen discount.

My Fair Lady ★
6000 Reseda Blvd., Unit O
Tarzana, CA 91356
818/881-1651

Hours: Mon-Sat: 10-5:30 Sun: 11-4:30
Credit Cards: AE, DISC, MC, V

My Fair Lady carries name-brand women's sweaters, knits, cottons, dresses, and designer pant suits at 40 to 70% below retail prices. Owner Jonathan Rick says, "We're not fancy, just top lines at the greatest bargains going." Their Blow-Out Room has super markdowns up to 90% off retail, and their recently added Five N' Dime room has everything priced at $10 or less. A mailer is sent out four times a year, so you'll want to get on their mailing list. Last but not least, you can save an additional 10% when you use your *Buying Retail Is Stupid!* coupon here. (Coupon not valid on items purchased during major clearance sales or from the Blow-Out or Five N' Dime rooms.)

Rotey's Boutique ★
2300 E. Walnut St.
Pasadena, CA 91107
818/793-7344

Hours: Mon-Sat: 10-6
Credit Cards: Cash or Checks Only

Some people have all the luck. The owner of Rotey's Boutique travels all over the world buying unusual clothing and accessories. You'll find local, national, and international goods discounted 35 to 80% below retail. Although one can buy outfits suitable for the office, the best stuff is for women with more worldly tastes. Rotey's Boutique has dresses, pants, and tops in wonderful fabrics and prints, and most are loose and comfortable. If you have a favorite brand not in their inventory, they'll try to get it for you at a discount. Sizes run petite to XXX-large. Make certain to get your name on their mailing list for special sales held throughout the year. Each sale features $10- and $20-racks with values up to $200. In addition, there is always something extra offered to customers during these sales. Sales in the past have included prizes (free cruises), three days of a professional make-up artist doing makeovers and offering advice, scissor sharpening, and more. Don't overlook Rotey's Barn in back of the store with clothing priced at $5, $10, and $20 (values up to $250). Your *Buying Retail Is Stupid!* coupon is redeemable for additional savings of 5% (good on nonsale items only).

Sara Designers Outlet ★
10216 Riverside Dr.
Toluca Lake, CA 91602
818/755-9070

Hours: Mon-Fri: 10:30-6:30 Sat: 10:30-5
Credit Cards: AE, DISC, MC, V
♦ **Senior Discount:** 10% **Age:** 55

Although we can't name names, Sara Designers Outlet has the same brands found in many high-end department stores at 40 to 80% below retail. They concentrate on career and after-five apparel with a European flair. The clothing is very well made with careful attention to details. The staff will help you put chic ensembles together, along with adding final touches from their selection of accessories. Sizes run from 3 to 16, and there are private dressing rooms. Recently added is a section of casual clothing for babies sizes 0 to 24. Every January and June Sara's has a sale in which items are discounted another 50%. For extra savings, use your *Buying Retail Is Stupid!* coupon, good for a 10% discount on nonsale items only.

Seymour Fashions ★
7040 Darby Ave.
Reseda, CA 91335
818/705-1911

Hours: Mon-Fri: 10-5:30 Sat: 10-4
Credit Cards: MC, V
♦ **Senior Discount:** 10% **Age:** 60

If you'd like to save money and customize your own wardrobe at the same time, then Seymour Fashions is your kind of place. Just about everything, in sizes small to XXXXL, is made to be mixed and matched. Most of the tops are appliquéd, and there is a large assortment of bottoms (shorts, pants, leggings, pocket pants, and three styles of skirts) made from the same fabric used in the appliqués. Not only can you mix and match, but also you can actually have anything you see in the store made in one of many available fabrics. The clothing here is not only versatile but also very well made. Don't be surprised to meet women who have flown in from various parts of California to update their expandable wardrobes. Put your name on the mailing list for notifications of special sales. Prices run about 20% off comparable items in boutiques, and you'll save up to 50% off their prices in the sale room. Don't forget your *Buying Retail Is Stupid!* coupon for an extra 10% discount (not valid with senior citizen discount).

Sideline Sales ★

818/762-4295

Hours: By Appointment Only
Credit Cards: MC, V

Since 1989, Sideline Sales has been going directly to homes and offices with several racks and tables of clothes at savings of 20 to 50% off retail. This "store to your door" concept offering women's contemporary sportswear is based on style, savings, and service. Most of their lines are featured in better clothing stores and sold to TV and movie productions. Not only do they offer home and office parties, but they also give an incentive to the hostess. You can use your *Buying Retail Is Stupid!* coupon to receive an additional 5% discount.

Susie's Deals ★

3837 Plaza Dr., #806
Oceanside, CA 92056

619/941-9914

Hours: Mon-Fri: 10-9 Sat: 10-7 Sun: 11-6
Credit Cards: DISC, MC, V

How's this for a bargain? Nothing in the store is more than $20, and it's true! You'll find the latest in styles for the younger set (junior sizes), with name brands such as Judy Knapp, Yes, No Excuses, and many others. They have lots of accessories which are priced individually or sold in twos or threes for more savings. If you present your *Buying Retail Is Stupid!* coupon, you'll receive an extra 10% discount.

Additional Locations:
10 other stores throughout Southern California

See Also: (refer to index)
    Blue Moon
    Dressed Up!

Sit down when trying on a new outfit, preferably in front of a mirror; clothes that look fine while you're standing do not look and fit the same when you're sitting down.

HARDWARE & SOFTWARE

Comp USA
9380 Warner Ave.
Fountain Valley, CA 92708
714/965-1169, 800/COMP-USA (266-7872)

Hours: Mon-Fri: 9-9 Sat: 10-7 Sun: 11-6
Credit Cards: AE, MC, V

Comp USA is a computer superstore, and they are user friendly! At 30 to 80% below retail, they make friends easily. These people really want to save their customers money. That's why there is no membership fee. This is a complete warehouse stocked with computers, software, printers, drives, monitors, modems, accessories, and everything else needed to allow you, and your computer, to live happily ever after. Would you like a few brand names? O.K., we'll name just a few. You'll find Toshiba, Panasonic, Packard Bell, Macintosh, Epson, NEC, Mitsubishi, Sony, and Fuji.

Additional Locations:
10 other stores throughout Southern California–call 800/266-7872.

Computer City Supercenter
465 S. Associated Rd. (Brea Plaza Shopping Center)
Brea, CA 92621
714/257-2400

Hours: Mon-Sat: 9-9 Sun: 11-6
Credit Cards: All Major

Computer City Supercenter is America's fastest growing computer retail chain. They carry a complete line of computers, printers, accessories, software, and related business products for Apple, IBM, AST, Compaq, Hewlett Packard, Packard-Bell, Microsoft, and Lotus. Their successful concept is having a distinctive competitive edge, noncommissioned sales staff, world-class customer service, and guaranteed great prices. Their stores have 5,000 in-stock items and another 15,000 available through their centralized electronic catalog, offering fast delivery right to your door. You'll find stores in Los Angeles, Orange, Riverside, and San Diego counties.

Additional Locations:
8 other stores throughout Southern California

Computer Palace ★
22401 Ventura Blvd.
Woodland Hills, CA 91364
818/224-3430

Hours: Mon-Sat: 9-6
Credit Cards: All Major

Computer Palace carries a wide range of most computers, including Macintosh- and IBM-compatible products, and will guarantee the best prices. Discounts range from 25 to 50% off retail. They are also an authorized dealer and service center for Hewlett Packard, Apple, and Epson products. Their friendly and patient salespeople will give you excellent service and can help arrange financing. Your *Buying Retail Is Stupid!* coupon gives you a $25 discount off any service fee of $50 or more.

Additional Locations:
Glendale–1029 E. Broadway, 818/241-2551
Los Angeles–444 S. Flower St., #160, 213/689-0808
West Los Angeles–11919 W. Pico Blvd., 310/478-4321

Computer Recycler ★
670 W. 17th St., Unit G-4
Costa Mesa, CA 92627
714/645-4022

Hours: Mon-Fri: 9-5
Credit Cards: All Major

These days we're recycling just about everything, so why not computers? Computer Recycler specializes in used Macintosh computers and peripherals at about 30% less than brand-new prices. All products carry a one-year warranty. If you buy a computer from them, your *Buying Retail Is Stupid!* coupon is good for an extra $25 discount.

New & Used Computer Store ★
10360 Sepulveda Blvd.
Mission Hills, CA 91345
818/837-3737

Hours: Mon-Fri: 10-6 Sat-Sun: 10-4
Credit Cards: MC, V

Whether you're a novice or a pro, everyone can benefit from the savings on computers—and everything that goes along with them—at the New & Used Computer Store. Discounts run 10 to 50% off retail on computer equipment, and up to 50% off retail on in-stock software. You'll save the most money on used equipment (all tested with a 30-day parts and labor warranty). For example, a few months ago we bought a switch box at a discount computer store for $25. The same model here, which looked brand new, was $5. Complete systems, not including printers, start at $200. If you already have an Apple, Macintosh, or IBM system and can't find parts or software, chances are you'll find what you need in this large (3,000 square feet), well-organized store. Price quotes are gladly given over the phone, something this family-owned-and-operated store does that many others don't. By the way, don't worry if you don't know anything about computers. The staff is very good about explaining things in lay terms. Just so you know, before any trade-in is purchased, full hardware and software diagnostics are run in their full-service department in back of the store. Your *Buying Retail Is Stupid!* coupon is good for a 5% discount on any of their used computer equipment.

Personal Support Computers

10431 Santa Monica Blvd.
West Los Angeles, CA 90015
310/474-1633

Hours: Mon-Sat: 10-6
Credit Cards: AE, MC, V

Personal Support Computers has the highest rating in Los Angeles for service and support. They guarantee lowest package prices and will train you on the use of your computer purchases. As the title states, "support" is their middle name. They are recognized as the largest Macintosh retailer in the United States and carry a large selection of computer accessories and software. You will also find many IBM compatibles, Hewlett Packard printers, and other brands such as Epson, NEC, and Hyundai. They have a large, Apple-authorized service department with five certified technicians and an inventory of 150,000 spare parts. Get on their mailing list so that they can inform you of their super blowouts. You can't go wrong here. They have been in business since 1980 and sell, lease, and service their products.

Not all "sale prices" are a bargain; often discounts come off of inflated retail prices.

SERVICES

Complete Computer Cure
1602 Lockness Pl.
Torrance, CA 90501
310/534-7900

Hours: Mon-Fri: 8-5
Credit Cards: DISC, MC, V
♦ **Senior Discount:** 10% **Age:** 65

If your computer should come down with a dreaded cold or flu, or even a virus, give these folks a call because they have the cure. They will pick up and deliver your computer for free; they even have loaners and offer maintenance contracts as well. So, for fast turnaround at a low cost (about 20% less than others), they will repair and do maintenance on all personal computers, terminals, printers, and drives.

Additional Locations:
6 other locations throughout Southern California–call 310/534-7900.

File receipts and warranties together, immediately after purchase, for easy access when needed.

Adray's
6609 Van Nuys Blvd.
Van Nuys, CA 91405
818/908-1500

Hours: Mon-Fri: 10-9 Sat: 10-8 Sun: 10-6
Credit Cards: All Major

You will save about 40% on almost everything at Adray's. They are the discount headquarters for major brands of TVs, VCRs, camera equipment, answering machines, small and major appliances, stereo systems, jewelry, perfumes and colognes, and more. You will find the salespeople knowledgeable but usually very busy. If you are planning a major purchase, we suggest that you do your homework about the product before going to Adray's. Shopping here is much different from shopping in a retail store, but once you see their prices, adapting won't be a problem. Adray's offers a one-year price guarantee.

Additional Locations:
Encino–15945 Ventura Blvd., 818/386-6868
Los Angeles–5575 Wilshire Blvd., 213/935-8191
Pasadena–3635 E. Colorado Blvd., 818/683-5400
Torrance–17502 Hawthorne Blvd., 310/793-2600
West Los Angeles–11201 W. Pico Blvd., 310/479-0797

Fedco
8450 La Palma
Buena Park, CA 90620
714/236-1800

Hours: Mon-Fri: 9-8 Sat-Sun: 10-6
Credit Cards: Cash, Checks, or Fedcharge

Fedco is the only member-owned, nonprofit mutual benefit corporation of its kind in California, and it must be doing something right, because it's been an unqualified success since 1949. Unlike other membership operations, Fedco charges a one-time fee of $10. At Fedco you do not need to buy in bulk to get the best deal. Fedco also accepts manufacturers' cents-off coupons. You'll find guaranteed lowest prices on TVs, camcorders, VCRs, major appliances, and tires. Fedco carries a complete selection of family clothing, jewelry, beauty aids, housewares, toys, and much more. Each location has a grocery and produce market, fresh bakery, and butcher shop. Members will also find prescription pharmacies and optical centers.

Additional Locations:
9 other stores throughout Southern California

JCPenney Outlet Store
6651 Fallbrook Ave.
Canoga Park, CA 91607
818/883-3660

Hours: Mon-Sat: 9:30-9 Sun: 10-7
Credit Cards: AE, DISC, JCPenney, MC, V

This is where JCPenney sells overstocked or discontinued items featured in their catalogs. You'll find this enormous store literally packed with first-quality merchandise. The inventory includes clothing, toys, furniture, stereos, linens, and more. In addition to the large selection, you'll love the 30 to 50% off retail on most items. Because they want to move merchandise in a hurry (new merchandise arrives daily), original prices are slashed dramatically before stock is put on the floor. Special sales are held during the year. So, if you are a JCPenney shopper, now you know where to go for terrific deals on their merchandise.

PriceCostco
5175 W. Marine Ave.
Hawthorne, CA 90260
310/643-8562

Hours: Mon-Fri: 11-8:30 Sat: 9:30-6 Sun: 10-5
Credit Cards: DISC

Though it can be dangerous, one of our favorite things to do is wander around PriceCostco. How can shopping be dangerous? With over 100,000 square feet of everything imaginable—groceries, computers, televisions, VCRs, stereo equipment, clothing, office supplies, furniture, appliances, housewares, hardware, jewelry, books, tires, toys (you name it and it's there)—the danger of spending much more than you had planned lurks in every aisle. The prices are so fantastic you may end up buying things you don't need. PriceCostco carries only quality name brands at substantially low prices. Most of their stores also have pharmacies, one-hour photo centers, optical departments, fresh meats, bakeries, tire centers, and food courts. To really save big bucks, call for information on how to become a PriceCostco member. If you happen to own a business, you'll be pleased to know PriceCostco offers delivery services to their business members. Store hours vary by location.

Additional Locations:
42 other stores throughout Southern California–call 800/774-2678.

Sam's Club

6345 Variel Ave.
Woodland Hills, CA 91367
818/710-8480

Hours: Mon-Fri: 7:30 a.m.-8:30 p.m. Sat: 7 a.m.-7:30 p.m. Sun: 10-6
Credit Cards: DISC, Sam's Credit Card

"Honey, don't buy that here. We'll get it the next time we go to Sam's Club." More and more people are taking on this money-saving attitude. After all, why would you pay $4.50 for an item weighing 12 ounces when you can get the same item at Sam's Club in 36 ounces for less than $4.50? Buying retail is stupid, you know! With Sam's Club, consumers don't have to wait for special sales to save money. They always have everyday low prices, up to 80% off retail, on a vast selection of top-quality, brand-name merchandise. With more than 100,000 square feet in each location, Sam's Club has everything needed for your home or business. They have bakery items, groceries and produce, clothing, hardware, furniture, tires, electronics, jewelry, and much more. Their inventory is consistent, but that doesn't mean you won't find some surprises on every visit. The buyers for Sam's Club are always on the hunt for great deals to pass on to their appreciative members. By the way, membership is $25 a year, and if you don't save that much the first time you shop here, you didn't buy anything!

Additional Locations:
18 other stores throughout Southern California

> Before making any purchase, be sure to ask yourself, "Do I really need this?"

FACTORY OUTLET MALLS

Camarillo Factory Stores
740 E. Ventura Blvd.
Camarillo, CA 93010
805/445-8520

Hours: 7 Days a Week: 10-8
Credit Cards: Varies with Vendor

Camarillo Factory Stores is the "hot spot" outside of Los Angeles. They feature some of the top department-store outlets as well as many top designers. For example, you'll find Barneys New York Outlet, Karen Kane, Kenar, Off 5th—Saks Fifth Avenue Outlet, Jones New York, Laundry, Osh-Kosh B'Gosh, Villeroy & Boch, and many more. Their large food court will allow you to "shop 'til you drop."

60 stores at one location

Citadel Factory Stores
5675 E. Telegraph Rd.
City of Commerce, CA 90040
213/888-1220

Hours: Mon-Sat: 10-8 Sun: 10-6
Credit Cards: AE, MC, V

This is the first factory outlet center to be opened in Los Angeles. Currently, it has 42 outlet stores, including Eddie Bauer, Old Navy, Laundry, Ann Taylor, Joan & David, Capezio, Corning Revere, Geoffrey Beene, and more. Prices are always discounted about 10 to 70% off retail. If shopping makes you hungry or thirsty, you can "wet your whistle" at Johnny Rockets, Subway Sandwich, Taipan Express, Pachanga-Mexican Grill, Sbarro (Italian food), or Steve's Ice Cream. As a point of interest, Citadel Factory Stores sits on the site of what once was a tire factory. The restored facade—a replica of an Assyrian castle—was built in 1929 and was once used as a backdrop in the movie *Ben Hur*.

42 stores at one location

Cooper Building
860 S. Los Angeles St.
Los Angeles, CA 90014
213/622-1139

Hours: Mon-Sat: 9:30-5:30 Sun: 11-5
Credit Cards: Cash or Checks Only*

This place is incredible! The Cooper Building is the original factory outlet mall. This "Tall Mall" is 11 stories high, with 6 selling floors all bulging with exciting merchandise in the heart of the wholesale garment district. You'll find quite a collection of outlet stores representing various manufacturers, famous retail stores, and discount stores. Whether you shop at the Cooper Building once a month or once a year, you always save 25 to 75% off retail prices every single day of the week. Shoppers can buy current designer and brand-name fashions for men, women, and children, leather fashions, shoes, handbags, fashion accessories, lingerie, and home fashions all under one roof. Why spend twice the amount on prestigious labels carried in expensive department stores when you can save a bundle buying the identical item at the Cooper Building? Wear comfortable shoes, so if the elevators are running slow, you can take the stairs. *Some vendors accept credit cards.

35 stores at one location

Desert Hills Factory Stores
48400 Seminole Rd.
Cabazon, CA 92230
909/849-6641

Hours: Mon-Fri, Sun: 10-8 Sat: 9-8
Credit Cards: All Major

While taking a pleasure drive to Palm Springs, make sure you stop at Desert Hills Factory Stores, where you'll save 25 to 65% on everything from designer fashions to national brand housewares. There are about 100 renowned manufacturers such as J. Crew, Anne Taylor, Cole Haan, Brooks Bros., Nike, Coach, Joan & David, Donna Karan, Esprit, Nautica, Timberland, Anne Klein, Guess?, Lenox, Oneida, Villeroy & Boch, and many more in their own outlet stores. There are two ATMs, as well as indoor and outdoor food courts for hungry shoppers.

100 stores at one location

Factory Merchants Barstow

2552 Mercantile Way

Barstow, CA 92311

619/253-7342

Hours: 7 Days a Week: 9-8

Credit Cards: Varies with Vendor

If brand-name factory outlets are your favorite sources for discount shopping, you'll find an oasis at Factory Merchants Barstow. Savings run 20 to 70% off retail. Some of the stores are Anne Klein, Polo, London Fog, OshKosh, Barbizon, Evan Picone, Levi, Coach, Brooks Bros., Banister, Oneida, and Royal Doulton. You'll find other outlets selling luggage, toys, greeting cards, paper products, and perfume. Your friends might think you're crazy for driving to Barstow to go shopping, but after they've seen your purchases and heard what you paid, they'll want to hitch a ride on your next trip. The mall is open daily except Thanksgiving and Christmas.

95 stores at one location

Lake Elsinore Outlet Center

17600 Collier Ave.

Lake Elsinore, CA 92530

909/245-4989

Hours: Mon-Sat: 10-8 Sun: 10-6

Credit Cards: MC, V

Lucky for us, we have relatives that live near Lake Elsinore Outlet Center. They probably see more of us since the mall was built because we really enjoy shopping at the large Liz Claiborne outlet. Other of the 45 outlets you'll find here are J H Collectibles, London Fog, Jones New York, Mikasa, Nine West & Co., Levi's (this outlet also carries Dockers), as well as most of the other popular outlets usually found in outlet malls. You can also get a bite to eat near the Liz Claiborne store.

45 stores at one location

Oxnard Factory Outlet

2000 Outlet Center Dr.

Oxnard, CA 93030

805/485-2244

Hours: Mon-Sat: 10-8 Sun: 11-6

Credit Cards: AE, DISC, MC, V

If it gets too hot to hit the outlet malls in the desert, point your car toward the mild climate of Oxnard. One of the newer outlet malls in Southern

California, Oxnard Factory Outlet has 36 stores featuring brands such as Carter's, Fila, GHQ, Gap, Bugle Boy, Geoffrey Beene, Nine West, Florsheim, Easy Spirit, Corning/Corelle, American Tourister, Harman Audio, and Benneton. Discounts range from 20 to 70% off retail. You'll also find places to get a quick bite to eat.

36 stores at one location

San Diego Factory Outlet Center
4498 Camino de la Plaza
San Ysidro, CA 92173
619/690-2999

Hours: Mon-Fri: 10-8 Sat: 10-7 Sun: 10-6
Credit Cards: All Major

You'll find a real variety among the 35 factory outlet stores here. Need some jeans? Stop by Levi's outlet. Sneakers—Nike outlet; shirts—Van Huesen outlet; cookware—Famous Brands outlet; dinnerware—Mikasa outlet. You'll also find outlets featuring labels such as Eddie Bauer, Bass, OshKosh, Carter's, Nine West, Dockers, Vans, Guess?, Ray Ban, Jockey, and others. For your convenience, if you don't feel like lugging a bunch of packages around, you can mail them home from the postal center. There is also a food court to satisfy hungry shoppers. Open since 1989.

35 stores at one location

San Diego North County Factory Outlet Center
1050 Los Vallecitos Blvd.
San Marcos, CA 92069
619/595-5222

Hours: Mon-Thur: 10-7 Fri-Sat: 10-8 Sun: 11-6
Credit Cards: MC, V

The next time you spend the weekend in San Diego, save a little energy so you can do some bargain shopping on the way home at San Diego North County Factory Outlet Center. Or, if you need some new clothes for the weekend, buy them on your way to San Diego. Adolfo II, Bugle Boy, Capezio, Famous Footwear, Designer Labels for Less, and L'eggs/Hanes/Bali are a few of the stores featuring clothing and shoes. You'll also find Sunglasses Outlet, Tiger Shark Golf, Discount Watches, Corning/Revere, and others. When it's time for a break, food and refreshments are available at Barron's Burgers & Brew.

25 stores at one location

SWAPMEETS & FLEA MARKETS

Alameda Swapmeet
4501 Alameda St.
Los Angeles, CA 90058
213/233-2764

Hours: Mon-Fri: 10-7 Sat-Sun: 8-7
Credit Cards: Varies with Vendor

When it's too hot to be outside, check in at the Alameda Swapmeet. This indoor swapmeet has about 200 booths selling a large variety of only new merchandise. Admission and parking are always free.

200 vendors at one location

Alpine Village Swapmeet
833 W. Torrance Blvd.
Torrance, CA 90502
Hours: Tues-Sun: 8-3
Credit Cards: Varies with Vendor

With at least 300 vendors, the Alpine Village Swapmeet has a nice selection of new and used merchandise. Vendors are both indoors and outdoors, plus you can have lunch at one of the German restaurants while you're there. Admission is 50¢, and parking is free.

300 vendors at one location

Antelope Valley Swapmeet
5550 Pearblossom Hwy. (Hwy. 138)
Palmdale, CA 93590
805/533-3433 (weekends only)

Hours: Sat-Sun: 6-3
Credit Cards: Varies with Vendor

The Antelope Valley Swapmeet, located where the Pearblossom and 138 highways meet, has been open since 1976. Selection varies from antiques and homemade foods to things found in the back of someone's garage. The kids can ride the ponies, and everyone can kick back and listen to some live entertainment. Admission is 50¢ on Saturday, and $1 on Sunday. Parking is free. The phone number Monday through Friday is 805/273-0456.

300 vendors at one location

Burbank Monthly Antique Market

1001 Riverside Dr.

Burbank, CA 90290

310/455-2886

Hours: Fourth Sunday of Each Month: 9-3
Credit Cards: Varies with Vendor

This event takes place the fourth Sunday of each month and comprises more than 125 dealers of antiques and collectibles. Thousands of items are for sale, including vintage textiles, quilts, garden furniture and accessories, china, silver, art, and more. Stop by and check it out.

125 vendors at one location

Colton Open Air Market

1902 W. Valley Blvd.

Colton, CA 92324

909/877-0790

Hours: Thur, Sat-Sun: 7:30-3
Credit Cards: Varies with Vendor

Depending on the time of year, you'll find 300 to 500 merchants at the Colton Open Air Market. You can buy everything from items for your home to clothing for your kids. On Thursdays at 10 a.m. they hold an antique auction. The entrance fee is 50¢ per adult on Thursdays and Saturdays. On Sundays entrance is free. Children under 12 and parking are always free.

300-500 vendors at one location

Escondido Swapmeet

635 W. Mission Ave.

Escondido, CA 92025

619/745-3100

Hours: Wed-Thur: 6:30-4 Sat-Sun: 6-4
Credit Cards: Varies with Vendor

In addition to people selling arts and crafts, collectibles, new and used merchandise, and everything else usually found at a swapmeet, you'll find a farmer's market at the Escondido Swapmeet. They have a great selection of eateries, too. Entrance fees are 50¢ on Wednesday and Saturday, 35¢ on Thursday, and 75¢ Sunday.

Indoor Swapmeet of Stanton

10401 Beach Blvd.

Stanton, CA 90680

714/527-1234

Hours: Mon, Wed-Fri: 10-7 Sat-Sun: 10-6 (Closed Tuesday)
Credit Cards: Varies with Vendor

You'll find more than 70 vendors selling everything from haircuts to silk flowers. Some of the brand names carried are Reebok, Panasonic, Levi, Jordache, Kenwood, Toshiba, Guess?, and Bugle Boy. As you can see by the small sampling of brand names, you are in for a shopping treat. This two-story, air-conditioned, 42,000-square-foot building was designed especially for swapmeets, and they have thought of everything. Even the aisles were made extra wide to accommodate wheelchairs.

70 vendors at one location

Oceanside Drive-In Swapmeet

3480 Mission Ave.

Oceanside, CA 92054

619/745-3100

Hours: Fri: 6-3 Sat-Sun: 6-4
Credit Cards: Varies with Vendor

We used to think that all swapmeets were held at drive-in theaters. The Oceanside Drive-In Swapmeet proves that they're still around. Wear comfortable shoes, because you have to cover more than 40 acres with more than 1,000 vendors. In addition to regular hours, they hold swapmeets on holidays that fall on a Monday (same hours as Fridays). Entrance is 50¢ on Saturday and holiday Mondays. Friday admission is 35¢, and Sunday will cost you 75¢. Parking is free.

1,000 vendors at one location

Ontario Open Air Market

7407 Riverside Dr.

Ontario, CA 91761

909/984-5131

Hours: Tues, Sat-Sun: 7:30-3
Credit Cards: Varies with Vendor

This is a swapmeet the entire family can enjoy. They have hundreds of vendors selling everything from jewelry to "garage sale" stuff, and also have pony rides for the kids! If you need a new "pet" for the backyard, check out the livestock auctions held every Tuesday. Dads, husbands, and boyfriends can no longer use an important ball game as an excuse to stay home because there's a beer and wine bar—they sell soft drinks too—with a widescreen TV. Admission on Tuesdays and Sundays is 50¢ and free for children under 12. Saturdays and parking are free.

350-500 vendors at one location

Orange County Marketplace
88 Fair Dr. (Orange County Fairgrounds)
Costa Mesa, CA 92626
714/723-6616

Hours: Sat-Sun: 7-4
Credit Cards: Varies with Vendor

This happens to be one of the best swapmeets around. What impresses us the most is the quality and variety of merchandise. Of course, you'll still find the same things found at most swapmeets, but the selection of new products is substantial. Some of the items we've purchased here include dried and silk flowers, jewelry, shoes, salon hair products, real plants, camping equipment, baskets of all shapes and sizes, handbags, backpacks, sheets, and the list goes on and on. There's a large refreshment center and quite a few food vendors scattered about. Do wear comfortable shoes because there's a lot of ground to cover. Admission is $1 for adults, and parking is free.

1,200 vendors at one location

Outdoor Antique and Collectible Market
Veterans Memorial Stadium (Conant St. & Lakewood Blvd.)
Long Beach, CA 90808
213/655-5703

Hours: Third Sunday of Each Month: 8-3
Credit Cards: Varies with Vendor

If you're looking to add a few antiques to your collection, it would probably be tough to beat the selection at the Outdoor Antique and Collectible Market, held at the Long Beach Veterans Memorial Stadium. It's held on the third Sunday of every month; in November, it's also held on the first Sunday of the month. Entrance is $4.50 a person, and children under 12 are free, as is parking.

At least 800 vendors at one location

> To keep your hands free and your valuables safe, shop with a fannypack instead of a handbag.

Pasadena City College Flea Market
1570 E. Colorado Blvd., CC214
Pasadena, CA 91106
818/585-7906

Hours: First Sunday of Each Month: 8-3
Credit Cards: Cash or Checks Only

Visit the PCC Flea Market located at Pasadena Community College and you'll save a bundle on antiques and records. The flea market is noted for great prices on high-end antiques and for garage sale merchandise with prices starting at 50¢. There are more than 75 record vendors found in the Record Swap section of the market. Admission is free.

475 vendors at one location

Rose Bowl Flea Market and Swapmeet
Rose Bowl Dr.
Pasadena, CA 91103
213/560-7469, ext. 11

Hours: Second Sunday of Each Month: 9-3
Credit Cards: Varies with Vendor

If we were asked to pick our favorite swapmeet or flea market, the one held at the Rose Bowl would definitely be among the top three. With at least 1,500 vendors selling a multitude of products, this is shopper's heaven. This outdoor marketplace isn't located inside the Rose Bowl as one might think, but totally surrounds it. Admission is $5 and free for children under 12 when accompanied by an adult. If you want to shop with antique dealers and retailers, the gates open at 6 a.m. (pretty early for a Sunday morning), and the entrance fee is $10. The box office closes at 3 p.m., and the whole thing shuts down at 4 p.m. Parking is free.

1,500 vendors at one location

San Bernardino Indoor Swapmeet
National Orange Showgrounds
San Bernardino, CA 92410
909/889-3100

Hours: Sun: 10-7
Credit Cards: Varies with Vendor

The San Bernardino Indoor Swapmeet offers new and used merchandise of every caliber. Whether you're looking for beauty supplies or an old rake, you'll probably be able to locate it here. Admission is $1, and children under 12 are free when accompanied by an adult.

40 vendors at one location

Santa Fe Springs Swapmeet
13963 Alondra Blvd.
Santa Fe Springs, CA 90670
310/921-9996

Hours: Wed-Thur, Sat-Sun: 5:30-3:30
Credit Cards: Varies with Vendor

Santa Fe Springs Swapmeet has a little bit of everything. There are hundreds of vendors selling a vast array of merchandise from antiques to clothing at discount prices. You'll have the biggest selection on weekends, when there are more vendors. Spend a little and get a lot while shopping at the Santa Fe Springs Swapmeet. There's an entrance fee of 50¢ on Wednesday, and 75¢ on Saturday and Sunday. Admission is free on Thursday. Starting the second week in April through October, the swapmeet is open Thursday and Friday evenings from 5 p.m. to 10 p.m. Night admission is 75¢.

300-650 vendors at one location

Saugus Swapmeet
22500 Soledad Canyon Rd.
Saugus, CA 91350
805/259-3886, 818/716-6010

Hours: Sun: 7-3
Credit Cards: Varies with Vendor

A friend of ours, who lives in Santa Monica, makes the drive several times a year to Saugus simply because she thinks this is one of the best swapmeets. You can buy just about anything for yourself as well as your family or home at the Saugus Swapmeet. Way back when, the grounds used to be the ranch of cowboy movie star Hoot Gibson. Admission is $1 for adults. Parking and children under 12 are free.

700 vendors at one location

Valley Indoor Swapmeet ★
6701 Variel Ave.
Woodland Hills, CA 91303
818/340-9120

Hours: Fri-Sun: 10-6
Credit Cards: Varies with Vendor

As the name implies, the Valley Indoor Swapmeet is located inside; it's air-conditioned during the summer and protected from the elements during the winter. This makes shopping a definite pleasure. Each location features hundreds of shops that display a huge array of top-quality goods such as clothes, jewelry, plants, art, antiques, and more. Vendors sell merchandise for 20 to 50% off retail. Admission is $1 per adult and is free for senior citizens and children. If you take along your *Buying Retail Is Stupid!* discount coupon, you'll get free admission at any of their locations!

Additional Locations:
Panorama City–14650 Parthenia St., 818/892-0183
Pomona–1600 E. Holt, 818/331-0123

When on a shopping trip, allow plenty of time; rushing around can lead to costly impulse buying.

ENTERTAINMENT & COMMUNICATION

All Systems Go ★

13050 San Vicente Blvd.
Los Angeles, CA 90049
310/393-2800

Hours: Mon-Sat: 10-5:30
Credit Cards: AE, MC, V
♦ **Senior Discount:** 20% **Age:** 65

All Systems Go is a full-service consumer electronics store. They carry pagers, cellular phones, phone systems, car audio, security systems, and custom home theater systems. Recently added to their inventory are DSS Satellites and residential phone systems. Personal service and attention to one's budget are always first when selling you these items. In fact, they even offer a *Buying Retail Is Stupid!* coupon that will save you an additional 20% on nonsale items only (not valid with senior citizen discount).

Discount Sales

8438 Sunland Blvd.
Sun Valley, CA 91352
818/768-6636

Hours: Mon-Thur: 10-6 Fri: 10-6 Sat: 10-5
Credit Cards: DISC, MC, V

Discount Sales has to be visited to be believed. You pay prices that are generally just 8 to 10% above cost and get the top brands in ceiling fans, stereos, TVs, VCRs, and camcorders. They buy in large quantities and sell in volume. Announcements are sent out to their customers when they have clearance sales on floor stock, so be sure to get on their mailing list. By the way, every summer they have a two-for-one sale on ceiling fans. Call the Upland store for hours.

Additional Location:
Upland–1405 E. Foothill Blvd., 909/985-3254

Harman Audio Outlet
2000 Outlet Center Dr., Suite #190
Oxnard, CA 93030
805/981-3800, 800/981-3810

Hours: Mon-Sat: 10-8 Sun: 10-6
Credit Cards: All Major

Subwoofers, surround processors and speakers, THX systems, Dolby pro-logic receivers, CD players, cassette decks—if these words mean anything to you, you'll want to stop at Harman Audio Outlet and receive 30 to 60% off retail prices. In addition, they have demo clearances and holiday and close-out specials. All products are sold with the full manufacturer's warranty and a 30-day return policy. Tap into their expert advice to help design your ideal home theater.

Olympic Electronics ★
6329 Hollywood Blvd.
Hollywood, CA 90028
213/467-4752

Hours: 7 Days a Week: 11-9
Credit Cards: DISC, MC, V
♦ **Senior Discount:** 20% **Age:** 65

Olympic Electronics is right on the corner of Hollywood and Ivar. They promise the lowest prices in the area on portable radios, cameras, and stereos for the home or car. They've got a store full of electronic wonders from all the major manufacturers, and most are priced at just 5 to 10% over cost. They are wholesale to the public, so shop here and save. Don't forget to take in your *Buying Retail Is Stupid!* coupon for a free Walkman radio with a minimum $50 purchase (not valid with senior citizen discount).

Shelley's Stereo Hi-Fi Center ★
1520 Wilshire Blvd.
Santa Monica, CA 90403
310/451-0040

Hours: Mon-Wed, Sat: 10-6 Thur-Fri: 10-8
Credit Cards: All Major
♦ **Senior Discount:** 10% **Age:** 55

Shelley's Stereo Hi-Fi Center has been in business since 1959 and can save you money on quality, brand-name stereo components, plus you get old-fashioned home service for custom wiring. Shelley's has some used equipment, accepts trade-ins, and has an excellent service department. They also guarantee the best prices on their merchandise. You can use your *Buying Retail Is Stupid!* coupon for an additional 10% discount on nonsale items only (not valid with senior citizen discount).

Additional Location:
Woodland Hills–6201 Topanga Canyon Blvd., 818/716-8500

Speaker City
115 S. Victory Blvd.
Burbank, CA 91502
818/846-9921

Hours: Mon-Sat: 10-6
Credit Cards: AE, DISC, MC, V

We have discovered a virtual candy store for speaker enthusiasts and audiophiles, at savings of at least 50%! All components needed to build speakers from scratch, and also complete kits for speaker systems, can be found here. They do "X-overs" too. One of the great things about Speaker City is you know exactly what you are buying. The price of a speaker, already built, is no longer a mystery, because lining the walls are the individual components that went into the speaker, along with the cost of each item. They carry speakers for the home and stock complete sound systems for your car (no installations). Stereo components are available by special order only. Customized speaker systems are available for both home and vehicles. Name brands include Focal, Dynaudio, Vifa, Versatronics, and Pyle. If you need any technical advice, talk to Wally Noss. He's not only an expert on sound systems, but also a professional musician.

See Also: (refer to index)
Asmara Overseas Shippers
Caston's T.V. & Appliance

PARTS, SUPPLIES & EQUIPMENT

All Electronics Corp.
14928 Oxnard St.
Van Nuys, CA 91411
818/997-1806, 800/826-5432

Hours: Mon-Fri: 9-6:30 Sat: 9-5
Credit Cards: AE, DISC, MC, V

This is a big surplus outlet for electronic parts and supplies. If you are handy with that sort of thing, and know your way around semiconductors, speakers, and transformers, you can save from 25 to 75% off retail prices on all of your purchases! Aside from regularly ordered merchandise, they also buy close-outs and end-of-line goods. As they have been in business since 1967, the folks at All Electronics Corp. know everything and have everything—from AC/DC adapters and potentiometers, to solid state relays and zener diodes—in their stores. If you enjoy shopping from home, call 818/904-0524 for their free, 60-plus-page catalog.

Additional Location:
Los Angeles–905 S. Vermont Ave., 213/380-8000

Ametron ★
1200 N. Vine St.
Hollywood, CA 90038
213/464-1144

Hours: Mon-Fri: 8:30-5:30 Sat: 8:30-5 Sun: 11-3
Credit Cards: AE, DISC, MC, V

A one-of-a-kind operation! Ametron covers nearly a city block with 60 parking places available for your convenience. Known throughout the nation as the "Supermarket of Electronics," they are relied upon by both business and industry for hard-to-get items. We won't even try listing the contents of this huge place, but rest assured, they have everything electrical that you could possibly need. Some brand names are Sony, Nakamichi, RCA, Zenith, Panasonic, NAD, Onkyo, Teac, Electro-Voice, Bogen, Sunnheiser, AKG, Neumann, and University Sound, among others. Go in; get what you want at deeply discounted prices. We almost forgot to tell you about another service they offer. Are you in search of a few props for the concert scene in the latest movie you're producing? Must you have several closed-circuit TVs added temporarily to your security system? You can rest easy. They rent just about anything to do with electronics. For rental rates and availability, the phone number is 213/466-4321. Your *Buying Retail Is Stupid!* coupon entitles you to a gift with any purchase over $75.

Filament Pro-Audio

143 E. Arrow Hwy.
San Dimas, CA 91773
909/592-2848

Hours: Mon-Fri: 9-6 Sat: 10-5
Credit Cards: AE, MC, OPT, V

You won't find any musical instruments here. What you will find are more than 200 lines of the best sound and lighting equipment for musicians and disc jockeys. Savings run about 35 to 40% off retail on items such as PA speakers, amplifiers, mixers, studio monitors, recorders, and cables. Filament Pro-Audio has been in business since 1968, and most of the merchandise in their 3,800-square-foot showroom is for rent. They keep their inventory to a minimum, but it takes only two to three days for special orders. Brand names include J.B.L., Shure, Fostex, Soundcraft, Rane, and Ampex.

> Scan newspaper ads to get an idea of costs of different items and brand names.

Balloons & Flowers By Joseph ★
13029 Victory Blvd.
North Hollywood, CA 91606
818/761-8600, 800/422-3933

Hours: Mon-Fri: 9:30-6 Sat: 9:30-5
Credit Cards: DISC, MC, V
♦ **Senior Discount:** 20% **Age:** 65

With guaranteed best prices from Balloons & Flowers By Joseph, you won't go broke preparing for your wedding, bar or bat mitzvah, or corporate event, or any other celebration. They offer a complete line of balloons and fresh flowers, as well as a full party-planning service. Use the *Buying Retail Is Stupid!* coupon for a free bride and groom balloon sculpture (value $150) when you purchase $200 worth of flowers or balloons (not valid with senior citizen discount). They also deliver balloon and floral arrangements throughout the San Fernando Valley, Los Angeles, and some parts of Ventura and Orange counties.

Boulevard West Florist ★
22829 Ventura Blvd.
Woodland Hills, CA 91365
818/225-0814

Hours: Fridays Only: 12-7
Credit Cards: AE, MC, OPT, V

Do you love fresh-cut flowers? Although Boulevard West Florist is a full-retail florist shop, once a week they offer savings of 50 to 200% off florist and supermarket prices. On Friday afternoons only, they open their "Back-Room Bargains" featuring fresh-cut flowers in bunches of 10 stems, at prices starting at $3 per bunch. The same flower that sells for $5 per stem at the supermarket runs 10 for $15 here on Fridays. The earlier you arrive, the better the selection. Make sure to take along your *Buying Retail Is Stupid!* coupon to receive a 15% discount. And don't forget, bargain prices are good only on Fridays. Note: Boulevard West also offers the same low prices at various farmers' markets and kiosks in Los Angeles County. Give them a call for other locations, days open, and hours.

Mimi's Flowers ★

818/841-6967

Hours: By Appointment Only
Credit Cards: All Major

With 14 years' experience in the floral industry, Mimi LaPorte will put the cherry on the top of your next affair with exceptional floral arrangements at discounted prices. Set up a morning, afternoon, or evening appointment with her for your wedding, banquet, or party. When the arrangements are completed, Mimi's will then make sure everything is displayed to your satisfaction. A specialty is arrangements for weddings, including bridal bouquet, table centerpieces, ceremony decorations, stands along the aisle, and much more. Prices average about 50% off retail. Mimi's services Los Angeles and Ventura counties. Use your *Buying Retail Is Stupid!* coupon and receive even greater savings of 10%.

The Orchid Man ★

1816 Laurel Canyon Blvd.
Los Angeles, CA 90046

213/848-8776

Hours: By Appointment Only
Credit Cards: Cash or Checks Only

Orchids for rent? Yes, it's true! With The Orchid Man, you can rent fresh and lovely orchids for your home or office. For as little as $12, including pickup and delivery, you can have a single-spike orchid for a month or more. When The Orchid Man picks up your "tired" orchid, he will deliver a new one and take the "used" orchid home to be cared for until it reblooms. If owning your own orchids is more your style, The Orchid Man will sell you some from his stock of 1,200 flowers in his greenhouse at a savings of 30% off retail. Use your *Buying Retail Is Stupid!* coupon for an extra 10% off your purchase.

Rhoda Kellys Floral Factory ★

Canoga Park, CA 91304

818/341-7256

Hours: By Appointment Only
Credit Cards: Cash or Checks Only

Rhoda Kellys Floral Factory provides floral arrangements for wedding services at 20 to 50% off retail. They have an entire selection of fresh flowers and offer friendly, personalized service. Flowers are arranged in the bride's choice of designs and within budget. In most cases, estimates include delivery, set-up, and waiting time. With the *Buying Retail Is Stupid!* coupon, you'll receive a free Bride and Groom Teddy Bear set with a purchase of $200 or more.

Roberto's Florist ★
11031 Balboa Blvd.
Granada Hills, CA 91344
818/368-8594, 800/942-0010

Hours: Mon-Sat: 9-7 Sun: 11-5
Credit Cards: All Major

If you're searching for flowers and arrangements at discounts of 20 to 35% below retail, look no more. Roberto's Florist is a discount florist that specializes in the procurement and distribution of arrangements for weddings and bar mitzvahs and large-volume orders. Whether your event has 1,200 people or 50, Roberto's can do it wonderfully and economically. They will even base prices on a per-person basis so that costs are carefully controlled. Roberto's invites all prospective customers to view products prior to their event to know exactly what they are getting. They also ship nationwide and have a 100% guarantee return policy. Take in your *Buying Retail Is Stupid!* coupon and you'll save an extra 10% off any purchase of wedding flowers.

Wholesale Flower Place
11533 Slater Ave., #E
Fountain Valley, CA 92708
714/434-1072

Hours: Mon-Thurs: 10-5:30 Fri: 10-6:30 Sat: 9-3:30
Credit Cards: MC, V

Whether you purchase a single-stem rose or flowers for a large wedding or special occasion, you'll get guaranteed lowest prices and service with a smile from Wholesale Flower Place. When flowers are in season, you can purchase roses, mums, lilies, carnations, tulips, exotics, and many other varieties, usually at 50 to 80% off retail. Flowers are available by the stem or in bunches. You can create your own bouquet, with or without assistance, then have the flowers beautifully arranged by the staff, free of charge. They will meet or beat any flower shop's advertised price. Spanish-speaking employees are also available. So make someone's day with a gift of flowers.

MARKETS

Bargain Circus

852 N. La Brea
Los Angeles, CA 90038
213/466-7231

Hours: 7 Days a Week: 8 a.m. to 9 p.m.
Credit Cards: AE, DISC, MC, V

A grocery store and so much more! In fact, you never know what you'll find at Bargain Circus. In addition to food products (they have the best prices in town on prepackaged foods for the Jewish holidays), Bargain Circus features clothing, electronics, beer, sundries, perfumes and colognes, champagne and wine, rugs, and an assortment of ceramics and dishes. The stock changes weekly, so it's like going to a new store every week. They buy inventory close-outs and job lots, so the prices are terrific. With this store having more than 35,000 square feet, not only do you have a large assorted selection, but also you have lots of area to cover. Watch for their newspaper ads for their latest specials.

Grand Central Public Market

317 S. Broadway
Los Angeles, CA 90013
213/624-2378

Hours: Mon-Sat: 9-6 Sun: 10-5:30
Credit Cards: Cash Only*

A visit to the historic Grand Central Public Market is a shopping and cultural experience at an international level. You'll find 45 vendors (in about 80,000 square feet) providing a multitude of foods and services. Along with nine snack bars, you'll find fresh produce, eggs, dried fruits, health foods, natural juices, nuts, bakeries, delicatessens, poultry, seafood, and hard-to-find spices and herbs. You can buy choice cuts of beef, veal, and lamb, as well as ethnic delicacies such as beef cheeks, brains, pig snouts, and lamb heads. We said this was an experience, didn't we? Don't worry if English isn't your native tongue. More than 20 languages are spoken here, including Arabic, Chinese, Japanese, Korean, Portuguese, Spanish, Tagalog, Yiddish, and of course, English. You'll need to take your own shopping bags (or buy them here), because they don't have shopping carts. Porters are available for assistance if you buy in large quantities. The Grand Central Public Market, opened in 1917, has never closed, not even during the Great Depression. Many of the vendors have been here for more than 40 years, continuing a sense of family, tradition, quality, and low prices. Wear comfortable shoes and don't forget your shopping bags. *Some vendors accept checks.

45 vendors at one location

Max Foods
1445 E. Foothill Blvd.
Upland, CA 91785
909/985-8894

Hours: 7 Days a Week: 7 a.m.-10 p.m.
Credit Cards: MC, V

You can save 10 to 15% on your groceries by shopping at Max Foods. Making volume purchases, along with low overhead (the warehouses are not fancy), enables them to pass along substantial savings to consumers. You'll find name-brand labels on food, produce, meat, general merchandise, and liquor. They provide bags for your groceries, but they'll pay you 5¢ for every grocery bag you bring from home and use. All manufacturer coupons are accepted. Food stamps are also accepted. Check hours at other stores, as they may vary.

Additional Locations:
22 other stores throughout Southern California–call 310/984-1200.

Smart & Final
10113 Venice Blvd.
West Los Angeles, CA 90034
310/559-1722

Hours: Mon-Sat: 7 a.m.-8 p.m. Sun: 8 a.m.-7 p.m.
Credit Cards: MC, V

Smart & Final is a pioneer when it comes to offering warehouse prices. You can save on groceries, frozen and deli items, beer and wine, janitorial supplies, coffee supplies, party supplies, paper products, and much more. You get warehouse prices without having to pay a membership fee. Brand names include Carnation, M & M's, Nestle, Procter & Gamble, Heinz, Best Foods, Hormel, and many more. Smart & Final caters mostly to food service businesses, schools, clubs, and offices, but you don't have to own a business` to take advantage of the low prices. In many cases, warehouse stores change brands and merchandise according to the best deals that are available. That isn't the case at Smart & Final, where you can rely on finding the same products on a regular basis.

Additional Locations:
More than 90 other stores throughout Southern California—call 800/894-0511.

Southland Farmers' Market Association

213/244-9190

Hours: Call for Hours
Credit Cards: Cash or Checks Only

Markets range in size from 15 to 70 farmers, and all products are sold directly by the producer, catcher, or collector. Shoppers often save from 20 to 30% over local markets on items including fresh fruits and vegetables, nuts, eggs, honey, fish, live plants, beefalo products, dried fruits, juices, olives, dates, and sprouts. The markets are open one day a week. Contact the Southland Farmers' Market Association for hours and information regarding the market nearest you. In addition to cash and checks, food stamps are accepted.

Additional Locations:
19 markets throughout Southern California–call 213/244-9190.

Trader Joe's

14443 Culver Dr.
Irvine, CA 92714

714/857-8108

Hours: 7 Days a Week: 9-9
Credit Cards: DISC, MC, V

If you've never visited a Trader Joe's store you're in for a treat. Trader Joe's carries a crazy combination of private and national brands of food, wine, and beer at exceptionally low prices. The products at Trader Joe's contain no artificial colors or flavors and no additives. Many products are from Europe, South America, and the Far East—so it's always an adventure shopping here. They have everyday low prices on their merchandise of unique grocery products, dried fruit, nuts, cheeses, entrees and fresh salads, dairy products, chocolates, snacks, juices, frozen foods, and domestic and imported wines and beers. Trader Joe's also has their Fearless Flyer, which is a 20-page combination of *Mad* magazine and *Consumer Reports*, with stories on more than 100 products. It's published three times a year and is available in all 44 stores. We're sure once you visit a Trader Joe's you'll be hooked!

Additional Locations:
43 other stores throughout Southern California—call 800/SHOP TJ'S (800/746-7857).

> To avoid overbuying,
> shop for groceries after you
> have eaten—that is,
> on a full stomach.

NUTS & CANDY

The Candy Factory ★
12530 Riverside Dr.
North Hollywood, CA 91607
818/766-8220

Hours: Tues-Fri: 9-5 Sat: 10-4 Sun: Private Parties Only
Credit Cards: MC, V
♦ **Senior Discount:** 10% **Age:** 65

The Candy Factory has one of the most complete inventories of candy-making supplies and molds anywhere. Candy is sold by one-pound packages or in bulk in 25- to 50-pound cases. They also have candy-making classes and will do custom candy. You'll even find "x-rated" molds in a discreet location of the store. Name brands include Merckens, Nestle, and Guittard. The Candy Factory is also a factory outlet for Sheftel's Original Products. Savings run 40% off retail on goodies such as chocolate-covered potato chips. Mark your calendar for special sales they hold in July. The Candy Factory can also create a fun and unforgettable birthday for your little ones (15 children minimum). Everything—birthday cake, punch, party favors, games—is included, plus the kids get to actually make their own chocolate candy. The parties are held at their factory, so you won't end up with chocolate everywhere. You'll receive an extra 10% discount with your *Buying Retail Is Stupid!* coupon (not valid with senior citizen discount).

Christopher's Nut Co.
14332 Calvert St.
Van Nuys, CA 91401
818/787-6303

Hours: Mon-Fri: 7-4
Credit Cards: Cash or Checks Only

Having a party? Even if you just need something to munch on, stop by Christopher's Nut Co. where you can purchase all kinds of nuts, dried fruit, and sugarless and regular candy, all at 35 to 55% below retail. Savings are even higher if you buy in bulk. One pound of macadamia nuts costs $6.40 here, while you might pay $12 to $14 elsewhere. They are the largest distributor for major-brand nuts in Los Angeles. Some brands you might recognize are Blue Diamond, Mauna Loa, and Dole. They deal with only top-of-the-line products. They also carry spices and are open on Saturdays the last three months of the year.

Clarice's Cake Decorating and Candy Making Supplies ★
22936 Lyons Ave.
Newhall, CA 91321
805/259-0352

Hours: Tues-Fri: 9:30-5:30 Sat: 9:30-4:30
Credit Cards: Cash or Checks Only
♦ **Senior Discount:** 15% **Age:** 60

The perfect wedding cake can be yours, for only $2 per person, from Clarice's cake Decorating and Candy Making Supplies. A minimum of 15 people is all it takes to have them prepare a wedding cake with butter or whipped cream frosting and a choice of 30 fillings. Clarice's can prepare cakes for more than 900 people. For do-it-yourselfers, they also sell supplies and offer classes for making your own wedding cake. Ask about their free on-the-spot instructions on baking and candy making. Friendly service is number one here. Don't forget your *Buying Retail Is Stupid!* coupon to save an extra 15% off (not valid on classes, bulk items, or senior citizen discount).

Nuts to You ★
901 S. San Pedro St.
Los Angeles, CA 90015
213/627-8855

Hours: Mon-Sat: 8-5
Credit Cards: MC, V

If you go nuts over nuts as we do, then you can really save money when you buy your nuts from Nuts to You. When we sit down to watch a football game or other sporting event, the cashews and pecans just seem to disappear. You'll save 20 to 50% off the retail price, but you have to buy five pounds at a time. The good news is you can buy an assortment to get to the five-pound minimum. They also have a large selection of dried fruit. Nuts to You has been in business since 1907. Nut lovers will be happy to know that there's an additional 10% discount with the *Buying Retail Is Stupid!* coupon.

Ye Olde Fashioned Candy Shoppe ★
690 W. Willow St.
Long Beach, CA 90806
310/427-6253

Hours: Mon-Sat: 9-6 Sun: 11-5
Credit Cards: AE, DISC, MC, V
♦ **Senior Discount:** 10% **Age:** 62

Ye Olde Fashioned Candy Shoppe carries all kinds of candy and gift items at savings of 20 to 50%. They take pride in saying that their candies are the "best in the U.S.A." They have sugar-free and salt-free candies, also. Name brands include Allen Wertz, Jelly Bellys, Chocolate Roses, and others. Chocolate prices start at $3.95 a pound. Candy starts at $1.95 a pound and is sold by the piece or in unlimited pounds. Ye Olde Fashioned Candy Shoppe also offers gift baskets and wedding favors. You can satisfy your sweet tooth and get a "sweet" deal at the same time when you use your *Buying Retail Is Stupid!* coupon for an additional 10% discount (not valid with senior citizen discount).

SPECIALTY & MISCELLANEOUS FOODS

Monterrey Food Products ★
3939 Cesar Chavez Ave.
Los Angeles, CA 90063
213/263-2143

Hours: Mon-Fri: 8-5
Credit Cards: Cash or Checks Only

This large warehouse of wholesale groceries and restaurant supplies specializes in Mexican foods. Even though it's a giant warehouse, 8,000 square feet, they pride themselves in personal attention to each customer. There are over 40 varieties of spices available by the pound, dry chiles, tamale steamers, Mexican grinding stones, and custom blends of spices for that special dish. They will even mail the merchandise to you. This place is a must for the Mexican gourmet! Get on their mailing list so you'll receive information about their big sale held toward the end of the year. Your *Buying Retail Is Stupid!* coupon can be redeemed for an extra 5% discount.

Nature Mart
2080 Hillhurst Ave.
Los Angeles, CA 90027
213/660-0052

Hours: 9 a.m.-10 p.m. Seven Days a Week
Credit Cards: MC, V
♦ **Senior Discount:** 10% **Age:** 65

Shop for all your vitamins, produce, grains, nuts, and cosmetics at discounted prices, and then take a break at their health food restaurant. Before or after shopping, fresh carrot juice and a good veggie burger always make one feel wholesome. That's why we're happy to tell you about Nature Mart. This is actually a three-in-one store. One part of the store has a terrific selection of vitamins, medicinal herb teas, personal care products, and many other natural goods, plus organic produce, frozen, dairy, and grocery departments. The area of Nature Mart with bulk bins offers bulk pricing on items such as wheat bran, hummus mix, granola, psyllium seed husks, yeast, oats, rice herbs, trail mixes, and coffee. Last but not least, their restaurant features garden burgers and made-to-order vegetable and fruit juices.

PAF-MART
830 E. 6th St.
Los Angeles, CA 90021
213/623-3433

Hours: Mon-Fri: 5-Noon Sat: 6-1
Credit Cards: Cash Only

Now you can buy direct from one of the largest fish distributors in Southern California. PAF-MART will sell you any type of frozen or fresh fish at 10 to 25% less than supermarkets. Varieties in stock include shark, mahi mahi, orange roughy, salmon, catfish, tuna, swordfish, all sizes of shrimp, whitefish, lobsters, clams, oysters, and more. If you have a special recipe calling for some type of unusual seafood they don't usually carry, they'll do their best to locate it for you. When buying fish, you generally must buy it whole, but don't worry, a filleting service is available at an extra cost of 75¢ per fish. Shopping at PAF-MART is an easy way to catch fish! You'll find plenty of free parking around the corner on Gladys Street.

Surfas, Inc. ★
8825 National
Culver City, CA 90232
310/559-4770

Hours: Mon-Sat: 9-5
Credit Cards: AE, MC, V

Don't expect carpeting and grand decor at Surfas, just fantastic wholesale prices on restaurant equipment and gourmet foods. Featured are more than 4,000 items such as china, glassware, cutlery, tableware, kitchen utensils, and cookware in their restaurant equipment department. Under the same roof you'll find gourmet delights from Van Rex—fresh goose liver pate, vegetable pate, snails and shells, smoked salmon, prosciutto, hams, bacons, teas, garden herbs, vinegars, and condiments from all over the world. Savings range 30 to 40% off retail, and you can save an additional 5% on food items with the *Buying Retail Is Stupid!* coupon.

WINE & SPIRITS

Los Angeles Wine Co.
4935 McConnell Ave., Unit #8
Los Angeles, CA 90066-6756
310/306-WINE (306-9463)

Hours: Mon-Sat: 10-6 Sun: 12-5
Credit Cards: MC, V

Los Angeles Wine Co. has cinder block walls and cement floors, but what they lack in ambiance is more than made up for in low prices. Not only will you find an incredible selection, but also you'll find it at 35 to 50% off retail prices! All wine is personally tasted prior to making it into their inventory. The staff is very knowledgeable, so don't hesitate to ask questions. Oenologists will appreciate brand names that include Jordan, Silver Oak, Beringer, Fetzer, Mondavi, Grgich Hills, Jadot, and Kendall-Jackson, and many more. They also produce a monthly newsletter announcing new items in their inventory and special purchase. Whether you are looking for a private-reserve cabernet sauvignon or a vintage port, you'll always find it at the best price at the Los Angeles Wine Co.

Additional Location:
Palm Desert–72-608 El Paseo (at Hwy. 111), #2, 619/346-1763

Martin's Guide To Wine Bargains ★
P.O. Box 1543
Culver City, CA 90232
310/474-7773, 800/986-WINE (986-9463)

Credit Cards: Checks or Money Orders Only

Bargain-hunting wine lovers can now learn where the best deals are through *Martin's Guide To Wine Bargains* newsletter. Martin Weiner, director of the Los Angeles School of Wines for 27 years, personally tastes all wines before writing about them in his twice-a-month newsletter which costs $58 yearly. It features exceptional bargains on close-outs, such as $40 wines on sale for under $15. Receive a 10% discount on your one-year membership with the *Buying Retail Is Stupid!* coupon.

> Subscriptions to newspapers or periodicals, whether published daily, weekly, or monthly, are usually much less expensive than buying them individually.

Topline Wine & Spirit Co.
4718 San Fernando Rd.
Glendale, CA 91204
818/500-9670, 213/665-8484
Hours: Mon-Sat: 10-6 Sun: 12-5
Credit Cards: DISC, MC, V

Do you enjoy a glass of wine or two with your evening meal? Topline Wine & Spirit Co. carries all your favorite brand names priced at 30% below supermarket prices. For example, Korbel Natural champagne, made in California, is $4 less here than at a discount supermarket chain. Other champagnes at low, low prices include Moet White Star, Dom Perignon, and Perrier-Jouet. Topline also carries a wonderful selection from California wineries such as Kendall-Jackson, Caymus, Opus I, Grgich Hills, Jordan, Beringer, Mondavi, Schramsberg, and many others. They also carry French and Italian wines, as well as a large variety of quality spirits at discount prices.

Twenty Twenty Wine/Bel-Air Wine
2020 Cotner Ave.
Los Angeles, CA 90025
310/447-2020
Hours: Mon-Sat: 10:30-6:30
Credit Cards: AE, MC, V

What's a discount wine and wine accessories company doing with a name like Twenty Twenty/Bel-Air Wine? Their address and their telephone are both 2020, naturally. It's also natural that you will find brand-name wines, wine lockers, and accessories at discount prices. Twenty Twenty carries such brands as Mumms, Dom Perignon, Mouton, Roederer, Cheval Blanc, and Heitz. So, at your next party, when you announce, "Cristal for all!," it won't break your pocketbook. Make sure to get on the mailing list for their "wine garage sales." The wines for these sales are gathered from private collections and restaurants. Serious wine collectors can be seen walking around at these sales with their noses buried in a reference book. If you don't have your own book listing fine wines, you can borrow one from Twenty Twenty. The West Los Angeles store also carries fresh caviar.

Additional Location:
West Los Angeles–10421 Santa Monica Blvd., 310/474-9518

Wine and Liquor Depot ★
16938 Saticoy St.
Van Nuys, CA 91406
818/996-1414

Hours: Mon-Sat: 10-6 Sun: 12-5
Credit Cards: DISC, MC, V

If you want a choice selection of imported and domestic wine, beer, or liquor at discount prices (8 to 15% above cost), you'll find it at Wine and Liquor Depot. With experience dating back to 1956, these people know exactly what it takes to make customers very happy. There are no off-name labels here, just the most popular in major brand names such as Mondavi, Budweiser, Beefeaters, Moet, and hundreds of others. There is one exception, and that's on single-malt scotch. By stocking more than 200 single-malt scotches—they have the best selection in Southern California—there are bound to be names you haven't heard of. The largest selection in the store belongs to wine. You can choose from inexpensive dinner wines to high-end wines for collectors. Make sure to ask about future wine tastings and classes. In addition, Wine and Liquor Depot offers simple to elaborate gift baskets at competitive retail prices. Your *Buying Retail Is Stupid!* coupon is good for an extra 5% discount.

Wine Club
2110 E. McFadden
Santa Ana, CA 92705
800/966-5432, 714/835-6485

Hours: Mon-Sat: 9-7 Sun: 11-6
Credit Cards: MC, V

Wine Club has the selection of a fine wine boutique with warehouse prices. They sell all your favorite wines at 12% above cost. You'll find wine from companies such as Grgich Hills, Caymus, Chateau Mouton Rothschild, Sterling, Robert Mondavi, Jordan, Dom Perignon, and Mumms. Get on their mailing list to receive a monthly newsletter filled with information and special purchases. You can shop at the store or have orders shipped to your home.

Wine Exchange
2368 N. Orange Mall
Orange, CA 92665
714/974-1454, 800/76-WINEY (769-4639)

Hours: Mon-Fri: 9-8 Sat: 9-7 Sun: 10-6
Credit Cards: DISC, MC, V

It's Saturday night and you're having a party. You want to impress your guests with some very special wine. Well, let the staff at Wine Exchange help you make a choice from their stock of more than 1,500 premium wines. Savings range from 20 to 35% off retail on wines from California, Oregon, France, Germany, Italy, Australia, and many other places. Remember to ask about receiving their free newsletter.

SERVICES

Superior Value Enterprises
2118 Wilshire Blvd., #552
Santa Monica, CA 90403
310/280-3436

Hours: Mon-Fri: 9-6
Credit Cards: Cash or Checks Only

You can purchase brand-name cereals including Kellogg's, Post, Nabisco, General Mills, and Quaker Oats, plus coffee such as Maxwell House, MJB, Hills Bros., and Folgers (regular and decaffeinated), for only $1 each. Here's how the offer works: prepay $30 and you'll receive a booklet with 30 coffee certificates or 30 cereal certificates (indicate when sending payment which offer you want). You'll be able to redeem your cereal and coffee certificates approximately once a week. The merchandise then will be mailed to your home or office at no additional charge. This is a fabulous way of getting cereal and coffee at next to nothing.

Yoganics ★
213/733-1888

Hours: Mon-Sat: 10-4
Credit Cards: MC, V

Save time and gasoline by ordering organic produce and groceries from Yoganics, a home-delivery service. Prices are comparable to, or less than, those at health food stores, but without your having to drive to a store, the savings add up. Items available are organic fruits, vegetables, flours, grains, pastas, oils, honey, dried fruits, nuts, and more. Once a week the items you order will be delivered to your home (you do not have to place an order each week). Prices start at $25 for a box of organic food. There is a one-time $25 registration fee which also includes a monthly newsletter full of useful information and great recipes. Your *Buying Retail Is Stupid!* coupon will save you $10 on your registration fee.

HOME FURNISHINGS

CHINA, COOKWARE, CRYSTAL & SILVER

AAA Eternal Stainless Steel Corp. ★
430 San Bernardino Rd.
Covina, CA 91723
818/331-7204

Hours: Mon-Fri: 9-5
Credit Cards: AE, MC, V

They carry a wide variety of household and kitchenware stainless-steel products, including such items as waterless cookware and china. There are 100 to 200 different items from which to choose. Depending on the item, you can expect to save 20% below retail. Regal Products are among the many name brands represented in their inventory. Special close-out items are offered at prices below the standard discounts. For any large-scale buying, you can arrange to have salespeople come to you. Under their lifetime guarantee policy, they will replace any defective item for the rest of your life. Make sure to use your *Buying Retail Is Stupid!* coupon and save an additional 10% on your next purchase.

Almost & Perfect English China ★
14519 Ventura Blvd.
Sherman Oaks, CA 91403
818/905-6650, 800/854-5746

Hours: Mon-Fri: 10-5:30 Sat: 10-5
Credit Cards: AE, DISC, MC, V

Don't let the name fool you. The Lalique, Waterford, and Baccarat crystal is first quality, and you save 15 to 20% off retail prices. You can save up to 80% on the English bone china because the firsts and seconds are mixed together. Frankly, the seconds are of excellent quality, and most have unnoticeable flaws. During their January and July sales, crystal is discounted an additional 5%, and some china an additional 15%! Stock is on open shelves, so you can pick what you want. You don't have to pay for entire place settings, thus saving even more money by purchasing only the items you need. You will find Royal Doulton, Wedgwood, Toby Mugs, Aynsley-Rosenthal, and lots more. They will special-order any out-of-stock item. Don't forget to use your *Buying Retail Is Stupid!* coupon for an extra 5% discount.

Chalmers
904 S. Robertson Blvd.
Los Angeles, CA 90035
310/289-7777, 800/959-3989

Hours: Mon-Fri: 9:30-6:30 Sat: 10-5:30 Sun: 12-4
Credit Cards: All Major

Chalmers's policy is to offer guaranteed best prices on fine china, silver, and crystal such as Villeroy & Boch, Lalique, Baccarat, Lenox, Mikasa, Royal Doulton, and more. They gift-wrap free and offer bridal registry services. Pick out the perfect gift with savings of 20 to 50% off retail.

The Dish Factory
310 S. Los Angeles St.
Los Angeles, CA 90013
213/687-9500

Hours: Mon-Fri: 8:30-5 Sat: 9-4
Credit Cards: DISC, MC, V (No Personal Checks)

If you have kids, you should probably have dishes made for restaurants. To the unassuming eye, they look the same as "normal" dishes, but in fact they're much more durable and more resistant to chipping (an absolute necessity for restaurants). You'll find stacks and stacks of dishes here in lots of bright, solid colors and familiar patterns. Most of the inventory consists of discontinued patterns, seconds, and overruns from large manufacturers. Unfortunately, we can't name names, but we can tell you that much of what you see can be found in many restaurants around town. In addition to restaurant china, they carry glasses, plastic dishes, pots and pans, and flatware. Also available are commercial refrigerators and ranges. Personal checks are not accepted, but business checks can be used with a $30 minimum purchase.

Additional Locations:
Colton–333 E. Valley Blvd., 714/370-4040
Reseda–18336 Sherman Way, 818/343-8555

Dishes a la carte ★
5650 W. Third St.
Los Angeles, CA 90036
213/938-6223

Hours: 7 Days a Week: 11-7
Credit Cards: All Major

With the low prices on dishware from Dishes a la carte, you can have a different place setting for every day of the week. They sell restaurant-quality, American-made overruns and seconds (only slight blemishes, no cracks) in a variety of colors and white. They have coffee mugs and plates for 75¢, Libby cobalt glassware at $2, ovenproof serving platters for $3, and much more. A large selection of gift items is also available, including hand-painted pasta bowls, vases, canister sets, cookie jars, and more. Take in your *Buying Retail Is Stupid!* coupon for an extra 10% off your purchase.

Additional Location: Glendale–113 W. Los Feliz Rd., 818/240-2329

Doin' Dishes ★
5016 E. 2nd St.
Long Beach, CA 90803
310/439-3474

Hours: Mon-Thur: 10-9 Fri-Sat: 10-9:30 Sun: 11-6
Credit Cards: MC, V

Since August 1993, Doin' Dishes has been selling quality kitchen and dinnerware products at or below wholesale prices. In order to do this, they purchase products in bulk directly from the manufacturer. There are thousands of dishes to choose from—solids to patterns, baking dishes to decorative pieces. With their mix-and-match colors and designs, you can buy one piece or 50. They also have a selection of table linens and glassware at 40 to 70% off retail. Look for their sale table where items are marked down an additional 30 to 50%, and a bargain table where dishes are $1 each. Four sidewalk sales a year offer even greater savings. Brand names you'll find are Los Angeles Pottery, Coors China, Guzzini, Fiestaware, Tag, Nancy Calhoun, and more. The *Buying Retail Is Stupid!* coupon offers an additional 10% off nonsale items only.

Additional Location:
Santa Monica–925 Montana Ave., 310/319-3474

Luna Garcia ★
201 San Juan Ave. (@ Main)
Venice, CA 90291
310/396-8026

Hours: Mon-Fri: 9-5 Sat: 9-2
Credit Cards: Cash or Checks Only

You'll find handmade pottery by Luna Garcia, in a satin-matte glaze, at 25 to 75% less than what pricey gourmet and specialty stores around the U.S. and Europe charge. For the most part, the merchandise consists of seconds and overruns from the on-premises studio. This oversized dinnerware is available in 12 colors, and there's also a selection with decorative designs. You'll also find platters, large bowls, mugs, and other various serving pieces. Prices range from $12.50 to $300. Get on the mailing list for the big sale in November. Save an extra 10% by presenting your *Buying Retail Is Stupid!* coupon.

Melamed & Co. ★
22400 Hawthorne Blvd.
Torrance, CA 90505
310/542-4438

Hours: Mon-Fri: 10-9 Sat: 10-7 Sun: 11-6
Credit Cards: All Major

Now you no longer have to wait for department store sales to get discounts on china, crystal, silver, and collectibles. Melamed & Co. has name-brand merchandise discounted 15 to 60% off retail. Lenox, Wedgwood, Haviland, Wallace, Towle, Reed & Barton, Baccarat, Lalique, and Waterford are just a few of the many brands found here. Make sure to get on their mailing list because they have a special sale every year for preferred customers. Your *Buying Retail Is Stupid!* coupon is good for an extra 15% discount on any nonsale items.

Mikasa Factory Outlet
20642 S. Fordyce Ave.
Carson, CA 90749
800/2-MIKASA (264-5272)

Hours: Mon-Thur, Sat: 9-5 Fri: 9-7 Sun: 10-5
Credit Cards: AE, DISC, MC, V

The Mikasa Factory Outlet isn't just for discontinued patterns. They have over 25,000 square feet of floor space, and more than 200 patterns in stock. You can buy new and discontinued patterns at 30 to 70% below retail prices. They carry china, crystal, flatware, stemware, gifts, candles, and table linens in a variety of brands; Mikasa, Studio Nova, Home Beautiful, and Christopher Stuart are just a few found at this store. They are close to the 710, 91, and 405 freeways. You can special-order, and they will ship your purchase anywhere in the continental U.S. for a nominal fee. Look for the blow-out sales held in June and November at their Carson warehouse.

Additional Locations:
8 other stores throughout Southern California–call 800/2-MIKASA (800/264-5272).

Old World Crystal Company
3825 Thousand Oaks Blvd. (North Ranch Mall)
Westlake Village, CA 91362
805/496-6411

Hours: Mon-Fri: 10-6 Sat: 10-5
Credit Cards: DISC, MC, V

Looking for a nice wedding or anniversary gift? You definitely won't be paying department-store prices for crystal at Old World Crystal Company. Importers of crystal direct from some of the largest and best manufacturers in Europe, Old World will save you 40 to 50% off retail prices. When we were comparison-shopping, a multi-colored crystal vase was $30 less than the sale price at a well-known department store. You'll find a very nice selection of vases, bowls, stemware, and many other items made of crystal. Always ask which lines are offered at discount prices. It's important you ask because they also carry name-brand crystal, china, and various other goods—including unusual Christmas ornaments made from antique molds—at full retail. Gift wrapping is free, and shipping is available. Call ahead for Sunday hours.

Pottery Ranch, Inc.
248 W. Huntington Dr.
Monrovia, CA 91016
818/358-1215

Hours: Mon-Sat: 9-6 Sun: 10-6
Credit Cards: MC, V

You'll find everything you need for your table at the Pottery Ranch in Monrovia. Dinnerware, gardenware, glassware, baskets, silk and dried flowers, and ceramic giftware are all sold here at discounts averaging 20% or more. They have a bridal registry, and specials are run all year. Brand names carried include Mikasa, Noritake, Royal Doulton, Wedgwood, Fiesta, Houtake, and Sango. They're nice people with good buys.

See Also: (refer to index)
      Surfas, Inc.

DECORATOR ITEMS

Collections '85 Inc. ★
12701 Van Nuys Blvd.
Pacoima, CA 91331
818/834-1538

Hours: Last Saturday of Each Month: 9-3
Credit Cards: AE, MC, V

Buy direct from the manufacturer and save 25 to 50%. Collections '85 Inc. manufactures middle- to high-end decorative accessories, lamps, and accent furniture for the home or office. Though they normally sell only to the wholesale customer, Collections '85 Inc.'s showroom is open to the general public the last Saturday of every month. Their accessories have been used in the movie industry and can be found in hotel chains worldwide, including the

Presidential Suite of the San Francisco Hilton. They are also sold in better furniture stores across the U.S., Middle East, South America, and Japan. All products are made in the U.S. and hand-finished. Purchases can be shipped nationwide, and all items are sold "as is" with a no-return policy. Take in your *Buying Retail Is Stupid!* coupon and you'll save an extra 5% off your purchase of $250 or more.

Crafters Guild
215 N. Moorpark Rd., Suite I
Thousand Oaks, CA 91361
805/373-1821

Hours: Mon-Sat: 10-7 Sun: 12-5
Credit Cards: DISC, MC, V

If you love handmade crafts but don't have the time to make them, stop by Crafters Guild where, depending on the time of year, there are anywhere from 100 to 300 crafter booths rented by local artisans. You'll save 30 to 60% off retail prices when you buy direct from Crafters Guild, and the variety is endless. You'll love the choices of handmade wreaths priced lower than what the materials alone would cost. Or, how about imagining you live on a farm by purchasing a barnyard wood animal for your front lawn? Other handmade items you'll find are wood toys, rag dolls, dried flower arrangements, handpainted children's and women's clothes, quilts, jewelry, gift baskets, hair accessories, and more. Some booths also offer antiques and collectibles.

Additional Location:
Torrance–2645 Pacific Coast Hwy., 310/539-5900

How & Wen? The 2nds Shop ★
1975 S. Sepulveda Blvd.
Los Angeles, CA 90025
310/477-7229

Hours: Mon-Sat: 10-5 Sun: 12-4
Credit Cards: DISC, MC, V

You'll find outstanding buys at How & Wen? The 2nds Shop. There is always a vast array of glazed ceramics for your home and kitchen. Most merchandise is priced at 50 to 70% below retail, with even bigger savings during their parking-lot sales. There's a potpourri of decorator merchandise. Perfect for gift giving, these various items are made of brass, silver, glass, wood, crystal, and more. Some items are duplicates that were on display at the LA Mart. Make sure you get on their mailing list, and for even greater savings, make use of your 15% *Buying Retail Is Stupid!* coupon.

Island Products Distributing

3311 W. MacArthur Blvd.
Santa Ana, CA 92704
714/540-6597

Hours: Mon-Fri: 9-5
Credit Cards: AE, MC, V

Get ready for a real treat. Eli Coloma, owner of Island Products, has handmade goods made of willow and rattan from the Philippines and China, plus lots of rustic baskets too. You can shop in his 13,000-square-foot warehouse in Santa Ana, which is open to the public, but the best buys to be had are found at the Orange County Marketplace on weekends. Eli says when you get there to ask anyone who works there, "Where's the crazy Filipino?" Eli offers an early-bird special at the swapmeet. From 7 to 9:30 a.m., you get an additional 15% off his regular 35-to-50%-below-retail prices. From 10 to 11 a.m., you get an additional 10% discount. However, there's one hitch! If you don't remember to ask for the discount before you pay for the merchandise, it's sorry, Charlie! As a bonus, no matter what time of day it is at the swapmeet, if you are pregnant and showing, Eli will give you an additional 15% discount, but you have to bring it up before money changes hands. No one said this would be easy. Island Products also extends a 15% discount to those of you in the police, fire department, or military.

Additional Location:
Costa Mesa–88 Fair Dr. (Orange County Fairgrounds), 714/723-6616

Italian Pottery Outlet

19 Helena
Santa Barbara, CA 93101
805/564-7655

Hours: 7 Days a Week: 10-5
Credit Cards: DISC, MC, V

It's worth a drive to Santa Barbara—not only to enjoy the ocean view and smell the clean, fresh air, but also to stop at Italian Pottery Outlet, the factory outlet for Parracca and other Italian handmade ceramics. The dinnerware and decorative pieces reflect the brilliant colors of sunny Sicily, and each comes with a certificate of origin. Savings range from 30 to 50% off retail. You have your pick of either first-quality goods or seconds. If you're not familiar with the Parracca line, call for a complimentary color flyer. You'll be hooked once you see the designs.

The J.R. Collection ★
612 Colorado Ave., #1
Santa Monica, CA 90401
310/450-6833

Hours: Mon-Sat: 10-6
Credit Cards: MC, V

Buy direct from the manufacturer and save 20 to 70% off retail prices of glass and iron home accessories from The J.R. Collection. Featured in the store are overruns and prototypes produced for finer department stores and catalogs. There are more than 40 styles in 15 colors to choose from. Don't forget your *Buying Retail Is Stupid!* coupon and save an extra 10% off your purchase of $30 or more.

Pier 1 Imports Clearance Store ★
17506 E. Colima Rd.
Rowland Heights, CA 91748
818/810-0774

Hours: Mon-Fri: 10-9 Sat: 10-8 Sun: 11-7
Credit Cards: AE, DISC, MC, V

Fans of Pier 1 will definitely want to know about this place. The clearance store will save you 50 to 90% off original Pier 1 retail prices. For those unfamiliar with Pier 1, they sell furniture, housewares, decorative home items, clothing, and accessories. Everything is first quality. Best of all, you can save an additional 10% with your *Buying Retail Is Stupid!* coupon.

Third Market, Inc. ★
401 N. Tustin
Orange, CA 92667
714/289-0350

Hours: Mon-Fri: 10-6 Sat: 10-5 Sun: 12-5
Credit Cards: DISC, MC, V

Third Market, Inc. guarantees the lowest prices on gift items, collectibles, and close-outs. They are a full-service store that offers free gift wrapping, shipping anywhere in the U.S., special orders, and 15 to 90% off many items. Some of the name brands you will find at Third Market are Lladro, Hummel, Swarovski, Cherished Teddies, and Lenox. On top of their already low prices, yearly sales such as the Spring Sale, Christmas in July Sale, and Pre-Christmas Sale will no doubt find you a great deal. Be sure to ask about their Birthday Club savings, and remember to take along your *Buying Retail Is Stupid!* coupon to save an additional 10% off any minimum $50 purchase (excluding Armani and Muffy Vander Bear).

Tuesday Morning

505 S. Villa Real Dr. (Vista Nohl Plaza)
Anaheim Hills, CA 92807
714/974-9580

Hours: Mon-Sat: 10-6 Sun: 12-6
Credit Cards: DISC, MC, V

Tuesday Morning is one of the best places around to get high-end decorator items, household accessories, linens, and more at 50 to 80% off retail. The chain deals with manufacturer close-outs, and you never know what you'll find. In the last few years, we've found terrific deals on crystal, luggage, vases, and all kinds of picture frames. Four times a year, the store closes for about a month. When they reopen, the stores have been entirely rearranged with new merchandise and a new theme. Turnover of inventory is fast, and new merchandise arrives several times a week. Sometimes they'll get a large amount of one item and just a few pieces of another. If you see something you like, buy it, because it probably won't be there the next time you go in. Every store has a "Casualty Corner" with goods that either have lost a mate or are one-of-a-kind or seconds. Make sure to get on their mailing list for special sale hours. They offer a 90-day refund policy with a sales receipt.

Additional Locations:
More than 21 stores throughout Southern California—call 214/387-3562.

See Also: (refer to index)
Designers' Bloopers

FURNITURE
Bedroom

A-1 Furniture Outlet

6002 S. Broadway
Los Angeles, CA 90003
213/758-3963, 213/753-3397

Hours: By Appointment Only, Mon-Fri: 10:30-5
Credit Cards: Cash or Checks Only

They have on display at least 100 bedroom sets and 100 mattress and box spring sets. On top of that, they also carry living room furniture, dining room sets, dinette sets, occasional tables, and much more. Many different brands are represented, and they encourage customers to comparison shop. When you've decided what you want, take the brand name and model number to A-1 Furniture Outlet, where you can get values as low as 10% over cost. Should you have any questions, call the staff, who will do their best to give you the information over the phone. They're open to the public by appointment only, so remember to check out the other stores before you call.

Alpert's Bedroom & Waterbed Warehouse ★
9848 Desoto
Chatsworth, CA 91311
818/718-9316

Hours: Mon-Fri: 10-7 Sat: 10-6 Sun: 11-5
Credit Cards: AE, DISC, MC, V

Alpert's has been selling at discount prices since 1962. They stock a large selection of bedroom furniture, specializing in solid-oak products, wall units, waterbeds, flotation units, four-poster beds, canopy beds, and innerspring mattresses. They also carry contemporary lacquer upholstered beds, futons, air beds, foam beds, and youth furniture such as chest beds and bunk beds. Everyday discounts range from 18 to 55% off original prices, with a 30-day price guarantee. Major brands include Spring Air, Vargas, Sealy, Somma, and many others. Most items are available for delivery within 24 hours. Offering the same discounts, store hours, and accepted credit cards, Alpert's Furniture in Canoga Park is a full-line furniture store for home and office. You'll save an additional 5% when you use your *Buying Retail Is Stupid!* coupon.

Additional Locations:
Canoga Park–Alpert's Furniture, 7631 Canoga Ave., 818/888-5060
Thousand Oaks–2895 E. Thousand Oaks Blvd., 805/497-4529

Bed Broker ★
300 E. Orangethorpe
Placentia, CA 92670
714/993-9953

Hours: Mon-Fri: 10-8 Sat: 10-6 Sun: 12-5
Credit Cards: DISC, MC, V
♦ **Senior Discount:** 5% **Age:** 65

Having almost 8,000 square feet of showroom, with a warehouse on the premises, makes Bed Broker the largest bedroom furniture store in Orange County. More than 70 mattresses are on display from 22 different manufacturers. They have more than 50 white iron and brass beds displayed and a selection of more than 1,000 to choose from. About 45 day beds, bunk beds, and various furniture for children are on display representing more than 400 available to customers. Most major brands are available, including Spring Air, Lady Englander, Bassett, Aireloom, Lady Americana, Elliott's, Wesley Allen, Springwall, Diamond, Tempo, and many more. Bed Broker offers savings of 50 to 70% off retail prices and guarantees lowest prices. Beyond their "never undersold" policy, quality and courtesy are strongly emphasized. In fact, you can deal directly with the owners seven days a week. Don't forget to use your *Buying Retail Is Stupid!* coupon for an additional 5% savings.

Brass Beds Direct ★
4866 W. Jefferson Blvd.
Los Angeles, CA 90016
213/737-6865, 800/727-6865

Hours: Tues-Sat: 1-5
Credit Cards: AE, DISC, MC, V

Brass Beds Direct offers the highest-quality brass beds and accessories available, at up to 65% off retail prices. They also sell wrought-iron products, home furnishings, and mattresses at 20 to 30% off retail. Call and inquire about specific items. Layaway and financing plans are available. Your *Buying Retail Is Stupid!* coupon will save you an extra 5%.

Bunk Bed Center & Valley Mattress ★
6875 Beck Ave.
North Hollywood, CA 91605
818/765-6451

Hours: Mon-Fri: 9-5:30 Sat: 9-5 Sun: 12-5
Credit Cards: DISC, MC, V
♦ **Senior Discount:** 10% **Age:** 55

With their motto "Comfort is our most important product," you know you'll be taken care of at Bunk Bed Center & Valley Mattress. Selling at 15 to 20% below retail, they have a large selection of space-saving children's bedroom furniture, and more than 50 bunks and lofts on display in their 5,000-square-foot store. Some of their more unusual styles are hard-to-find space-savers, trundle bunks that sleep three, chest bunks that include nine drawers of storage, and study centers which include a loft bed, desk, and chest. A layaway plan is available. Make sure you take in your *Buying Retail Is Stupid!* coupon for an additional 10% savings (not valid with senior citizen discount).

Electropedic Adjustable Beds ★
907 Hollywood Way
Burbank, CA 91505
818/845-7489, 800/727-1954

Hours: Mon-Fri: 10-5 Sat: 10-4 Sun: 12-4
Credit Cards: All Major
♦ **Senior Discount:** $100 **Age:** 50

When one of our husbands unfortunately threw his back out playing paddle tennis, we decided an electric bed was a good choice for a quick recovery. And it was. Electropedic Adjustable Beds is a factory outlet that sells these comfortable beds at savings of 40 to 50% off retail. These beds are available in twin, full, queen, king, dual king, and dual queen. They also carry lift-chairs and electric scooters. Don't forget to take in your *Buying Retail Is Stupid!* coupon for an extra $100 discount, which, by the way, is also valid with the senior citizen discount!

Richard Pratt's Mattress Warehouse ★
18717 Parthenia St.
Northridge, CA 91324
818/349-8118

Hours: Mon-Fri: 9-8 Sat-Sun: 9-6
Credit Cards: DISC, MC, V

Why pay department-store prices for mattresses when you can buy them at Richard Pratt's Mattress Warehouse? The Pratt family has owned and operated this store since 1968. Brands include Spring Air, Aireloom, Serta, Diamond, Springwall, and more. You can get all sizes and models, from twin to California king, plus roll-away and day beds. Buying up what others can't sell results in savings for their customers of 30 to 70% off retail. You're likely to recognize department-store labels on many of their beds. They also have close-outs and mismatched sets. Because everything is already in stock, immediate delivery is available. Take in your *Buying Retail Is Stupid!* coupon to receive a 10% discount when you purchase a mattress set.

RTC Mattress Warehouse ★
5142 Clareton Dr., Unit 140
Agoura, CA 91301
818/991-5868

Hours: Mon-Sat: 10-6 Sun: 11-5
Credit Cards: DISC, MC, V

You'll save 15 to 40% off retail prices when you shop at RTC Mattress Warehouse for Simmons, Beautyrest, Backcare, and Maxipedic. Savings are even higher on mismatched mattress sets. The motto here is "Who cares if the covers don't match?" They offer same-day, local delivery and will even haul your old mattress away. All sizes of mattress sets are available, plus trundle beds, roll-aways, and bed frames. You can also purchase mattresses and box springs separately. If you live within a 40-mile radius of the Agoura or San Marcos store, not only is your *Buying Retail Is Stupid!* coupon good for a free bed frame, but also they'll deliver, set up your new set, and haul away the old one free of charge with any $250 minimum purchase.

Additional Location:
San Marcos–947 Rancheros Dr., 619/746-7442

Sit'N Sleep ★
3824 Culver Center
Culver City, CA 90230
310/842-6850, 800/675-3536

Hours: Mon-Fri: 9-9 Sat: 9-6 Sun: 10-5
Credit Cards: AE, DISC, MC, V
♦ **Senior Discount:** 5% **Age:** 55

You'll find 20 to 40% savings off manufacturer list prices here. Sit'N Sleep carries name-brand mattress sets in all sizes and firmnesses. Not only do they stock 150 different mattress styles, but they also have a large selection of adjustable electric beds, all at guaranteed best prices. In fact, if they can't beat an advertised price, you'll get the bed for free! Sit'N Sleep offers four-hour local delivery, a 30-day price guarantee, and a 30-night sleep trial. The 2,100 mattresses in stock mean "Buy it today and try it tonight." If you already know what brand, size, and style you want, just give them a call and handle the entire transaction by phone. The staff is very pleasant. Get an extra 5% discount with the *Buying Retail Is Stupid!* coupon (not valid with senior citizen discount).

Spencer's Mattress Factory Outlet ★
15460 Devonshire St.
Mission Hills, CA 91345
800/350-6332

Hours: Mon-Fri: 11-6 Sat: 10-5 Sun: 12-5
Credit Cards: AE, DISC, MC, V
♦ **Senior Discount:** 10% **Age:** 55

You can save 30 to 50% buying your new mattress here. As a manufacturer, Spencer's allows you to order a custom mattress and watch it being made. Delivery is free anywhere in L.A. County, and it's possible to sleep on your ready-made mattress the day you buy it. A layaway plan is available. Children get free balloons on weekends, and you can use your *Buying Retail Is Stupid!* coupon for an extra 10% discount (not valid with senior citizen discount).

Wooden Ships Waterbeds and Futons ★
10181 Indiana Ave.
Riverside, CA 92503
909/359-3131, 800/233-7005

Hours: Mon-Fri: 10-8 Sat: 10-7 Sun: 12-6
Credit Cards: AE, DISC, MC, V
♦ **Senior Discount:** 5% **Age:** 55

You'll find downright honest salespeople who tell you like it is and won't try to sell you something you don't need. Wooden Ships wants their clients to be satisfied for life, and makes sure they are. A customer, trying to decide whether to replace a waterbed at a cost of several hundred dollars or to repair it, was advised by a Wooden Ships salesperson to patch it at a cost of $10. They work on a lower profit margin than most other waterbed stores, so you'll save 10 to 30% on your purchases. You'll find excellent buys on their waterbed accessories and futons, too. The store in Riverside has a special section with close-outs and special purchases where you can save at least 50% off retail. Don't forget to use your *Buying Retail Is Stupid!* coupon for a 15% discount on nonsale items only (not valid with senior citizen discount).

Additional Locations:
Palm Springs–2777 N. Palm Canyon Dr., 619/778-1313
San Bernardino–217 E. Club Center Dr., Suite C, 909/422-1313

Home Furniture

Al's Discount Furniture ★
4900 Lankershim Blvd.
North Hollywood, CA 91601
818/766-4289, 213/877-4783, 800/746-4257

Hours: Mon-Fri: 9-9 Sat: 9-6 Sun: 10-6
Credit Cards: AE, DISC, MC, V

Family owned and operated, Al's Discount Furniture has been selling name-brand furniture at discount prices since 1962. You'll find contemporary and traditional furniture, and they always have the latest in furniture trends. Also available are Spring Air mattresses, including the Four Seasons line. Aside from a large showroom of furniture for every room in your house, there are additional selections from more than 200 furniture catalogs. Everything comes with a 30-day price guarantee, and financing is also available. Be sure to use your *Buying Retail Is Stupid!* coupon, and you'll save an additional 5%.

Additional Locations:
West Los Angeles–2234 Sepulveda Blvd., 310/444-1470
Woodland Hills–22039 Ventura Blvd., 818/340-0300

All In 1 Home Furnishings ★
382 N. Allen Ave.
Pasadena, CA 91106
818/795-1143, 213/681-1476

Hours: Tues-Fri: 10-5:30 Sat: 10-5
Credit Cards: DISC, MC, V

If you already know what you want in the way of home furnishings, then stop by All In 1 Home Furnishings to check their in-house catalogs—they sell everything you need in the way of furniture at about 35% below retail. Window coverings are discounted 50 to 75%, and wall coverings 30%. Brand names include Stanley, Lane, Sealy, Universal, Parkview, and many more. All you have to do is give them the brand name and model number of the item you want. If you pay by cash or check, you can use your *Buying Retail Is Stupid!* coupon for an extra 5% discount. Coupon is not valid if payment is made with a credit card.

Additional Location:
Lomita–2041A Pacific Coast Hwy., 310/539-4002

Angelus Home Center ★
3650 E. Olympic Blvd.
Los Angeles, CA 90023
213/268-5171

Hours: Wed-Sun: 10-6
Credit Cards: MC, V

Angelus Home Center offers top-quality, name-brand furnishings at discounts of 30 to 70% off retail. You'll find furniture for every room in your house from manufacturers such as Stanley, Guildcraft, Broyhill, Bassett, Thomasville, and more. If you don't see a name or item you want, they'll special-order it for you. When you visit, make sure to put your name on their mailing list. Throughout the year they hold special sales advertised only to those on the mailing list. Your *Buying Retail Is Stupid!* coupon is good for a 5% discount which is redeemable even on sale items. Call the Huntington Beach store for hours.

Additional Location:
Huntington Beach–Angelus Furniture Mart, 7227 Edinger Ave., 714/373-4071

Byrne Home Furnishings ★
3516 W. Magnolia Blvd.
Burbank, CA 91505
818/845-0808, 800/660-3516

Hours: Tues-Sat: 9-5
Credit Cards: MC, V

Located in Burbank, Byrne Home Furnishings' showroom has 10,000 square feet of home and office furniture displayed in room-like settings. Feast your eyes on beautiful and unique furniture as well as decorator items for the entire house at 25 to 40% below retail prices. Century, Harden, Aireloom, Simmons, Stiffel, Lane, Bernhardt, Lexington, and Waterford are just a few of the many fine brand names they carry. The owners are very particular about quality materials and workmanship. If a well-known manufacturer starts to cut corners—such as using particle board instead of hardwood—the manufacturer is simply eliminated from Byrne's inventory. They also offer California state certified designers. Your *Buying Retail Is Stupid!* coupon will save you an extra 10% on framed artwork or any sofa floor sample.

Cort Furniture Rental Clearance Center ★
5435 San Fernando Rd. West
Los Angeles, CA 90039
818/543-3728, 800/448-5595

Hours: Mon-Fri: 9-6 Sat: 10-5
Credit Cards: AE, MC, V

Cort offers quality used furniture at a savings of 30 to 70% off original retail prices. They carry a complete line of office and residential furniture including sofas, dining room and bedroom sets, and office chairs. All purchases usually are delivered within 24 hours, and your *Buying Retail Is Stupid!* coupon entitles you to 10% off your purchase.

Designer Interiors ★
9132 Jordan Ave.
Chatsworth, CA 91311
818/709-9918

Hours: Mon-Tues, Thurs-Sat: 10-5 Sun: 12-5
Credit Cards: MC, V

Have you ever wondered what happens to all the gorgeous furniture and accessories in model homes? Much of it ends up at Designer Interiors selling at 30 to 70% below original retail prices. Most of the furniture and decorator accessories are originally from high-end manufacturers, including quite a selection of white sofas and sectionals. Shoppers will always find unique pieces among the selection of "typical" contemporary furniture. Designer Interiors also carries new stock at discounted prices. On one visit we fell head over heels for an elegant, hand-carved dining room set from Italy priced at $2,200 instead of $6,000 retail. Shipments arrive every two to three weeks, so inventory is always changing. All sales are final, so look things over very carefully before purchase. Layaway and storage are also available. Your *Buying Retail Is Stupid!* coupon is good for an extra 5% discount (not valid with previously reduced items or with other discount offers).

Designers Furniture Mart ★
300 S. Brand
Glendale, CA 91204
818/244-3061, 800/799-7879
Hours: Mon-Fri: 11-8 Sat: 10-7 Sun: 11-5
Credit Cards: All Major

Designers Furniture Mart has been providing exceptional service and
guaranteed best prices on name-brand furniture since 1984. Their toll-
free number makes it easy to acquire quotes over the phone. Featured are
slip-covered sofas, wrought-iron and pine bedroom sets, sofa sleepers,
and all types of futon beds. Financing options such as no interest and
deferred payment plans are available. Don't forget your *Buying Retail Is
Stupid!* coupon for additional 10% savings.

Designers' Bloopers ★
12600 Washington Blvd.
Los Angeles, CA 90066
310/398-9396
Hours: Tues-Sat: 10-6 Sun: 12-5
Credit Cards: MC, V

Designers' Bloopers offers unusual pieces of quality art and furniture for
your home—without the high prices that usually go with them. Their
furniture, lamps, carpets, art, and accessories were specially ordered for
someone else, but were too dark, too light, too long, too short, too
dramatic, too subtle, too modern, too traditional, too curvy, too angular,
too soft, too hard, or just too many. Wrong for someone else could be
exactly right for you. The most important aspects of Designers' Bloopers
is that almost everything is one-of-a-kind and the prices are often below
wholesale. They've been known to have prices better than parking-lot
sales at the Pacific Design Center. Furthermore, you can take along your
Buying Retail Is Stupid! coupon for an additional 5% off.

Eddie Gold Furniture, Inc. ★
4935 McConnell Ave., Bldg. 3
Los Angeles, CA 90066
213/870-3050
Hours: Tues-Fri: 9-5 Sat: 11-5
Credit Cards: DISC, MC, V

It may take you a while, but when shopping here, you'll eventually notice
that there aren't any pushy salespeople hanging around. What you will
find hanging around is quality furniture for your entire home. Brand
names include Bernhardt, Lane, Lexington, Sealy, Stanley, Universal,

and others at about 40% below retail. And if you happen to get in on one of their floor sample sales, savings can run as high as 70% off retail. Not many stores in today's marketplace can say they've been in business for three generations, but this one can. This family-owned business has kept their customers happy with low prices since 1951. Don't forget that your *Buying Retail Is Stupid!* coupon is good for an extra 10% discount (close-outs and previously reduced items not included in discount offer).

Eurostyle Furniture

19511-1/2 Business Center Dr.
Northridge, CA 91324
818/993-5772

Hours: Mon-Sat: 10-6 Sun: 11-5
Credit Cards: MC, V

If you love ornately designed European furniture, have we got a deal for you. Eurostyle imports all of their merchandise from Italy and sells it directly to the public at up to 50% off retail. And discounts run higher if you buy several pieces. You can customize your furniture by selecting from one of many wood finishes and nearly 1,200 fabrics. In fact, if you mention *Buying Retail Is Stupid!*, you will receive an extra 10% discount. Customers are important to Eurostyle, and you'll always find one of the owners on the floor. Appointments are available after business hours, and, if it's more convenient, they will come to your home for a free consultation. Financing is available.

Additional Location:
Thousand Oaks–720 E. Thousand Oaks Blvd., 805/494-7900

Finders Keepers Furniture Outlet ★

2912 El Camino Real
Tustin, CA 92680
714/730-6590, 800/622-FIND (622-3463)

Hours: Mon-Fri: 10-8 Sat: 10-6 Sun: 11-6
Credit Cards: All Major

You'll love Finders Keepers Furniture Outlet. They are a true furniture outlet selling close-outs, discontinued items, overruns, and mis-shipped merchandise from many prestigious East Coast furniture manufacturers with savings of 40 to 70%. Some brand names you'll find here are Lexington, Pulaski, Stanley, Lane, Broyhill, and Universal. Greater savings are available during their tent sales (twice a year) and truck unloading sales (four times a year). In addition, your *Buying Retail Is Stupid!* coupon will save you an extra 10% (not valid on Starburst items).

Furniture Liquidators ★
6900 Deering Ave.
Canoga Park, CA 91303
818/719-0220

Hours: Mon-Fri: 10-6 Sat-Sun: 10-5
Credit Cards: All Major

"Quality at Discount" is the theme at Furniture Liquidators, and that's just what you'll find. Their prices range from 50 to 70% below major department stores and 20 to 30% below other discount furniture stores. You'll find savings on all types of furniture, bedding, lamps, decorator items, and tables featuring brand names such as Universal, Sandberg, and Sheffield. Make sure to use your *Buying Retail Is Stupid!* coupon for an extra 5% discount.

Furniture Trends ★
2585 Cochran St.
Simi Valley, CA 93065
805/584-0116

Hours: Mon-Fri: 10-7 Sat: 10-6 Sun: 12-4
Credit Cards: DISC, MC, V

Furniture Trends is known for "Upscale Furniture . . . Downscale Prices." See their large collection of fine country, traditional, contemporary, and Southwestern styles. With 20 to 50% savings on popular brand names such as Cal-Style, Broyhill, Pacific Motif, and many others, you'll get lots of value for your money. They also have outstanding values in dining room, living room, and bedroom sets. Financing is also available. Take in your *Buying Retail Is Stupid!* coupon for a 5% discount (not valid with other special offers or discounts).

Goochey's Furnishings & Lighting
14241 Ventura Blvd., #104
Sherman Oaks, CA 91423
818/986-4772, 213/872-1113

Hours: Mon-Fri: 10-6 Saturday & Evenings By Appointment Only
Credit Cards: Cash or Checks Only

Goochey's Furnishings & Lighting can help you decorate your entire home or office. They carry wallpaper, carpeting, furniture, light fixtures, draperies, blinds, and even china. You'll save at least 35% off retail on all your decorating needs at this one-stop shop. Additional discounts as high as 75% below retail are also available whenever Goochey's acquires special purchases from manufacturers.

IKEA
20700 S. Avalon Blvd.
Carson, CA 90746
310/527-4532

Hours: Mon-Fri: 11-9 Sat: 10-7 Sun: 11-6
Credit Cards: DISC, MC, V

Because IKEA has more than 100 stores in 25 countries, their huge worldwide buying volume translates into low manufacturing costs which they pass along to the consumer. By designing most of their products themselves in Sweden, they are able to reduce costs even further and offer the lowest everyday prices, while still keeping design and quality high. You'll find more than 12,000 unique items and coordinated home furnishings—all at affordable prices. There are more than 70 coordinated room settings offering hundreds of home decorating ideas. They have 12 shops in their marketplace with thousands of accessories—offering everything from cookware to lighting, rugs, and plants. There's a supervised play area for children, a Swedish-style restaurant that offers baby food and child-size meals, a baby changing room with free diapers, and strollers to push around the little ones while you're shopping. All in all, IKEA offers everything you need to turn your house into a home. With four football fields of home furnishings to choose from, you better make sure you wear comfortable shoes. Hours listed above are for the Carson store. Call other locations for hours.

Additional Locations:
Burbank–600 N. San Fernando Blvd., 818/842-4532
City of Industry–17621 E. Gale Ave., 818/912-4532
Fontana–17284 Slover Ave., 909/829-4532
Tustin–2982 El Camino Real, 714/838-4000

Mark Friedman Furniture
1437 4th St.
Santa Monica, CA 90401
310/393-2338

Hours: Mon-Tues, Fri-Sat: 11-5 Wed-Thurs: 11-7
Credit Cards: Cash Only

This store has home furnishings for every room in the house. They carry every style, including contemporary, traditional, country, and classic. You can furnish living rooms, dining rooms, and bedrooms with their mattresses and box springs, dinettes, carpeting, lamps, slip-covered sofas, curios, leather, and occasional items. They have all famous national brand names at 10% above cost. And for even greater savings, check out their floor sample sales. Two hours of free parking is available directly across the street at parking structure #5.

Old World Ironmongers Factory Outlet ★
13282 Paxton St.
Pacoima, CA 91331
818/897-8233

Hours: Mon-Sat: 10-4
Credit Cards: MC, V

Old World Ironmongers offers hand-forged, interior iron furniture at 33 to 70% off retail. In addition to their original designs made of solid (not hollow) iron, they carry a variety of furniture: e.g., floor and table lamps, coffee, end, and dining tables, credenzas, chairs, room dividers, and beds. Ask about their yearly inventory clearance sale. Take in your *Buying Retail Is Stupid!* coupon for an additional 5% savings.

Sears Outlet Store
2401 S. Vineyard
Ontario, CA 91761
909/923-5960

Hours: Mon-Fri: 10-7 Sat: 10-6 Sun: 11-5
Credit Cards: AE, DISC, MC, SEARS, V

Furniture and appliances from your local Sears store can be found here at huge savings of 20 to 60% off the original retail prices. Merchandise from their stores is sent to the surplus stores to make room for new stock. You may find one-of-a-kind items, discontinued merchandise, floor samples, and dented, scratched, or reconditioned items. With new shipments arriving daily, inventory changes constantly. So, when you see something you want, buy it! It might not be there tomorrow.

Additional Locations:
Corona–492 N. Main St., 909/340-4269
Lancaster–44247 10th St. West, 805/726-0344
Santa Ana–500 W. Warner Ave., 714/754-6188
Woodland Hills–22940 Victory Blvd., 818/594-8621

Sitting Pretty Inc.
7115 Darby
Reseda, CA 91335
818/881-3114

Hours: Mon-Sat: 10-6 Sun: 12-5
Credit Cards: AE, DISC, MC, V

Sitting Pretty offers factory discounts on bars, bar stools, dinettes, game sets, wall units, and chairs. They have more than 20,000 square feet of beautiful merchandise in decorator designs. Expect to save 25 to 50% off retail prices on brand names such as Dinaire, Chromcraft, Stakmore, Kessler, and many more.

Additional Location:
Los Angeles–1888 S. Sepulveda Blvd., 310/478-3608

Woodpeckers
4111 Vanowen Place
Burbank, CA 91505
818/841-5485, 800/826-5556

Hours: By Appointment Only, Mon-Sat: 8-4
Credit Cards: MC, V

Getting a hand-built, customized piece of furniture doesn't have to cost a bundle. Have Woodpeckers build the entire piece for you. Woodpeckers is a family operation of woodworkers creating unique, quality furniture at retail prices or less. They offer a free design service to help create exactly what you want, and specialize in handmade chairs, dining tables, beds, chests of drawers, and much more. Do-it-yourselfers can call them about evening workshops where they'll help you build your piece, select and buy the wood (at a 20% discount), and cut the parts for a cost of $149.

See Also: (refer to index)
Pier 1 Imports Clearance Store
Prince of Wales

Infants' & Children's Furniture

Baby Toytown, Inc.
15979 Piuma Way
Cerritos, CA 91703
310/860-5358

Hours: Mon-Sat: 10-6 Sun: 12-5
Credit Cards: AE, DISC, MC, V

Baby Toytown carries everything you may need for babies and toddlers, plus a very nice selection of furniture for up to age 13. Major brands, including Simmons, Bassett, Stanley, Childcraft, and many others, are available at about 20 to 40% below retail. You'll find every item and accessory ever made for babies, except for clothing. Apples to apples, they'll match a lower price on current merchandise seen elsewhere by confirming the information by phone. With such a vast selection of individual items, there are prices suitable for most anyone's budget. In fact, the only drawback we can see about shopping here is having to narrow the choices so a decision can be made. They also offer an efficient baby shower registry at no charge. A major sale takes place each January, when customers are willing to wait two hours just to get through the door.

Additional Location:
Reseda–18719 Sherman Way, 818/881-4441

Babyland & Kids Furniture ★
1901 E. Colorado Blvd.
Pasadena, CA 91106
818/578-7500

Hours: Mon-Fri: 10-7 Sat: 10-6 Sun: 11-5
Credit Cards: AE, MC, OPT, V

Babyland & Kids Furniture will save you 30 to 40% on fine furniture and accessories from Italy. They buy direct from the factory, do away with the middleperson, and pass on the savings directly to you. Use the *Buying Retail Is Stupid!* discount coupon for a free mattress with every three-piece room set purchased.

Additional Locations:
West Los Angeles–1782 S. La Cienega Blvd., 310/836-2222
Woodland Hills–7134 Topanga Canyon Blvd., 818/704-7848

Carousel Baby Furniture
1726 E. Colorado Blvd.
Pasadena, CA 91106
213/684-0457

Hours: Mon-Thur, Sat: 9:30-6 Fri: 9:30-9
Credit Cards: MC, V

Roll those dice. Baby needs a new pair of shoes. If not, then a new car seat might be in order. You won't have to take any gambles at Carousel Baby Furniture. This large store has everything—strollers, playpens, mattresses, clothing (including a selection for premature babies), layettes, and many other furniture items such as rocking chairs and glider rockers. For brand-new mommies, there are breast pumps, diapers, and bassinets. You'll also find mirrors, headboards, books, lamps, replacement pads, and parts. When buying Simmons, Childcraft, or Aprica, you can expect to pay up to 50% off retail prices. If it has anything to do with babies, you'll be sure to find it here. Carousel Baby Furniture has been serving the community since 1957 and always has the latest information about baby safety available in English and Spanish.

Nine Months and More ★
25381 Alicia Pkwy., #Q
Laguna Hills, CA 92653
714/699-0093

Hours: Mon-Fri: 10-8 Sat: 10-6 Sun: 12-5
Credit Cards: AE, DISC, MC, V

Nine Months and More is a 5,000-square-foot store that guarantees the lowest prices on baby furniture and accessories. Within 30 days, if you have found a lower price, they will match or beat it. Prices are 10 to 15% below retail on name-brand items such as Aprica, Century, Graco, Simmons, Childcraft, and Combi. Take in your *Buying Retail Is Stupid!* coupon for an additional 5% off your purchase of any item, excluding sale merchandise.

Sid & Me ★
7522 Sunset Blvd.
West Hollywood, CA 90069
213/874-1787

Hours: Mon-Sat: 10-6
Credit Cards: MC, V

Sid & Me, "Your Baby and Kids' Headquarters," is an institution where you can find everything in baby furniture and clothing for infants. There are all the necessities, of course, such as strollers and car seats. Sid & Me carries major brands such as Simmons, Ragazzi, Childcraft, Aprica, Graco, Century, Morigeau, and many others at 10 to 40% below retail. They offer free layaway, free shower registry, a most knowledgeable staff, and big savings! Families have been shopping for their baby needs at Sid & Me since 1951. With a $100 purchase of regularly priced items, you will receive a $10 discount using your *Buying Retail Is Stupid!* coupon.

Additional Location:
Los Angeles–8338 Lincoln Blvd., 310/670-5550

The Stork Shop ★
1868 S. La Cienega Blvd.
Los Angeles, CA 90035
310/839-2403

Hours: Mon-Sat: 10-5:30
Credit Cards: MC, V

The Stork Shop promises a fun visit. They have everything you could possibly want in furniture and clothes for your baby. In fact, they also carry more than 20,000 garments for boys and girls up to age 14. Their layettes are beautiful, and you'll love the many designer styles of furniture and accessories. You'll save 20 to 50% off retail prices on most of your purchases too! If you spend over $45, you'll receive an extra $5 off when you use your *Buying Retail Is Stupid!* coupon.

See Also: (refer to index)
Jazzy's World

Unfinished Furniture

Froch's Woodcraft Shop, Inc.
6659 Topanga Canyon Blvd.
Canoga Park, CA 91303
818/883-4730, 800/228-4877
Hours: Mon-Thur: 9-6 Fri: 9-5 Sat: 9-6 Sun: 12-5
Credit Cards: AE, DISC, MC, V

Froch's Woodcraft Shop, a large store with standard and unusual pieces, is by far the best unfinished furniture store we've ever seen. They manufacture their unfinished furniture in the San Fernando Valley with their own craftspeople. This allows for the fantastic savings of 50% off retail. You can remodel or build your kitchen with cabinetry available in different styles and sizes. If you're ready to revamp your closets, Froch's has various units you can mix and match to suit your own particular needs. Everything is all wood, and you won't find any particle board.

Additional Location:
Panorama City–7945 Van Nuys Blvd., 818/787-3682

Woody's Un-Finished Furniture
1222 Commerce Center Dr.
Lancaster, CA 93534
805/945-0551, 800/238-8667
Hours: Mon-Fri: 10-9 Sat-Sun: 10-6
Credit Cards: All Major

You can save 40 to 50% off retail furniture prices by applying the finish yourself. Woody's carries only solid-wood furniture (absolutely no particle board) in pine, oak, alder, maple, and ash. If you've never finished furniture before, take advantage of their free classes. They have furniture for every room in your house, such as dining room tables and chairs, entertainment centers, buffets, corner nooks, barstools, appliance carts, bunk beds, computer and office furniture, desks, and shelves. Brand names include Whittier, Rods, Master Craft, Maco, and Union City.

Additional Location:
Palmdale–20th St. East, 805/265-7410 (10-6 Daily)

LAMPS & LIGHT FIXTURES

Castle Chandeliers & Lighting Co. ★
4617 Van Nuys Blvd.
Sherman Oaks, CA 91403
818/986-7077

Hours: Mon-Fri: 9-6 Sat: 9:30-6 Sun: 12-5
Credit Cards: AE, DISC, MC, V
♦ **Senior Discount:** 5% **Age:** 55

If it has to do with lighting fixtures, Castle has it all. They stock lamps, fans, chandeliers, track lights, exterior lighting, shades, and more. Products they haven't manufactured themselves are imported from Europe. All merchandise is offered at factory-direct prices. With the biggest showroom in Southern California, you are bound to find what you are looking for with over 1,000 of the finest lamps from which to choose. You'll receive an additional 10% discount buy presenting your *Buying Retail Is Stupid!* coupon.

Lampmart ★
5821 S. Main St.
Los Angeles, CA 90003
213/234-5320

Hours: Mon-Fri: 9-5 Sat: 9-4
Credit Cards: MC, V

One of the largest lamp, lighting fixture, and lampshade inventories in the greater Los Angeles area can be found here. Their prices are 20 to 33% below retail on lamps, lampshades, chandeliers, fans, and mirrors. If you've got a lamp or chandelier that needs to be fixed, refinished, or restored, they can do it. If you need to have your fixtures installed, they can handle that too. Custom lampshades and duplications are also available. In business since 1945, Lampmart offers terrific pricing and also carries top name brands. You'll get a 5% discount when you present your *Buying Retail Is Stupid!* coupon.

The Lampshade Outlet
23552 Commerce Center Dr., Suite J
Laguna Hills, CA 92653
714/859-2832

Hours: Mon-Sat: 10-5:30 Sun: 12-5
Credit Cards: All Major
♦ **Senior Discount:** 10% **Age:** 60

If your cat's been using one of your lampshades as a scratching post, or if a few of your lampshades didn't quite make it during your last move, your worries are over. The Lampshade Outlet carries an inventory of at least 7,000 lampshades at $5 to $10 less per shade than most stores charge. Prices start at $9.95 and go up to $100. For the best results, take your lamp(s) with you.

Lighting Liquidators, Inc.
561 W. Colorado St.
Glendale, CA 91204
818/545-0470

Hours: Wed-Fri: 10-7 Sat: 10-6 Sun: 10-5
Credit Cards: MC, V

Lighting Liquidators has factory-new, first-quality fixtures and lamps at discounts of 40 to 80% below retail. They carry a full line of indoor and outdoor fixtures, floor and table lamps, chandeliers, kitchen and bathroom fixtures, and ceiling fans. Lighting Liquidators is the number one industry source for close-outs and liquidations, and their inventory continuously changes. All sales are final with a no refund or exchange policy.

Ray Ferra's Iron & Antique Accents
342 N. La Brea Ave.
Los Angeles, CA 90036
213/934-3953

Hours: Tues-Fri: 10-5 Sat: 10-3
Credit Cards: AE, DISC, MC, V

If you've been looking for replacement glass for an antique lamp, then Ray Ferra can come to your rescue. If the problem isn't replacement glass, he also does rewiring for most lamps, ceiling fixtures, and crystal chandeliers. Commercial and residential lighting is also one of his specialties. He carries reproduction and original Tiffany lamps, handles, and many hard-to-find lighting items. You can also find reproductions of art deco and art nouveau wall sconces made with original molds from the 1920s and 1930s. He's been providing excellent service since 1968, and you can save 20% or more off retail prices, even if you could find it elsewhere. Parking is available in back of the store.

See Also: (refer to index)
Goochey's Furnishings & Lighting
McNally Electric

LINENS

Al Greenwood Bedspread King

2750 E. Pacific Coast Hwy.
Long Beach, CA 90804
310/498-9277

Hours: Mon-Sat: 10-5:30 Sun: 12-5
Credit Cards: MC, V

When a man calls himself The Bedspread King, you expect to find one of the country's largest selections of bedspreads. Well, it's true. In addition to the incredible selection of quilted bedspreads in designer fabrics at savings of 20 to 50% off retail, Al Greenwood stocks hooked and ready-to-hang draperies, many in fabrics made to match the bedspreads. Matching fabrics are also available for do-it-yourself drapes, pillows, and other decorator accessories. Call the South Gate store for hours.

Additional Location:
South Gate–8468 State St., 213/566-9393

Bed Bath & Beyond

11801 W. Olympic Blvd.
West Los Angeles, CA 90064
310/478-5767

Hours: Mon-Sat: 9:30-9 Sun: 9:30-7
Credit Cards: AE, DISC, MC, V

With their prices, Bed Bath & Beyond says, "We make you laugh at white sale prices." We found their prices to start at about 20 to 25% below retail. When price shopping for a particular set of matching bathroom accessories, we discovered the everyday prices at Bed Bath & Beyond to be 25% lower than prices at a discount chain store. Their large stores are filled with giant selections of sheets, towels, bedspreads, comforters, pillows, kitchenware, dinnerware, cookware, gift items, toss pillows, shower curtains, everything! You'll find Martex, Fieldcrest, Wamsutta, Nettlecreek, and Mikasa, just to name a few brands.

Additional Locations:
7 other stores throughout Southern California—call 310/478-5767.

Bedroom & Window Creations ★

1301 Beach Blvd., #6
La Habra, CA 90631
310/902-2600

Hours: Mon-Fri: 9-6 Sat: 10-5
Credit Cards: AE, DISC, MC, V
♦ **Senior Discount:** 5% **Age:** 60

As the manufacturer for their own stores, Bedroom & Window Creations (A.K.A. Bedspread Creations) is able to offer factory-direct wholesale prices to people lucky enough to know about them. They have about 2,000 square feet with more than 400 bedspreads in stock. With more than 2,000 different fabrics to choose from, they will make anything you want (comforters, bedspreads, canopies, valances), even if you wish to furnish your own fabric. They also carry comforters, pillows, mini- and vertical blinds, window shades, and all the other items necessary to make them your one-stop decorating center. Name brands include Bedspread Creations, Pacific Designs, India Ink, Waverly, and many others. You'll save an additional 5% with your *Buying Retail Is Stupid!* coupon. Deals don't get much better than this.

Additional Location:
Anaheim Hills–8018 E. Santa Ana Canyon Rd., #104, 714/282-2986

The Linen Club

100 Citadel Dr., #136
City of Commerce, CA 90040
213/721-2444

Hours: Mon-Sat: 9-8 Sun: 10-6
Credit Cards: MC, V

Victor, the owner of The Linen Club, guarantees not to be undersold. If you're looking for bedspreads, comforters, blankets, sheets, or towels, you need look no further. The store is filled with linens, including most designer names such as Wamsutta, Cannon, Fieldcrest, Martex, Laura Ashley, and more, at savings of 35 to 70% off retail. They also have accessories for your powder room. If you need a warm comforter for your Aunt Tilley in Montana, you can phone your order in and have it shipped just in time for her birthday. The Linen Club has been satisfying their customers since the early 1980s, so they must be doing something right.

See Also: (refer to index)
Burlington Coat Factory Warehouse
Doin' Dishes
Fedco

SERVICES

ADCO
818/340-9910

Hours: By Appointment Only
Credit Cards: Cash or Checks Only

Jean Chapman works on an extremely low mark-up which enables you to buy furniture, mattresses, and window coverings at deep discounts. They work completely from catalogs at ADCO (since 1955) and will even give price quotes over the phone. After you have made a decision regarding the product you want, call them with the manufacturer's name, the model number of the item, and any other pertinent information. A 25% deposit is required, and you can pick up the merchandise when it arrives or make arrangements for delivery. By the way, they do not handle carpeting, appliances, or electronic equipment.

Consumers Guild, Inc. ★
17036 Devonshire St.
Northridge, CA 91325
818/363-3900

Hours: Mon-Fri: 10-6 Sat: 10-5 Sun: 12-5
Credit Cards: AE, MC, V

Consumers Guild in Northridge has been specializing in catalog discount sales since 1961. With low overhead, no fancy showroom, no warehousing, fewer salespersons, and less advertising, they are able to pass on discounts of 20 to 50% off retail prices to their customers on such quality brand-name furniture as Bassett, Lane, Henredon, Simmons, Sealy, Stanley, Universal, and almost 200 other manufacturers. In addition to furniture, they offer lamps and window treatments. Delivery and installation are also available. Remember to use your *Buying Retail Is Stupid!* coupon for an extra 5% discount.

Dean Interior Designs
13045 Ventura Blvd.
Studio City, CA 91604
818/783-5904

Hours: Mon-Fri: 9-5
Credit Cards: Cash or Checks Only

You can change the look of your home or office with expert advice from Ken Dean, interior designer. By dealing directly with manufacturers, he will save you 30% below retail on fabrics, furniture, flooring, draperies, carpets, wallpaper, ceramic tiles, and most other products for the home or office.

Design Direct—Pacific Design Center
8687 Melrose Ave., #M-23
West Hollywood, CA 90069
310/657-9422

Hours: Mon-Fri: 10-5
Credit Cards: MC, V

Shop at the same stores where top interior designers purchase furniture, lighting, fabric, and accessories without paying high retail prices. Design Direct is a purchasing service located in the Pacific Design Center—better known as the Blue Whale. Typically, you'll pay 20% above wholesale cost at Design Direct. Just visit any of the 200 showrooms and jot down what item you're interested in purchasing. Design Direct will do the rest—handle the ordering and delivery of the merchandise. Think of this service as having your personal interior designer, but without the expense.

Valley Upholstering ★
18165 Napa St., Unit 8
Northridge, CA 91325
818/349-4336

Hours: Mon-Fri: 8:30-4:30
Credit Cards: Cash or Checks Only
♦ **Senior Discount:** 10% **Age:** 55

Valley Upholstering is a labor wholesaler to hotels, major department stores, and design firms. Now also open to the public, Valley can save you about 50% off retail on upholstering services. You can use your own fabrics, or select brand-name fabrics from one of their sample books featuring Waverly, Schumacher, Barrow, Robert Allen, and many more. Fabrics are discounted 20 to 30% off retail. They also manufacture custom furniture at discounted prices. In-home design consultation is available by appointment. If you have them reupholster your sofa, you'll receive two free accent pillows with your *Buying Retail Is Stupid!* coupon.

Comparison-shop before making
expensive purchases.

Bes International Jewelry
607 S. Hill St., #334
Los Angeles, CA 90014
213/626-1075

Hours: Mon-Fri: 9:30-5 Sat: 10-3:30
Credit Cards: AE, DISC, MC, V

Here's a complete line of jewelry at wholesale prices. You will save at least 50% in their glittering showroom filled with 14K and 18K gold! Owner Evelyn LeVine has bracelets, necklaces, chains, rings, engagement sets, earrings, and more. Custom designing is available, and repairs are done while you wait. In fact, if you are bored with some of your old jewelry lying around, let Bes redesign or remount it for you in a new modern style. They've been in business since 1977, and parking is validated.

Beverly Loan Co.
9440 Santa Monica Blvd., #301
Beverly Hills, CA 90210
310/275-2555

Hours: Mon-Thur: 9-5 Fri: 9-6
Credit Cards: MC, V (No Checks)

Since 1938, Beverly Loan Co.'s main business has been making loans of virtually any amount secured by the pledge of fine jewelry (gold watches, diamonds, etc.) or objets d'art. Since loan terms are comparatively low, most borrowers redeem their Rolexes and Cartiers. However, if the loan is not paid off, the merchandise is sold to dealers and the public at prices 50% off retail and often below wholesale. They are located in the Bank of America Building.

California Jewelsmiths
250 S. Beverly Dr.
Beverly Hills, CA 90212
213/272-5364, 310/275-5364

Hours: Mon-Sat: 9:30-5:00
Credit Cards: AE, MC, V

California Jewelsmiths has been in business since the 1940s and has maintained three generations of clients strictly by word of mouth. They don't advertise the great savings, usually 30% or more off retail, on their fine diamond jewelry, bracelets, necklaces, rings, precious and semiprecious stones, charms, pendants, chains, and watches. Check them out when shopping for a dependable jewelry store. Custom design is also a specialty. Repair work is done on the premises.

Claydon's Jewelers
2772 Artesia Blvd., Suite 101
Redondo Beach, CA 90278
310/542-0501

Hours: Tues-Fri: 10-6 Sat: 10-4:30
Credit Cards: AE, DISC, MC, V
♦ **Senior Discount:** 10% **Age:** 55

We found Claydon's Jewelers from a woman's letter saying she was their new customer for life. Why? She saved $500 there on a diamond and didn't write to us about it until she had done some apples-to-apples comparison shopping. Claydon's can do everything for you from custom-designing a piece of jewelry using rare gemstones in unusual shapes, to repairing silver and pewter items such as candle holders, tea sets, or frames. All this is done on their premises. They also do antique jewelry restoration and watch repairs, string pearls, and engrave your merchandise. Always wanting to do just a little more for their customers, Claydon's will schedule appointments during and after their normal business hours. Now, we'd say that this is a one-stop jewelry shop.

Denny Lesser Fine Jewelry Manufacturing ★
9927 Topanga Canyon Blvd.
Chatsworth, CA 91311
818/772-4278

Hours: Mon-Sat: 9:30-6 Sun: 10-5
Credit Cards: MC, V

Since 1970, Denny Lesser Fine Jewelry has been providing its customers with great service and values on the finest gold and silver jewelry. All items are 30 to 50% below retail, and Denny Lesser will negotiate with customers to make sure they are satisfied. In addition, one weekend a year several stone importers and wholesale manufacturers meet at the store to offer customers "better than downtown prices." All products are unconditionally guaranteed, and customers may even watch the work being done if it makes them feel more comfortable. With your *Buying Retail Is Stupid!* coupon, they will pay your sales tax!

The Diamond Mine
2508 Hamner Ave.
Norco, CA 91760
909/735-7447

Hours: Mon-Fri: 9:30-5:30 Sat: 9-3
Credit Cards: AE, DISC, MC, V
♦ **Senior Discount:** 40% **Age:** 55

Why not save yourself at least 50% below mall jewelry-store prices by checking out The Diamond Mine? You can buy on sight or design what you want in 14K and 18K gold. In addition, they carry loose diamonds and gemstones, and they do their own castings. If you are longing for a solid-gold watch in 14K or 18K gold, with or without diamonds, head for The Diamond Mine. Though owner Dan Shevitski doesn't keep expensive watches like this in stock, he'll get one for you for only 10% over what he is charged. Customer service is of the utmost importance here. For example, a very good friend of ours needed to have a sapphire replaced in her ring. When she returned to pick it up, Dan wasn't happy with the quality of the new sapphire and had it replaced with a better stone at no extra charge. Knowing that the same item costing $100 at retail jewelry stores will cost only $40 at The Diamond Mine, why would anyone want to shop anywhere else? The Diamond Mine has been in business since 1985.

J. Rothstein & Co. ★
8950 W. Olympic Blvd., Suite 209
Beverly Hills, CA 90211
310/858-3800

Hours: Mon-Fri: 10-6 Sat: 10-3
Credit Cards: MC, V
♦ **Senior Discount:** 5% **Age:** 55

Good things come in small packages, and if you are looking for a gift for someone special, J. Rothstein & Co. can really help you out. As an importer and wholesaler of fine jewelry, they are able to extend deep discounts to their customers. J. Rothstein sells all gold jewelry without gemstones by the gram weight. The prices run at least 50% off retail, but since many stores mark their jewelry up so high, discounts can run much higher. In addition to gold jewelry, they have a beautiful selection of very unusual pieces. You'll find rare and exotic pearl jewelry, including authentic biwa pearls, and fine jade, too. Most of these pieces are one-of-a-kind and are set in handmade mountings made specifically for the featured stone(s). Men's and women's Seiko watches are also available at 40% below retail. Repairs, restringing, and ear piercing are also available. Whatever you do, don't let the Beverly Hills address scare you off. J. Rothstein & Co. has terrific prices to fit everyone's pocketbook and even better customer service. Custom work is available, and during most of the year, special orders take about a week. If your watch needs a new battery, take in your *Buying Retail Is Stupid!* coupon and you'll get a new battery free of charge.

John Moyen's Jewellery Connection ★
2806-A Townsgate Rd.
Westlake, CA 91361
818/707-1230, 805/494-8114
Hours: Tues-Fri: 10-6 Sat: 10-5
Credit Cards: All Major
♦ **Senior Discount:** 10% **Age:** 65

It's hard to top jewelry as a gift. If you're tired of shopping in run-of-the-mill jewelry stores, John Moyen's Jewellery Connection will be a welcome breath of fresh air. Not only will you find many very unusual pieces, but you'll also discover that high quality and low prices (about 40 to 60% off retail) go hand-in-hand here. Should you find a particular ring but would prefer, for example, the center stone to be a ruby instead of a sapphire, switching stones is no problem. Of course, the price will be adjusted up or down, depending on the type and quality of the stone you choose. When shopping here, you know exactly what you are buying because it's all listed separately on the tag. (They even separate the weight of round and baguette diamonds.) The staff here goes the distance for customers. On one visit, a gentleman came in needing a pin for his watchband. Less than five minutes later he was out the door with his watchband fixed at no charge. John Moyen started as a wholesaler in the industry in the early 1960s and opened his doors to the public in 1985. John says, "Shopping here is always better than a sale–guaranteed." Every purchase is backed by a 30-day, money-back guarantee. You can save an extra 10% off your purchase if you remember your *Buying Retail Is Stupid!* coupon. The coupon can be used for everything except loose stones.

Lord of the Rings ★
607 S. Hill St., Suite 850
Los Angeles, CA 90014
213/488-9157
Hours: By Appointment Only
Credit Cards: AE, DISC, MC, V
♦ **Senior Discount:** 5% **Age:** 60

Lord of the Rings has been open since 1983 and offers all types of fine jewelry, precious stones, engagement rings, and wedding bands to the public at wholesale prices. In addition, owner/gemologist David Barzilay offers a free mini-class on "everything you always wanted to know about diamonds but were afraid to ask." Generally, your savings will run about 50% below retail. They are open six days a week and some evenings if requested. Please call them to set up an appointment. They will also accept your *Buying Retail Is Stupid!* coupon for an additional 5% discount on your purchase.

Patsy Comer's Jewelry & Coins ★
7249 Reseda Blvd.
Reseda, CA 91335
818/345-1631

Hours: Mon-Fri: 10-5 Sat: 10-4
Credit Cards: Cash Only

At Patsy Comer's you'll find plenty of recycled, fine, and costume jewelry (old, antique, and estate in sterling, gold-plate, and 14K or 18K gold). This small store is staffed by people who love their work as well as their customers. Most of the gold jewelry is sold by gram weight, making it possible to buy gold jewelry at least 50% below retail. On one visit we spotted a bracelet in 14K gold with very unusual links priced at $300. We found a similar bracelet in a high-end department store for $1,300. The only real difference between the two bracelets was the boxes they came in, and for that price, we'll take the cardboard box. About half the store is filled with old and antique costume jewelry, including plenty of items for men such as tie tacks and cuff links. In addition to all kinds of jewelry, coin collectors can purchase coins and all related supplies at discounted prices. By the way, the ticking you hear is from kitchen timers. The timers are set so that customers won't get tickets when the one-hour parking meters expire. Don't forget to take your *Buying Retail Is Stupid!* coupon for an extra 10% discount.

St. Vincent Jewelry Center
640 + 650 S. Hill St. (@ 7th)
Los Angeles, CA 90014
213/629-2124

Hours: Mon-Sat: 9:30-6
Credit Cards: Varies with Vendor

St. Vincent Jewelry Center, the single largest jewelry exchange in the world, is home to more than 400 wholesalers and manufacturers. This is the place to go for jewelry of any kind; we don't care what you want—it's here. Opened in 1982, the many individual jewelry stores offer you factory-direct prices at savings of 40 to 70% below retail. Whatever you need or desire is here and fits any budget. You can spend $25 or $1,500,000. True jewelry lovers will think they've hit buried treasure. Generally speaking, the higher the floor you're on, the higher the quality, and of course, the higher the prices. Aside from ready-made jewelry, you'll find businesses specializing in custom design, loose stones, repair, and restoration, and you'll also find gold, precious-metal, and jewelry buyers. It's hard to believe that this fabulous selection of 400 vendors is all under one roof, and when you see the prices, you won't believe the savings either. In addition to the above address, they are located at 659 S. Broadway. Call to get a free directory listing all stores.

400 vendors at one location

San Pedro Jewelry Mart

317 W. 6th St.
San Pedro, CA 90731
310/548-1000

Hours: Tues-Sat: 10-5
Credit Cards: AE, DISC, MC, V

If you're in the market for better jewelry at 30 to 60% below mall prices, head on over to San Pedro Jewelry Mart. You have a choice of ready-made jewelry or customized work. In addition, they have diamond everything—cocktail, engagement, and wedding rings, necklaces, earrings, and bracelets—set in either 14K or 18K. They also have a nice selection of pearls and colored stones. Jewelry lovers have been buying from this manufacturer since 1978.

Silver Connection

100 N. La Cienega, #222
Los Angeles, CA 90048
310/652-3787

Hours: Mon-Thur: 11-9 Fri-Sat: 11-10 Sun: 11-8
Credit Cards: All Major
♦ **Senior Discount:** 10% **Age:** 55

You can get super deals on sterling-silver jewelry: earrings, rings, bracelets, charms, bangles, pill boxes, money clips, key chains, pendants, anklets, and much more at the Silver Connection. They even sell "one ear-pierced" earrings for those who enjoy being a little different. They're overflowing with 1,000 charms, 2,000 pairs of earrings, 3,000 rings, and more from India, Mexico, U.S., Italy, Thailand, Nepal, Israel, and Bali at savings 20 to 50% off retail, sometimes more! Silver Connection is located in the Beverly Connection.

400 vendors at one location

Steven & Co. Jewelers

437 N. Bedford Dr.
Beverly Hills, CA 90210
310/274-8336

Hours: Mon-Fri: 9:30-6
Credit Cards: All Major

Dreams turn into reality here. Steven & Co. has jewelry with diamonds, emeralds, rubies, sapphires, and pearls at 10 to 20% above cost, as well as watches, clocks, and gold jewelry. They carry such brand names as Rolex, Cartier, Ebel, Movado, and others. You'll also find period jewelry at discount prices. Expert repairing of watches and jewelry, custom designing, redesigning, and ear piercing are available. They also purchase and appraise estates. Free parking is available at 461 Bedford. Get on their private mailing list for special sales. Private appointments are also available.

Watch Connection ★

3033 S. Bristol
Costa Mesa, CA 92626
714/432-8200

Hours: Tues-Fri: 11-5:30 Sat: 11-5
Credit Cards: All Major

The Watch Connection carries one of the largest selections of fine wristwatches (at least 2,500) we've ever seen. Discounts average about 25% off suggested retail prices on brand names such as Movado, Omega, Piaget, Rado, Tag Heuer, Hublot, Seiko, and many others. In addition to wristwatches, along with batteries and watchbands, they offer complete watch repair. This family-owned business was started in 1979. When you use your *Buying Retail Is Stupid!* coupon, you'll get an extra 10% discount.

See Also: (refer to index)
Collector's Eye
Nebraska Bead Co.

Check return policies
before buying.

DRUG STORES & PHARMACIES

Consumer Discount Drugs
6542 Hollywood Blvd.
Hollywood, CA 90028
213/461-3606

Hours: Mon-Sat: 9:30-8 Sun: 10:30-6:30
Credit Cards: DISC, MC, V

You can save an average of 30% off the retail price on most items in this fully stocked drug store. Consumer Discount Drugs carries everything from vitamins and brand-name cosmetics to health and beauty aids. Every week, they feature at least 10 to 20 special sale items, so check those out for extra savings!

Discount Medical Pharmacy
2716 Griffith Park Blvd.
Los Angeles, CA 90027
213/661-8366

Hours: Mon-Fri: 9-7:30 Sat: 10-5
Credit Cards: All Major
♦ **Senior Discount:** 10% **Age:** 55

Bodybuilders will definitely want to stop at Discount Medical Pharmacy, where bodybuilding supplements such as Met RX, RX Fuel, Creatin Fuel Plus, Gainers Fuel, and more are available at 15% above cost. They also supply HIV medications at the lowest prices in town, fill regular prescriptions at competitive prices, and will handle all your insurance billing. Customer service and excellent prices will be found here.

P X Drugs No. 2 ★
6312 Van Nuys Blvd.
Van Nuys, CA 91406
818/785-0441

Hours: Mon: 8:30-6:30 Tues-Fri: 8:30-8 Sat: 9-1
Credit Cards: MC, V

Everything in this drug store is discounted: prescriptions, health and beauty aids, greeting cards, cosmetics, and food items such as soft drinks, ice cream, and lots of munchies. The pharmacy honors most insurance plans. Presentation of your *Buying Retail Is Stupid!* coupon will get you an additional 10% discount on anything in the store, except prescriptions.

Riverside Pharmacy ★
11655 Riverside Dr.
North Hollywood, CA 91602
818/985-7230

Hours: Mon-Fri: 9:30-6 Sat: 9:30-1
Credit Cards: All Major

With prescription prices on the rise, here's a place that will keep money in your pocket; Riverside Pharmacy has been selling prescriptions at a discount since 1969. They are always available for consultation on medications and offer fast in-store service—10 minutes or less. If you live in the San Fernando Valley, your prescription can be delivered for $1 to $2 (depending upon location). Bring in your *Buying Retail Is Stupid!* coupon and save 40% off greeting cards and 20% off gift items.

Super-Rite Drugs Inc. ★
14425 Burbank Blvd.
Van Nuys, CA 91401
818/787-2552

Hours: Mon-Fri: 9-6 Sat: 9-3
Credit Cards: AE, DISC, MC, V

With the high cost of medications, it's wise to shop around for the best price. Super-Rite Drugs will guarantee the lowest price on any prescription with verification of pricing from another pharmacy. While you wait for your prescription, free coffee and cookies are offered as a special touch. You can also browse around the store examining their low prices (about 20 to 50% off retail) on vitamins, health and beauty aids, cosmetics, and greeting cards. Super-Rite ships prescriptions anywhere in the United States. If you have a new prescription or have an existing one transferred from another pharmacy, your *Buying Retail Is Stupid!* coupon will save you an extra 5% on your first order.

See Also: (refer to index)

MEDICAL SUPPLIES & EQUIPMENT

Anders Orthopedics & Prosthetics

1825 N. Western Ave.
Los Angeles, CA 90027
213/461-4279

Hours: Mon-Fri: 9-12, 1-5
Credit Cards: Cash or Checks Only

From braces to wheelchairs, Anders carries everything in orthopedic and prosthetics lines. They have more than 25 years of experience, so you will receive knowledgeable, professional service, plus savings of 30 to 50% off retail. They also have corsets, trusses, orthopedic shoes, surgical stockings, crutches, and many other necessary items. Just ask for Johnny Anders. Open only during the week, the store is closed each day from noon to 1 p.m.

Kagan Surplus Sales ★

8050 Webb Ave.
North Hollywood, CA 91605
818/768-1422

Hours: Mon-Thur: 8:45-5:45 Fri: 8:30-5:15 Sat: 10-4:30
Credit Cards: DISC, MC, V

Kagan Surplus Sales specializes in recycled home-care medical equipment. This 4,000-square-foot warehouse offers items that have been completely refurbished (repaired, painted, and recovered if necessary). Savings range from 50 to 90% off what you would pay if these items were brand new. The price is the only way to tell that the wheelchairs (always a large selection) and various walkers are used. Don't forget to use your *Buying Retail Is Stupid!* coupon for additional savings. You'll save 5% if your purchase is under $100, and 10% if your purchase is $100 or more.

Quickmed Supplies Inc.

3421 San Fernando Rd., #H
Los Angeles, CA 90065
213/259-1000, 800/966-1111

Hours: Mon-Fri: 9-5
Credit Cards: Cash or Checks Only

Quickmed Supplies is your one-stop shop for all medical supplies, such as wheelchairs, orthopedic goods, portable commodes, gauze, bandages, and cotton. They carry back supports, canes, knee braces, and other related products. This is a discount warehouse where you can save 20 to

40% off retail prices. If it's portable, you'll find everything related to medical recuperation at Quickmed Supplies.

See Also: (refer to index)
> Electropedic Adjustable Beds

OPTICAL SERVICES

For Eyes Optical of California, Inc.

18712 Ventura Blvd.

Tarzana, CA 91356

818/705-4020

Hours: Mon-Fri: 10-7:30 Sat: 10-6 Sun: 12-5
Credit Cards: DISC, MC, V
♦ **Senior Discount:** 10% **Age:** 65

This full-service optical company sells prescription, sun, sport, and other eyewear in its own stores coast-to-coast. It was started in the early 1970s by two opticians who decided to save the public money. As a result, you can now visit any For Eyes and save 25 to 50% on all prescription and nonprescription glasses. Each pair is custom made, but the stores maintain a "one price" policy of $49 for regular-line frames and lenses. A second pair purchased at the same time is $30. There are no added charges for plastic, tinted, or oversized lenses. You can select such designer names as Anne Klein, Pierre Cardin, Armani, and Calvin Klein. We have good news for moms and dads—a guarantee is provided for one year against breakage on children's glasses! Eye exams are not available at most locations.

Additional Locations:
6 other stores throughout Southern California—call 800/FOR-EYES (800/367-3937).

Frame-N-Lens

488 E. 17th St.

Costa Mesa, CA 92627

714/548-6739

Hours: Mon-Fri: 10-7 Sat: 10-6
Credit Cards: DISC, MC, V

You should know about these convenient, price-worthy stores if you're in the market for eyeglasses. Frame-N-Lens will make your first pair of single-vision glasses for $50 and a second pair with the same prescription for $35. With over 500 frames to choose from, there are styles to please everyone. Designer frames are also available at an additional cost. Eyeglass repairs and adjustments are free. Store hours vary with location.

Additional Locations:
More than 150 stores throughout Southern California—call 800/GLASSES (800/452-7737).

PS Optical ★
8165 E. Wardlow Rd.
Long Beach, CA 90808
310/598-7673

Hours: Mon-Fri: 9:30-6 Sat: 9:30-5
Credit Cards: All Major
♦ **Senior Discount:** 5% **Age:** 65

PS Optical offers frames, lenses, and contacts at wholesale prices. Save 20 to 50% on your favorite styles including Giorgio Armani, Liz Claiborne, Christian Dior, Ray Ban, Polo, Gucci, Guess?, and more. PS Optical will even customize lenses for swimming goggles and diving masks, and offer the same service for most other sports. As owner Gene Hoffman states, "Service and value are our trademarks." Bring in your *Buying Retail Is Stupid!* coupon, and you'll receive a free second pair of frames from their special collection using the same prescription (not valid with senior citizen discount).

See Also: (refer to index)
　　　　Fedco
　　　　PriceCostco

With private store owners, ask if there is an additional discount when paying with cash.

MUSIC, MOVIES & LIVE ENTERTAINMENT

MUSIC & MOVIES

Aron's Record Shop
1150 N. Highland Ave.
Hollywood, CA 90038
213/469-4700

Hours: Mon-Thur: 10-10 Fri-Sat: 10-Midnight Sun: 11-8
Credit Cards: All Major

You'll always save 10 to 30% off new items such as CDs, cassettes, laser discs, and LPs. Aron's Record Shop has everything in current release, plus a wide selection of Japanese and European imports, audiophile pressings, and small local labels. Alternative and international music are specialties. They put out at least 1,000 used CDs and records each day at special discount prices. If your preferred style of music has changed, take in any of your CDs, albums, tapes, and laser discs for trade value toward the purchase of anything in the store. For extra savings, give them a call to find out when they'll be having their next parking-lot sale.

Dave's Video: The Laser Place
12144 Ventura Blvd.
Studio City, CA 91604
818/760-3472, 800/736-1659

Hours: 7 Days a Week: 10-9
Credit Cards: All Major

For the largest selection of new, used, rental, and sale laser discs in the country, try Dave's Video: The Laser Place. Every day at Dave's you can find discounts on used discs (30 to 80%) and sale prices on new discs (20 to 70%), along with more than 8,000 competitively priced new titles. Dave's will also pay cash for your laser discs. All discs are shipped free via UPS. The store also has a selection of home-theater electronics, laser disc players, and big-screen TVs at great prices.

db cooper's WHOLESALE Music Exchange ★
1724 W. Verdugo Ave.
Burbank, CA 91506
818/563-2222
Hours: Mon-Sat: 11-10 Sun: 12-7
Credit Cards: AE, MC, OPT, V

Whether you have a few CDs in your collection or hundreds, paying $13.99 to $16.99 per CD can really add up. db cooper's Wholesale Music Exchange has plenty of used CDs, and most are priced at $5.50 and $6.47. Newly acquired CDs are displayed on shelves around the store so regular customers don't have to thumb through the alphabetized CD bins. Also, with at least 15,000 new and used LPs, the largest selection in the store belongs to vinyls. All used products are guaranteed (48 hours for exchange or credit with receipt). If you want to sell some of your old music, trade-ins are accepted at any time during posted hours. You can get cash or store credits ($10 cash equals about $15 in store credits). Signing up for their mailing list is well worth it. Mailings go out five times a year, and if you're a music lover, you won't want to miss out on specials like an extra 50% off their discounted LPs (available only if you present the mailer upon purchase). When you buy three CDs, you'll receive a fourth one free if you present your *Buying Retail Is Stupid!* coupon.

Disc-Connection Compact Discs, Records & Tapes ★
10970 W. Pico Blvd.
West Los Angeles, CA 90064
310/208-7211
Hours: Mon-Thur, Sat: 11-7 Fri: 11-9 Sun: 11-9
Credit Cards: AE, DISC, MC, V

Eighty thousand albums in one room! Find me a sales clerk, quickly! Of course, with that many records, you'll always find what you want, especially since they specialize in hard-to-find movie soundtracks and Broadway show tunes or original-cast albums. They also carry cassettes (blank and pre-recorded), CDs, and records, plus tape-cleaning paraphernalia, books, and record collecting magazines. But that's not all, ladies and gents: they have a large stock of comedy and personality albums. And this store gives you money! Bring in your unwanted LPs, CDs, or cassettes, and they'll pay you cash or give you credit toward purchases. Take in your *Buying Retail Is Stupid!* coupon for an additional 10% discount on used CDs and LPs only.

Lasers Unlimited ★
2006 N. Glenoaks
Burbank, CA 91504
818/845-2219

Hours: Mon-Thur: 10-8 Fri-Sat: 10-9
Credit Cards: AE, DISC, MC, V

For the sophisticated video viewer—you know who you are—Lasers Unlimited will rent you first-run laser disc videos for $3 per day. But wait, the deal gets better. Bring in your *Buying Retail Is Stupid!* coupon or mention you have the book and you save the $5 lifetime membership fee. Once a member, you can rent three discs or more on Friday and keep them all weekend, rent two discs on Monday and Tuesday and keep them two days, and on Wednesday and Thursday rent two discs for the price of one. The same goes for thousands of older titles on disc. New laser discs are 10% off retail, and used ones can be obtained for up to 70% off. Lasers Unlimited has a new and used disc sale twice a year.

Moby Disc ★
1835 Newport Blvd., #A104
Costa Mesa, CA 92627
714/897-2799

Hours: 7 Days a Week: 10-10
Credit Cards: DISC, MC, V

Moby Disc sells new and used CDs. All used merchandise is priced as follows: CDs, $1.99 to $8.99; CD singles, 49¢ to $3.99; cassettes/LPs, 25¢ to $4.99. If you have any unwanted CDs, cassettes, or LPs, take them in for credit against your purchase. You can also get cash for your trade-ins. You'll find most of your favorite recording artists here at a "whale" of a savings. Your *Buying Retail Is Stupid!* coupon is good for a 10% discount on nonsale items only.

Additional Locations:
7 other stores throughout Southern California

Music Exchange ★
210 W. Colorado St.
Glendale, CA 91204
818/240-6539

Hours: Mon-Fri: 12-10 Sat: 11-10 Sun: 12-9
Credit Cards: MC, V

Are the prices of new CDs putting a pinch in your music budget? You can buy recycled CDs here for 99¢ to $10. Used CDs make up about half of the store and are alphabetized in bins according to artist. Before making your purchase, you can listen to any used or new CD over headsets on one of their eight CD players. If you have a few CDs lying around that you no longer listen to, take them to Music Exchange for cash or credit. All new releases are carried, and the top 30 hits are always on sale. Special orders are no problem, and they can tell you if what you're looking for is already in stock, new or used. They want their customers to be happy. All new and used CDs are guaranteed against defects. If you use your *Buying Retail Is Stupid!* coupon, you'll receive an extra 20% discount on used CDs.

Odyssey Video
11910 Wilshire Blvd.
Los Angeles, CA 90025
310/477-2523

Hours: 7 Days a Week: 9-Midnight
Credit Cards: AE, DISC, MC, V

If you've felt as if it's been an odyssey lately finding that special movie you've wanted to see, then look no more! The Odyssey carries more than 10,000 movies. And they have the lowest prices in town! Tuesdays and Thursdays their movies are 99¢ per day, and they charge only $2.49 on the other days. Musicals, westerns, children's films, and selected new releases are 99¢ every day. It takes no Herculean effort to get there, so you can cocoon the whole weekend.

Additional Location:
North Hollywood–4810 Vineland Ave., 818/769-2001

Penny Lane
1349 Third St. Promenade
Santa Monica, CA 90401
310/319-5333

Hours: 7 Days a Week: 10-Midnight
Credit Cards: All Major

Whether you prefer mainstream or eclectic music, Penny Lane has it all from A (acid jazz) to Z (zydeco), new or used, current and not so current. If you don't know where to start, there are dozens of new releases preloaded in their listening stations. In fact, you can listen to anything, new or used, prior to making a purchase. They offer a low-price guarantee, as well as trade-in allowances on used CDs and CD-ROMs. For future savings, you might want to buy one of their T-shirts. Anyone wearing a Penny Lane T-shirt always receives an extra 10% discount. Hours vary with store and season, so make a call before making the drive.

Additional Locations:
Pasadena (Old Town)–12 W. Colorado Blvd., 818/564-0161
Venice–62 Windward Ave., 310/399-4631
Westwood Village–1080 Gayley Ave., 310/208-5611

Record Surplus
11609 Pico Blvd.
West Los Angeles, CA 90064
310/478-4217

Hours: Mon-Thur: 11-9 Fri-Sat: 11-10 Sun: 11-7
Credit Cards: AE, DISC, MC, V

Record Surplus (A.K.A. The Last Record Store) has used records and tapes starting as low as 46¢ and CDs starting at 92¢. They have all styles and categories of music—rock, jazz, soul, classical, movie soundtracks, and collectibles—guaranteed to tickle anyone's fancy. You can also get cash for your old LPs, CDs, cassettes, and videos. Each store provides listening stations for customers to use prior to making purchases. Customer satisfaction is guaranteed.

Rockaway Records
2395 Glendale Blvd.
Los Angeles, CA 90036
213/664-3232

Hours: 7 Days a Week: 10-9:30
Credit Cards: AE, MC, OPT, V

Music lovers can save plenty of money on preowned CDs, LPs, and 45s at Rockaway Records. CD prices start at $2.99 from a collection numbering in the thousands. To give you an idea of the vast selection, during their parking-lot sales more than 20,000 CDs are featured with prices starting at 49¢ each. That's a lot of CDs! Parking-lot sales are held four times a year. Other than CDs, you'll find records and everything else in the store discounted an additional 10 to 50%. Call to find out when the next parking-lot sale will be held.

Second Time Around Records ★
7704 Melrose Ave.
Los Angeles, CA 90046
213/852-1982

Hours: Mon-Sat: 11-9 Sun: 12-8
Credit Cards: AE, DISC, MC, V

Love isn't the only thing better the second time around. Go to Second Time Around Records and you'll see what we mean. Shoppers will find new and used records, CDs, tapes, and videos as well as used stereo equipment. Because they love a good challenge, they'll hunt down and find any record you want. Elvis and Beatles lovers will find collectibles among their memorabilia. Used records sell for as little as 99¢, and during their weekend sales, prices start at 10¢. Don't forget to take along your *Buying Retail Is Stupid!* coupon to receive an additional 10% discount. Some stores may be called Discount Records.

Additional Locations:
Buena Park–8682 Beach Blvd., 714/821-1985
Costa Mesa–2750 Harbor Blvd., 714/662-1983
El Toro–23720-B El Toro Rd., 714/587-1987

Super Pops Record Detective ★
1242 3rd St., #102
Santa Monica, CA 90401
310/395-1344

Hours: Mon: 1-5 Tues: 2-5 Fri-Sat: 1-6 Sun: 1-5
Credit Cards: Cash or Checks Only
♦ **Senior Discount:** 20% **Age:** 62

You'll find used CDs and tapes here, but the focus is on rare LPs. The hours are limited because the primary business is searching for out-of-print records or CDs, which is done free of charge. All you have to do is give them a call (or leave a message on the answering machine), and they will do their best to find the long-lost album of your dreams. Prices start at $1 for records and go up depending on the age and condition. CDs and imports start at $6. You'll receive a 10% discount on your purchase when you present your *Buying Retail Is Stupid!* coupon (not valid with senior citizen discount).

Tower Outlet
14621 Ventura Blvd.
Sherman Oaks, CA 91403
818/783-8810

Hours: 7 Days a Week: 10-10
Credit Cards: All Major

It seems as though every time you turn around another chain of retail stores is opening an outlet. The music industry is no exception. Tower Outlet is filled with new CDs, new and viewed movies on video, laser discs, LPs, and cassettes at deeply discounted prices. Most of the store is devoted to videos that were previously used as rentals in the Tower retail stores. Prices for used videos run 99¢ to $14.95 in every category. Laser discs at Tower Outlet are new, and titles vary from visit to visit, with prices starting as low as $3.95. Although the store doesn't sell used CDs, the prices are as low as those at many used CDs stores. Prices are 99¢ to $8.99 (up to $17.99 retail) for all types of music, with the largest selection devoted to rock, classical, and jazz. Sometimes they have CDs that are currently being sold in their retail stores. There's a small selection of new cassettes for 49¢ to $3.99, and LPs are 25¢ to $4.99. In this same area are discounted accessories such as CD and cassette racks. You may be surprised to see discounted books in the store. Tower also has book stores out of the area and sends all excess stock to this location.

The Tune-Up Shop
173 Pier Ave.
Santa Monica, CA 90405
310/314-1621

Hours: Mon-Fri: 11-7   Sat: 11-6   Sun: 12-5
Credit Cards: AE, MC, V

Tired of paying top dollar for your favorite music? Stop by The Tune-Up Shop, where you can find new and used CDs at savings of 20 to 40%. They have a wide selection of music including alternative, rock, soul, jazz, and world beats with prices starting at 99¢. The Tune-Up Shop will also buy your old CDs.

See Also: (refer to index)
> Green Ginger Bookshop
> Pasadena City College Flea Market

LIVE ENTERTAINMENT

Audiences Unlimited, Inc.

100 Universal City Plaza, Bldg. 153
Universal City, CA 91608
818/753-3470

Hours: Mon-Fri: 9-6

We love telling you about free things—here's one to paste on your refrigerator. Audiences Unlimited offers you a chance to be in the audience for such hit TV shows as *Roseanne, Grace Under Fire, Cybil, Married With Children*, and many more. Just send a self-addressed, stamped envelope for a show schedule for the month. There are more than 40 network shows to choose from. You can make reservations by phone or mail. The telephone number above will give you all the details. This can be a fun evening activity for your out-of-town guests.

Hollywood Bowl

2301 N. Highland Ave.
Hollywood, CA 90068
213/850-2000

Hours: Tues, Thur-Fri—Call First
Credit Cards: Free

If you really enjoy great music and really appreciate the simple pleasures in life, keep your ears tuned for the FREE Hollywood Bowl performance rehearsals that take place July through September. They usually rehearse Tuesdays, Thursdays, and Fridays between 9 and 11 a.m., but be sure to call first to check on the season's schedule.

"On the House" ★

P.O. Box 5215
Santa Monica, CA 90409
310/392-7588

Hours: Tues: 1-5 Wed-Fri: 11-5
Credit Cards: Checks Only

Once in a while, you'll hear about something that seems "too good to be true," but that's not the case with "On the House." It is a theater membership club in which members pay annual dues of $149, for two people, to receive 12 months of free tickets to every event their service offers (25 to 40 events each week). You could literally attend a different performance every night of the week if time allowed. "On the House" doesn't advertise, so members just pass the good news along to friends. You will enjoy everything from live theater, small theaters, large theaters, movie screenings at major picture studios, and nightclub shows to dance events. There's a special reservation number and a private 24-hour hot line announcing what shows are available. Your *Buying Retail Is Stupid!* coupon has two different offers. If you're interested in a membership, the coupon is good for a 10% discount on membership fees. If you want to test the waters before joining, you can use the coupon for a free pair of tickets. All you have to do is give them a call. After you speak to them about times and dates, send them your coupon, and they'll send you the free tickets.

Theatre LA—The Discount Ticket Outlet
Los Angeles, CA 90017
213/688-ARTS (688-2787)

Hours: Tues-Sat: 12-5
Credit Cards: AE, MC, V

Do you love going to the theater but just can't afford the high prices? Here's the perfect solution to seeing your favorite shows at up to 50% off the regular price. First, call Theatre LA's information line at 213/688-ARTS, open 24 hours, seven days a week. You'll hear a complete list of events: theater, music, dance, fine and performing arts, and special museum events. Each category offers details about dates, times, names and addresses of where events are being held, and phone numbers for more information. There's something suitable for everyone. When we placed a call to the information line, just a few of the places mentioned were Cerritos Center for the Arts, Actors Alley, Tiffany Theatre, Gene Autry Museum, and Watts Towers. In order to take advantage of the discounts, you must be an associate member. Annual fees are $35. You can sign up over the phone by calling their direct line at 213/614-0556. Membership information is also available on the main menu of the information line (213/688-2787). After receiving your membership card, you can present the card at the box office for your discount. Have a wonderful time at all the cultural events Los Angeles has to offer!

> Network with friends and family regarding special sales and favorite discount stores—a list of everyone's favorite places may be a gold mine.

MUSIC STORES

Ace Music
1714 Wilshire Blvd.
Santa Monica, CA 90403
310/828-5688

Hours: Mon-Sat: 10-6
Credit Cards: AE, DISC, MC, V

Finally, a store that quotes discount prices over the telephone without hemming and hawing. They just tell those customers what they want to hear. That may be because this store has had continuous ownership since 1964, guaranteeing interest in the customer after the sale. As far as guitars are concerned, a lifetime service warranty of their own accompanies every guitar purchased here. A recent addition is a complete repair facility for guitars. They have brand-name musical instruments, such as Fender, Gibson, Martin, Gretsch, and Guild, and all makes and models of electric and acoustic guitars, amps, and PA equipment. Every instrument is serviced prior to being added to the sales floor. They service all the products they sell and have complete teaching facilities. They offer a special in-store warranty beyond what the manufacturers offer. You can expect to save 20 to 50% off retail prices.

Amendola Music, Inc. ★
1692 Centinela Ave.
Inglewood, CA 90302
310/645-2420

Hours: Tues-Fri: 11-6 Sat: 10-5
Credit Cards: AE, MC, V
♦ **Senior Discount:** 5% **Age:** 55

At Amendola Music, you can save up to 40% off the manufacturer's retail price on musical instruments, amplification systems, professional sound systems, deejay equipment, and other accessories. They carry such names as Ovation, Yamaha, Tama, Ludwig, Zildjian, Paiste, Shure, Bach, Peavey, Gemini, and more. They also have a complete repair center, and financing is available. Use your *Buying Retail Is Stupid!* coupon for an extra 20% discount.

Goodman Music

3501 Cahuenga Blvd. West
Los Angeles, CA 90068
213/845-1145

Hours: Mon-Sat: 10-6
Credit Cards: All Major

You'll find that Goodman Music has discounted prices on a large selection of keyboards and professional audio gear—including direct-to-disc and digital multi-track recording equipment—and microphones. They also carry a full line of synthesizers and software. Brand names include Apple, Sony, Digidesign, Roland, Yamaha, Korg, Peavey, and Lexicon. Make sure you put your name on their mailing list. During special sales, savings can run up to 80% off retail.

The Guitar Store ★

496 E. Holt Ave.
Pomona, CA 91767
909/623-6448

Hours: Mon-Fri: 10-7 Sat: 10-6
Credit Cards: AE, DISC, MC, V

This discount music store, offering up to 50% off retail prices, is a dream come true for professional bands. They have 10,000 square feet stocked with a full line of guitars, amplifiers, drums, keyboards, sound systems, recording equipment, stage lighting, and accessories. With their seven departments staffed by experts, you'll get straight answers to your questions. Some of the brands carried are Yamaha, Roland, JBL, Tama, and Fender. They handle both new and used items and offer a school band rental program through NEMC (National Educational Music Co.). Trade-ins are accepted, and they buy used equipment. Financing is available. Need new guitar strings? When you buy a set, you'll get a second set free (a $7 to $60 value) with your *Buying Retail Is Stupid!* coupon.

Musician's Warehouse

1878 N. Placentia Ave.
Placentia, CA 92670
714/528-3370

Hours: Mon-Thur: 10-8 Fri: 10-7 Sat: 10-6 Sun: 11-5
Credit Cards: All Major

Anyone working at Musician's Warehouse is a musician—which is a great selling point, since they specialize in after-sales support on purchases of their guitars, keyboards, amps, PA systems, recording equipment, and drums. Their customer service is fantastic, and the "extras" are a real bonus: seminars and special one-time artist events; private guitar, piano, and drum lessons with recitals; and special student discounts. Plus, you save 20 to 50% off retail prices. They also have a complete computer hardware and software sales and support department. Brand names you'll recognize are Korg, Roland, Digitech, Alesis, Fender, Taylor, SWR, Marshall, Studiomaster, Anvil, Tama, Shure, Ampex, and many more. If you have a nagging urge to perform, every Friday is "Open Mike" night and is completely free to the public. There are five sales during the year, so get on their mailing list.

Nadine's Music
6251 Santa Monica Blvd.
Hollywood, CA 90038
213/464-7550

Hours: Mon, Fri, Sat: 10-6 Tues-Thurs: 10-7
Credit Cards: All Major

Nadine's has been in the music biz since the 1970s, selling guitars, amps, keyboards, multi-track tape recorders, acoustic drums, microphones, PA systems, speakers, computers, and software at a minimum of 20% below retail prices. They carry such brand names as Fender, Gibson, Roland, Korg, Peavey, Akai, Mackie, Alesis, Electro-Voice, and JBL. There is no high-pressure salesmanship; the people are all friendly and knowledgeable and really want to help. Great prices and good service—what more could you want?

Sightsinger Music
3203 S. Harbor Blvd.
Santa Ana, CA 92704
714/540-1441

Hours: Mon-Fri: 10-8 Sat: 10-6 Sun: 12-5
Credit Cards: AE, DISC, MC, V

Looking for discounts starting at 20% off retail on the best in electronic keyboards, synthesizers, music computers, music software, guitars (acoustic and electric), amplifiers, PA systems, drums, or accessories? At Sightsinger Music, you'll find name brands such as Roland, Yamaha, Korg, Fender, Taylor, Martin, Takamine, Ovation, JBL, Ibanez, Mackie, Alesis, Ampeg, Gibson, and Ramsa. They have one of the largest selections in musical gear, along with a very service-oriented and knowledgeable staff. Satisfied musicians have been buying equipment at Sightsinger Music since 1964. Financing is available.

West L.A. Music
11345 Santa Monica Blvd.
Los Angeles, CA 90025
310/477-1945, 818/905-7020
Hours: Mon-Fri: 11-7 Sat: 10-6
Credit Cards: All Major

This is THE music store, where you can find everything in professional audio equipment, everything in musical instruments, and everyone who is anyone in the music/recording industry. The recording stars aren't on Hollywood Boulevard or Sunset. They're at West L.A. Music, buying the equipment they need for their studios, band members, and tours. West L.A. Music will beat any deal you can get anywhere else, and they have guitars, speakers, drums, microphones and stands, keyboards, synthesizers, computers and music software, recording equipment, and all accessories. They are usually the first in town to get the newest items, and they have frequent special sales, so check them out often if music is your beat. If you're interested in a particular item, call to see when a factory rep will be doing a demo. You'll find helpful and knowledgeable salespeople to assist you in every department.

Woodlowe Music Center
21410 Ventura Blvd.
Woodland Hills, CA 91364
818/883-0050
Hours: Mon-Fri: 10-8 Sat: 10-6
Credit Cards: MC, V
♦ **Senior Discount:** 15% **Age:** 55

Woodlowe Music Center offers a terrific range of merchandise and service, at 20 to 40% off retail prices. In addition to selling quality instruments, such as guitars, drums, clarinets, flutes, trumpets, and violins, they have one of the finest teaching staffs in the San Fernando Valley. Among other related items carried are amplifiers, sheet music, books, and microphones. They have provided fantastic service since 1960, along with instrument rentals and repairs.

Test small electrical products
in the store prior to completing
the purchase.

PIANOS & KEYBOARDS

Hollywood Piano Rental Co.
1647 N. Highland Ave.
Hollywood, CA 90028
213/462-2329, 800/881-7426

Hours: Mon-Fri: 9-5:30 Sat: 9-4 Sun: 12-5
Credit Cards: MC, V

Family owned since 1928, Hollywood Piano Rental Co. offers savings of 10 to 20% on all types of pianos and organs for home or professional needs. They have about 400 pianos for rent, and they also sell both new and used pianos in all styles. In-house financing is available.

Keyboard Concepts Inc.
5600 Van Nuys Blvd.
Van Nuys, CA 91401
818/787-0201, 800/818-PIANO (800/818-7426)

Hours: Mon-Sat: 10-7 Sun: 12-5
Credit Cards: All Major

Keyboard Concepts has a very large selection of new and used acoustic and digital pianos and home keyboards on display in a 12,000-square-foot showroom. You'll save 30 to 50% on such brand names as Yamaha, Steinway, Baldwin, Schimmel, Young Chang, and more. With each purchase of a new keyboard, they offer free lessons. In addition to pianos and keyboards, they have plenty of sheet music and keyboard accessories, such as stands, pedals, software, and more. Need to rent instead of purchase? Keyboard Concepts can solve the problem. Owners Dennis and Jeff are committed to serving their customers—so, give them a call.

Keyboard Country Inc. ★
551 N. Azusa Ave.
West Covina, CA 91791
818/858-6100, 800/PIANO-88 (742-6688)

Hours: Mon-Fri: 10-8 Sat: 10-6 Sun: 11-6
Credit Cards: All Major
♦ **Senior Discount:** 10% **Age:** 55

Learning about Keyboard Country Inc. will be music to your ears. They have the largest selection in Los Angeles of digital pianos and organs, featuring Roland, Kurzweil, Korg, Technics, Young Chang, and many more. Best of all, they guarantee the lowest price—otherwise, you receive the difference plus $200. With your *Buying Retail Is Stupid!* coupon and purchase of a new organ, you'll receive lifetime free music lessons plus free organ delivery.

Merrill's Music ★
1428 4th St.
Santa Monica, CA 90401
310/393-0344

Hours: Mon-Fri: 10-7 Sat: 10-6 Sun: 12-5
Credit Cards: All Major

Merrill's Music is the place to go for pianos, keyboards, and professional audio products. Discounts run 20 to 50% off retail on all major brands such as Yamaha, Kawai, Technics, Roland, Casio, and others. If within 60 days of purchasing an item from Merrill's you see it for less money, you can get a refund of the difference. Rentals start at $10 for acoustic pianos and $15 for electronic keyboards. Should you buy from Merrill's and later decide to trade up, you get the full price credited to your new purchase. This trade-in policy is good for one full year on electronic keyboards and for five years on acoustic keyboards. For the best deals, check out their used pianos and keyboards. The prices are usually lower than what you would pay a private party and include a full 10-year parts and labor warranty, plus delivery and tuning in your home. Also, they have a "music software bar." They don't carry drums or guitars. You'll receive an extra 10% discount when you use your *Buying Retail Is Stupid!* coupon.

Piano & Keyboard Finders
13370 E. Firestone Blvd., Unit A
Santa Fe Springs, CA 90670
310/926-6666, 800/576-3463

Hours: Mon-Fri: 11-6 Sat: 10-5 Sun: 12-5
Credit Cards: AE, MC, V

You won't have to dream anymore about owning a grand, vertical, or digital piano, portable keyboard, or organ. Now you can save 50% or more on privately owned used pianos, new discontinued models, and bank and finance company repossessions from Piano & Keyboard Finders, the largest supplier of used pianos in the United States. Featured in their showroom are name brands such as Steinway, Kawai, Mason & Hamlin, Samick, Chickering, Yamaha, Kimball, Kohler & Campbell, Baldwin, Roland, Suzuki, and more. Call their 800 number and receive a free copy of their piano trader publication. "The Vance Piano Trader" features 35 to 70 listings of privately owned, used pianos that are still located in sellers' homes. If you want to list your piano in their publication, there's a charge of $29.95.

REPAIRS

United Band Instrument Co.
3833 W. Avenue 43
Los Angeles, CA 90041
213/257-7514

Hours: Tues-Sat: 10-5
Credit Cards: Cash or Checks Only

If you have a woodwind or brass instrument in need of repair, take it to
United Band Instrument Co. They have been in business since 1954 and
know their stuff! Repairs cost about 30% less than you'd pay elsewhere.
They also carry musical accessories, and you can find bargains on used
instruments when available.

> Unless you pay off your credit
> card balance monthly, pay
> with cash or check instead—
> interest payments on credit card
> balances can wipe out any
> discounts and more.

ONE-STOP SUPPLIERS

A 'N B Stationery ★

12338 Ventura Blvd.
Studio City, CA 91604
818/760-0244, 213/877-8466

Hours: Mon-Fri: 9-5:30 Sat: 10-5
Credit Cards: AE, MC, OPT, V

This is a small, personal store, but their stock and service are large. A 'N B Stationery carries a complete line of office supplies, office furniture, accounting and computer supplies, and even gifts and greeting cards. You will discover all major brands at a 20-to-50% savings. Call to find out about A 'N B Stationery's quarterly sales for even bigger discounts. There's an additional 10% discount when you present your *Buying Retail Is Stupid!* coupon (nonsale items only).

Office Depot

675 E. Hospitality Lane
San Bernardino, CA 92408
909/885-0097

Hours: Mon-Fri: 7 a.m.-9 p.m. Sat: 9-9 Sun: 10-6
Credit Cards: All Major

Office Depot is a warehouse store with low prices, and you don't have to sacrifice service for savings. Their knowledgeable sales staff will assist you or answer any questions you may have about office supplies, equipment, or furniture at this one-stop shop. They offer discount prices on thousands of best-selling, top-quality, brand-name office products in their huge, no-frills warehouse stores. Hours can vary from location to location, and some stores are closed Sundays.

Additional Locations:
52 other stores throughout Southern California—call 800/685-8800.

> Scanners aren't always correct; make certain that the scanned price is the same as the shelf price.

BUSINESS MACHINES

Arttype Business Machines ★
15420 Devonshire St.
Missions Hills, CA 91345
818/893-8066, 800/530-COPY (530-2679)

Hours: Mon-Fri: 8:30-5 Sat: 10-2
Credit Cards: AE, MC, V
♦ **Senior Discount:** 10% **Age:** 65

Arttype has copiers, computers, fax machines, typewriters, word-processing calculators, and supplies. Bob Lowry guarantees the lowest prices around, and they handle most name brands such as IBM, T/A Adler-Royal, Sharp, Brother, and Panasonic. The best buys of all are on refurbished copiers and fax machines that come with a 90-day warranty. Arttype is a warranty service center for most brands and has friendly, knowledgeable service. Your *Buying Retail Is Stupid!* coupon is good for a 10% discount on all supplies such as ribbons and ink cartridges (not valid with senior citizen discount).

Star Office Machines
11353 Santa Monica Blvd.
Los Angeles, CA 90025
310/477-6091

Hours: Mon-Fri: 9:30-6 Sat: 10-5
Credit Cards: MC, V

You can save up to 50% on typewriters, answering machines, cash registers, dictating machines, calculators, copy machines, and more. Star Office Machines carries Canon, IBM, Sanyo, Olympia, Sharp, Texas Instruments, Brother, and Smith-Corona and provides in-house service. An extra 3% discount is available for cash transactions.

NEW & USED OFFICE FURNITURE & EQUIPMENT

A.B.E. Corporation
3400 N. Peck Rd.
El Monte, CA 91732
818/443-4223, 800/564-4223

Hours: Mon-Fri: 8-6 Sat: 9-5
Credit Cards: MC, V

A.B.E. Corporation has specialized in purchasing, recycling, and selling high-quality, pre-owned office furniture and equipment since 1964. They buy from savings and loans and other failed businesses, so they can pass on huge savings (up to 90%). There is a multi-million-dollar inventory to choose from in their 40,000-square-foot showroom, which is one of the largest in California; they have another 125,000 square feet of warehouse and a fleet of trucks for pick-up and delivery. They boast being the largest company specializing in recycled office furniture; from what we can tell, there is no disagreement. By the way, as with all recycled merchandise, quality and selection vary from visit to visit.

Affordable Used Office Furniture ★

16028 Sherman Way
Van Nuys, CA 91406
818/785-4010

Hours: Mon-Fri: 8-5 Sat: 10-3
Credit Cards: AE, MC, OPT, V
♦ **Senior Discount:** 10% **Age:** 65

Affordable Used Office Furniture's goal is to offer affordable used furniture to new and start-up companies. They say, "We don't have the largest selection of stock, but what we have is priced to move." Their reupholstered chairs—available in a variety of colors—cost far below the prices of new ones. Stock varies from week to week, and deliveries are usually available the same day of purchase. Affordable also buys and trades furniture. Owner Myron Thomas has advised us that every price is negotiable. So get out your Herb Cohen *How to Negotiate Anything* book, and brush up on your skills. Bring your *Buying Retail Is Stupid!* 10% coupon for additional savings (not valid with senior citizen discount).

American Surplus ★

18643 Parthenia St.
Northridge, CA 91324
818/993-5355

Hours: Mon-Fri: 8:30-5:30 Sat: 10:30-3:30
Credit Cards: MC, V

American Surplus specializes in Holga office furniture and has 6,000 square feet of desks, secretarial chairs, executive chairs, file cabinets, lateral files, storage cabinets, shelf files, bookcases, and computer furniture. You'll find new items, which are factory seconds, used furniture, and industrial shelving. You can anticipate saving 15 to 60% off retail, but if you use your *Buying Retail Is Stupid!* coupon, you'll save an additional 10%!

M.L.E. The Office Furniture Warehouse
260 N. Palm St.
Brea, CA 92621
714/680-6831

Hours: Mon-Fri: 8:30-5:30 Sat: 9-5
Credit Cards: AE, DISC, MC, V

The motto of M.L.E. The Office Furniture Warehouse is "No one, but no one, sells for less!" Their 32,000-square-foot store has filing cabinets, chairs, desks, tables, lamps, computer furniture, and much more by names such as Hon, Globe, Bevis, and Microcentre. They guarantee the best price, even below the superstores. If you see a lower price on the same brand name and model number, they'll confirm the information by phone. Comparing apples with apples, if the price is lower than theirs, they'll beat the price. Generally prices are 40 to 60% off retail. Delivery service also is available. Ask about their parking-lot sales featuring prices below cost.

See Also: (refer to index)
Cort Furniture Rental Clearance Center

> When going through the daily newspaper, keep alert for going-out-of-business sales.

Party & Paper Goods

COSTUMES

Magic World ★
10122 Topanga Canyon Blvd.
Chatsworth, CA 91311
818/700-8100

Hours: Mon-Fri: 7:30-6:30 Sat: 9-6
Credit Cards: All Major

If you're tired of showing up in the same Halloween costume every year, have we found a deal for you. Magic World runs a special every October, in which you can rent just about any of their 15,000 costumes for the entire month for a one-day rental fee. Most costumes, available in everything from ancient Roman to Zorro, rent for $25 to $85, with the average price running about $45. The only costumes that aren't included in the rental special are their one-of-a-kind costumes, such as an elaborate Henry VIII costume made of heavy brocade and velvet for $200 a day, or their plush animal or food (tomato, banana, hot dog, or hamburger) costumes. In addition to rentals, Magic World sells costumes, accessories, and theatrical make-up, plus magician supplies (amateur to professional), at 20% below retail. If you're having a party, you can get 60 balloons, ribbon, and a tank for $19.95. Take in your *Buying Retail Is Stupid!* coupon for an extra 5% discount.

Shelly's Discount Costumes and Accessories ★
2091 Westwood Blvd.
Westwood, CA 90025
310/475-1400

Hours: Mon-Sat: 10-6 Sun: 11-4
Credit Cards: AE, DISC, MC, V

If you want to be someone else for a night, and we do mean anyone, this is a great place to shop. The studios shop here because Shelly's has costumes and accessories year-round. Accessorizing your costume can be the most fun of all. Shelly's has at least 50 styles of gloves in 100 colors, and more than 500 styles of hats. They also have a full line of FX make-up (including the gory stuff), wigs, wands, swords, wings, masks, and lots more. Discounts on these items run 20 to 40% off retail. Comparison-shopping costumes for this store is difficult, because for the most part, it is impossible to compare apples with apples. When *The*

Little Mermaid movie was popular, Shelly's had the costumes priced for $30 to $50. We found Little Mermaid costumes in other stores in the same price range, but what a difference in the product. The costume at Shelly's was much more elaborate in fancy fabrics with lots of attention to detail. Most costumes come complete with accessories; all you have to do is supply the makeup and shoes. The store in Tarzana, Apparel Warehouse, also carries costumes and accessories, but the selection is quite a bit smaller than at the Westwood store. Your *Buying Retail Is Stupid!* coupon is good for an extra 20% discount.

Additional Location:
Tarzana–Apparel Warehouse, 6010 Yolanda St., 818/344-3224

See Also: (refer to index)
        Jim's One Stop Party Shop

PARTY & PAPER SUPPLIES

Alin Party Supply ★
4929 Woodruff Ave.
Lakewood, CA 90713
310/925-5501

Hours: Mon-Fri: 9-9 Sat: 9-6 Sun: 10-5
Credit Cards: AE, DISC, MC, V

This store is the greatest! Whatever you need for your next celebration can be found at Alin Party Supply at 10 to 50% below retail. They carry a complete line of supplies for banquets, parties, weddings, and receptions, including invitations (regular, religious, Spanish, Mormon, and Jewish). You'll find supplies for anniversaries, luaus, bar mitzvahs, Quince Anos, and more. Have a wedding coming up? Select your invitations from more than 20 sample books, all of which are available at full-priced competitors, and save up to 30% on your order. They have a great selection of wrapping supplies and low rental rates for tables and chairs. Buy as much or as little as you need, and don't forget your *Buying Retail Is Stupid!* coupon good for a 10% discount.

Additional Locations:
Downey–12270 Paramount Blvd., 310/862-1661
Fountain Valley–17070 Magnolia St., 714/847-1688
Riverside–6493 Magnolia Ave., 909/682-7441

Box City ★
16113 Sherman Way
Van Nuys, CA 91406
818/901-0336, 800/992-6924

Hours: Mon-Sat: 9-6 Sun: 10-4
Credit Cards: AE, DISC, MC, V
♦ **Senior Discount:** 10% **Age:** 62

If you need a box of any kind, this is definitely your sort of place. Gift boxes, mailing boxes, shipping boxes, and moving boxes—whatever kind of box you need they have, plus all necessary supplies for shipping and moving. Not only do they have every kind of box imaginable, but also you can expect to save big bucks! We can't mention any names, but Box City is 30 to 50% lower than a well-known do-it-yourself moving business that most of us have used in the past—and wait; it gets better! Box City charges 50% less for their boxes than your major moving companies, and the owner will accept a 10% *Buying Retail Is Stupid!* coupon (not valid with senior citizen discount).

Additional Locations:
North Hollywood–12800 Victory Blvd., 818/982-5675
Pasadena–2650 E. Colorado Blvd., 818/432-1678
Valencia–23403 Lyons Ave., 805/254-1178
West Los Angeles–10775 W. Pico Blvd., 310/474-5144

Box Connection
120 Industry Ave.
La Habra, CA 90631
714/525-7697

Hours: Mon-Fri: 8-5 Sat: 8-12
Credit Cards: AE, MC, V

Save 25 to 35% on all moving accessories at Box Connection. They carry a huge assortment of professional-grade boxes and supplies. All boxes are suitable for moving or shipping cross-country via UPS, air freight, rail, or van lines. They offer free packing tips as well as free local delivery, and guarantee the lowest price. Box Connection also has an exclusive "Recycling Incentive Plan," which states that when you've completed your move, they'll pick up your used boxes at no charge and refund 20% of your purchase price.

Current Factory Outlet

2150 Nevada St., #110
Corona, CA 91720
909/270-0166

Hours: Mon-Sat: 10-6 Sun: 11-5
Credit Cards: DISC, MC, V

This hidden treasure is one of four outlet stores (and more coming) in Southern California selling discontinued merchandise from Current mail-order catalogs. Their stock consists of cards, gifts, stationery, and gift wrap. Savings are generally 50 to 80% off retail prices. Their number one goal is customer service, and they offer to promptly replace your order or refund your money if you're not satisfied with their products or service. Call about their special sales offering an additional savings of 40%. Hours vary from location to location.

Additional Locations:
Covina–1404 N. Azusa, 818/332-1869
El Cajon–173 Fletcher Pkwy., 619/440-4292
Escondido–1054 W. Valley Pkwy., 619/738-7181
Oxnard–1863 Ventura Blvd., 805/981-9191
Stanton–12781 Beach Blvd., 714/893-6068

Individual Paper Products

5333 Downy Rd.
Vernon, CA 90058
213/583-4121, 800/464-4121

Hours: Mon-Fri: 7-5
Credit Cards: Cash or Checks Only

This store is family owned and has been in business since 1926. This is a no-frills warehouse where you can save big bucks on paper, plastic, and aluminum products. They also carry cleaning supplies. If you don't care what is imprinted on the paper plates, napkins, and cups, you will save even more than the usual 25 to 50% off retail, because they buy the overruns from manufacturers. Get on their mailing list so you'll be in on their special sales.

> Once a year, buy birthday, anniversary, and generic cards, plus wrapping paper, to save individual trips to the store for each occasion.

Party Corner Discount Center ★
11422 Laurel Canyon Blvd.
Mission Hills, CA 91345
818/365-6909

Hours: Mon-Sat: 10-6 Sun: 11-4
Credit Cards: All Major
♦ **Senior Discount:** 10% **Age:** 65

Party planning is a cinch with Party Corner's large selection of party supplies, which includes decorations, wedding invitations, crepe paper, garlands, and decorations for cars. They'll blow your balloons up for you, or you can rent a helium tank and do it yourself. Expect to find discounts in the neighborhood of 10 to 50% off retail prices, and greeting cards are always 50% off. Can't think of anything to wear as a costume for that come-as-you-are party? You'll find it and much more at Party Corner Discount Center. They rent and sell costumes, along with accessories, wigs, and masks. They have more than 1,000 costumes, so you can definitely attend your party in style! When you use your *Buying Retail Is Stupid!* coupon, you'll save 10% more on your purchase (not valid with senior citizen discount).

Additional Locations:
North Hollywood–11371 Riverside Dr., 818/506-4785
Tarzana–6038 Reseda Blvd., 818/343-3343

Party World
25410 Marguerite Pkwy.
Mission Viejo, CA 92691
714/768-3850

Hours: Mon-Fri: 10-8 Sat: 9-6 Sun: 10-4
Credit Cards: MC, V

There are 20 Party World stores in Southern California. Each store is a one-stop center for all your party needs. Save 10 to 70% on everything from invitations to helium tanks and balloons. If you are going to have a party for your child, you'll be pleased to know they have more than 27 birthday patterns available. To give your next bash a personal touch, make sure to inquire about their custom imprinting service. Whether you're having a party for 2 or 2,000, Party World has it all.

Additional Locations:
19 other stores throughout Southern California

See Also: (refer to index)
        Haz Equipment Rentals
        Smart & Final

PARTY RENTALS & SERVICES

Calligraphy by Gary Mond
6524 Ventura Canyon Ave.
Van Nuys, CA 91401
818/786-6085

Hours: Mon-Fri: 8:30-6 Sat: By Appointment Only
Credit Cards: Cash or Checks Only

Add that special touch to your envelopes, placecards, diplomas, poems, awards, stationery, and certificates with Calligraphy by Gary Mond. Since 1984, he has personally calligraphied (by hand, not computer) unique designs at savings of 20 to 25% off other calligrapher prices. There are 10 calligraphy styles to choose from, and he can produce your product in gold, white, or silver ink for an additional charge. The turnaround time is quick for most projects. Calligraphy is not a hobby for Gary. He's a professional calligrapher and is always available to new as well as present clients.

Jim's One Stop Party Shop ★
7918 Foothill Blvd.
Sunland, CA 91040
818/352-8893

Hours: Mon-Fri: 9-6 Sat: 8-4:30
Credit Cards: DISC, MC, V
♦ **Senior Discount:** 10% **Age:** 62

Whether you are throwing a backyard wedding, a home party, a picnic, or a corporate event, Jim's One Stop Party Shop will create, plan, coordinate, cater, and clean up for just one low cost. For $8.99 per person (minimum 50 people), Jim's will deliver tables, chairs, paper goods, coffee, punch, bread, cold meats, cheese, condiments, salads, a gazebo, and a uniformed server. Most caterers charge nearly that much for the food alone. The same package with hot food is $14.99 per person. Also, Jim's has more than 10,000 costumes for sale or rent. Any kind of costume imaginable can be found, including tuxedos, at savings ranging from 25 to 40% off retail. Remember to take in your *Buying Retail Is Stupid!* coupon and you'll save an extra 10%.

Jukeboxes 4 Rent ★
818/366-9400, 800/JUKE-KIX (585-3549)

Hours: 7 Days a Week: 10 a.m.-10 p.m.
Credit Cards: Cash or Checks Only

It's party time and you need some music to liven it up. Try an alternative to a disc jockey or live musicians and rent a jukebox from Jukeboxes 4 Rent.

Cost for a one-day rental starts at $150 (a deejay usually costs $300 to $400). They have record selections dating back to 1913 (hear Al Jolson sing) as well as the current sound, including country & western. You'll have more than 4,000 songs from which to choose. Rental price includes delivery and pick-up in the San Fernando Valley. There's an additional nominal charge for out-of-area deliveries and hauling a jukebox over steps, lawn, gravel, or dirt. Bring in your *Buying Retail Is Stupid!* coupon and save an additional 5% off your rental.

Sir Michael's Limousine Service ★

2625 West Ave. 32
Los Angeles, CA 90065
213/225-5466

Hours: 7 Days a Week: 24 Hours a Day
Credit Cards: AE, MC, V
♦ **Senior Discount:** 10% **Age:** 60

If your special event requires you to arrive in style, or you are just looking for a fun night on the town, we have the answer. Since 1983, Sir Michael's Limousine Service has been offering rates 20% below their competitors. Sir Michael's has an entire fleet of limousines including Rolls Royce, Mercedes, Cadillac, Lincoln, and 15 passenger vans. Rates are $55 per hour with a three-hour minimum, and include tax and gratuity! In addition, reservations made for Sunday through Thursday for at least four hours receive a fifth hour free. Sir Michael's Limousine Service will not be undersold; and they guarantee the best prices in town. Remember your *Buying Retail Is Stupid!* coupon and you'll save an extra 10% off two limousines ordered at one time (not valid with senior citizen discount).

See Also: (refer to index)
Clarice's Cake Decorating and Candy Making Supplies

When getting bids for any kind of work, try for a minimum of three—and don't automatically go for the lowest bid; first check referrals.

Birds Plus
14041 Burbank Blvd.
Van Nuys, CA 91401
818/901-1187

Hours: 7 Days a Week: 10-6
Credit Cards: MC, V

Birds Plus specializes in exotic birds, cages, and supplies at savings of 20 to 40% off the prices charged in retail pet stores. They carry all name-brand pet products. Whether you're feeding a parakeet or a pelican, they can help you with any of your bird needs or problems. They offer boarding and consulting on breeding, and groom for free. Call to find out about their special sales held throughout the year.

Bracken Bird Farm
10797 New Jersey St.
Redlands, CA 92373
909/792-5735

Hours: Mon, Wed-Sun: 9-5 (Closed Tuesday)
Credit Cards: DISC, MC, V (Checks accepted only for under $100)

For all of you bird lovers out there, we have found a place where many pet store owners buy their stock. The Bracken Bird Farm is an acre filled with hundreds of birds from which to choose. You'll find macaws, cockatoos, finches, and parakeets. Lovebirds run $30 to $50, cockatiels are $35 to $60, and parrots start at $100. They have hand-fed baby parrots and also carry bird supplies. If you are looking for a bird for one of your children, it would be well worth the drive. The beautiful grounds in this pastoral setting feature a walk-through aviary, pygmy goats, turkeys, exotic chicks, llamas, Texas long-horn steer, a camel, and various ducks. You can save 25 to 50% below retail on your bird selection.

The Buzzard House
11052 Limonite Ave.
Mira Loma, CA 91752
909/736-0197

Hours: Mon-Fri: 10-7 Sat: 10-6 Sun: 10-5
Credit Cards: MC, V

Don't you love the name of this place? Open seven days a week, The Buzzard House has a complete selection of pet supplies at discount prices; you can save 10 to 25% off the retail prices of other pet stores. They buy in large quantities and pass on the savings. If you're in need of dog food, bird food, bird supplies, or nonprescription medicinal items, this is the place to go. You'll also appreciate the devoted animal lovers working at The Buzzard House.

Consolidated Pet Foods ★
1840 14th St.
Santa Monica, CA 90404
310/393-9393, 800/479-4977

Hours: Mon-Wed, Fri: 8-5 Thurs: 8-7
Credit Cards: Cash or Checks Only

You can save approximately 15% off retail buying food for the furry members of your family at Consolidated Pet Foods. Brand names include Nature's Recipe, Science Diet, Eukanuba, Iams, Eagle, Solid Gold, and Nutro Max. In business since 1946, they also have their own line of food—regular and specially formulated for animals on special diets—made with only natural ingredients. As we all know, time is money, and you'll save both with free deliveries from Consolidated Pet Foods. Their delivery area is bordered by Oxnard, Ontario, and San Clemente. If you give them a call, they'll deliver a free sample of pet food the next time they're in your area. Although they take only cash or checks, charge accounts are available to regular customers. You'll receive a 15% discount on your first order when you use your *Buying Retail Is Stupid!* coupon.

Discount Pet Food ★
17641 Vanowen St.
Van Nuys, CA 91406
818/996-2066

Hours: Mon: 10-7 Tues-Fri: 10-6 Sat: 10-5 Sun: 10-4
Credit Cards: DISC, MC, V

At Discount Pet Food you can buy the four-legged loved one in your life just about all brand-name products. This huge store is filled with food and all kinds of supplies for furry friends priced 20 to 50% below retail.

Canned foods for cats and dogs are sold at case prices. Whether you buy one can or a case, the price per can is the same. Dog biscuits are sold in bulk, and brand names include Milk Bone, Natures Recipe, Bonz, Triumph, Old Mother Hubbard, Breeders Choice, and Iams. Rawhide is a good way to keep your pooches chewing something of your choosing— not theirs—and you have 28 varieties to choose from. They even have cow hooves for the same purpose. You can also get products for rabbits, hamsters, rats, guinea pigs, horses, turtles, chickens, ferrets, chinchillas, hermit crabs, reptiles, and tropical fish. Bird food is available for parrots, parakeets, cockatiels, large hookbills, pigeons, doves, canaries, and finches. There is also a low-cost veterinarian and trainer/groomer in the store. Take in your *Buying Retail Is Stupid!* coupon for a 10% discount on a $20 minimum purchase of food or supplies.

Discount Tropical Fish ★

561 W. La Habra Blvd.
La Habra, CA 90631
310/691-2037, 714/772-9997

Hours: Mon-Fri: 10-9 Sat-Sun: 10-8
Credit Cards: DISC, MC, V

If it's freshwater or saltwater fish you're wanting for your tank or outdoor pond, make sure to stop at Discount Tropical Fish. They carry all kinds of fish, and carry both dry and live foods. You will find basic tropical fish such as guppies, neons, and angel fish, to fancy goldfish, koi, African chiclid, live coral, sea anemone, and invertebrates. Their tanks run 10% over their cost, power filters run 25 to 50% below retail, fish are discounted 10 to 50%, and all dry goods are discounted 10%. If you have been longing for a koi pond in your backyard, Discount Tropical Fish can make recommendations for having one built or assist you in setting up a small one. If you buy an entire aquarium set (tank, filter, gravel, etc.) they'll throw in $10 worth of free fish. Also, your *Buying Retail Is Stupid!* coupon is redeemable for a 10% discount.

Donna's Bird House ★

1571 E. Walnut
Pasadena, CA 91106
818/795-8584

Hours: Tues-Sat: 10-6 Sun: 11-5
Credit Cards: AE

Donna's Bird House has discounts of 10 to 60% on birds and bird supplies. All birds are hand-raised, and Donna's has access to almost every species, even rare and unusual birds. They also have a wide range of brand-name products including Kaytee, Pretty Bird, Presidente, and Hoei. Donna's buys, sells, and trades birds and bird cages, and also offers consignment sales, grooming, and discount boarding. Have a question? Give them a call. Free advice is always available. Your *Buying Retail Is Stupid!* coupon will save you an extra 15% off your purchase (excludes live stock and birds).

Elliot's Pet Emporium ★

891 S. "E" St.
San Bernardino, CA 92408
909/824-5011

Hours: Mon-Fri: 9-9 Sat-Sun: 9-7
Credit Cards: V, MC
♦ **Senior Discount:** 10% **Age:** 65

This is one of the world's largest pet stores, with more than 25,000 pet items at discount prices. They buy in huge volume and pass the savings on to their customers. Savings run at about 25% below retail. They carry everything you need to make your dogs and cats happy. In addition, you can buy birds, reptiles, and fish along with all necessary supplies and equipment. You'll save an extra 10% with your *Buying Retail Is Stupid!* coupon (not valid with senior citizen discount).

For Pet's Sake Pet Shop ★

3208 Thousand Oaks Blvd.
Westlake Village, CA 91362
805/496-3430

Hours: Mon-Sat: 10-6 Sun: 11-5
Credit Cards: DISC, MC, V

This is one pet shop you'll really enjoy. The animals at For Pet's Sake are known to be the healthiest in the area. They carry birds, kittens, reptiles, small animals, and fish, and they also have pet supplies, beds, houses, and books on animal care. The store is very clean, and all skin and flea products, as well as pet foods, are guaranteed. The salespeople are knowledgeable and can answer almost any question you might have. For Pet's Sake has built quite a reputation by treating dog and cat disorders naturally, without drugs! Savings run about 20% off retail, and you can save another 10% if you remember to use your *Buying Retail Is Stupid!* coupon.

Norm's Feed Store
11708 South East End Ave.
Chino, CA 91710
909/628-7016

Hours: Mon-Sat: 8-6 Sun: 8:30-12
Credit Cards: Cash or Checks Only

When was the last time you walked into a store and really felt that the management was there to help you? Norm's Feed Store is that kind of place. You'll find very friendly salespeople, knowledgeable about the food your dogs and cats eat. They have pet and vet supplies, and you can even pick up hay, straw, and alfalfa cubes. Delivery is available for large orders.

Pedley Veterinary Supply Inc.
8978 Limonite Ave.
Riverside, CA 92509
909/685-3511

Hours: Mon-Sat: 9-5
Credit Cards: MC, V

Do-it-yourself vaccinations for your dogs, cats, and horses and even some available for your goat! Purchasing a dog's vaccination here, for example, can save you quite a bit of money. A parvo vaccination for your dog can run from $15 to $25 when administered by your vet. Do it yourself, and a parvo vaccination costs only $2.50. Most of the vaccinations are ready to go in a syringe, and antibiotics are also available. While not vets, the animal lovers employed at Pedley's are very knowledgeable about your pets' needs. They also carry over-the-counter medical supplies and vitamins, plus most pet supplies.

Red Barn Feed & Saddlery Inc. ★
18601 Oxnard St.
Tarzana, CA 91356
818/345-2510

Hours: Mon-Fri: 9-6 Sat: 9-5 Sun: 11-4
Credit Cards: MC, V

In business since 1952, this store has one of the largest inventories of pet products in the Los Angeles area. They carry Nutro, Iams, Science Diet, Pedigree, Whiskas, Friskies, Breeders Choice, Purina, Cycle, and many other brand names. You can save 20 to 40% off retail prices. There are always in-store specials, and if you live in the Los Angeles area, keep an eye out for Red Barn's discount coupons in local newspapers. They also carry foods and supplies for your pet chicken, pig, rabbit, horse, goat, ostrich, or elephant. All employees are animal owners and can answer any questions based on personal experience. They are also very involved with local animal organizations. If you need firewood, hay (sold by weight, not by bale), tack, or cages, Red Barn Feed & Saddlery has it all. You'll save an additional 5% by using your *Buying Retail Is Stupid!* coupon.

Don't assume that everything in a discount store is a bargain; items at full retail can be mixed in with the bargains—it pays to know the normal retail price in advance.

Bel Air Camera, Audio & Video
1025 Westwood Blvd.
Los Angeles, CA 90024
310/208-5150
Hours: Mon-Fri: 9-7 Sat: 9:30-6 Sun: 11-4
Credit Cards: MC, V

Bel Air is one of the largest camera, audio, and video stores on the West Coast. They offer cameras, camera accessories, video cameras and recorders, tape recorders, televisions, enlargers, and more. You can get these items daily at about 10% above their cost. They have Nikon, Minolta, Pentax, Vivitar, Panasonic, Olympus, Sony, Speedotron, Hasselblad, and others. Unless it's a close-out or discontinued item, Bel Air will meet any locally advertised price. They're always running specials, and if you get on their mailing list you'll receive information regarding classes and seminars.

Camera City ★
12236 W. Pico Blvd.
Los Angeles, CA 90064
310/477-8833
Hours: Mon-Fri: 9:30-6 Sat: 10-5
Credit Cards: AE, DISC, MC, V

Camera City has been at their present location since 1969, with prices discounted at 20 to 50% below what you'd pay at other retail stores. In photo equipment, they carry camera lenses, flashes, cases, and tripods. Rentals and repairs are available on brands such as Canon, Minolta, Ricoh, Sharp, Vivitar, Kodak, and Polaroid. Camera City is happy to say that they service what they sell. Student discounts are offered, and your *Buying Retail Is Stupid!* coupon is good for an extra 10% discount on regularly priced items.

Frank's Highland Park Camera
5715 N. Figueroa St.
Los Angeles, CA 90042
213/255-0123, 800/421-8230
Hours: Mon-Sat: 9:30-6
Credit Cards: MC, V

The Vacek family has been selling all types of cameras in their 10,000-square-foot store since 1969. They have bargain tables that offer even greater savings than their standard 6% over wholesale pricing. You can also find everything you need for your darkroom, including paper, chemicals, and equipment. If you'd like to trade in your camera, or pick up a used one, see Frank's Highland Park Camera.

Hooper Camera and Video Centers ★
5059 Lankershim Blvd.
North Hollywood, CA 91601
818/762-2846

Hours: Mon-Sat: 9-6
Credit Cards: AE, DISC, MC, V
♦ **Senior Discount:** 5% **Age:** 62

If it takes a picture, you can buy it at cost plus 5 to 10% at Hooper Camera and Video Centers. Merchandise other than cameras is sold at 10 to 35% off retail prices. This is the largest chain of photographic stores in the combined areas of San Fernando Valley and Conejo Valley. They carry everything you need in photographic equipment and supplies, at prices you can't beat. They carry all the major brands and have special sales during the year. Eight of their stores have in-house labs for custom, economy, as well as one-hour photo finishing. Full industrial and digital imaging, as well as photo portrait studios, are also available. You'll find helpful, knowledgeable salespeople to assist you. Take your *Buying Retail Is Stupid!* coupon with you for an additional 5% off your purchase of nonsale items only (not valid with senior citizen discount).

Additional Locations:
8 other stores throughout Southern California—call 800/322-6372.

Simon's Camera Discount Store ★
1316 N. Western Ave.
Hollywood, CA 90027
213/463-8585

Hours: Mon-Sat: 9-6
Credit Cards: AE, DISC, MC, V

Simon says, "See us first." He'll sell you top-brand cameras such as Nikon and Canon at the best discount prices around. In fact, cameras and supplies are usually marked at only 5 to 10% above cost, so you know you'll be finding good bargains here. Simon's also rents and services cameras. One-hour photo service is also available, and you'll save an extra 20% on this service when you use your *Buying Retail Is Stupid!* coupon. Their low pricing is based on cash and carry, so your purchase will be 3% higher if you use your credit card.

SERVICES

E.V.S. Productions ★
18356 Oxnard St., #8
Tarzana, CA 91356
818/996-5810

Hours: Mon-Fri: 8-6 Sat: 9-1
Credit Cards: MC, V

E.V.S. Productions is the place to go for video duplication and film-to-video transfers. When they do a film-to-videotape transfer, everything is done by hand on the premises. All videotape is timebased corrected. They do PAL, SECAM, and NTSC transfers, and customers are welcome to view the tape before transferring, but only by appointment. The film viewing is free, as well as any consulting necessary—whatever the customer needs. They use Fuji and Panasonic film and equipment. Most of all, the people at E.V.S. Productions are very professional. Be sure to take along your *Buying Retail Is Stupid!* coupon for a 10% discount off their already discounted prices.

Faces N' Places Photos ★
44910 18th St. West
Lancaster, CA 93534
805/945-4252

Hours: Mon-Fri: 10-6 Sat: 10-4
Credit Cards: Cash or Checks Only
♦ **Senior Discount:** 20% **Age:** 55

Wesley and Rosemary Jones have an alternative to the usually expensive family or wedding photographic session. Their complete package will average less than $600 with a guarantee of satisfaction, or no charge above the $150 deposit. They specialize in the intimate, family-oriented, or modestly organized wedding. Their emphasis is on spontaneous, impromptu shots that bring back the fondest memories of the happy occasion. What started out as a hobby has turned into a growing business. The Joneses are flexible, are easy to work with, and pride themselves on listening to their customers' needs. They work mostly within the Los Angeles and Antelope Valley areas. When you use their services, your *Buying Retail Is Stupid!* coupon is good for a free 8 × 10 plus 12 wallet-sized photos.

PLANTS, LAWN & GARDEN

LAWNMOWERS

Lee Lawnmower ★
2115 S. Bristol
Santa Ana, CA 92704
714/546-6334

Hours: Mon-Sat: 7-6 Sun: 9-3
Credit Cards: MC, V

If you are looking for great service and buys, find your way to Lee Lawnmower, in business since 1960. You can usually get same-day service if something goes wrong with your gas, electric, or diesel lawnmower. Lee Lawnmower guarantees that nobody can beat their prices or especially their service. In addition to lawnmowers, you can find blowers, edgers, hedge trimmers, weed-eaters, and of course most parts and supplies. They carry Astron, Briggs & Stratton, Echo, Homelite, and Power Trim to name just a few of their brand names. If you can't find what you are looking for, just ask. Should you find something you absolutely must have and can't afford to pay cash, ask about their own financing with no interest. Take your *Buying Retail Is Stupid!* coupon with you for an additional discount of 10% (valid only on nonsale items and repairs).

Additional Location:
Buena Park–Paul's Lawnmower, 7942 Commonwealth, 714/523-1600

NURSERIES

American Wholesale Nurseries
5000 Bennett Rd.
Simi Valley, CA 93063
805/582-2800

Hours: Mon-Sat: 8-5
Credit Cards: MC, V

Wow! They have about 35 acres filled with 500,000 plants. If that isn't enough to wow you, you also have 500 varieties from which to choose. As a grower of annuals, perennials, shrubs, and trees, American Wholesale Nurseries offers an enormous selection priced far below retail nurseries. Plus, discount chain and warehouse stores have a tough time beating their prices. In addition to their own, many other name brands are available. You

305

can fill your truck bed with plants and bulk soil blends, or even better, just have everything delivered by their on-time staff.

Additional Location:
Newhall–23915 San Fernando Rd., 805/259-2900

Baron Brothers Nursery ★
7568 Santa Rosa Rd.
Camarillo, CA 93012
805/484-0085

Hours: Mon-Sat: 7-5 Sun: 9-4
Credit Cards: DISC, MC, V
♦ **Senior Discount:** 10% **Age:** 55

Baron Brothers Nursery is the largest family-owned and operated nursery in Ventura County selling plants, floral, and feed. They grow their own plants and trees, from one-gallon plants up to 84" box specimen trees on their 110 acres. Savings range from 20 to 50% off retail prices. They deliver from San Diego to Sacramento in their own enclosed trucks. Remember your *Buying Retail Is Stupid!* coupon for 10% savings on O.H. Kruse Feed (coupon not valid with senior discount).

California Cactus Center ★
216 S. Rosemead Blvd.
Pasadena, CA 91107
818/795-2788

Hours: 7 Days a Week: 10-5
Credit Cards: AE, MC, OPT, V
♦ **Senior Discount:** 10% **Age:** 55

One way to save water is to plant a cactus garden instead of grass. California Cactus Center is one of the largest growers of cacti and succulents in the U.S. With plants starting at 2" and going to 20' you can save 15 to 30% off retail. Close your eyes and try to imagine a 20' cactus—that's mighty big! It might be the perfect gift, at the perfect price. Their staff offers landscaping, installation, and transplanting services. Check out their annual holiday sale November 28 to December 31. Used with the purchase of nonsale items, the *Buying Retail Is Stupid!* coupon will get you a free starter-size bag of cactus mix.

Dirt Cheap Plant Co. ★
440 E. 17th St., Unit A
Costa Mesa, CA 92627
714/645-4553

Hours: 7 Days a Week: 10-6
Credit Cards: MC, V

Dirt Cheap Plant Co. is just that. Assorted houseplants and potted flowers, from 4" pots to giant jungle monsters in the 4'-to-8' range, are for sale at dirt-cheap prices. Check out their outrageous selection of baskets and other plant-related items too. All flowers and plants are first quality and greenhouse fresh and at savings of 40 to 60% off retail. They are always running specials of some sort, so give them a call to see what's happening. Well, what are you waiting for? Get those green thumbs moving! Before you go, remember your *Buying Retail Is Stupid!* coupon for a 20% discount on nonsale items only.

Krystal Gardens ★
6501 Chagall Dr.
Moorpark, CA 93021
805/529-6264

Hours: Mon-Sat: 8-4:30 Sun: 10-4:30
Credit Cards: MC, V
♦ **Senior Discount:** 10% **Age:** 65

We love the words "wholesale to the public." This means 30 to 50% savings on trees and plants from Krystal Gardens. You can choose from white birch, agapanthus, day lilies, pine trees, fruit trees, redwoods, African iris, lantana, roses, general shrubs, and groundcovers. Save an additional 10% with your *Buying Retail Is Stupid!* coupon on everything except sod, turf, and sale items (not valid with senior citizen discount).

Nursery Liquidators
1500 S. State College Blvd.
Anaheim, CA 92806
714/533-4065

Hours: Mon-Tues, Thur-Sun: 10-4:30
Credit Cards: MC, V ($20 Minimum Purchase)

Nursery Liquidators has been around since 1962, selling plants and trees at prices you wouldn't believe. Save as much as 40 to 70% off the prices of other nurseries. They have more than two million plants (few of which are houseplants) and trees for your selection. They grow about 70% of their own inventory, so they can pass on the savings to you. If you're doing some landscaping, this is the place to shop.

Okada Nursery, Inc.
18715 S. Western Ave.
Gardena, CA 90248
310/324-1514

Hours: Mon-Sat: 7-5
Credit Cards: Cash or Checks Only

Anyone who likes puttering around in the garden will certainly appreciate the fine bedding and groundcover plants for sale at Okada Nursery. Because about 90% of their inventory is grown right on the premises, you can be sure that anything you buy is in great condition. Prices run 20 to 50% less than those at other retail outlets. Gardeners "in the know" have been buying healthy plants here since 1952. They close at 4 p.m. during the winter.

Valley Sod Farms
16405 Chase St.
North Hills, CA 91343
818/892-7258, 800/662-8873

Hours: Mon-Sat: 7:30-5
Credit Cards: DISC, MC, V

Blue grass, blue rye, fescue, dwarf fescue, hybrid Bermuda, and St. Augustine—no, we're not talking about race horses. These are all the different types of grass sod you can buy at the only sod farm in the San Fernando Valley. They'll deliver anywhere in the area, and if you are out of the area, they can make delivery arrangements with some of their affiliates. Delivery for six yards or more is free in the San Fernando Valley, and there's a minimum delivery charge of $35 in all other areas. So, if you're looking for sod, seed, or bulk amendments, check them out. The cost for the average yard will run 40 to 60% below most nursery prices.

POTS, PLANTERS & FOUNTAINS

Mainly Seconds—Pottery, Plants & Things
4562 Beach Blvd.
Buena Park, CA 90621
714/994-0540

Hours: Mon-Fri: 9-9 Sat: 9-8 Sun: 9-6
Credit Cards: MC, V

If you're looking for those room accessories that make your house a home and display your personality, then this is where you need to shop. Mainly Seconds carries pottery (clay, stoneware, plastic, ceramic), baskets, plants, plant foods, potting soils, cacti, silk flowers, vases, dried flowers, macramé, and wrought iron at 40 to 60% below retail. Each of their locations has over 6,000 square feet and is always stuffed with goodies.

Additional Locations:
Costa Mesa–1785 Newport Blvd., 714/548-7710
Orange–789 S. Tustin Ave., 714/744-2559
North Hollywood–12144 Magnolia Blvd., 818/985-4499

Pottery Etc. ★
7403 Canoga Ave.
Canoga Park, CA 91303
818/704-0741

Hours: Mon-Fri: 8-6 Sat-Sun: 9-5
Credit Cards: MC, V

This is the place to go for an enormous selection of unusual and standard pottery in just about every size imaginable. Prices run 5 to 50% off retail on pottery from all over the world. Animal lovers will find planters in all kinds of animal shapes (cats, lambs, rabbits, cows, pigs, swans, ducks, etc.). If you're in search of unique items, take a look at one of their catalogs. You'll find all kinds of pottery, statues, pedestals, and fountains that can be special-ordered. Family-owned and operated, Pottery Etc. hopes you'll find it a pleasure shopping here. You'll receive a 10% discount and a free 2" clay pot when you use your *Buying Retail Is Stupid!* coupon. During the winter, the store closes at 5 p.m. Monday through Friday.

Pottery Manufacturing & Distributing, Inc.
18881 S. Hoover St.
Gardena, CA 90248
310/323-7754

Hours: Mon-Sat: 8-4:30
Credit Cards: AE, DISC, MC, V

Pottery Manufacturing & Distributing, Inc. is a factory outlet with over two acres of red clay pots. You can save up to 50% off retail on factory seconds, overruns, and close-outs. They carry pots ranging in size from 1-1/2" to 40". You'll also find imported Italian stoneware, "poly-planters," and statuary items such as fountains and birdbaths. For extra savings, there are always monthly specials. If you mention *Buying Retail Is Stupid!,* you'll receive a surprise gift with your purchase.

The Pottery Store
10761 Venice Blvd.
Los Angeles, CA 90034
310/558-3124

Hours: 7 Days a Week: 9-5:30
Credit Cards: Cash or Checks Only

The Pottery Store has one of the largest inventories of indoor and outdoor decorator vases, pots, and planters in Los Angeles. Their ceramic and stoneware inventory includes Italian terra cotta to California red clay styles. The Pottery Store also carries a large selection of plants, trees, and budding flowers. Whether you are decorating your home, office, or restaurant, you'll find what you need here at a discount usually 20 to 50% below retail.

Santi's Fountains ★
18888 Van Buren Blvd.
Riverside, CA 92508
909/780-0622

Hours: Mon-Tues: 9-4 Wed-Sun: 9-5
Credit Cards: DISC, MC, V

This is definitely not your run-of-the-mill operation. Descendants of one of the most influential painters of the Italian Renaissance, Raphael, the Santi family has quite a few generations behind them of knowledge and expertise in hand-crafted artworks. You will at last be able to find the perfect fountain for your courtyard or patio. In addition, they have pottery, birdbaths, and bench sets. Because the manufacturing is done right on the premises, they have more of a selection than most others. Call them for sale dates during December. Plan to save 15% on your purchases here, plus save another 10% with your *Buying Retail Is Stupid!* coupon.

Sig's Pottery & Nursery ★
17825 Devonshire St.
Northridge, CA 91325
818/368-5171

Hours: Mon-Sat: 9-6 Sun: 9:30-6
Credit Cards: DISC, MC, V

Sig's has seconds of glazed ceramic pots priced 50 to 75% off retail. They also have first-quality red clay, concrete, and ceramic pots at 20% off retail. You'll find a large selection (half an acre, to be exact), consisting of Mexican, American, Italian, and Asian stoneware and plastic pottery. Plants for your new pots (indoor and cactus) and more than 200 cement fountains and 50 birdbaths are discounted 15 to 20%. If you don't see what you want, just ask. Special orders are no problem at Sig's. From November 1 through February 28, Sig's closes an hour earlier than usual. Remember to use your *Buying Retail Is Stupid!* coupon for an extra 5% discount.

See Also: (refer to index)
Pottery and Floral World

Shop out of season for super deals—barbecues and air conditioners in winter, heaters and parkas in summer.

BARBECUES

Barbeques Galore
324 S. Mountain Ave.
Upland, CA 91786
909/985-1522

Hours: Mon-Sat: 10-6 Sun: 11-5
Credit Cards: AE, DISC, MC, V

Just thinking about a Saturday afternoon barbecue makes my mouth water. Barbeques Galore has approximately 200 barbecues on display (gas, electric, and charcoal), along with smokers, accessories, fireplaces, and fireplace accessories. Some brand names carried are Ducane, Charbroil, Arkla, and Weber. For those chefs who enjoy experimenting, they stock the unusual, as well as products from other countries. Their knowledgeable staff will be able to answer all of your questions regarding your particular needs. In addition to offering assembly and delivery on all products, Barbeques Galore discounts everything in the store 20 to 50% off retail. For even higher savings, watch for their special weekly sales.
Additional Locations:
10 other stores throughout Southern California

Half Price Stores Inc.
6367 Van Nuys Blvd.
Van Nuys, CA 91401
818/780-6844, 800/573-6722

Hours: Mon-Fri: 10-6:30 Sat: 10-6
Credit Cards: DISC, MC, V

If you could use a new gas barbecue, you'll find a quality line of discounted barbecues in the unlikeliest of places. Half Price Stores Inc. has been a "a little bit of this and a little bit of that" store since 1967. In a small room in back of the store, you'll find Broilmaster barbecues discounted at about 40%. There are several assembled models on display, and each is available in several configurations (with or without wheels, natural gas or propane, etc.). It's important to know that in order to keep prices low, Half Price Stores does not assemble or deliver barbecues. They also carry all kinds of replacement parts such as burners, racks, and cooking grids. Although they carry only Broilmaster barbecues, replacement parts are available from most makers. On your way to the back of the store, you'll pass bargains of all sorts—

sundries, school supplies, household items, cleaning aids, and much more at 10 to 70% off retail. All sales are final.

Woodland Hills Fireplace Shop ★
21140 Ventura Blvd.
Woodland Hills, CA 91364
818/999-2174

Hours: Mon-Sat: 9-6 Sun: 12-3
Credit Cards: AE, DISC, MC, V
♦ **Senior Discount:** 5% **Age:** 65

If it's too hot, get out of the kitchen. What better way to do that than by barbecuing? If you don't have a barbecue, or if the one you have now has seen better days, this is the place to shop. The sign painted on the window of the store says, "Guaranteed Lowest Prices," and it's true! Savings usually run 35 to 40% off suggested retail prices, and you'll find the prices to be 15 to 20% lower than their discount competitors. Brands include names such as Charmglow, Ducane, Fire Magic, Arkla, Weber, and Broilmaster. During the season, there are always at least 18 models of free-standing barbecues on display, plus another six built-in models. If your existing barbecue is collecting dust because of missing parts, replacements are also available. In addition to barbecues, the shop carries tools and accessories for outdoor cooking. Everything is available promptly, as their huge warehouse is only minutes from the store. By the way, during the fall and winter months, the store turns into a fireplace shop with the same terrific discounts on prefabricated chimneys and fireplaces, glass doors, screens, tool sets, and all other related accessories. Contractors and customers alike drive in from all over Southern California to take advantage of their low prices. During September they have an inventory sale with all barbecues priced at 5% above cost. You can get an additional 10% discount by using your *Buying Retail Is Stupid!* coupon on nonsale items only (not valid with senior citizen discount).

INDOOR & OUTDOOR FURNITURE

ABC Pool & Patio ★
24449 Hawthorne Blvd.
Torrance, CA 90505
310/373-0935

Hours: Call for Hours
Credit Cards: AE, DISC, MC, V

Established in 1958, ABC now has 16,000 square feet of patio furniture, barbecues, fireplace accessories, pool and spa supplies, and gifts. Tropitone furniture and PGS barbecues are among the various brand names represented. You can expect to save 35% off retail prices on patio furniture. You'll save 10 to 20% off their barbecues and other items. Don't miss their special sales on the Fourth of July and Labor Day. Be sure to use your *Buying Retail Is Stupid!* coupon and you'll save an additional 5%!

Berks
2520 Santa Monica Blvd.
Santa Monica, CA 90404
310/828-7447, 800/622-3757

Hours: Mon-Sat: 9-6 Sun: 10-5
Credit Cards: AE, MC, V

If you are looking for a complete selection of outdoor and casual indoor furniture, and you'd like to pocket savings of 20 to 60%, then shop at Berks. They've been selling everything you need to furnish your patio or porch since the 1950s. You can purchase items such as tables, chaise lounges, and umbrellas by makers such as Brown Jordan, Tri-Comfort, Terra Teak, and others. Customers always find a variety of styles and colors, and Berks offers immediate, free delivery. If you find it advertised cheaper anywhere else, show it to them; they guarantee the lowest prices. Check out their special sales during the year for extra savings.

Cottage Shops ★
7922 W. 3rd St.
Los Angeles, CA 90048
213/658-6066

Hours: Mon-Sat: 9:30-6 Sun: 11-5
Credit Cards: AE, DISC, MC, V
♦ **Senior Discount:** 10% **Age:** 65

This discount store, in business since the late 1940s, has a complete selection of pool and patio furniture, lounges, umbrellas, and much more. Cottage Shops will save you about 30% and more off retail on most items, and they really stand behind what they sell. Brand names include Tropitone, Allibert, Ducane, Woodard, Lane Venture, and Barlow Tyrie Teak. Delivery and layaway services are available, and they can refurbish your old pool and patio furniture. You'll find free parking in back of the store. Don't forget to use your *Buying Retail Is Stupid!* coupon for an extra 10% discount (not valid with senior citizen discount).

Deforest's Patio and Fireside
22105 Ventura Blvd.
Woodland Hills, CA 91364
818/348-5040

Hours: Mon-Sat: 9:30-6 Sun: 11-5
Credit Cards: DISC, MC, V

Love relaxing in your backyard sipping on ice tea, but don't have any outdoor furniture to sit on? Deforest's Patio and Fireside can take care of all your needs so you can have fun in your backyard. They carry quality, name-brand patio furniture such as Brown Jordan, Tropitone, Woodard, and much more, including umbrellas, cushions, and accessories—all at discounts of 20 to 40% off retail. Round out the entire outdoor experience by purchasing one of their discounted barbecues. And if you're not an outdoor person but love a romantic evening by your fireplace, you'll be able to purchase an assortment of fireplace tool sets, wood baskets, screens, and custom glass doors at 20 to 30% off list. Mark your calendars for their floor clearance sale held every year after Labor Day.

Rattan Depot
10588-1/2 W. Pico Blvd.
Los Angeles, CA 90064
310/839-9003

Hours: Mon-Sat: 10-6 Sun: 12-5
Credit Cards: MC, V

Rattan Depot carries rattan and wicker for the living room, dining room, and bedroom. Their prices are 20 to 50% below retail store prices. You'll find a good selection, and they are very helpful in assisting you with your decorating decisions. If you don't see what you want, special orders are no problem. They also offer good prices on repair, refinishing, and reupholstery services. You can go into the store, or they will come to your home for a free estimate. Delivery is available.

Wicker Mart ★
36 W. Main St.
Alhambra, CA 91801
818/576-1313, 818/281-4711

Hours: Mon-Sat: 10-6 Sun: 12-5
Credit Cards: DISC, MC, V
♦ **Senior Discount:** 15% **Age:** 65

If you want wicker furniture, custom rattan furniture, cane planters, cane seat repairs, and accessories, come to Wicker Mart and save 20 to 50% off retail and enjoy their extensive selection. Custom upholstery and a layaway plan are also available. For higher discounts, keep your eyes open for their summer sales. Take in your *Buying Retail Is Stupid!* coupon for an extra 10% discount (not valid with senior citizen discount).

Woodland Casual ★
19855 Ventura Blvd.
Woodland Hills, CA 91364
818/348-6000

Hours: Mon-Sat: 10-6 Sun: 11-5
Credit Cards: AE, DISC, MC, V

Well, here it is, the largest selection of patio furniture in the San Fernando Valley. There are four entire floors of patio furniture, wicker, rattan, dinette sets, sofas, bedroom furniture, and baker's racks to choose from. You can expect to find such brands as Tropitone, Mallin, Homecrest, and Pastel to name a few. With the purchase of $1,000 or more, delivery is free. You can look forward to saving 25 to 40% off retail on most items. For even more savings, your *Buying Retail Is Stupid!* coupon will give you an extra 5% discount.

Patio Furniture Repair

Patio Guys, Inc.
1635 E. Del Amo Blvd.
Carson, CA 90746
310/639-8480, 800/310-4897

Hours: Mon-Fri: 8:30-5
Credit Cards: MC, V

Why buy new patio furniture when you can have it completely refurbished to look showroom-new by Patio Guys? Their workmen will take your old piece of outdoor furniture, remove the lacing, sandblast the frame to bare metal, weld any breaks, apply a powder-coat paint, bake it in a blast furnace, and restrap your chair with vinyl in colors to match the frame. Estimated savings of refinishing your old furniture can be 40 to 50% compared with purchasing new. They offer free quotes over the phone, and pick-up and delivery of furniture. Greater savings are offered October 1 through January 31.

POOL SUPPLIES & SPAS

J. B. Sebrell Co. ★
365 S. Central Ave.
Los Angeles, CA 90013
213/625-2648

Hours: Mon-Fri: 9-5:30 Sat: 9-5
Credit Cards: DISC, MC, V
♦ **Senior Discount:** 10% **Age:** 60

Swimming pool equipment and supplies, all marked at savings of 20 to 40% below list price, are available for you at J. B. Sebrell. They have everything—heaters, pumps, ladders, chemicals, skimmers, diving boards—plus equipment for spas, fish ponds, fountains, even above-ground pools. They accept trade-ins, buy and sell used equipment, and do repairs. Ask for their free catalog and shop by phone. They've been in business since 1938, and you'll save money on everything stocked in their huge inventory. You'll save even more when you use your *Buying Retail Is Stupid!* coupon for an extra 10% discount (not valid with senior citizen discount).

Spa Broker
12436 Ventura Blvd.
Studio City, CA 91604
818/980-0066

Hours: Mon-Sat: 10-5 Sun: 11-4
Credit Cards: AE, DISC, MC, V

Dave English has been selling spas since before they were the "in" thing. You can view quite a variety of spas and gazebos in Spa Broker's large showroom. Brand names include Anton, Grecian Swim Spas, and more. Shopping here will result in savings of $300 to $700 per spa. Keep in touch with Spa Broker to find out when they are offering even greater savings with their special sales. Financing is available.

For any type of specialty work (construction, electrical, roofing, plumbing, etc.), instead of picking a company blindly out of the phone book, ask satisfied friends and neighbors for referrals.

Valley Spa Warehouse ★
14626 Beach Blvd.
Westminster, CA 92683
714/898-5688

Hours: Mon-Sat: 9-7 Sun: 10-6
Credit Cards: MC, V

Valley Spa Warehouse offers the public wholesale prices on all spas, spa covers, and equipment at 20 to 50% below retail. This is the oldest spa store in Orange County and features L.A. Spas and Coleman, in addition to their own Valley Spa brand. Different models go on sale every month, and owner Stu Robertson will negotiate pricing. Use your *Buying Retail Is Stupid!* coupon and you'll receive extra jets free with your purchase.

On lengthy shopping trips, with lots of stops, plan the most direct route to avoid zigzagging all over town.

SAFES & VAULTS

1st Security Safe and Lock Co.
900 S. Hill St.
Los Angeles, CA 90015
213/627-0422

Hours: Mon-Fri: 8:30-5:30 Sat: 9:30-4:30
Credit Cards: Cash or Checks Only
♦ **Senior Discount:** 10% **Age:** 65

You will save so much money using this book, you're going to need a safe to keep it in. 1st Security Safe and Lock Co. specializes in jewelry safes, floor safes, and wall safes at 10 to 30% below retail. Not only do they sell safes, but they also install and service their products, plus offer locksmith services. Arrangements can be made if you'd like to finance your purchase.

Dean Security Lock & Safe
8616 Woodman Ave.
Arleta, CA 91331
818/892-1234

Hours: Mon-Fri: 7:30-5:30 Sat: 10-2
Credit Cards: MC, V

Rather than having to use a safety-deposit box during banking hours, many people are opting for the convenience of 24-hour access to a safe in their own homes. Dean Security Lock & Safe has more than 100 safes from renowned manufacturers priced 15 to 50% below retail. While comparison-shopping an in-home safe Dean's has for $300 ($600 retail), we found that the lowest comparable price was $380 at a well-known, discount chain store. Customers will appreciate their great selection of residential and commercial safes—free-standing, wall, in-floor, rotary and front-loading, fire, and burglary—with dial or digital electronic locks. Most safes are U.L.-rated. If they don't have what you're looking for, from tiny to enormous, their custom safes are a specialty. They also buy and sell used safes. Licensed and bonded, over the years they've built such a good reputation that safe manufacturers send them prototypes for input on pros and cons. Delivery, installation, moving, and service are provided by an efficient, in-house staff.

In-A-Floor Safe Company ★
Cedar Glen, CA 92321

909/337-9116

Hours: Mon-Fri: 9-6
Credit Cards: Cash or Checks Only

In business since 1925, In-A-Floor Safe Company is the originator of in-floor safes, receiving a patent in 1932. Because the company is family owned and operated, you can expect to receive service not always available elsewhere. In addition to the in-floor safes at up to 40% off retail, you can get fire safes and media/data safes at 35 to 40% off list prices. Low-cost installation is available, and they also service all brands of safes. In-A-Floor Safe Company will take an extra 10% off your purchase with your *Buying Retail Is Stupid!* coupon.

International Security Products
5311 Derry Ave., Suites G & H

Agoura Hills, CA 91301

818/991-9083

Hours: Mon-Fri: 8-4
Credit Cards: Cash or Checks Only

Buy direct from the manufacturer and save 30% on all wall safes and vaults. International Security Products manufactures a variety of wall safes, in-room vaults, hide-a-vaults, and car safes in different sizes and depths. All products are lined with felt, include shelves, and are made 100% in the U.S.

Always wear comfortable walking shoes for extended shopping trips.

California Mart Manufacturers' Saturday Sale

CA Mart Exhibit Hall–Los Angeles St. @ Olympic Blvd.

Los Angeles, CA 90015

213/623-5876

Hours: Hours Vary—Call for Information
Credit Cards: Cash Only

We think everyone has heard of the California Mart, but most people are unaware of how to get in. In general, they are not open to the public, but during their Saturday Super Sales, they allow the public in for a small entrance fee (currently $1). The "buys" at these special sales are absolutely incredible! You will have access to name-brand apparel and all kinds of accessories. Most items are either from excess stock or orders that didn't ship to retailer accounts. Just one visit will make you a true believer in our *Buying Retail Is Stupid!* philosophy. Although Saturday Super Sales are usually held on the last Saturday of the month, they've been known to throw in an extra Saturday, especially during November and December. Hours and dates can vary, so call the phone number listed above to find out about their next sale, or keep an eye out for their ads in major newspapers. Don't forget to take plenty of cash with you because they don't accept checks or credit cards.

79 vendors at one location

JB Unique Needlework, Inc.

19505 Business Center Dr.

Northridge, CA 91324

818/993-3999

Hours: Mon-Wed: 10-5 Thurs-Sat: 10-5
Credit Cards: MC, V

During the month of January, JB Unique Needlework, Inc., has a once-a-year sale on items that are rarely offered at discount prices. Those who do needlework will think they must be dreaming when first entering this store. That was our experience! JB Unique Needlework represents the equivalent of at least 20 needlework shops, maybe even more, in this 4,000-square-foot store. (A relative couldn't believe that we would even think about taking her to such a place, with only 45 minutes to shop.) They have absolutely everything necessary from equipment and fabrics by the yard, to expert advice for beginning to advanced needlepoint, cross stitch, and crewel embroidery. All popular brands are carried such

321

as Dimension, Bucilla, Needle Treasure, Elsa Williams, and many more. They also have hard-to-find brands such as Elizabeth Bradley, Rita Klein, Lavender & Lace, and Winterthurs. All regular stock is discounted 20% during their January sale. Aside from the 20% discount on regular stock, JB's Bargain Corner, already priced 30 to 50% below retail, is reduced another 20% off the last ticketed price. Even completed projects featuring discontinued kits are deeply discounted ($120 ready-to-hang needlework pieces go for $35). The sale usually lasts one week. Mark your calendars in November or December as a reminder to give JB Unique Needlework a call for the next sale. Or, write to them about being added to their mailing list for notification of the January sale and other specials held throughout the year.

Lancaster Chamber of Commerce Flea Market
554 W. Lancaster Blvd.
Lancaster, CA 93534
805/948-4518

Hours: Third Sunday in May, First Sunday in October: 9-5
Credit Cards: Varies with Vendor

Now, this is definitely worth waiting for. Established in 1966, and held only twice yearly, the Lancaster Chamber of Commerce Flea Market has everything a genuine flea market should have: plenty of vendors (they tell us up to 1,000) selling new and old merchandise, jewelry, antiques, collectibles, arts and crafts, and items that fall under the "you name it, we got it" category. Also, you'll find all kinds of ethnic and American foods. Admission and parking is $2.

500 to 1,000 vendors at one location

Mikasa Warehouse Sale
20642 S. Fordyce Ave.
Carson, CA 90749
800/2-MIKASA (264-5272)

Hours: Call for Sale Hours
Credit Cards: AE, DISC, MC, V

Twice a year, Mikasa has huge blow-out sales featuring much deeper discounts than are usually found in their outlet stores. The sales are held in one of their enormous warehouses with stacks and stacks of merchandise. Plan on spending at least two hours to see everything. Employees continually bring out new goods, so it's quite possible that whenever you return to an area, you'll find new items there. The sales are held one weekend in June, and in November during the first weekend after Thanksgiving (perfect timing for holiday gifts). So, whether you need crystal champagne flutes, flatware, or a new set of dishes, it's well worth waiting for these sales. On our last visit, we were there for nearly four hours and really got our money's worth. Our purchases would have cost nearly $800 retail, not including sales tax. Our tab for the day was less than $250.

St. John Knits, Inc.
17422 Derian Ave.
Irvine, CA 92713
714/863-1171

Hours: Open to the Public Once a Year
Credit Cards: Cash or Checks Only

If you're a devotee of St. John Knits, you'll be happy to know that once a year they open their doors to the public. The sale features items from their classic apparel collection. There are quite a few restrictions to this sale, but the savings are well worth the trouble. In October, call or write for information about this special sale which usually occurs toward the end of November. Location of the sale varies from year to year. By the way, men are not allowed at the sale because there is open dressing.

Trouble Shooter's Antiques & Collectibles Round-Up
Douglass Rd. adjacent to Arrowhead Pond
Anaheim, CA 92806

Hours: First Sunday in June & October: 6-3*
Credit Cards: Varies with Vendor

You can find some great deals on antiques and collectibles and do a good deed at the same time. In June and October (first Sunday of the month), the *Orange County Register* sponsors the Trouble Shooter's Antiques & Collectibles Round-Up, in which all profits are donated to nonprofit agencies in Orange County. In addition to quite a selection of various antiques and collectibles, you can have your family heirlooms appraised at the Appraisers booth. There are more than 800 vendors displaying their wares at the Tejas Partners Parking Lot off the 57 Freeway in Anaheim (Katella Avenue exit, at Katella and Douglass Road).

*General admission from 9 a.m. to 3 p.m. is $5 per adult, and if you want to get a jump on the selection, Early Bird Hours begin at 6 a.m., and admission is $10 per adult. Children under 12 with adults are free.

800 or more vendors at one location

BICYCLES

All Pro Bicycles ★
2381 Tapo St.
Simi Valley, CA 93063
805/583-4296

Hours: Mon-Fri: 10-6 Sat: 10-5 Sun: 11-4
Credit Cards: AE, DISC, MC, V
♦ **Senior Discount:** 10% **Age:** 60

A great place to buy a new bike, All Pro Bicycles carries Diamond Back, Trek, GT, Nishiki, and Balance bikes at everyday low prices. If you find any advertised price lower in the Santa Clarita, Conejo, San Fernando, and Simi valleys than All Pro's, they will refund 125% of the price difference to you. They boast the largest selection of bikes in Simi Valley. You'll find a knowledgeable staff, including people who are experts at wheel building. They carry all the accessories you will need and have an excellent service department. If you have your heart set on a bicycle but are short on cash, financing is available. Their two other stores are Chatsworth Cyclery and Joe's Cycle Center in Newhall. Don't forget to use your *Buying Retail Is Stupid!* coupon for a 10% discount on any of their regularly priced bicycles or accessories (not valid on previously reduced merchandise).

Additional Locations:
Chatsworth–21112 Devonshire St., 818/886-5404
Newhall–24727 San Fernando Rd., 805/255-7871

Beverly Hills Bike Shop ★
854 S. Robertson Blvd.
Los Angeles, CA 90035
310/275-BIKE (275-2453)

Hours: Mon-Fri: 10-7 Sat: 9-6 Sun: 10-6
Credit Cards: All Major
♦ **Senior Discount:** 10% **Age:** 60

For serious discounts and incredible package deals, stop by Beverly Hills Bike Shop. They will match or beat competitors' advertised prices and will give you lifetime tune-ups on your new bike; also, they offer a lifetime guarantee against defects in workmanship on the frame and moving parts. Beverly Hills Bike Shop carries an entire line of bikes (child to pro), parts, and accessories including helmets, gloves, baby joggers, trailers, clothing, and more. They offer good, old-fashioned customer service, six-month 0% financing, and worldwide shipping. Also, every September, they have a huge monster sale. Remember to take in your *Buying Retail Is Stupid!* coupon and you'll save an extra 10% off your purchase (not valid on bikes with senior citizen discount).

Bikecology–Santa Monica
501 Broadway @ 5th St.
Santa Monica, CA 90401
310/451-9977

Hours: Mon-Wed: 10-7 Thur-Fri: 10-8 Sat: 9-6 Sun: 9-5
Credit Cards: AE, DISC, MC, V

You can save 10 to 25% below retail on the very best brands in bicycles, and savings run higher on bicycling apparel, parts, and accessories. Bikecology has been named California's number one volume dealer for many popular brands such as Specialized, Gary Fisher, and Diamond Back. There are bicycles for ages 2 to 102, and they even have baby joggers made for one baby or two. In addition, Bikecology has the latest in everything for professional cyclists. For deeper discounts, their Famous Moonlight Madness sales occur four times a year. Ask for a catalog (which is very informative), and make sure you get on their mailing list.

Criterium Cycle Sport ★
16935 Vanowen St.
Van Nuys, CA 91406
818/344-5444

Hours: Mon-Wed, Fri: 10-6 Thurs: 10-8 Sat: 9-5 Sun: 11-4
Credit Cards: AE, DISC, MC, V
♦ **Senior Discount:** 15% **Age:** 65

The folks at Criterium Cycle Sport carry new bicycles and a large selection of cycling accessories. This is not a self-service operation; they have professional salespeople who take the time to make sure you select the right bike for your needs. They carry brands such as Nishiki, Bianchi, Proflex, Manitou, Merlin, GT, and many others. They also provide repairs and offer customers a lifetime warranty on all bicycle purchases. You'll receive an additional 10% discount with your *Buying Retail Is Stupid!* coupon, so you can ride away with an even better deal! (Discount coupon not valid with senior citizen discount.)

Supergo ★

8850 Warner Ave.
Fountain Valley, CA 92708
714/842-3480

Hours: Mon-Wed: 10-7 Thur-Fri: 10-8 Sat: 9-6 Sun: 9-5
Credit Cards: AE, DISC, MC, V

Riding a bicycle is a great way to have fun and get some exercise at the same time. Supergo has bicycles, along with all necessary apparel and equipment, at prices below retail. Discounts on bicycles run 10% off retail, and all accessories are discounted 15%. They guarantee to have the lowest prices around. In fact, they have a 30-day price-protection policy, and savings run higher during special sales. For example, at the end of June they hold a sale in which savings run an additional 25%. They carry major brands such as Diamond Back, Univega, Raleigh, Mongoose, Litespeed, Klein, and many others. Major bike enthusiasts will find name-brand, high-tech components. So, when you get ready to invest in a new bicycle, take your *Buying Retail Is Stupid!* coupon to Supergo for an extra 10% discount (valid on nonsale items only).

Tuazon's Bike Shop ★

3375 Iowa St., Suite I
Riverside, CA 92507
909/684-6255

Hours: Mon-Sat: 9:30-6
Credit Cards: MC, V
♦ **Senior Discount:** 10% **Age:** 60

More and more people are finding alternative ways to get to work, have fun on the weekends, and get some exercise. As a result, the bicycle is a vehicle that is growing in popularity. At Tuazon's, you'll find excellent prices (guaranteed best price) on racing, mountain, and folding bicycles. If you think that your balance may not be as sharp as it used to be, you can buy a three-wheeler adult bike from Tuazon's, which would definitely make getting around in your community a breeze. Repairs are done on all makes. Don't forget to redeem your *Buying Retail Is Stupid!* coupon for an extra 10% savings on any bicycle not on special sale. (Discount coupon is not valid with senior citizen discount.)

Shoes should fit and feel comfortable when you first try them on, not six months down the road.

EXERCISE EQUIPMENT

Busybody
27221 La Paz Rd.
Laguna Niguel, CA 92656
714/362-6573

Hours: Mon-Fri: 10-7 Sat: 10-6 Sun: 12-5
Credit Cards: All Major

Just looking over Busybody's huge selection of fitness equipment, at guaranteed lowest prices, will get your adrenaline going. They carry treadmills, home gyms, exercise bikes, stair climbers, Nordic skiers, benches, weights, fitness accessories, heart rate monitors, reading racks, weight belts, and gloves. You'll receive professional service from their trained fitness consultants, certified service technicians, delivery persons, and installers. They also offer free commercial/home fitness center design and a 30-day satisfaction, no-sweat guarantee. Get extra savings on their used equipment. If you're ready to upgrade your equipment, they accept trade-ins.

Additional Locations:

16 other stores throughout Southern California

The Fitness Store Outlet Store ★
17632 Chatsworth St.
Granada Hills, CA 91344
818/831-5520

Hours: Mon-Fri: 10-6 Sat: 10-5 Sun: 12-5
Credit Cards: AE, DISC, MC, V

If you've been thinking about working off some excess poundage, buying recycled exercise equipment at The Fitness Store Outlet Store can save you hundreds of dollars. We've seen $1,199 reconditioned Trotter treadmills that originally retailed for over $2,000. With its new rollers and new belt, we couldn't tell the difference between this one and one that was brand new. The outlet has a large selection of exercise equipment suitable for anyone's work-out level. All goods come with a warranty ranging from 30 days to one year. In addition to used equipment and floor models from their six retail stores, you'll find some new equipment that comes with a price guarantee. Model for model, if you buy a piece of equipment and see it advertised for less, they'll refund the difference in price within 30 days of purchase when you take in the dated ad. In business since 1981, they are licensed by the state of California and the Los Angeles Police Department. You'll save an extra 5% with your *Buying Retail Is Stupid!* coupon.

L.A. Gym Equipment ★
1660 S. La Cienega Blvd.
Los Angeles, CA 90035
310/285-9944
Hours: Mon-Fri: 10-7 Sat: 10-6 Sun: 10-5
Credit Cards: AE, DISC, MC, V
♦ **Senior Discount:** 10% **Age:** 55

L.A. Gym Equipment's motto is "Total service equals total satisfaction—no surprises—no hidden costs." Their showroom features new, used, and rental gym equipment for commercial gyms, homeowners, schools, condos, and hospitals—ranging from one-pound dumbbells to treadmills. Prices are 20 to 50% off retail, with guaranteed best prices. Their professionally trained fitness consultants offer in-depth product knowledge and personal service. Don't forget to use your *Buying Retail Is Stupid!* coupon for an additional 10% discount (not valid with senior citizen discount).

Additional Locations:
Laguna Niguel–28251 Crown Valley Pkwy., Units K+L, 714/831-4348
Lynwood–11132 Long Beach Blvd., 310/603-5689
Sherman Oaks–4561 Van Nuys Blvd., 818/784-6200

GAME ROOM "TOYS"

Billiards & Barstools ★
1394 W. 7th St.
Upland, CA 91786
909/946-1366
Hours: Mon-Fri: 10-7 Sat: 10-6 Sun: 11-5
Credit Cards: MC, V

Billiards & Barstools is your one-stop shop for home recreation. Whether you are a dart thrower or billiard player, everything you need can be found here in standard or customized form. You'll find at least 30 styles of billiard tables made by World of Leisure and Brunswick. You can also spice up your game room with a nostalgic jukebox, a slot machine, or even a carousel horse. If playing pool makes you thirsty, you can put your favorite beverages in an old Coke machine found here. If you're short on space but still want a pool table, check out their dining–pool table combination. Because Billiards & Barstools buys factory direct, you will spend 30 to 50% below retail and sometimes a lot less! They've been in business since 1967, so they're not behind the eight ball, and neither will you be when you use your *Buying Retail Is Stupid!* coupon for an additional 10% discount on accessories. Coupon is good only at the Upland and Victorville stores.

Additional Location:
Victorville–12420 Amargosa Rd., 619/241-7665

Crown Billiards & Bar Stools

2090 E. Main St.
Ventura, CA 93001
805/653-5255

Hours: Mon-Fri: 8-5:30 Sat: 10-5 Sun: 12-5
Credit Cards: AE, DISC, MC, V

For savings of 20 to 25% below suggested retail prices on pool tables and bar stools, Crown Billiards is the place to go. They feature a large selection of name brands: Brunswick, Global, Mevcci, Adams, Walton Bars, Cal Style, Mikhail-Durafeev, and Gomez, to name a few. If you are looking for a pool table to complement the decor of your home, they can even match your furniture with the legs on the pool table. If you don't find just the right thing you're looking for, they have lots of catalogs to give you an even wider variety of products to choose from.

Discount Billiards, Inc. ★

6445 Sunset Blvd.
Los Angeles, CA 90028
213/462-2616, 800/366-8125

Hours: Mon-Sat: 10-6
Credit Cards: All Major
♦ **Senior Discount:** 10% **Age:** 65

Enjoy the game of pool in your home with a table from Discount Billiards. Used pool tables start at $600 (retail $1,800), with an additional $150 for delivery and installation. New commercial 8' tables—including delivery, installation, and accessories—start at $1,250 (retail $1,800). Discount Billiards also has a large selection of pool table accessories, foosball tables, and darts at prices 30 to 40% off retail. Tables are available on a rent-to-own basis. Also, watch for their seasonal and parking-lot sales where you can save even more on their already discounted prices. Remember to take in your *Buying Retail Is Stupid!* coupon and you'll save an extra 10% off your purchase.

Eldorado Games

911 S. East St.
Anaheim, CA 92805
714/535-3300

Hours: Mon-Sat: 9:30-7
Credit Cards: Cash or Checks Only

If you're a pinball wizard or want to be one, then Eldorado Games is a place you must visit. Whether for personal or commercial use, this is the home for coin-operated entertainment. The best buys are on recycled machines, on which you can save anywhere from $1,200 to $2,500 off new retail prices. Eldorado will also do their best to locate hard-to-find or rare games. Repair work is available, and they sell manuals and schematics for old games. They have a warehouse filled with brand names such as Williams, Bally, Nintendo, Merit, and Atari. Pinball machines share the showroom with video games and foosball tables. If you have any questions, give George a call for free advice and information. If he doesn't have an answer for you, he'll be happy to refer you to another resource.

Golden West Pool Tables ★
4553 Van Nuys Blvd.
Sherman Oaks, CA 91403
818/888-2300

Hours: Mon-Tues, Thur-Fri: 9-6 Wed: 9-7 Sat: 9-5 Sun: 12-5
Credit Cards: AE, MC, V
♦ **Senior Discount:** 10% **Age:** 65

Buy factory direct and save on pool tables at Golden West. They always have at least 20 tables of every size and style on display with prices starting at just over $1,700. Their prices represent a savings of 20 to 25% off retail stores. Golden West has been in business in California since 1962. They have a big selection of lamps, cue racks, custom cues, custom oak bars and bar stools, and game tables, too. You can give them a call if you have a table in need of repair. By the way, don't overlook their Brunswick antique tables. You'll save an extra 5% when you remember to use your *Buying Retail Is Stupid!* coupon (not valid with senior citizen discount).

Jukeboxes Unlimited ★
818/366-9400, 800/JUKE-KIX (585-3549)

Hours: 7 Days a Week: 10-10 (By Appointment Only)
Credit Cards: Cash or Checks Only

Since 1971, Jukeboxes Unlimited has been selling and servicing jukeboxes for the stars. They carry Seeburg, Wurlitzer, Rockola, and NSM. Savings are 20% off retail prices, so why not sit back and relax to the music. You can use your *Buying Retail Is Stupid!* coupon to save an additional 5% (not valid with any other coupon offer or discount).

Sign up for store mailing lists;
retailers often have pre-sales limited
to regular customers.

GOLF

Desert Empire Golf Center
74-121 Hwy. 111
Palm Desert, CA 92260
619/568-4644

Hours: Mon-Sat: 9-5 (June, July, August: 10-4)
Credit Cards: MC, V

If you like to golf, you will want to look good walking or riding the course. Here's a place to get top name-brand golf wear for women at savings of 15 to 70% off retail. Desert Empire has been in business since 1978 and has a 2,800-square-foot store. You can expect personal service even though the prices are sliced, and it won't be rough to find additional savings during the summer or other seasons. You'll find yourself on the right course for slacks, warm-ups, tops, shorts, and sweaters, but don't get teed off because they carry clothing only for women. Desert Empire has grown through word of mouth, which is the best kind of advertising.

Golf Balls Plus
29716 Avenue Banderas
Rancho Santa Margarita, CA 92688
714/589-4600, 800/682-6299

Hours: 7 Days a Week: 8-5
Credit Cards: AE, MC, V

Golf Balls Plus retrieves golf balls from lakes and ponds and sells them at prices 40 to 50% off the cost of new balls. All balls are in perfect condition, and your order will get you brand names such as Top-Flight, Slazenger, Titleist, and many more. All orders can be shipped nationwide.

Golf Faire ★
17635 Vanowen
Van Nuys, CA 91406
818/343-2454

Hours: Mon-Sat: 9:30-6 Sun: 10-5
Credit Cards: MC, V

You may be wondering where all the golf fanatics go. Well, stop by the Golf Faire, which has one of the largest selections of equipment in the Southland. These people are serious, claiming "absolutely no lower prices on all name brands." For Foot-Joy and Dexter Shoes, Reebok clothing, bags, putters, videos, balls, gloves, and all accessories, don't drive past the Golf Faire. They carry Pro-Line clubs, and brand names include Ping, Hogan, Wilson,

Lynx, MacGregor, Powerbilt, Titleist, and Spaulding too. They also offer one-day repair service and regripping while-U-wait. Your *Buying Retail Is Stupid!* coupon is good for an extra 10% discount.

The Golf Passbook
800/950-4653
Hours: 7 Days a Week: 9-5
Credit Cards: AE, DISC, MC, V

If you'd like to save money playing 150 California golf courses, you ought to look into The Golf Passbook. Green fees run at about 50% off the regular price, and your golf cart is included in the fee. Play is limited on several of the desert courses to certain months (June 1 to September 30 or December 31), while others offer year-round play. Golf courses include Indian Wells, La Quinta, Pala Mesa, Rancho Mirage Country Club, PGA West, and many others. You'll also find Arizona courses. Fees usually run at about $25 a round—the low is $7; the high, $60. Some courses offer two rounds, while others offer unlimited rounds. Each player must have his or her own passbook. If you happen to be playing one of these courses with a partner who doesn't have a passbook, your partner will be charged regular green fees—and will most likely have to pay half the normal charge for a golf cart. In addition to discounted fees, The Golf Passbook offers golf hotel and resort packages at special prices. The Golf Passbook is $45, but if you mention *Buying Retail Is Stupid!* when you call, you'll receive two books for the price of one.

Los Angeles Washington Golf Center ★
5450 Wilshire Blvd.
Los Angeles, CA 90036
213/931-7888

Hours: Mon-Fri: 10-8 Sat: 10-6 Sun: 12-4
Credit Cards: All Major
♦ **Senior Discount:** 5% **Age:** 50

Golf, anyone? Cart yourself over to a new store in town—Los Angeles Washington Golf Center. Their 11,000-square-foot store offers name-brand golf clubs, clothes, shoes, and accessories at 20 to 30% below retail. Special sales offer extra savings—so, call about their five holiday sales. Also, you can save an additional 5% with your *Buying Retail Is Stupid!* coupon on nonsale items only (not valid with senior citizen discount).

Lumpy's Discount Golf and Fashion Place
67625 Hwy. 111
Cathedral City, CA 92234
619/321-2437

Hours: Mon-Sat: 9-6 Sun: 10-5
Credit Cards: AE, DISC, MC, V

Lumpy's is the largest discounter in the area for clubs, accessories, and apparel. Everything they carry in stock is 10 to 50% below retail, and they guarantee "we will meet or beat advertised prices on golf merchandise in stock, or give you the item free." They have plenty of stock on hand in brand names such as Hogan, Titleist, Lynx, Foot-Joy, Cobra, Spalding, Lion, Wilson, Etonic, Callaway, Dexter, Yonex, and many more. Just for walking in the door, they'll provide a free swing analysis with their sport tech analyzer. Lumpy's has been in business since the early 1980s, and they treat their customers just like neighbors.
Additional Location:
La Quinta–Hwy. 111 & Washington, 619/346-8768

Pro Golf Discount ★
1472 Los Angeles Ave.
Simi Valley, CA 93065
805/520-9801

Hours: Mon-Fri: 10-7 Sat: 10-6 Sun: 10-4
Credit Cards: AE, DISC, MC, V

If you live in Simi Valley, Pro Golf Discount is a great place to shop for all your golf equipment needs. Pro Golf's discounts run from 20 to 50% off retail prices on brand names such as Spaulding, Foot-Joy, Etonic, Taylormade, Ram, and Maxfli. They boast the greatest selection of clubs in Simi Valley. A selection of left-handed golf clubs is available, and clubs are matched to individual needs. Most repairs are done in the store, and satisfaction is guaranteed. Use your *Buying Retail Is Stupid!* coupon and you'll receive an additional 10% discount (golf balls excluded from discount).

Shamrock Golf Shops
1425 N. Main St.
Santa Ana, CA 92701
714/542-4981, 800/333-9903

Hours: Mon-Fri: 11-7 Sat: 9-5
Credit Cards: DISC, MC, V

Here's one for the golfers! It seems as if a lot of golfers feel they can change their game by changing their equipment. For this type of golfer or for the beginner, Shamrock Golf Shops carry brand-name equipment at discounts up to 40% below retail. They stock Callaway, Cobra, Hogan, Ping, Wilson, Taylormade, Mizuno, Titleist, and Shamrock. The prices posted are based on payment by credit card; you will save an additional 2% if you pay with cash or check. The money you save could allow you to press on the back nine!

Additional Locations:
Costa Mesa–375 Bristol St., #375, 714/751-0736
Los Angeles–11776 W. Pico Blvd., 310/478-8627
Pasadena–1250 E. Green St., 818/793-3165

Woodland Hills Discount Golf ★
19836 Ventura Blvd.
Woodland Hills, CA 91364
818/999-4477

Hours: Mon-Thur: 9-6 Fri: 9-7 Sat: 9:30-6 Sun: 10-5
Credit Cards: MC, V

You'll find whatever you need for the links at Woodland Hills Discount Golf priced 20 to 30% below retail. In fact, golfers from all over the world buy clubs from these nice people. They carry all your favorite brands, always have a large selection of straw hats, caps and visors, and are an authorized Ping dealer. They also have putters galore starting as low as $7.49. Every December they hold a sale in which prices are discounted another 20%. Special orders are no problem, and you still get discount prices. Your *Buying Retail Is Stupid!* coupon will get you an extra 10% discount (not redeemable on golf balls or special sale items).

SPORTING GOODS

Lake Balboa Skates
16105 Victory Blvd.
Van Nuys, CA 91406
818/782-1234

Hours: Mon-Fri: 10-8 Sat-Sun: 9-7
Credit Cards: All Major

O.K., all you in-line skating fans, Lake Balboa Skates has the highest-quality skating and hockey equipment at guaranteed best prices. They also rent in-line skates and routinely stock more than 1,000 pairs, including Rollerblade, Bauer, Roles, and more. Each skate sale comes with a free group lesson, free skate tune-ups, and free rental passes for your friends.

Additional Location:
Santa Clarita–27209 Camp Plenty, 805/252-3388

Oshman's Warehouse Outlet

901 S. Hill St. (@ 9th)

Los Angeles, CA 90015

213/624-2233

Hours: Mon-Sat: 10-6 Sun: 11-5
Credit Cards: All Major

Everything carried in regular Oshman stores eventually ends up here; merchandise usually runs 25 to 50% off whatever the price was in the retail store. For example, a Louisville Slugger softball bat that started out at $36.99 later went on sale for $29.99. When this bat made it to the outlet store, the price was dropped to $19.98. This enormous store (14,000 square feet) is fed by about 150 Oshman retail stores. The inventory consists of discontinued items, floor models, and last season's inventory. When they close a retail location, the current inventory also goes to this warehouse outlet. Because they are an outlet, the selection varies from visit to visit. One week they may have only one basketball, and the next they'll have 5,000. This is also a great place for men's and women's athletic shoes. When you visit this store, make sure to ask if they are running one of their in-store specials. In-store specials are unadvertised and often offer additional discounts of 20 to 40% off the lowest ticket price. Returns are accepted, and parking next to the building is validated with purchase.

Play It Again Sports

30317 Canwood St.

Agoura Hills, CA 91301

818/879-5083

Hours: Mon-Fri: 11-7 Sat: 10-6 Sun: 12-5
Credit Cards: AE, DISC, MC, V

It seems as though we're recycling just about everything these days, and sporting goods and equipment are no exception. Play It Again Sports stores are sprouting up all over the country buying, selling, and trading-in used sports equipment at savings of about 50% off retail. Buying recycled goods can save you from investing hundreds of dollars in a sport that you or your child might find boring in six months. Inventory can include everything from hockey equipment, tennis rackets, and in-line skates, to wet suits and exercise equipment. As with any type of store selling used goods, selection always varies from visit to visit. If you, like many others, have purchased a piece of equipment with the best of intentions but all it's doing is collecting dust, Play It Again will buy it from you outright or will sell it on consignment (usually a 50-50 split). The stores also carry new merchandise, but the best deals are on recycled goods. Each store posts its own hours and may be run a bit differently from the policy quoted above.

Additional Locations:
17 other stores throughout Southern California—call 612/520-8500.

Sport Chalet Warehouse Outlet ★

5161 Richton St.
Montclair, CA 91763
909/946-1517

Hours: Mon-Fri: 11-7 Sat: 10-6 Sun: 11-5
Credit Cards: AE, DISC, MC, V

The Sport Chalet Warehouse Outlet carries quality name-brand merchandise from its retail chain stores at a savings of up to 60% off. They have an entire line of sporting goods, clothing, athletic shoes, and more. Name brands include Nike, Reebok, Rawlings, Adidas, Timberland, Wilson, and Coleman. Take in your *Buying Retail Is Stupid!* coupon and receive 10% off any purchase of $50 or more.

Super Pro Image Outlet Store ★

740 Ventura Blvd.
Camarillo, CA 92230
805/383-3115

Hours: Mon-Sat: 10-8 Sun: 10-6
Credit Cards: All Major

Die-hard sports fans can buy authentic and replica sports apparel, accessories, memorabilia, and other licensed goods discounted 10 to 90% below retail. The licensed products are what your favorite teams wear in professional football, basketball, baseball, and hockey, plus most college and university teams. We spotted a Miami Dolphins traditional team jacket—wool with leather sleeves and team logo in full-thread embroidery—for $110 instead of $220. Sports-team caps that sell for $20 to $23 can be purchased at the outlet store for $7. This is the only outlet in Southern California for Super Pro Image stores. Everything is first quality. Most apparel is unisex and available in sizes small to XX-large for adults, youth sizes 8 to 20, toddlers 2T to 5T, and infants 0 to 24 months. Most sports are represented year-round, not just seasonally. If you want the entire gang to be properly attired as all die-hard fans should be, group discounts are available for large-quantity purchases. Take in the *Buying Retail Is Stupid!* coupon and you'll score an extra 10% discount (not valid on group discounts).

See Also: (refer to index)
　　　　　Army-Navy Surplus
　　　　　Real Cheap Sports

WINTER & WATER SPORTS

Aqua Flite
818/759-9963, 800/581-7916

Hours: By Appointment Only
Credit Cards: DISC, MC, V

Aqua Flite can save you 30 to 40% on your next diving suit. Aqua Flite visits your home or office with its selection of wet and semi-dry suits. All suits are custom made in the U.S. and come with a two-year guarantee.

Coral Reef Dive & Surf & Wet Suit Factory ★
14161 Beach Blvd.
Westminster, CA 92683
714/894-3483

Hours: Mon-Fri: 10-9 Sat: 10-7 Sun: 10-6
Credit Cards: AE, DISC, MC, V
♦ **Senior Discount:** 10% **Age:** 65

There's a whole new world under the sea that many of us have not visited. Coral Reef Dive & Surf & Wet Suit Factory will get you ready for the adventure and not break the bank. They manufacture their wet suits and offer savings up to 50% off retail. Purchase a custom-measured wet suit and receive a lifetime warranty on any seam repairs. On dive and surf equipment, their policy is to meet or beat any competitor with valid advertisement. Their prices are so low, you probably won't be looking elsewhere. Save an additional 10% with your *Buying Retail Is Stupid!* coupon.

Divers' Discount Supply ★
3575 Cahuenga Blvd. West
Univeral City, CA 90068
800/34-SCUBA (347-2822)

Hours: Tues-Fri: 11-7 Sat-Sun: 11-5
Credit Cards: All Major

Beginners and pros alike can save money at Divers' Discount Supply on just about anything related to diving. Prices run 20 to 50% below retail on all scuba equipment, with brand names such as Apollo, Oceanquest, Sherwood, TUSA, and many others. You'll find an unbelievable selection of wet suits, B.C. jackets, gloves, booties, and other items in sizes 3X-small to 8X-large. Beginners can get plenty of help and advice, because all employees are qualified and experienced divers. They have a variety of certification programs guaranteed to fit any schedule. If you're already an experienced diver, you can take your tanks in for airfills. Should you find an item advertised for less within 30 days of purchase, you'll receive a store credit for 150% of the price difference. These people are so involved in the world of diving that they sponsor a free service through the *Orange County Register*. It's called the Diving Info Hotline at 714/550-4636, extension 1991. If you take in your *Buying Retail Is Stupid!* coupon, you'll receive a free plush slap strap or T-shirt just for stopping in and saying, "Hi!"

Additional Locations:
Montclair–9197 Central Ave., Unit H, 909/621-5000
San Diego–4560 Alvarado Canyon Rd., 619/285-1000
Santa Fe Springs–14104 E. Firestone Blvd., 310/404-0000

H & H Jobbing Company
840 S. Los Angeles St.
Los Angeles, CA 90014
213/627-6861

Hours: Mon-Sat: 9-5
Credit Cards: MC, V

Whether you need tennis, golf, or ski clothing, this is the place to go for high-end brands at low-end prices (40 to 70% off retail). H & H does an excellent job at getting super deals on top brands and then passing the savings on to customers. If they can't get a super deal, they pass it on. That's why sometimes you see a brand on one visit and won't on another. Some of the labels we spotted were Bogner, Ellesse, Escada Sport, Fila, Head, and Kaelin, as well as many others. When you go to H & H, don't overlook a section in back of the store filled with close-outs, odds and ends, samples, and discontinued items. By the way, don't worry if you see racks of women's clothing when you walk into the store because H & H is located on the second floor, and you must walk through a store called Ladies Apparel in order to get to the stairs.

Additional Location:
Redondo Beach–2772 W. Artesia Blvd., 310/793-9150

Mike Murphy's Ski Shop
10795 San Sevaine
Mira Loma, CA 91752
909/681-6083

Hours: Mon-Sat: 10-5 Sun: 11-4
Credit Cards: All Major

Mike Murphy's Ski Shop offers down and dirty prices (20 to 40% off retail) and excellent customer service on water skis, wakeboards, kneeboards, wet suits, dry suits, and tubes. They've been offering equipment and accessories suitable for beginners to professionals since

1974. So, if you enjoy water sports, this is definitely a place to visit.

P F McMullin Co.

1530 E. Edinger, #9
Santa Ana, CA 92705
714/547-7479

Hours: Mon-Fri: 10-9 Sat: 10-6 Sun: 12-5 (Closed May, June, July)
Credit Cards: MC, V

P F McMullin Co. has been clothing families in Southern California who love to ski since 1965. What's great about this store is they can fit children starting at size 2 up to men's XX-large to help make your skiing experience a memorable one with the whole family. They have excellent choices of socks, pants, sweaters, jackets, gloves, goggles, and much more, with discounts ranging from 20 to 50% off retail. In addition, they have special apparel for snowboarding. The hours above are for the height of ski season, which is October through February. Off-season hours (August, September, March, and April) are Monday through Friday, 10-6. They are closed during the months of May, June, and July.

Wetsuits For Less

310/535-5945

Hours: By Appointment Only
Credit Cards: DISC, MC, V

Wetsuits For Less has the best prices on wetsuits in all sizes for all water sports. They carry a variety of suits for surfing, jet skiing, and windsurfing priced 35 to 40% below retail. Wetsuits For Less does not have a shop. They will visit your home or office and determine which suit is best for you. All suits come with a two-year warranty and can be shipped nationwide.

Check classified ads for bargains
on goods advertised as "like new,"
"used once," or "never used."

Army-Navy Surplus
503 N. Victory Blvd.
Burbank, CA 91502
818/845-9433

Hours: Mon-Fri: 9:30-6:30 Sat: 9:30-6 Sun: 10-5
Credit Cards: AE, DISC, MC, V

Going hunting? Do you need something to wear? Levi jeans are here, plus shoes, T-shirts, and camouflage pants. They also carry tents, tent poles, boats, and tarps in poly and canvas. Everything already mentioned, plus car covers and hard-to-get surplus items, is all at 20 to 50% above cost.

Additional Locations:
Hollywood–6664 Hollywood Blvd., 310/463-4730
Santa Barbara–631 State St., 805/963-3868
Santa Monica–1431 Lincoln St., 310/458-4166

Major Surplus & Survival ★
435 W. Alondra Blvd.
Gardena, CA 90248
310/324-8855, 800/441-8855

Hours: Mon-Fri: 8-5 Sat: 8-4
Credit Cards: All Major
♦ **Senior Discount:** 10% **Age:** 60

Major Surplus & Survival is one of the largest earthquake preparedness and survival stores in the country. They specialize in hard-to-find and unusual surplus items, canned and freeze-dried foods, and military meals. Major Surplus is the sole distributor of military M.R.E.s (Meals Ready to Eat) and buys them directly from the manufacturer that supplies the U.S. Armed Forces. They also carry numerous first-aid and emergency supplies, in addition to a full line of tents, backpacks, boots, and cutlery items. Ask about their twice-yearly warehouse sales known for spectacular markdowns. Remember to take in your *Buying Retail Is Stupid!* coupon and you'll save an extra 10% off your purchase of $5 or more (not valid with senior citizen discount).

Van Nuys Army & Navy Store ★
6179 Van Nuys Blvd.
Van Nuys, CA 91401
818/781-3500

Hours: Mon-Sat: 8:30-9 Sun: 9:30-6:30
Credit Cards: AE, DISC, MC, V

You will find this to be one of the best-stocked surplus stores in the area. It's filled with Levi's, jackets, belts, caps, camping gear, sleeping bags, pea coats, sweats, thermal pants, boots, and a million other items for both men and women. You can find Coleman coolers here, plus motorcycle boots, Swiss army and Buck knives, Schott leather jackets, outdoor products, MA-1 and M65 field jackets in both nylon and leather, soft packs, and duffels. Their complete military department stocks camouflage from at least six different companies. Extra savings come into play when they have close-outs. In business since 1950, Clara, Paul, and Ben head the Van Nuys store, and Marc oversees the one in Reseda. Both stores will meet or beat their competitors' prices. Check out the Air Force sunglasses and Halloween costumes too. Call the Reseda store for hours. Your *Buying Retail Is Stupid!* coupon will save you an extra 10%.

Additional Location:
Reseda–7116 Reseda Blvd., 818/344-0237

> Make sure everything (zippers, seams, buttons, etc.) is perfect before purchase.

Computer Games Plus ★

1839 E. Chapman Ave.
Orange, CA 92667
714/639-8189

Hours: Mon-Fri: 12-6 Sat: 12-3
Credit Cards: MC, V

Computer Games Plus carries computer software and video game cartridges at 25 to 30% off retail. Sega and Genesis games can run as low as $9.95. Make sure to ask about their specials that feature discounts of up to 90% off. You'll save even more when you use your *Buying Retail Is Stupid!* coupon for an extra 10% discount.

Dolls By Sandra

7700 Rhea Ave.
Reseda, CA 91335
818/343-4842

Hours: By Appointment Only
Credit Cards: Cash or Checks Only
♦ **Senior Discount:** 10% **Age:** 60

Sandra Borenstein, owner of Dolls By Sandra, says her company is a business of love. Now, we'd like a little of that. Sandra specializes in hospital care for dolls by repairing porcelain, china heads, composition, paper mache, fabric, and furry little creatures back to lovable condition again. Her service is priced to be affordable. She also creates dolls to order, such as portrait dolls, and teaches dollmaking.

LEC World Traders ★

249 N. First St.
Burbank, CA 91350
818/295-3794

Hours: Mon-Fri: 9-4 Sat: 9-5
Credit Cards: DISC, MC, V

For whatever reason, kids never seem to have enough toys. Parents can save lots of money on toys for kids of all ages at LEC World Traders. Brand names include Mattel, Playskool, Little Tikes, Tyco, Leyco, Kenner, Milton Bradley, and many others. You'll find 5,000 square feet filled with dolls, model race sets, games, cars and trucks, blocks, and all kinds of other fun stuff. Keep them in mind for the Christmas holidays, because one week after Thanksgiving they have a three-day sale with even deeper discounts. Special holiday hours are 9 a.m. to 8 p.m. Monday through Friday, 9 a.m. to 5 p.m. Saturday, and 10 a.m. to 4 p.m. Sunday. Regular discounts run at about 25% off retail, but LEC offers deeper discounts of 40 to 50% to charitable organizations. As a special offer to our readers, LEC will extend a free membership to their exclusive discount club—just present your *Buying Retail Is Stupid!* coupon for your free membership and discount card for savings of 50% off retail prices.

Los Angeles Toy Loan Program

Los Angeles, CA 90031
213/226-6286

Hours: Mon-Fri: 8-5

The Los Angeles Toy Loan Program began in 1935 and provides toys to needy children, especially those living in disadvantaged areas. Thirty-four loan centers are located throughout the county; the program is a resource for more than 150 teachers, educators, and county personnel, who borrow toys, books, and games to enhance learning and stimulate communication in therapy. Toys are lent freely, and there are no membership dues or fines for late returns. For a child to borrow toys, all that is needed is an application card signed by a parent or responsible adult. Call the main office (213/226-6286) for hours and toy loan center near you.

Additional Locations:
33 other locations throughout Southern California—call 213/226-6286.

Play Co. Toys

1193 Broadway
Chula Vista, CA 91911
619/420-2858

Hours: Mon-Fri: 9:30-9 Sat: 9-7 Sun: 10-6
Credit Cards: DISC, MC, V

We like to think of ourselves as "young at heart." So, of course, visiting a toy store is one of the "fun" things we like to do. Especially Play Co. Toys, where their policy is to match any competitor's advertised price—guaranteeing you the lowest price. The stores are located throughout Southern California and feature the most up-to-date toys on the market. You'll find name brands such as Nintendo, Sega, Fisher Price, Playskool, Mattel, Kenner, Hasbro, Parker Bros., Little Tikes, and many more. All stores carry toys, home video games and accessories, as well as a tremendous selection for the radio control, model rocketry, and model railroading enthusiast. Hours may vary from store to store.

Additional Locations:
16 other stores throughout Southern California—call 800/752-9261.

Toy Liquidators
100 Citadel Dr., Suite 144
City of Commerce, CA 90040
213/722-1998

Hours: Mon-Sat: 10-8 Sun: 10-6
Credit Cards: DISC, MC, V

Toys, toys, and more toys at 40 to 70% off retail can be found at Toy Liquidators in factory outlet malls. You can count on finding all your favorite brand names here, including Mattel, Playskool, Tyco, and Hasbro. They also carry battery-operated toys such as Nintendo games, Sega games, and Game Boy. These stores stock last season's hottest sellers and current manufacturer overruns.

Additional Locations:
6 other stores throughout Southern California

Uncle Tom's Toys
2281 Honolulu Ave.
Montrose, CA 91020
818/249-1557

Hours: Mon-Wed, Sat: 9:30-6 Thur-Fri: 9:30-8:30 Sun: 11-5
Credit Cards: DISC, MC, V
♦ **Senior Discount:** 10% **Age:** 55

Are your children always hitting you up for the latest toy they saw while watching cartoons on Saturday? You can buy whatever your little one's heart desires at Uncle Tom's Toys, at 10 to 60% off retail. In business since 1966, Uncle Tom's Toys has 6,000 square feet filled with fun stuff for youngsters and oldsters who are young at heart. They carry at least 200 brand names, adding up to thousands of different items from which to choose. You'll find an extensive selection of Barbie everything, Playmobil play centers (dollhouses, pirate ships, etc.), Little Tikes, rows of Lego sets, Illco, and more. They also have an aisle filled with games from Milton Bradley and Parker Brothers. Toward the back of the store, there is a large section devoted to Breyer animal figures, sold individually and in sets. Uncle Tom's Toys is a friendly place, staffed with people who enjoy playing as much as their customers do.

Additional Location:
Santa Barbara–Tom's Toy World, 1200 State St., 805/564-6622

MODEL TRAINS

Allied Model Trains
4411 S. Sepulveda Blvd.
Culver City, CA 90230
310/313-9353

Hours: Mon-Thur, Sat: 10-6 Fri: 10-9
Credit Cards: AE, DISC, MC, V

This is a place that will make a model railroader's heart beat faster, because we have discovered the world's largest model train store! They carry all brands and sizes of kits, tools, scenery supplies, and automobile and aircraft models. Most everything you see is priced at 20 to 50% off retail. You'll see name brands such as Lionel, LGB, American Flyer, Athearn, Fleischmann, and more, in sizes Z Gauge (the smallest at 1" to 2") to G Gauge (the largest at 18"). You'll also find many other interesting items, but for the most part, they are priced at retail. Allied Model Trains, a replica of Union Station, has 11,500 square feet for hobbyists to explore! For your enjoyment, they have several very interesting, extremely detailed operating displays. Owner Allen Drucker even had steps built below the large display windows to make viewing easier for little ones. Expert repairs are available, and they also buy old trains and toys.

The Roundhouse Train Store ★
12804 Victory Blvd.
North Hollywood, CA 91606
818/769-0403

Hours: Mon-Thur: 10-6:30 Fri: 10-7 Sat: 10-6 Sun: 11-5
Credit Cards: AE, DISC, MC, V

No longer are electric train sets a pastime strictly for children. Adults who enjoy collecting trains can be found browsing at one of the largest train stores in Southern California. The Roundhouse Train Store carries such brand names as LGB, Playmobil, Lionel, American Flyer, HO, N & Z Gauge, and more. Thousands of HO-scale detail parts are in stock. As a matter of fact, the movie industry is constantly buying parts to be used for special effects. Different specials run every week, in addition to their regular discounted prices. Whatever you do, don't forget to bring your *Buying Retail Is Stupid!* coupon for added savings of 10% off nonsale items only. Make certain to get on their mailing list for updates on their sales and new merchandise arrivals.

LUGGAGE & TRAVEL ACCESSORIES

California Luggage Outlet
18110 Euclid St.
Fountain Valley, CA 92708
714/540-5878

Hours: Mon-Sat: 9-7 Sun: 10-5
Credit Cards: All Major

One of the Southland's largest selections of luggage and leather goods at 20 to 50% off retail can be found at California Luggage Outlet. Featured are Tumi, Hartmann, Delsey, Andiamo, Lark, Samsonite, Skyway, and more. You'll find additional savings on discontinued luggage. There's also a full-service, on-site repair shop for your convenience.

H. Savinar Luggage ★
4625 W. Washington Blvd.
Los Angeles, CA 90016
213/938-2501, 800/877-TOTE (877-8683)

Hours: Mon-Sat: 9-5
Credit Cards: MC, V

This is a good example of why *Buying Retail Is Stupid!* was written. Why pay retail prices, when you can go to stores like H. Savinar, enjoy big savings, have a more complete selection than any retail store offers, and be waited on by helpful and knowledgeable salespeople? Their 14,000-square-foot warehouse is stocked with major-brand luggage, tote bags, travel-related accessories of all kinds, briefcases, portfolios, and small leather goods. The Savinar family has been in business since 1916, so if you want to buy the best for less, be sure to visit them. Gift wrapping and monogramming services are free. Call the Canoga Park store for hours. With any $50 purchase, your *Buying Retail Is Stupid!* coupon is good for a free, inflatable neck cushion.

Additional Location:
Canoga Park–6931 Topanga Canyon Blvd., 818/703-1313

LAX Luggage
2233 S. Sepulveda Blvd.
West Los Angeles, CA 90064
310/478-2661

Hours: Mon-Sat: 10-6 Sun: 11-5
Credit Cards: MC, V

Find name-brand luggage here at discounted prices. At LAX Luggage you'll see luggage made by Ricardo, Samsonite, Skyway, Lucas, Delsey, Hartmann, Andiamo, Tumi, and Lark, just to name a few. They also carry attachés, briefcases, agendas, travel items, and Seiko clocks. If your luggage is in need of repair, they do authorized airline luggage repair as well.

Additional Location:
Inglewood–11010 S. La Cienega Blvd., 310/417-2307

Luggage 4 Less ★
5144 Lankershim Blvd.
North Hollywood, CA 91601
818/760-1360, 800/665-8442

Hours: Mon-Sat: 10-6 Sun: 11-5
Credit Cards: All Major

Luggage 4 Less has all kinds of luggage at prices 25 to 70% below retail. Owner Fred Cohen has been in the luggage business for more than 30 years. He and his low-key staff are very helpful in finding what you need within your budget, and since no one works on commission, high-pressure sales are nonexistent. All goods are of first quality, and on occasion they do have close-outs. Customers are always informed if they're buying a close-out, because finding matching pieces would probably be impossible. In addition to luggage, they carry attaché cases and small leather goods. Most repairs are done on the premises, and monogramming is free on all items purchased here. Also featured are beautifully reconditioned antique steamer trunks. If you don't see a brand or an item that you want, you can place special orders and still get discounted prices. Although they don't quote prices over the phone, they will beat any verified price. Your *Buying Retail Is Stupid!* coupon is good for a 5% discount. Free parking is located in back of each location.

Additional Location:
West Los Angeles–11667 Wilshire Blvd., 310/268-6698

Rooten's Luggage Outlet
17775 Main St.
Irvine, CA 92714
714/250-0774

Hours: Mon-Fri: 9-6 Sat: 10-5 Sun: 11-5
Credit Cards: AE, MC, V

Whether you're traveling overnight to San Francisco, or touring Europe for a month, Rooten's Luggage Outlet will help you choose the perfect luggage for your journey. They have discounted prices (20 to 50% off retail) on all first-quality, name-brand luggage such as Andiamo, Tumi, Hartmann, Boyt, Lark, Skyway, Samsonite, Delsey, and more. Attachés and brief and computer cases are also available at discount prices. And while you're at it, why not get your initials monogrammed on your new luggage or briefcase, free of charge.

See Also: (refer to index)
Asmara Overseas Shippers

TRAVEL ARRANGEMENTS & SERVICES

Around The World Travel ★
6012 Reseda Blvd.
Tarzana, CA 91356
818/996-3000, 800/356-3330

Hours: Mon-Fri: 9:30-5:30
Credit Cards: All Major
♦ **Senior Discount:** Varies **Age:** 55

Taking a vacation is our favorite thing to do—well, second to getting a great deal on traveling. Around The World Travel guarantees the best prices on airfares and cruises. You can expect to save 10 to 50% on fares and receive professional service with a personal touch. They can also book tours, cars, hotels, and trains, and arrange corporate, group, and incentive travel programs. Why not try a cruise on one of their many famous lines: Crystal Cruises, Royal Cruise Line, Radisson Diamond, Royal Caribbean, Princess, Carnival, Royal Viking, Holland America, and more. Receive an additional 5% savings and a special gift with your *Buying Retail Is Stupid!* coupon with the purchase of a $1,000-per-person (double occupancy) cruise. Happy traveling!

Automobile Club of Southern California
2601 S. Figueroa St.
Los Angeles, CA 90007
213/741-3330

Hours: Mon-Fri: 9-5
Credit Cards: MC, V

The Automobile Club of Southern California offers its 4.2 million members the following benefits: roadside assistance services, travel planning, maps, tour books, reservations, automotive testing and analysis, automobile buying services, auto pricing information, and competitively priced auto insurance. All this for a first-time membership fee of $60. Annual renewal fees are $40. With just one road service tow, you'll probably recoup your investment. Membership entitles you to four free tows a year. When you're planning a trip, stop by and pick up some of their excellently written tour books. They have a wealth of information and can suggest many places to use your membership card for additional discounts while traveling. Many retailers in Southern California offer extra savings to Automobile Club of Southern California members.

Additional Locations:
78 other offices throughout Southern California

Crystal Blue Vacations
1827 Ximeno Ave., #311
Long Beach, CA 90815
310/434-2400, 800/995-BLUE (995-2583)

Hours: Mon-Fri: 7:30-6 Sat: 10-6 Sun: 10:30-5
Credit Cards: AE, MC, V

Since Crystal Blue is one of the nation's largest bookers of Club Med Vacations (sending approximately 150 travelers monthly), they guarantee the best rate of any agency on any Club Med Vacation. If you don't want to hassle with thinking about what to do while on holiday, a Club Med Vacation might be perfect for you. Price of trip includes: accommodations, three meals daily with unlimited wine and beer at lunch and dinner, sports activities with lessons and equipment, nightly entertainment, plus all taxes and gratuities. All you have to do is enjoy yourself! Bon voyage!

Flight Coordinators
2950 31st St., #140
Santa Monica, CA 90405
310/581-5600, 800/544-3644

Hours: Mon-Fri: 9-5:30 Sat: 10-2
Credit Cards: AE, DISC, MC, V

Offering 40 years of experience in low-cost airfare, Flight Coordinators say they can save you plenty on your overseas flights, especially if you need to fly on one day's notice. They deal mostly with overseas flights, but they do handle some domestic flights at a discount. Depending on where you're off to, you can expect to save from 5 to 50% on your airline tickets. You'll save more money if you pay by money order or cashier's check.

Freighter World Cruises
180 S. Lake Ave., #335
Pasadena, CA 91001
818/449-3106

Hours: Mon-Fri: 9-5
Credit Cards: Cash or Checks Only

You can save money, while enjoying quiet days at sea, when cruising on a freighter across the Atlantic. Freighter World Cruises books freighter travel, a cheaper cruising alternative with fares typically costing approximately $110 per day (normal cruises are 30 to 50% higher). Traveling this way requires allowing two to four weeks to cross the Atlantic, depending on the destination. Call Freighter World Cruises for a free information packet and sample copy of their newsletter; mention that you have a copy of *Buying Retail Is Stupid!* to receive the materials without cost.

Hotel Reservations Network
800/964-6835

Hours: Mon-Fri: 4 a.m.-2 p.m.
Credit Cards: AE, DISC, MC, V

When you need inexpensive or deluxe hotel rooms in San Francisco, Chicago, New York, Washington, DC, Boston, Paris, London, or any other major city in the world, make Hotel Reservations Network your first call. Hotel rates are up to 65% off regular prices, and the network always has low-cost rooms available. Book three nights or more and receive 500 frequent-flyer miles on Northwest or Continental Airlines.

Montrose Travel ★
2343 Honolulu Ave.
Montrose, CA 91020
213/245-3158, 818/248-9081

Hours: Mon-Thur: 8:30-6 Fri: 9-6 Sat: 9-2
Credit Cards: All Major

If cruise brochure prices have blown you out of the water, your dream of cruising the oceans of the world may yet be close at hand, because for the most part, cruise lines are discounting their "retail" prices. Montrose Travel is terrific at finding and negotiating travel discounts, and have been providing their clients with excellent service since the early 1960s. With the contacts made over the years, and the volume of trips they book (they have 40 full-time employees), Montrose Travel is often given special deals. Of course, you can book any other type of travel, too. They do their best to find their clients the best deals and, as with most travel agencies, are privy to information not available to the public. They deal only with reputable suppliers and make certain that the "specials" you call them about are actually specials. All Montrose agents are travelers, and no matter where your destination, someone there has experienced it firsthand and can tell you all the ins and outs—good and bad—that alluring brochures can't or won't convey. Your *Buying Retail Is Stupid!* coupon is good for an extra 5% discount on any excursion booked through Montrose Travel.

Spur Of The Moment Cruises, Inc.
411 N. Harbor Blvd.
San Pedro, CA 90731
310/521-1070, 800/4-CRUISE (427-8473)

Hours: Mon-Fri: 9-5
Credit Cards: Cash or Checks Only

So, you have some time on your hands and don't know what to do? Call Spur Of The Moment Cruises and hop on board a cruise. They are a clearing house for last-minute and unsold cruises. This means savings of 50 to 75% to you. Each month you can send them a self-addressed, stamped envelope and receive a list of their last-minute cruises. Ask about their senior citizen discounts, which vary with each cruise.

Trading Homes International ★
P.O. Box 787
Hermosa Beach, CA 90254
800/877-8723, 310/798-3864

Hours: 24-Hour Answering Service
Credit Cards: AE, MC, V

Invest $75 per year and you might have an entire vacation with no hotel expense, no rental car expense, and no kennel fees for your pets, plus save on your meals. You say, "How is this possible?" Trading Homes International is a company that publishes three directories per year, putting you in touch with members around the world who want to trade their homes with you. Exchanges vary from a weekend to a year. Some members also exchange cars, care for each other's pets, water gardens—the choice is yours. You can save thousands of dollars on accommodations, food, cars, etc., and visit some of the most exotic places in the world. Your membership fee also gets you a free listing in a directory for one year. Mention *Buying Retail Is Stupid!* when joining and receive $10 off yearly membership.

Vacation Exchange Club ★
800/638-3841

Hours: 6 a.m.-1 p.m.
Credit Cards: DISC, MC, V

Take a vacation anywhere in the world and pay only for transportation to and from your destination. Since 1950, the Vacation Exchange Club has offered members the opportunity to have "free" accommodations worldwide by exchanging their home for the use of another member's home. Possibilities could include a villa in the south of France, a seaside apartment off the coast of Italy, or a 350-year-old, thatched-roof home in the British countryside. Vacation Exchange Club's 15,000 members may even exchange cars or boats, and care for each other's pets or gardens. Cost for membership is $78 per year, and this entitles you to five publications and an ad for your home in one publication. Call for a free information packet. With your *Buying Retail Is Stupid!* coupon, you'll save 10% off your membership fee.

See Also: (refer to index)
       The Golf Passbook

VARIETY & THRIFT STORES

GENERAL MERCHANDISE

99¢ Only Store ★
13061 Harbor Blvd.
Garden Grove, CA 92643
714/539-5999

Hours: 7 Days a Week: 9-9
Credit Cards: Cash Only

If your lucky number is 99, then this is the store for you! Absolutely everything in the store is sold for 99¢. You can really get some great bargains on such items as sundries, food, glassware, paper goods, and small gift items, plus much more. New merchandise arrives daily, and there is never any limit on quantities purchased. Brand names include Revlon, Kraft, Hershey, Mattel, Fruit of the Loom, and more. Believe it or not, 99¢ Only Stores offer bridal gift certificates for thrifty future brides. Most stores now accept ATM cards, MasterCard, and Visa.

Additional Locations:
39 other stores throughout Southern California—call 213/LUCKY-99 (582-5999).

Bargain Fair ★
7901 Beverly Blvd. (@ Fairfax)
Los Angeles, CA 90048
213/655-2227

Hours: Mon-Fri: 9-7 Sat-Sun: 10-6
Credit Cards: DISC, MC, V

In business since the early 1960s, Bargain Fair is an adventure in shopping and a great place for people setting up their first apartment. As a buyer of close-outs and discontinued merchandise, they are always turning over their inventory of household items. Selection varies from visit to visit, but normally you'll find everything from dinnerware from Japan or Germany to Revlon shampoo at 25 to 75% off retail. Some of the names we've seen in the past are Anchor Hocking, Mikasa, Libby, Sterilite, Regal, and Crown Corning. Parking is validated with a $6 minimum purchase, and you can save an extra 10% by using your *Buying Retail Is Stupid!* coupon.

Bargain Saver
5500 Hollywood Blvd. (@ Western)
Los Angeles, CA 90028
213/466-5383

Hours: Mon-Sat: 10:30-7 Sun: 12-6
Credit Cards: MC, V

With almost everything you can imagine in this catch-all store, you've got to see it to believe it! Bargain Saver has household items, clothing, cookware, drinking glasses, jogging shoes, pillows, comforters, blankets, towels, toys, soap, rugs, statues, and a lot of odds and ends. Yes, we said odds and ends. Nonetheless, discounts on whatever you happen to find run 20 to 50% off retail.

Bargains Galore ★
2272 Honolulu Ave.
Montrose, CA 91020
818/957-2528

Hours: Mon-Sat: 9:30-6 Sun: 11-5
Credit Cards: MC, V

Bargains Galore, a discount store on the tree-lined, pedestrian-friendly main street of Montrose, is filled with close-outs, overruns, and insurance salvage goods. Prices here are even lower than sale prices at major discount chains. Although they carry a little bit of everything, they're different from similarly themed stores in that they are very particular about the goods carried. Just because they can get a great deal on an item doesn't mean they'll buy it. This philosophy translates into an unusual inventory. In one aisle you could find car wax and in another silk blouses. Because the majority of goods are a one-time buy, if you see it and like it, buy it. Chances are very good that on your next visit the item will be gone. They also have a nice selection of greeting cards that are always priced at 50% off retail. The people at Bargains Galore also offer a service that is unusual for a store of this nature: if you have something special in mind, they will do their best to find it for you, and at a bargain to boot. If you spend $10 or more, your *Buying Retail Is Stupid!* coupon is good for an extra 10% discount.

Pic 'N' Save
2090 E. Lincoln Ave.
Anaheim, CA 92806
714/776-0973

Hours: Mon-Sat: 9 a.m.-10 p.m. Sun: 9-9
Credit Cards: DISC, MC, V

We absolutely love exploratory shopping at Pic 'N' Save. They have a little bit of everything—play clothes for the kids, cosmetics, sundries, school supplies, linens, silk flowers, decorator items, housewares, hardware, food items, and more—at super-discounted prices. The fun part is that you never know what you'll find. Much of the merchandise is made up of close-outs, so if you see it, buy it. We learned this lesson the hard way. One day we spotted lots of gorgeous, handpainted picture frames, and when we went back the next day to make our purchase, not one was to be found. New goods arrive weekly, so selection is always on the move. Keep Pic 'N' Save in mind when the holidays roll around. You'll find Christmas products of all kinds at or below prices normally found in many retail day-after-Christmas sales.

Additional Locations:
120 stores throughout Southern California—call 800/800-9992.

United Discount Center ★
10340 Sepulveda Blvd.
Mission Hills, CA 91345
818/898-0099

Hours: Mon-Sat: 9-9 Sun: 9-8
Credit Cards: DISC, MC, V

United Discount Center is one of those everything stores that have "a little of this and a lot of that" at bargain prices. They do their utmost to make sure their prices are lower than most discount stores and supermarkets. Some of the best deals are on household items and sundries. A can of cleanser runs 40% less here than at your local market. They have a small section of electronic goods (radios, phones, portable stereos, etc.) that come with an extended one-year warranty. If something goes wrong within one year, as long as you save the original box and your receipt, they'll swap it for a new equivalent item. The store in Sun Valley is called Golden Dollar Discount. Your *Buying Retail Is Stupid!* coupon is good for an extra 10% discount on any nonsale item.

Additional Location:
Sun Valley–8367 Laurel Canyon Blvd., 818/504-9377

See Also: (refer to index)
       Bargain Circus
       Half Price Stores Inc.

Check return policies
before buying.

NEW & USED MERCHANDISE

Ad-Mart
9937 Commerce Ave.
Tujunga, CA 91402
818/353-1447
Hours: Mon-Sat: 9-5
Credit Cards: Cash or Checks Only

Everything you see in Ad-Mart is sold on consignment, and believe us when we say you never know what you'll find. They have clothing for the whole family, with the largest selection of men's jeans (priced $5 to $15) we've ever seen in a store like this. There are quite a few household items and also a large bin filled with linens. Ad-Mart, a family-owned business, has been serving their community since 1947. Consignments are taken Monday through Friday from 9 to 10 a.m., and again at 1 to 2 p.m., and on Saturday 9 to 10 a.m. only. No goods are accepted during the last week of the month.

Aunt Fannie's Attic
7146 Reseda Blvd.
Reseda, CA 91335
818/705-9429
Hours: Mon-Fri: 9-4:30 Sat: 10-4
Credit Cards: MC, V
♦ **Senior Discount:** 20% **Age:** 65

Aunt Fannie's Attic is a charity thrift shop for the National Asthma Center. Inventory—clothing, housewares, and sometimes furniture—is always on the move, and they have quarterly sales to make room for incoming merchandise. There's always a rack with everything priced at $1, and believe it or not, they have a layaway plan and dressing rooms, too. Usually there are new items donated by manufacturers, and if you have a few items around the house you no longer use, donations are always welcome. Senior citizens receive an additional 20% discount, but only if they ask.

Cinema Glamour Shop
343 N. La Brea
Los Angeles, CA 90036
213/936-9060
Hours: Mon-Fri: 10-4
Credit Cards: Cash Only

Now you can purchase items worn and used by movie stars. Cinema Glamour Shop's entire stock of merchandise consists of donations from the movie industry. Anything and everything donated to them by the industry is for sale here, so you never know what you are going to find. If you go down to the Cinema Glamour Shop to do some exploring, leave your checkbook and credit cards at home. This thrift shop operates strictly on a cash basis.

Collateral Loans, Inc. ★
18520 Sherman Way
Reseda, CA 91335
818/345-9600
Hours: Mon, Wed-Sat: 9-5
Credit Cards: Cash or Checks Only

This is really a loan corporation store, where all of the merchandise has been preowned, but not necessarily used. You can save as much as 80% on video equipment, typewriters, jewelry, crystal, bicycles, stereos, household appliances, and more. Some personal property was collateral on loans; other items have been bought outright from individuals and estates. You'll see some items still in factory-sealed cartons from IBM, Nikon, Pioneer, Martin, Zeiss, and more. If you happen to be looking for a particular item, put your name on their wish list and they'll call you if it becomes available. If you pay with cash, your *Buying Retail Is Stupid!* coupon is good for an extra 20% discount. Ask for Sam, and be sure to inquire about their twice-yearly sales. Parking is free.

Out of the Closet Thrift Store/Hollywood
1408 N. Vine St.
Hollywood, CA 90028
213/466-7601
Hours: Mon-Sat: 10-7 Sun: 12-7
Credit Cards: MC, V

Scouring thrift shops is a great way to save money, and occasionally it's possible to stumble across a "treasure" of some sort—also, the money you spend at many thrift stores goes to a worthy cause. Out of the Closet Thrift Store/Hollywood benefits Aunt Bee's, a free laundry service to bed- and home-bound people living with AIDS. Also, at least 250 articles of clothing are donated weekly to the homeless. Donations come from many sources, including excess clothing from the wardrobe department of major studios. They do their best to make sure their prices are lower than other similar stores. Everything is divided neatly into sections featuring middle-to high-end brand names. There is also a very good selection of used books. So, if you're downsizing instead of acquiring, drop off your excess goods—family clothing, shoes, accessories, dishes, linens, towels, working appliances, or whatever, at Out of the Closet Thrift Store/Hollywood. Anyone interested in the client services provided by Aunt Bee's should call 213/468-0744.

Additional Locations:
7 other stores throughout Southern California

4

Directory of Discount Mail-Order Companies

Money-Saving Shopping Without Leaving Home

DIRECTORY OF DISCOUNT MAIL-ORDER COMPANIES

MONEY-SAVING SHOPPING WITHOUT LEAVING HOME

Buying from catalogs is a huge part of the consumer scene and growing all the time. Mail-order purchasing has become significant to individuals who want to buy conveniently from their home, locate articles that may not be readily available in stores, and save money through discounts and low prices due to reduced overhead. No salespeople or fancy facilities are needed by catalog operations.

Initially, people may be hesitant to send money to an unknown entity for something they haven't seen, touched, or tried on—especially with the publicity sometimes given to rip-offs. However, with increased numbers of people reporting positive experiences and with guaranteed satisfaction and return policies, reservations are diminishing. Once someone overcomes hesitancy and becomes a first-time buyer, that person frequently becomes a regular mail-order purchaser.

The following strategies are aimed at maximizing benefits and minimizing risks. In using these suggestions, you will probably find—like millions of others—that mail-order buying can be convenient, fun, and cost-effective.

- Start your own discount mail-order library by writing for catalogs of companies that interest you. Catalogs are free in most cases. You can locate these companies by using the *Buying Retail Is Stupid!* catalog section as well as other sources.
- As the catalogs arrive, have fun looking through them. Mark any items that you may be interested in purchasing. Make a separate list indicating the company name, page number, item, and cost.
- Compare the retail price for desired items with the mail-order price.
- From those that appear to be "good buys," experiment by first ordering a few low- or medium-priced items.
- Before ordering, call to verify delivery, return, and satisfaction guaranteed policies. Many companies have 800 numbers.

- For higher-priced items, especially involving companies with which your experience is limited, you may want to ask for the names of one or two purchaser references. Prepare specific questions, and contact these references.
- Develop confidence with particular companies; establish your favorites, and deal with them regularly.
- Establish a working relationship with a specific person at the company.

The companies listed in this chapter are arranged in alphabetical order by product category (for example, appliances are listed before furniture) and then by company name within each product category. "See Also" is used to indicate stores in Chapter 3 that also carry the product and will mail directly to customers. Refer to the Index of Discount Stores & Outlets for the page numbers of these stores.

If you know the name of a company you wish to find out about or contact, the quickest way is to look it up in the alphabetical index of mail-order companies in the back of the book.

Always buy clothing that fits now, not for after you lose 10 pounds.

ABC Vacuum Cleaner Warehouse
6720 Burnet Rd.-BR
Austin, TX 78757
800/285-8145

Cost: Free

Some people are skeptical and do not understand how ABC Vacuum Cleaner Warehouse sells vacuum cleaners for such low prices. Well, here's the inside secret. They buy from suppliers that are overstocked or going out of business and do not have an expensive overhead. They try to have the lowest prices, but if you find it lower give them a call for an opportunity to beat their competition. All merchandise is new and in the original factory carton and comes with a warranty from ABC Vacuum Cleaner Warehouse. Among the brands are Royal, Oreck, Sharp, Sanyo, Panasonic, Simplicity, Lenhaus, Kirby, Rainbow, and Filter Queen.

Sewin' in Vermont
84 Concord Ave.
St. Johnsbury, VT 05819
800/451-5124

Cost: Free

If you do your own sewing, check out Sewin' in Vermont. They carry brand-name sewing machines, serges, presses, and notions at unbelievable prices.

The Sewing Machine Outlet
8814 Ogden Ave.
Brookfield, IL 60513
800/642-4056, 708/485-2834

Cost: Free

Shop at The Sewing Machine Outlet and save at least 25%. The Sewing Machine Outlet features sewing machines from New Home, Singer, and White. They also sell Oreck vacuum cleaners. Brochures are available, but you can call for a free price quote. All sewing machine orders that exceed $300 include a free carrying case (a $38 value).

Suburban Sew'N Sweep, Inc.
8814 Ogden Ave.
Brookfield, IL 60513
800/642-4056

Cost: Free

Suburban Sew'N Sweep carries the complete selection of Singer, White, and New Home sewing machines and serges. All machines are new, with full factory warranties, and shipped UPS. Savings range from 30 to 50%.

See Also: (refer to index)
Barrett's Appliances
Vinotemp International

Check labels for fabric content.
Natural fibers usually last longer.

ART SUPPLIES

Daniel Smith Artists Materials
4150 First Ave. South
Seattle, WA 98134
800/426-6740

Cost: Free

Daniel Smith Artists Materials has a beautiful catalog and offers 10 to 35% savings for the artistically minded. They manufacture their own lines of professional-quality oils, acrylics, watercolors, and printmaking inks. In addition, they carry a wide selection of brushes, paint, paper, frames, and other equipment. You'll also find that ordering from them is a pleasure. They are very customer oriented.

Ott's Discount Art Supply
102 Hungate Dr.
Greenville, NC 27858
800/356-3289

Cost: Free

Ott's claims to supply the most creative people in the world with art supplies at up to 75% off retail. Their goal is to make sure you are completely satisfied. If there are any problems, contact them within 30 days for a refund.

Pearl Paint Co., Inc.
308 Canal St.
New York, NY 10013
800/221-6845, 212/431-7932

Cost: $1

Get your creative juices flowing and call Pearl Paint Co. for any artist, graphic, and craft supplies you need. They have 11 floors and 3 buildings filled with these items at savings of up to 70% off retail. With more than 450,000 items, Pearl is your one-stop creative resource—the ultimate source for art, craft, and graphic supplies, tools, and furniture at 10 to 70% off retail. They also carry the following: kids' crafts, unique gifts, prints and posters, frames, fine writing instruments, computer furniture and accessories, stationery, daily planners, scrapbooks, and much, much more.

CRAFT & FLORAL SUPPLIES

Craft King
P.O. Box 90637
Lakeland, FL 33804
800/769-9494

Cost: Free

Craft King is dedicated to providing you with the highest-quality craft supplies at super-low prices, every day. The first catalog (more than 100 pages) you'll receive represents only a portion of their products. With your first order, they will forward their largest catalog (200 pages) with the latest craft materials available. Choose from more than 180 categories of items such as art sets, bead kits, bridal supplies, crystals, glues, Styrofoam shapes, music, candle-making kits, miniatures, and much more. Returns are accepted 30 days from receipt of materials.

Creative Craft House
P.O. Box 2567
Bullhead City, AZ 86430
520/754-3300

Cost: $2 (refundable upon order)

This no-frills catalog features hundreds and hundreds of craft items, including a Bonus Section of 32 pinecone and seashell projects. Depending on the amount you spend, they offer selected items with an additional 10 to 30% savings off their already low prices. You won't have to wait long for your merchandise because all orders are processed within two working days.

Gettinger Feather Corp. (A.K.A. AA Gettinger Feather Co.)
16 W. 36th St.
New York, NY 10018
212/695-9470

Cost: $2 (for price list with samples)

Be daring and dress up your evening wear with a feather boa from Gettinger's. You'll find every type of feather for any purpose. Want to restuff your old feather pillows? Why not buy their bedding feathers? Or for crafts, how about trying some of their pheasant, turkey, duck, goose, rooster, peacock, or ostrich feathers? Gettinger's is a landmark in New York, serving the public with savings of up to 50% off retail since 1915.

Hats By Leko
2081 Buffalo St.
Casper, WY 82604
800/817-HATS (817-4287)

Cost: $5

Hat lovers, we have hats for you straight from the importer. Hats By Leko offers you unfinished hats, hat supplies, flowers, and trims, all at discounted prices. Orders are shipped within two working days. There is a $30 minimum, and all sales are final.

Leather Unlimited Corp.
7155 Hwy. B, Dept. BRS96
Belgium, WI 53004
414/994-9464

Cost: $2

Leather Unlimited has been offering a wide array of leather, leather accessories, findings, buckles, leather kits, and finished products since 1970. Leather findings include buckles, snaps, zippers, belts, leather care, books, beads, and more. Finished products include sheepskin accessories, wallets, handbags, belts, hats, Indian jewelry, and other quality items. You can expect to save 25 to 60% off retail.

Roussel's
P.O. Box 476
Arlington, MA 02174
508/443-8888

Cost: 50¢

Roussel's specializes in parts for making earrings and necklaces. Their catalog offers up to 70% off retail. They are a no-frills company with great prices.

Smiley's Yarns
92-06 Jamaica Ave.
Woodhaven, NY 11421
718/847-2185

Cost: Free (with self-addressed, stamped envelope)

Smiley's Yarns is the ultimate yarn source for people who take their knitting seriously. Since 1935, they have offered first-quality, name-brand yarns at discounts of 40 to 80% off retail. Some brand names they feature are Phildar, Pingouin, Bernat, and Patons. If, for any reason, you aren't completely satisfied, return the yarn for an immediate refund. They offer "Only the best, always for less."

Warner Crivellaro Stained Glass Supplies
1855 Weaversville Rd.
Allentown, PA 18103
800/523-4242

Cost: $3

One of the most complete catalogs of stained glass and related supplies in the world! This catalog has everything for the beginner up to the expert, all at low wholesale prices. Their extensive inventory includes more than a thousand colors of glass, lamp bases, bevels, tools, books, brass filigree, metal sculptures, and project kits. They are continuously introducing new products and ideas for the stained glass industry. This catalog is a must for any stained glass enthusiast.

FABRICS & NOTIONS

The Button Shop
P.O. Box 1065
Oak Park, IL 60304
708/795-1234

Cost: Free

Don't let the name of this store fool you. The Button Shop, in addition to a large selection of buttons (hearts, elephants, dogs, ice cream cones, rocking horses, military, etc.), carries every type of basic sewing notion, such as zippers, thread, elastic, shoulder pads, needles, and scissors, at 20 to 50% off retail.

The Fabric Center
485 Electric Ave.
Fitchburg, MA 01420
508/343-4402

Cost: $2

The Fabric Center has been in business since 1929. They are the country's foremost mail-order distributor of the finest home decorating fabrics available. Their years of experience have given them the expertise to bring first-quality fabrics to the public at savings of 25 to 50% off the national average retail price. Orders are usually shipped within 24 hours. Their 164-page, award-winning catalog contains color photos of thousands of fabrics.

Global Village Imports
3439 N.E. Sandy Blvd., #263
Portland, OR 97232
503/236-9245

Cost: $5

Buy direct from Global Village Imports and save 20 to 50% off retail on their wide variety of handwoven fabrics and trims from Guatemala. Fabrics include brocades, ethnic novelties, ikats, and contemporary designs in 36" widths. Trims are available in many colors and several widths. All goods are 100% cotton, handwoven on large footlooms, and most are machine washable. Send $5 (applicable to first order) and receive a substantial swatch pack. They also donate a percentage of your purchase to organizations working for peace and justice in Guatemala.

Thai Silks
252 State St.
Los Altos, CA 94022
800/221-SILK (221-7455), 415/948-8611

Cost: Free

Exotic silks, in more than 400 designs, make Thai Silks one of the leading suppliers of silk fabrics to the public. You can get a sample collection of all their styles and various types of silks for $20, which is refunded if the samples are returned within 30 days. They also carry a selection of silk lingerie. All this is offered at 30 to 50% savings.

HOBBIES

Abracadabra Magic
Catalog Dept. C685, 125 Lincoln Blvd.
Middlesex, NJ 08846
908/805-0200

Cost: $2

You can do magic! Beginners are their specialty, and they offer delightful, professional-quality magic tricks for ages 3 to 103. Amaze friends with easy-to-do tricks—cards, coins, floating ghosts, scarves, fire, and more. Abracadabra has started thousands of folks like you performing magic, including many world-famous magicians. See why Abracadabra has grown to be the world's largest magical supply company. Order a one-year subscription for $8 (postpaid); order a two-year subscription and you receive the third year for free.

American Science and Surplus
3605 Howard St.
Skokie, IL 60076
847/982-0870

Cost: $2

This catalog is chock full of science and educational kits, toys, tools, surplus, and arts and crafts at savings of up to 50%. How about some of these: a plastic bird-shaped whistle, growing creatures in eggs, or an inflatable globe? All these items can make for a fun party or just keep your kids busy.

Astronomics
2401 Tee Circle, Suites 105/106
Norman, OK 73069
800/422-7876

Cost: Free

The nice thing about Astronomics is that they talk with you first about what you want to do with your telescope, where you're going to use it, and how you're going to use it—before they talk about their discounted prices. Then they recommend the telescope or accessory that they honestly feel best fits your needs. Honest advice like that is hard to come by these days. Their prices are 5 to 60% off retail. They can't guarantee they'll beat everyone's price—but definitely give them a try. A 30-day return policy is offered.

Orion Telescope Center
P.O. Box 1815
Santa Cruz, CA 95061
800/447-1001, 408/464-5710

Cost: Free

Orion Telescope Center claims they have the best customer service in the telescope industry. Savings are 15 to 40% off retail prices on items such as astronomical telescopes, binoculars, spotting scopes, and accessories. Their user-friendly catalog features a full page of information on "how to choose a telescope," as well as 73 pages of merchandise. If you are not completely satisfied with your purchase, just return it in new condition within 30 days of delivery for a prompt refund.

Precision Movement
P.O. Box 679
Emmaus, PA 18049
800/533-2024

Cost: Free

Their 64-page color catalog is filled with quartz clock movements, weather instruments, music box movements, and other clock-making supplies. Precision deals directly with factories all over the world to bring you the finest merchandise available at savings of 20 to 30%. Orders placed in September get an additional 10% off.

For Other Arts, Crafts & Hobbies Sources, See Also: (refer to index)

Buy goods that can be mixed and matched with your existing wardrobe.

AUTOMOBILE NEEDS

J.C. Whitney & Co.
P.O. Box 8410
Chicago, IL 60680
312/431-6102

Cost: Free

Shop America's best automotive catalogs and save up to 50%! J.C. Whitney has been the number one source for quality accessories and parts for over 80 years. Select from a huge inventory of more than 55,000 products. Ask for the 200-page General Catalog, as well as their separate catalogs for Jeep Vehicles, Volkswagen, Sport Utility Vehicles, Recreational Vehicles, Pickups, Motorcycles, and Automotive Tools (limit three).

See Also: (refer to index)
        Battery Specialist/Powerline
        Pacific Audio & Alarm
        Sonny's Radiator Exchange

> For special occasions, rent a gown or cocktail dress for a fraction of the price it would cost to buy a drop-dead gorgeous outfit you'll wear only once.

Beauty by Spector, Inc.
Dept. BRS-96
McKeesport, PA 15134
412/673-3259

Cost: Free

Exciting designer styles of wigs, wiglets, falls, extensions, and cascades for women are available in more than 60 colors with discounts of up to 50% off at Beauty by Spector. They also offer custom-type and stock hairpieces for men. Specify women's or men's styles when requesting information. They have an extensive list of additional catalogs on jewelry, precious jewelry, skin care and cosmetics, lingerie, and much more. There is a minimal charge for some of the additional catalogs.

Essential Products Co., Inc.
90 Water St.
New York, NY 10005
212/344-4288

Cost: Free

Why pay up to $315 an ounce for designer perfumes? Beautifully packaged in their own distinctive gift box and individually wrapped, Naudet fragrances make wonderful gifts at huge savings. Just let them know your favorite perfume or cologne such as Joy, Giorgio, Opium, or Obsession, and they'll send you an ounce of a similar-smelling scent for $20, or $11.50 for a half ounce. Men's fragrances sell for $11 for four ounces. If you're not satisfied with your purchase, return it within 30 days for a prompt refund. Send a large (#10 size) self-addressed, stamped envelope to receive five scent cards free, a fragrance list, and an order form.

See Also: (refer to index)
> Perfume City
> Perfumes West for Less
> Shaky Wigs of Hollywood
> Wilshire Beauty Supply Co.

Daedalus Books

P.O. Box 9132
Hyattsville, MD 20781
800/395-2665

Cost: Free

From the thousands of books offered by publishers as remainders every year, Daedalus chooses only those books that, in their judgment, are of lasting value. They believe that the quality of remainders in their catalog demonstrates that they're not "books that didn't sell," but rather books whose publishers' stock was larger than the projected future sales. Many of the finest books published every year are remaindered at some point to make room for another season's hopefuls. They feature categories such as fiction, history, poetry, children, gardening, and the arts. Books are generally 50 to 90% off retail. They also sell new books at up to 30% off.

Freebies

1135 Eugenia Pl., Box 5025
Carpenteria, CA 93014
805/566-1225

Cost: $8.95 one year, $12.95 two years

Even though this Freebies catalog is not free, you'll find it's well worth the cost when you see all the great items listed. How about free dinosaur tattoos for the kids, or a 24-page booklet on how to save time and money by properly caring for your clothes, home security tips and alarm warning stickers, or a dog training manual and $5 worth of coupons from Friskies? Some items require self-addressed, stamped envelopes, or $1 to $2 to cover shipping and handling.

Jessica's Biscuit

P.O. Box 301
Newtonville, MA 02160
800/878-4264

Cost: Free

Can you imagine looking through 72 pages of delicious, scrumptious, delectable cookbooks? Within this catalog are cookbooks featured in their "special sale selection" at 30 to 70% off retail prices. Even brand-

new titles are on sale at 10 to 50% off retail. Call for any title—
Jessica's Biscuit stocks more than 4,000 cookbooks, including ones
that are hard to find.

U.S. Government Books
Superintendent of Documents
U.S. Government Printing Office
Washington, DC 20402-9325

Cost: Free

Government publications, for people of all ages, are available through
this catalog. This is an unbelievable source for government books on all
subjects. Covering everything from agriculture, military equipment, and
foreign policy to travel, exercise, and nutritional needs, more than 21,000
different publications are available. Some items, such as informational
booklets, are $1, and historical documents reproduced on parchment
paper run $2 (great for student projects). Also listed are their locations in
various states where you can browse to your heart's content.

> Because tuxedos rarely go out of
> style, frequent tux wearers should
> buy, not rent, them.

ARCHITECTURAL STRUCTURES

Chadsworth's 1.800.Columns
277 N. Front St.
Wilmington, NC 28401
800/COLUMNS (265-8667)
Cost: $5

Chadsworth's is a stocking dealer of authentically correct architectural columns. They have hundreds of styles, including neoclassical, classical, and colonial, available in wood, fiberglass, stone, or marble. Interior and exterior columns are available in all sizes. They also have a complete selection of pillars, pilasters, and posts. Chadsworth's offers competitive pricing and job site delivery anywhere in the world.

DOORS & WINDOWS

Arctic Glass & Window Outlet
565 County Rd. T
Hammond, WI 54015
800/428-WARM (428-9276)
Cost: Free

Unlike with most large companies, the president and owner of Arctic Glass & Window Outlet, Joe Bacon, is still accessible, should you have a problem or unanswered questions about windows, doors, sunrooms, and skylights. Joe emphasizes fairness, fast service, quality products, and the lowest prices possible. They are committed to helping people use insulated glass for energy efficiency, ventilation, and decoration.

FLOOR COVERINGS

Johnson's Carpets
3510 Corporate Dr.
Dalton, GA 30721
800/235-1079, 706/277-2775
Cost: Free

No need to spend days looking for the perfect carpet at the best price, because Johnson's Carpets manufactures carpets and sells direct to you, with savings as high as 80%. Samples are available for all carpets they manufacture, so you can feel the weight and select exactly the right color before placing an order.

S & S Carpet Mills
P.O. Box 1568
Dahon, GA 30722
800/241-4013

Cost: Free

S & S Mills manufactures residential and commercial carpet and sells mill-direct to you, thereby avoiding the middleperson and costly mark-ups. Savings are approximately 50% off retail prices. All carpets are manufactured using the highest-quality raw materials and the most stringent quality-control measures. They offer defect-free carpet with a 100% satisfaction guarantee.

Warehouse Carpets, Inc.
P.O. Box 3233
Dalton, GA 30721
800/526-2229

Cost: Free

Save as much as 50% on brand-name carpets such as Mohawk, Aladdin, Diamond, Galaxy, Mannington, Shaw, Coronet, and many more. Warehouse Carpets has been operating since 1977 as a specialist in mail orders and direct home delivery.

HARDWARE

Abbey Tools
1132 N. Magnolia Blvd.
Anaheim, CA 92801
800/225-6321, 714/772-7222

Cost: Free

Whether you are a construction worker, a homeowner, or a craftsperson, a call to Abbey Tools mail-order company will guarantee low prices on more than 3,000 first-quality tools. They specialize in power tools and accessories for woodworking. Major brands include Makita, Milwaukee, Delta, Black and Decker, Bosch, Skill, Hitachi, and many more. Savings are up to 40 to 50% off retail, and orders over $50 are shipped free, except to Alaska and Hawaii. Abbey also has a "no-hassle" return policy.

Direct Line
7721 Pillsbury Ave. South
Richfield, MN 55423
800/241-2197

Cost: Free

This 64-page catalog from Direct Line features power washers, generators, electric motors, power tools, hand tools, water pumps, and much more at savings of 40 to 60% below retail. This is a "digest of discounts" for the professional and do-it-yourselfer. Catalogs are published four times a year and feature brands such as Honda, Hydroquick, Coleman, Briggs, Master, Agri Fab, and more. All purchases are shipped within 24 hours, and unused items can be returned within 30 days with a return authorization.

Faucet Outlet
P.O. Box 547
Middletown, NY 10940
800/444-5783

Cost: $5 (refundable upon first order)

You won't believe the variety of faucets, plumbing fixtures, and home improvement products available from Faucet Outlet. Their 80-page catalog only touches the surface of the thousands of different faucets and plumbing fixtures they offer at 20 to 50% off retail. Products from American Standard, Chicago Faucets, Delta, Elkay, Jado, Moen, Price Pfister, Kohler, Delta, St. Thomas Creations, Swanston, and Grohe are featured. So be creative and add a new look to your kitchen and bathroom.

Tools On Sale
216 W. 7th St.
St. Paul, MN 55102
800/328-0457

Cost: Free

This is the perfect bedside or bathroom reading catalog for people who are do-it-yourselfers—or just plain handy. You can get lost in this 480-page catalog looking at all the tools. Prices are up to 40% off retail, with no shipping charges on orders placed within the continental U.S. Also, when calling to place an order, make sure to ask if the item has a special sale price.

WINDOW & WALL TREATMENTS

American Discount Wallcoverings
1411 Fifth Ave.
Pittsburgh, PA 15219
800/777-2737

Cost: Free

You'll find more than 100 brands of wallpaper, window treatments, and upholstery fabrics at substantial savings of 10 to 50% off retail. They don't have a catalog, but they'll send you a list with most of the brand names they carry. After you've shopped around, call American Discount Wallcoverings with book names and pattern numbers.

Robinson's Wallpaper and Interiors
225 W. Spring St.
Titusville, PA 16354
800/458-2426

Cost: $2

Walk from room to room with Robinson's catalog in hand and visualize the beautiful decor you can create. Do-it-yourself decorators have been shopping at Robinson's since 1919.

Silver Wholesale Club
3001-15 Kensington Ave.
Philadelphia, PA 19134
800/426-6600, 215/426-6600

Cost: Free

Silver Wholesale Club has an extensive selection of first-quality wallcoverings, borders, and fabrics, in virtually every pattern manufactured in the country. Call them with the name of the book and the pattern number to receive their discounted prices of up to 81% below retail. They also sell Croscill bed linens and matching accessories.

Smith & Noble Windoware
P.O. Box 1838
Corona, CA 91718
800/248-8888

Cost: Free

We've never seen a catalog so user-friendly as Smith & Noble Windoware's for blinds, shutters, and shades. First, there are instructions on an easy, step-by-step process that the pros use to get perfect-fitting custom window treatments; then there are tips on custom fits and installation and on giving your rooms the right look and right light. Their selection is endless—hand-crafted wood blinds from premium kiln-dried hardwood, super energy-saving window covers, natural-fiber shades, and of course, Levolor blinds, verticals, cellular shades, valances, and roller shades. Their lowest-price guarantee offers you a reduction of 5% below any other price you find elsewhere. This catalog is a real find.

For Other Building & Remodeling Sources, See Also: (refer to index)
Discount Tile Center
Interior Motives
The Kitchen Store

> When shopping for clothing, ignore brand names. Look instead for well-made items using good fabrics and notions.

CLOTHING

Alberene Scottish Cashmeres
435 Fifth Ave.
New York, NY 10016
800/843-9078, 212/689-0151

Cost: Free

Prepare yourself for cooler weather with cashmere items from Alberene Scottish Cashmeres. Here you'll find a huge inventory of the finest Scottish cashmere sweaters, coats, capes, scarves, and accessories for women and men with savings of 40 to 50% off retail. But don't let the low prices fool you; everything at Alberene is exactly the same quality as the most famous and expensive Scottish brands. Alberene offers free shipping within the United States and a 30-day, full-refund return policy.

Arctic Sheepskin Outlet
I–94 at Hammond Exit
Hammond, WI 54015
800/428-9276

Cost: Free

If you're heading for cold country and need to keep your ears warm, or just want the comfort of luxurious sheepskin as a bicycle seat cover, then Arctic Sheepskin Outlet is the place for you. Savings of 20% are possible on hats and slippers and up to 50% on seat covers, rugs, mittens, car seats, bicycle seats, steering wheel covers, and more. Children's slippers are also available. There is an $8 shipping charge per order. Their merchandise is also guaranteed to be free of defects for one year.

Baby Clothes Wholesale
60 Ethel Rd. West
Piscataway, NJ 08854
800/568-1940

Cost: $3

If you're in the market for name-brand baby clothes, invest $3 for their catalog. You'll find boys' and girls' clothing from sizes infant to 4-toddler at 50% off retail. The catalog features a variety of fashions, from Mickey

Mouse and Goofy jacket sets with pants to a five-pocket, flowered overall with floppy hat. Baby Clothes Wholesale carries all major brands including Gerber, Hopscotch, Goodlad, Spencers, and Dundee and stands behind everything with a 30-day, money-back guarantee.

Dance Distributors
P.O. Box 11440
Harrisburg, PA 17108
800/33-DANCE (333-2623)

Cost: Free

If you are a dancer or know one, Dance Distributors is the place for dance shoes, bodywear, and accessories. Their prices are at least 25% below list; also, look for their special sales to save even more. They carry their own lines as well as Capezio, Danskin, Crishko, Sansha, Mirella, and more. If an item is not listed in their catalog, they can special-order it (no returns). Regular returns are accepted within 30 days; their normal shipping cost is $5 for the first item and 30¢ for each additional one.

The Deerskin Place
283 Akron Rd.
Ephrata, PA 17522
717/733-7624

Cost: $1

Choose from a wide selection of jackets (biker, bomber, suede-fringe, and more), handbags, shoes, moccasins, gloves, and wallets for men and women made from cowhide, sheepskin, and deerskin, and save up to 50%. You can even order a coonskin cap.

Rubens & Marble, Inc.
P.O. Box 14900-S
Chicago, IL 60614-0900

Cost: Free with self-addressed, stamped envelope

Since 1890, Rubens & Marble, Inc. has been supplying infant garments to hospitals all over the country. You'll save up to 60% on shirts, gowns, kimonos, sheets, stay-up stretch diapers, training and waterproof pants or panties, and terry bibs for sizes ranging from infant to 36 months. Most items are cotton irregulars with small knitting flaws, but first quality is available. A package of two irregular undershirts costs $1.99. Request a free brochure by sending a self-addressed, stamped business-size envelope.

Sport Europa
7871 NW 15 St.
Miami, FL 33126
800/695-7000

Cost: Free

Here are some of the sexiest bathing suits for men and women at savings of up to 50% off retail. You should order this catalog just to see what someone can dream up! Your body will definitely get a tan in all the right places. They also carry sexy ladies' dresses made of cotton/lycra, training wear for men and women, workout gloves, men's cotton baggie pants, and diver suits.

Sportswear Clearinghouse
P.O. Box 317746Y3
Cincinnati, OH 45231
513/522-3511

Cost: Free

Surprise, surprise, surprise! That's what you'll receive when you order T-shirts, sweatshirts, visors and caps, socks, and shorts from Sportswear Clearinghouse. They have overruns from other manufacturers with a logo on the goods. When ordering, you can specify only the size; the rest will be a surprise when you receive the goods.

LINGERIE

Charisma California
14550 Apache Ave.
Largo, FL 34644
800/TRY-HOSE (879-4673)

Cost: Free

If you're tired of spending too much money replacing panty hose, then call Charisma. They are the U.S. distributor for sheer 20 denier stockings that wear durably and carry a money-back guarantee. The run-resistant hosiery comes in 19 colors and ranges in sizes from petite to queen. Hosiery is sold in dozen lots only and starts at $34 per dozen (you may mix the colors). You'll save a bundle by not having to continuously replace your nylons.

L'eggs, Hanes, Bali, Playtex Outlet Catalog
P.O. Box 748
Rural Hall, NC 27098
800/300-2600

Cost: Free

Ladies, you'll be able to cover your legs with some of the lowest-priced panty hose around. Savings are up to 60% off retail on L'eggs, Hanes, Bali, and Playtex. This 50-page catalog carries bras, pantyhose, undies, and slips as well as active wear for men and women.

SHOES

California Best
970 Broadway
Chula Vista, CA 91911
800/225-2378

Cost: Free

You can purchase men's and women's athletic shoes, apparel, and accessories from California Best at 30 to 40% off retail; they also guarantee the best prices. They carry brand-name shoes such as Nike, Reebok, Asics, Saucony, and even EE and EEEE in New Balance shoes for men. If you know the exact shoe you're looking for, call and place your order, or request a free catalog.

Justin Discount Boots and Cowboy Outfitters
P.O. Box 67
Justin, TX 76247
800/677-BOOT (677-2668)

Cost: Free

Whether you build roads, ranch, dance the two-step, or just like making an impression with a knock-out-look boot, Justin Discount Boots will definitely fit the bill. Justin has the world's largest selection of cowboy boots—and they stand behind their product. If you're not satisfied, returns can be made within a reasonable length of time. Styles for men, women, and children come in a variety of colors such as forest green, burgundy, and turquoise, and of course all your standards. Featured in the catalog are western belts and shirts, men's and ladies' Wrangler jeans starting at $19.99, and toddler jeans for $16.95.

Okun Brothers Shoes
356 E. South St.
Kalamazoo, MI 49007
800/433-6344

Cost: Free

Save up to 35% off retail on shoes for the entire family through this catalog service. Okun Brothers Shoes handles brand names such as New Balance, Soft Spots, Clarks, Hush Puppies, Daniel Green, Florsheim, Dexter, Rockports, Reebok, Avia, and Timberland, and many more. They can provide nearly every shoe size in widths from AAA to EEEE. They say, "Shop by mail, no traffic, no parking, no babysitters, and no fuss!"

For Other Clothing & Accessories Sources, See Also: (refer to index)

Buy shoes toward the end of the day when feet are a bit larger.

Creative Computers' MacMall
2645 Maricopa St.
Torrance, CA 90503
800/222-2808

Cost: Free

Now you can order Apple Macintosh computers by mail. This 140-page catalog will save you up to 90% on software with the purchase of a new Macintosh and offers the lowest prices on Apple brand products. You'll have a 30-day, money-back guarantee on many products (specially identified in catalog), and for an additional $3, you can have your merchandise shipped overnight.

Crutchfield
1 Crutchfield Park, Dept. BRS
Charlottesville, VA 22906
800/955-9009

Cost: Free

Find exactly what you're looking for in car and home stereos, and save money too! Take advantage of great discount prices on hundreds of name-brand components, including Sony, Kenwood, Pioneer, JVC, Polk, Bose, and Infinity. Depend on Crutchfield's 30-day, total-satisfaction guarantee! You'll love how their detailed product descriptions, exclusive comparison charts, and helpful buying advice make it easy to choose what's best for you. Call now for your free copy! Discover how easy it can be to shop and save from the comfort of your own home.

Heartland America
6978 Shady Oak Rd.
Eden Prairie, MN 55344
800/229-2901

Cost: Free

How about a Lumiscope Blood Pressure Monitor for $99.99 (retail $155.99), a Uniden Laser/Radar Detector for $89.99 (retail $149.95), or Hamilton Beach Indoor Steam Grill for $39.99 (retail $64.99)? Heartland America offers a little bit of everything. The catalog features close-outs with even greater savings.

S & S Sound City

58 W. 45th St.
New York, NY 10036
800/326-1677, 212/575-0210

Cost: Free

S & S Sound City prides itself on giving excellent service and prices since 1975. They inventory a large stock of electronics such as TVs, video equipment, telephones, hi-fi stereo equipment, closed-circuit TV equipment, and personal electronics.

See Also: (refer to index)
Asmara Overseas Shippers
Comp USA
Speaker City

If you know you'll be trying on a lot of clothing, wear slip-ons instead of shoes that tie, and wear an outfit that's easy to get into and out of.

Caviarteria Inc.

502 Park Ave.
New York, NY 10022
800/4-CAVIAR (422-8427)

Cost: Free

Dine like the rich and famous with Caspian Beluga and Sevruga caviar, plus American sturgeon, whitefish, and salmon caviar, but without the high prices. Caviarteria, established in 1950, is the largest distributor of caviar in the U.S. and features discounts from 20 to 60% off retail. Call for their catalog which features a wide variety of other gourmet treats such as smoked salmon and much more. If you are ever in the New York area, treat yourself to affordably elegant dining in Caviarteria's Caviar and Champagne Tasting Bar.

New England Cheesemaking Supply Co., Inc.

85 Main St.
Ashfield, MA 01330
413/628-3808

Cost: Free

If you're a health nut or just want to experiment with something new, try making your own cheese. It's less expensive, less fattening, and lower in cholesterol, and it has no preservatives—can't beat that! Ricki Carrol has been offering home dairying supplies for more than 18 years. Cheesemaking kits range in prices from $12.95 for a Mascarpone kit (a delicious fresh Italian cheese made from cream) to $210.95 for the Wheeler Cheese Press handcrafted in England, constructed from hardwood and stainless steel, and made to last a lifetime.

San Francisco Herb Co.

250 14th St.
San Francisco, CA 94103
800/227-4530

Cost: Free

The prices at San Francisco Herb Co. are so low, you really won't believe them until you place an order for yourself. For example, lovers of peppermint teas can get about 250 tea bags (one pound) for less than $6.

At the supermarket 24 tea bags cost around $2.25. How about some garlic powder for $4.30 a pound. There are hundreds of herbs, dehydrated veggies, botanicals, shelled nuts and seeds, and baking and food items—even potpourri ingredients along with recipes. The hook here is that you must order a minimum of $30—so, get a couple of friends together for lots of savings. If you're on the East Coast, you probably want to order from their sister company, Atlantic Spice Co. in North Truro, Maine, by calling 800/316-7965.

Wood's Cider Mill
Road 2, P.O. Box 477
Springfield, VT 05156
802/263-5547

Cost: Free (with self-addressed, stamped envelope)

If you like traditions, make sure you purchase some unsweetened cider jelly and other fine apple products made by the same family on the same farm since 1798. They start with fresh apples and squeeze the juice on their century-old cider press. The cider is then boiled over a wood fire until it is thick enough to gel, with nothing added. Let your tastebuds carry you back to the good ol' days with their cider jelly, boiled cider syrup, and maple syrup, all at very reasonable prices.

HEALTH FOODS & VITAMINS

Jaffe Bros. Inc.
P.O. Box 636
Valley Center, CA 92082
619/749-1133

Cost: Free

If you're one of the many who like to eat healthful foods, then order Jaffe Bros.' 20-page catalog featuring organically or naturally grown dried fruits, nuts, seeds, beans, wholewheat pastas, oils, honey, and more. They keep prices down by selling a minimum of five pounds on most items or three jars of such items as organic low-salt sauerkraut or organic flax seed oil. They are now offering many items in two-pound packages for those who wish to try out new foods.

Sunburst Biorganics
832 Merrick Rd.
Baldwin, NY 11510
800/645-8448

Cost: Free

Save up to 70% on more than 4,000 vitamin products from Sunburst Biorganics. You can get alfalfa tablets, brewer's yeast, cod-liver oil, herbal laxatives, spirulina tabs, wheat germ oil gels, and a large variety of vitamins for you and even your pet. All their supplements are made from natural ingredients, with no sugar, starch, salt, or preservatives added. So, stay healthy and take some vitamins.

The Vitamin Factory
201 Route 22
Hillside, NJ 07205
800/619-1199

Cost: Free

The Vitamin Factory is committed to giving you the highest quality, lowest prices, and best possible service anywhere on more than 200 varieties of vitamins. If you are not completely satisfied with your purchase, return the unused portion within 30 days for a full refund.

SPIRITS

Brew City Supplies
P.O. Box 27729
Milwaukee, WI 53227
414/425-8595

Cost: Free

In this catalog from Brew City Supplies, find all the necessary hardware and ingredients to make great beer at home. Save 30 to 50% on brand names such as Scmidling Malt Mills, Northwestern Extracts, Yeast Lab, Coopers, Breiss Malts, John Bull, and more. Most orders are shipped within 24 hours, and Brew City will beat any competitor's advertised prices.

Brewers Resource
409 Calle San Pablo, #104
Camarillo, CA 93012
800/827-3983, Advice Line: 805/445-4100

Cost: Free

Brewers Resource claims to have the most comprehensive collection of home-brewing equipment and supplies, including hard-to-find and specialized products at 10 to 30% below retail. Their nationwide catalog features newly added yeast strains, the Complete Yeast Culturing Kit, and many helpful yeast culturing accessories.

The Cellar
14411 Greenwood Ave., N
Seattle, WA 98133
800/342-1871

Cost: Free

The Cellar has everything you need for brewing beer and making wine and liqueur at the best prices around. Their catalog features free recipes, and if you have a problem, there's an expert on duty to help you Monday through Saturday 10 a.m. to 6 p.m. and Sunday noon to 4 p.m. PST. Just call 206/365-7660.

Wine Link
440 Talbert St.
Daly City, CA 94014
800/231-1171

Cost: Free

If you enjoy a glass of wine and are sensitive to the chemicals and pesticides used on the grapes, then Wine Link is for you. They import French and Italian wines made from certified organically grown grapes. This means no chemical fertilizers, no herbicides, and no fungicides are used in the grape-growing process. They also have a selection of wines with no added sulfites. Get all this and savings of 15% off retail.

For Other Food & Beverage Sources, See Also: (refer to index)

CHINA, COOKWARE, CRYSTAL & SILVER

A Cook's Wares
211 37th St.
Beaver Falls, PA 15010
412/846-9490

Cost: $2

Tired of looking for new accessories for your Cuisinart? In "A Cook's Wares" catalog you'll find almost every type of blade and accessory for any type of Cuisinart appliance. Byron and Gail Bitar, owners since 1982, are constantly seeking the finest cookware and utensils and offering them at 20 to 40% off retail. The 63-page catalog features cutlery such as Henckels, and appliances such as direct infusion coffee makers, espresso makers, pasta machines, Rosti bowls, cookbooks, condiments, bakeware, porcelains, pepper mills, and "Try Me" specials.

Barrons
P.O. Box 994
Novi, MI 48376
800/538-6340

Cost: Free

Barrons provides you with the finest giftware, collectibles, crystal, dinnerware, and flatware at 30 to 60% off retail. They have the largest in-stock selection in the United States. Brand names include Hummel, Royal Doulton, Lenox, Mikasa, Oneida, Gorham, and many more. A bridal registry service is also available.

Beverly Bremer Silver Shop
3164 Peachtree Rd., N.E.
Atlanta, GA 30305
404/261-4009

Cost: Free

Missing a piece of your sterling silver flatware? Beverly Bremer Silver Shop keeps in stock more than a thousand patterns of new and beautiful-as-new sterling, so they can help you locate exotic as well as practical flatware items for your collection. They also have new and antique silver gift items. Contact them if you are interested in selling your sterling silver.

Buschemeyer's Silver Exchange
515 S. 4th Ave.
Louisville, KY 40202
800/626-4555

Cost: Free

This is a source for approximately 1,400 different active, current, and discontinued sterling, silverplate, and stainless patterns. New and estate pieces of holloware are also available at discount prices. They will be glad to find your pattern and quote prices. Send for brochures listing active sterling silver, silverplate, or stainless patterns which are available from Buschemeyer's Silver Exchange at discount prices.

Chef's Catalog
3215 Commercial Ave.
Northbrook, IL 60062
800/338-3232

Cost: Free

Chef's Catalog is filled with products for indoor and outdoor cooking. You'll find items for basic food preparation and specialized equipment for unusual or complicated recipes. This catalog has the largest selection of world-class cookware and bakeware in a variety of shapes, sizes, and materials, barbecues (indoor, outdoor, large, and small) and accessories, ice cream makers, and many other culinary necessities. There are also lots of professional kitchen tools that chefs won't be able to live without.

Colonial Garden Kitchens
P.O. Box 66
Hanover, PA 17333-0066
800/245-3399

Cost: Free

If you enjoy unique, cleverly designed products that in many cases aren't available in any store, you'll be glad to know that this catalog is full of interesting and unusual products that can make cooking and entertaining easier. So, go ahead and buy now, and pay later.

Kaiser Crow
14998 W. 6th Ave., #500
Golden, CO 80401
800/468-2769

Cost: Free

Kaiser Crow offers first-quality Oneida flatware at guaranteed lowest prices. Your money will be promptly refunded if you're not completely satisfied with your purchase.

Midas China & Silver
4315 Walney Rd., Dept. BRS
Chantilly, VA 22021
800/368-3153

Cost: Free

Pass on the memories of fine china and sterling flatware from Midas China & Silver. Your children and grandchildren will enjoy receiving items from their elegant selection. A national bridal registry service is available. Only the finest merchandise is in this catalog, with savings of up to 70%.

Ross-Simons
9 Ross Simons Dr.
Cranston, RI 02920
800/556-7376

Cost: Free

If you're looking for beautiful tableware and collectibles, Ross-Simons offers them priced at 20 to 60% below retail. Enter in their national bridal registry by calling 800/82-BRIDE (822-7433) with your choice of china, flatware, and crystal patterns. You needn't be limited to items featured in the catalog; they carry most famous brands and can locate almost any pattern.

Thurber
2256-C Dabney Rd.
Richmond, VA 23230
800/848-7237

Cost: $1

The color catalog from Thurber showcases both fine tableware and gifts with savings of 20 to 60%. Their Christmas holiday catalog features limited-edition plates and ornaments. Satisfaction is guaranteed, and returns are accepted within 30 days.

DECORATOR ITEMS

Emperor Clock Company
Emperor Industrial Park, P.O. Box 1089
Fairhope, AL 36533
334/928-2316

Cost: $2

You will absolutely flip over the exquisite grandfather clocks, cuckoo clocks, mantel clocks, wall clocks, and curio kits available for purchase from this catalog. By assembling these items yourself, you can save 30 to 60% off the retail prices. The kits come with only premium-grade solid hardwoods such as cherry, oak, and walnut. The Emperor collection also includes a full line of furniture kits. Factory craftspeople precision-cut all parts including miters, mortises, and tenons. As an added convenience, the more difficult parts are pre-assembled for you. You truly will enjoy looking through this catalog. Emperor Clock Company is the world's largest grandfather clock kit company.

Hanover House
P.O. Box 2
Hanover, PA 17333
717/633-3377

Cost: Free

Hanover House is a multifaceted sourcebook for gifts and seasonal, household, and novelty items. Great bargains are available on decorating items for any room of the home. Their 72-page catalog is printed four times a year.

Plexi-Craft Quality Products Corp.
514 W. 24th St.
New York, NY 10011
800/24-PLEXI (247-5394), 212/924-3244

Cost: $2

Buy direct from the manufacturer and save up to 50% with Plexi-Craft's own line of lucite and plexiglass. Their 16-page catalog features acrylic furnishings and accessories such as telephone and television stands, chairs, luggage racks, vanities and stools, magazine units, kitchen organizers, bathroom fixtures, and much more. They also do custom work.

Tapestry
P.O. Box 46
Hanover, PA 17333-0046
800/577-2288

Cost: Free

If you enjoy adding the final touches to a room with tasteful yet inexpensive decorator items, you're going to love Tapestry. You'll find items such as cachepots, planters with stands, nesting tables, lamps, magazine racks, storage items, screens, and chests in a variety of styles and price ranges. They also carry dishes, glasses, and linens.

FURNITURE

Adirondack Designs
350 Cypress St.
Fort Bragg, CA 95437
800/222-0343

Cost: Free

Purchase direct from the manufacturer of outdoor redwood furniture at savings of 30 to 50% off retail. They carry chairs, love seats, lounges, foot rests, and more with easy assembly. Satisfaction is guaranteed or you get a full refund. Adirondack Designs is operated by Parents & Friends, Inc., a non-profit organization that employs persons with developmental disabilities.

The Bartley Collection
65 Engerman Ave.
Denton, MD 21629
800/787-2800

Cost: Free

Choose from more than 300 antique reproduction furniture kits to build yourself a furniture piece from The Bartley Collection—for example, the graceful Chippendale Hooded Cradle, the Pad Foot Table, or the English Muffin Stand. Available in solid mahogany or cherry, these kits have become all-time favorites among customers, are easy to build, and have endless uses around the home. All kits are guaranteed for 30 days, and The Bartley Collection will replace at no charge any missing, defective, or shipment-damaged parts.

Cohasset Colonials
10 Churchill Rd.
Hingham, MA 02043
800/288-2389

Cost: $3

If you appreciate classic furniture design but cannot afford the originals or high-priced reproductions, then you will love this 32-page do-it-yourself catalog from Cohasset Colonials. They offer faithful reproductions of pieces from the most prestigious museums and private collections. All pieces are inspected by museum curators during every step of production to assure that designs equal the originals in quality. Cohasset then adds their own technical know-how and woodworking expertise to create a finished piece that is economical, fun, and easy to assemble. All pieces come with a 30-day, money-back guarantee.

Coppa Woodworking, Inc.
1231 Paraiso Ave.
San Pedro, CA 90731
310/548-5332

Cost: Free

You'll save a bundle on Adirondack chairs, wood screendoors, butcher block tables, and dressing screens from Coppa Woodworking. They offer 10 to 40% savings and will do whatever is necessary to find something that fits your needs. Wood screendoors come in a variety of 90 styles that can be painted too. A lifetime repair guarantee is available.

Shaker Workshops
P.O. Box 8001
Ashburnham, MA 01430
800/840-9121

Cost: Free

Shaker Workshops' furniture kits are produced to rigid specifications by their own skilled craftspeople, based on specific Shaker pieces in museums and private collections. Whenever possible, they use the exact same grade and species of wood used in the originals. They buy from mills with as many as five generations of experience in selecting and seasoning lumber. Only common hand tools are needed to assemble their kits. You'll discover the simplicity of Shaker furniture in its beauty and easy assembly. Some of the kits are replicas of furniture dating back to 1850.

Sobol House of Furnishings
Richardson Blvd.
Black Mountain, NC 28711
704/669-8031

Cost: Free

Shop around and compare brand names and cost on your next furniture purchase, then call Sobol House of Furnishings. They'll save you 40 to 50% off retail prices on their selection of traditional, 18th-century, or modern furniture.

Wicker Warehouse
195 S. River St.
Hackensack, NJ 07601
800/989-4253

Cost: $5

Wicker Warehouse promises top quality, great selection, and savings of 30 to 50% off wicker and rattan furniture. Brand names you'll recognize are Clark, South Sea, Weathercraft, Whitecraft, Braxton, and many more. They are customer-service oriented and definitely out to please you.

Wood Classics
Osprey Lane, Box 96-VB
Gardiner, NY 12525
914/255-5599

Cost: Free

For considerable savings, plus a lot of fun, you can assemble classic American furniture kits from Wood Classics. They come with precision-made parts and clear, detailed directions. All kits are made of the finest quality of solid woods (cherry or oak). The design of furniture featured in the catalog is simple yet elegant. Choose from bedroom sets, chairs, dining and coffee tables, lamps, desks, dressers, and mirrors. There is also a complete line of classically styled outdoor furniture made of solid teak or mahogany. So, if you are a stockbroker, teacher, salesperson, doctor, or lawyer and you're not interested in chucking the old life but would enjoy a chance for self-expression, get a kit from Wood Classics.

LAMPS & LIGHT FIXTURES

Golden Valley Lighting
274 Eastchester Dr., Suite 117A
High Point, NC 27262
800/735-3377

Cost: $5 (refundable with purchase)

At Golden Valley Lighting, they pride themselves in staying at the leading edge of lighting design. Since 1926, they have followed one simple rule: quality comes first. From brass to glass, they create designs that, whether contemporary or traditional, enhance the beauty of your home. Prices are generally 40 to 60% off retail. Their 170-page catalog features hundreds of beautiful chandeliers: ceiling, wall, chain, and cord drop; and also bath and outdoor lighting fixtures, with prices that meet or beat any other mail-order company. Visit your local lighting showroom, jot down manufacturers' names and model numbers, then call for a competitive price.

King's Chandelier Company
Hwy. 14, Box 667, Dept. BRIS
Eden, NC 27289
910/623-6188

Cost: $3.75

"We love our work" is the motto at King's Chandelier Company. The King family has been collecting, designing, making, and selling chandeliers for generations. Every fixture is especially made for you with crystal parts from such places as Venice, Czechoslovakia, and Austria, and metal parts from the U.S. or Europe. They do their own designing and importing and therefore can offer top-quality products at manufacturers' prices. For the serious minded, King's Chandelier Company will furnish you with a color VHS video cassette tape showing the chandeliers from all angles and specifying their dimensions. Advise them of up to six chandeliers from their catalog that you'd like them to tape. A required $25 deposit is refundable when you return the tape.

LINENS

The Company Store
500 Company Store Rd.
La Crosse, WI 54601-4477
800/285-3696

Cost: Free

The Company Store has been in business since 1911, keeping people warm and toasty with their plush down products. Their comforters, in a variety of styles and grades, are all covered in downproof fabric with a minimum 232 thread count. You can get high-quality merchandise without paying department-store prices. Featured in their catalog is a section on "What Every Shopper Should Know About Down Comforters."

Domestications
P.O. Box 40
Hanover, PA 17333-0040
800/746-2555

Cost: Free

Sleeping will never be the same after you receive Domestications. This 100-page catalog features a wide selection of sheet sets, quilts, comforter sets, napkins, and tablecloths in fantastic designs. They also offer a range of discounts.

Eldridge Textile Co.
277 Grand St.
New York, NY 10002
800/635-4399, 212/925-1523

Cost: $3

Eldridge Textile Co. features the latest fashions on comforters, sheets, pillow cases, valances, curtains, and just about anything else you need to beautify your bedroom. They carry only the most recognized design studios in the industry, such as Benetello, Williamsburg, Martex, and Wamsutta. You never have to wait for a sale when purchasing from Eldridge Textile Co. They offer guaranteed lowest prices and will beat any competitor's advertised price on any item you find in another catalog.

Harris Levy, Inc.
278 Grand St.
New York, NY 10002
800/221-7750, 212/226-3102

Cost: $2 (refundable with first purchase)

Discounting up to 40%, Harris Levy will send you linens for your bed, bath, and table. Their motto is "The very best at the least."

For Other Home Furnishings Sources, See Also: (refer to index)
Brass Beds Direct
Goochey's Furnishings & Lighting
Mark Friedman Furniture
Sid & Me
Wicker Mart

Watch Depot
1738 Thomas St.
Hollywood, FL 33020
800/GO-WATCH (469-2824)

Cost: Free

At Watch Depot, there are thousands of watches to choose from: Citizen, Seiko, Swiss Army, Movado, Swatch, Timex, Lorus, Pulsar, and many more—watches that will dial a phone for you, take your pulse, or monitor your blood pressure, and those that just tell time. The kids will love the Disney design watches—especially one for each of Snow White's seven dwarfs. Prices are up to 55% off retail.

> Check labels for fabric care.
> Dry cleaning or handwashing can
> add time and money to the care
> of an item.

AARP Pharmacy Service
500 Montgomery St.
Alexandria, VA 22314
800/456-2277

Cost: Free

Save up to 50% on your prescription drugs when ordering through AARP Pharmacy Service. Just call their 800 number to check prices. Orders are sent within seven days. Make sure to ask for their free catalog.

See Also: (refer to index)
Quickmed Supplies Inc.

Renting instead of buying bridal gowns or bridesmaid dresses can save hundreds of dollars.

Cable Films and Video
Country Club Station, 7171
Kansas City, MO 64113
913/362-2804

Cost: Free

Established in 1976, Cable Films features film classics. You will find films from the '30s and '40s, silents, Chaplin short features, Hitchcock and Sherlock Holmes mysteries, westerns, an excellent animated library, Bela Lugosi films, and much more.

Rick's Movie Graphics
P.O. Box 23709
Gainesville, FL 32602
800/252-0425

Cost: Free

"Sooner or later . . . everybody comes to Rick's." That's if you're looking for authentic movie advertising posters—the actual posters used in movie theaters. Rick's has thousands of posters from the mid-1970s and earlier that are in good to near-mint condition, as well as posters from the 1980s and all current and upcoming releases. Prices start at $15. Make sure to get on their mailing list to receive catalogs featuring sales where you can save up to 60% off their already low prices.

> Stay away from fad clothing
> and lean toward classic styles.

MUSICAL INSTRUMENTS

Interstate Music Supply

P.O. Box 510865
New Berlin, WI 53151
800/982-2263

Cost: Free

If you're in need of any musical instrument, we're sure you'll find it at
Interstate Music Supply. They've been serving schools since 1971 with
their large inventory of band instruments and accessories. Brand names
you'll find in their 250-page catalog are Yamaha, Korg, Gibson, Ludwig,
Roland, and more at savings of 20 to 60% off retail.

Shar Products Company

P.O. Box 1411
Ann Arbor, MI 48106-1411
800/248-7427

Cost: Free

Shar Products is the largest supplier of musical merchandise geared to
string musicians. Celebrating 34 years in business, Shar Products
publishes a 64-page catalog offering 20 to 50% off retail prices on
violins, bows, cases, rosin, sheet music, strings, tuners, and much more.

The Woodwind & The Brasswind

19889 State Line Rd.
South Bend, IN 46637
800/348-5003

Cost: Free

You won't believe how huge the catalog is from The Woodwind & The
Brasswind company. It features up to 50% off on string instruments,
drums, keyboards, guitars, amps, woodwind and brasswind instruments,
and a large selection of resource books for educators. This catalog is an
absolute must for anyone interested in musical instruments.

The Check Gallery
P.O. Box 17400
Baltimore, MD 21203
800/354-3540

Cost: Free

What's unique about this check-printing company are checks printed on recycled paper with biodegradable, soy-based inks. Plus you get a free checkbook cover made of recycled vinyl at no extra cost! Not only do you get 200 checks at $4.95 for your first order, but you're also helping the planet. Now that's a deal!

Custom Direct Check Printers
P.O. Box 145439
Cincinnati, OH 45250
800/272-5432

Cost: Free

Nowadays we need to think about saving on everything we use—even the checks we write. Custom Direct Check Printers offers a choice of 22 styles of 200 checks for $4.95 on first orders. The trick about ordering from this check company, or any check company, is to order out-of-state so that there is no sales tax. Prices are competitive, but make sure to note the cost of reorders, which is usually more than first orders. In any event, the cost is still much less than that of ordering checks from your bank.

Make your food shopping list to match the layout of your favorite grocery store.

Fidelity Products

5601 International Pkwy.
New Hope, MN 55428
800/328-3034

Cost: Free

You'll find a quality selection of office supplies, boxes, graphic products, furniture, and equipment at the lowest prices guaranteed. If you find a current price lower than the prices shown in their catalog, send them a copy of the ad or catalog page within 30 days of purchase and you'll receive a refund of the difference.

See Also: (refer to index)
        M.L.E. The Office Furniture Warehouse
        Office Depot

> Shop with a pocket calculator
> to compare the cost per
> measurement units of products—
> the larger-size packages don't
> always translate into savings.

Contact Lens Replacement Center

P.O. Box 1489
Melville, NY 11747
800/779-2654

Cost: Free

So, you lost your contact. Well, don't get depressed; just call Contact Lens Replacement Center with your prescription, and they will guarantee the lowest price for replacing your contacts. They also carry sunglasses (Ray Ban, Serengeti, Revo, Vuarnet, Suncloud, and Randolph Engineering). Most orders are shipped within 24 hours and carry a 30-day guarantee.

Hidalgo Inc.

45 La Buena Vista
Wimberley, TX 78676
512/847-5571

Cost: Free

Hidalgo offers sunglasses and prescription glasses at 30 to 60% discounts. Their unique "try-on" program allows you to order frames to try on in the privacy of your own home before you make a buying decision. They carry many name brands, lenses for special uses, polarized glass and plastic lenses, aviation chronograph watches, and even hand-carved, scale-model desk-top model airplanes. Hidalgo assures their customers full satisfaction with their 30-day, money-back guarantee.

National Contact Lens Center

4930 Pinecroft Way
Santa Rosa, CA 95404
800/326-6352

Cost: Free

Is the doctor in? You bet! National Contact Lens Center claims they are the only mail-order contact lens replacement center that has a doctor available for questions, and if the doctor is not in at the time of your call, he or she WILL call you back. Their prices are 20 to 70% off retail, and they guarantee the lowest prices. Prescriptions can be taken from the original vials if necessary, but written prescriptions are preferred. There's a money-back guarantee when lenses are returned in their original vials within 30 days.

407

Prism Optical, Inc.
10992 N.W. 7th Ave.
Miami, FL 33168
800/637-4104

Cost: Free

You won't believe your eyes! Save 30 to 70% off prescription and nonprescription eyewear and contact lenses. Designer frames and sunglasses include brand names such as Giorgio Armani, Carrera, Bolle, Revo, Calvin Klein, Serengeti, and others. Prism Optical offers an unconditional, money-back guarantee. All contact lenses are factory sealed and guaranteed against defects.

Sunglasses U.S.A.
469 Sunrise Hwy.
Lynbrook, NY 11563
800/USA-RAYS (872-7297)

Cost: Free

Now you can buy everyone's favorite sunglasses, Ray Bans, at genuine wholesale prices. You'll pay the same price as your local optometrist when you order from Sunglasses U.S.A. Their catalog offers quite a large selection of shades (75 categories on the price list) from which to choose, and they'll wave the customary $2 shipping and handling charge on your first order.

> Try local farmers' markets for deals on fresh fruits and vegetables.

PARTY & PAPER GOODS

Current

The Current Building
Colorado Springs, CO 80941
800/525-7170

Cost: Free

For stationery, wrapping paper, note cards, and gifts, Current offers a unique line of fine-quality products suitable for every occasion, at lower than card-shop prices. You can also find personal checks at up to 60% below bank prices and fees. Their selection of items, with nature and animal themes, bound to please children and adults alike. Gift wrapping perfectionists will appreciate the multitude of styles and colors available, individually or in sets. The catalog that comes out in time for Valentine's Day is not to be missed.

Stumps

One Party Place, P.O. Box 305
South Whitley, IN 46787
800/22-PARTY (227-2789)

Cost: Free

You won't believe the possibilities on how to make your parties the talk-of-the-town. Stumps mail-order party place has the unusual—how about a 10´-tall, giant star entrance; an 18'-tall, giant tuxedo with 135 twinkle lights (great for a black-tie affair); or a 12'-high giant Hollywood clapboard for an entertainment theme party. That's just a sampling of the fantastic things available from Stumps. They also carry, at great prices, items such as glassware, napkins, keytags, ribbons, balloons, streamers, and much more. You name the event—weddings, reunions, birthdays, proms, anniversaries, Valentine's Day, Mardi Gras, Christmas, New Year—they have the decorations.

PET & ANIMAL SUPPLIES

Omaha Vaccine Company
P.O. Box 7228
Omaha, NE 68107
800/367-4444

Cost: Free

There are 282 pages in the Omaha Vaccine Company catalog with everything imaginable for your animals. They refuse to be undersold—so the savings are considerable.

R.C. Steele
1989 Transit Way
Brockport, NY 14420
800/872-3773

Cost: Free

This catalog offers dog equipment and kennel supplies at wholesale prices! You can order books, grates, cages, grooming supplies, toys, treats, nutritional products, and training aids, plus anything else found at your local pet store, but at bargain prices. They require a minimum order of $50.

United Pharmacal Co., Inc.
P.O. Box 969
St. Joseph, MO 64502
800/444-8651

Cost: Free

Since 1952, UPCO has cared about serving you and your animal's needs. They offer products at the lowest possible prices, backed by guaranteed service. You'll find everything for your pet in their 190-page catalog. Orders are shipped on the same day received, and shipping is free in the continental U.S.

Bi-Rite Photo and Electronics
20 E. 39th St.
New York, NY 10016
800/223-1970

Cost: Free

You can save up to 60% on cameras and accessories, typewriters, video equipment, telephone systems, and more.

Porter's Camera Store, Inc.
P.O. Box 628
Cedar Falls, IA 50613
800/553-2001

Cost: Free

Whether you're a professional or an amateur photographer, you'll appreciate the savings (10 to 88% off retail) found in this catalog. In addition to cameras, lenses, filters, tripods, and all other necessary camera accessories, Porter's Camera Store carries everything you need in darkroom equipment and supplies. Backdrops, light meters, slide viewers, film, and projectors are just a few more items carried in their extensive inventory.

See Also: (refer to index)
Frank's Highland Park Camera

Buying basic products such as flour, salt, sugar, vinegar, and bleach with generic or store brand names is a good way to save money.

PLANTS, GARDENS & POOLS

Burpee–W. Atlee Burpee & Co.
300 Park Ave.
Warminster, PA 18974
800/888-1447

Cost: Free

Home gardeners in all parts of the country have been buying seeds, bulbs, and plants from Burpee for years. Make your garden more beautiful with flowers, roses, vines, trees, and shrubs. Chefs can enhance dishes with vegetables and herbs picked fresh from the backyard. You can also order tools, supplies, and specialized products for gardening.

Harris Seeds
60 Saginaw Dr., Dept. 96161, P.O. Box 22960
Rochester, NY 14692-2960
800/514-4441

Cost: Free

Treat yourself to the finest vegetable and flower seeds and plants, including many seed-starting and home-gardening supplies. For 117 years, Harris Seeds catalog has been in business providing high-quality merchandise and exclusive proprietaries.

In The Swim Discount Pool Supplies
320 Industrial Dr.
West Chicago, IL 60185
800/374-1500

Cost: Free

In The Swim can help reduce the cost of maintaining your pool by up to 54%. They offer factory-direct prices on chlorine, solar blankets and reels, winter covers, accessories, and much more. All products have a 30-day return policy. Orders are shipped the same day, free of shipping charges—so, take a dip and have some fun today!

Water Warehouse
801 Lunt Ave.
Elk Grove Village, IL 60007
800/574-7665

Cost: Free

Since 1964, Water Warehouse has been offering guaranteed lowest prices on pool and spa supplies. Take advantage of their expert staff to help with any questions you might have. Not only can you purchase supplies, but also, how about a game of volleyball, badminton, or basketball played in your pool? What a nice way to spend the day.

See Also: (refer to index)
      J. B. Sebrell Co.

> File discount coupons by
> subject for easier retrieval.

Bart's Water Sports
7581 E. 800 N., P.O. Box 294
North Webster, IN 46555
800/348-5016

Cost: Free

For over 22 years, it's been the goal of Bart's to offer the lowest prices in the country on every item needed to enjoy water sports. You'll find wet suits, wakeboards, water skis, boat covers, lifts and props, personal watercraft accessories, lifts, and covers as well as swimwear, dock accessories, gauges, and more! Bart's 64-page color catalog is full of top-quality watersport equipment at savings of up to 40% off retail (up to 60% off retail in special Closeout Section!). If in the unlikely event you see a printed price that is lower than Bart's (on the same equipment), call and ask for "Betty Price Beater"—who will let you know whether Bart's can beat the price! You'll be pleased to know Bart's has a no-hassle, 60-day, money-back guarantee on unused merchandise.

Berry Scuba Co.
6674 N. Northwest Hwy.
Chicago, IL 60631
800/621-6019

Cost: Free

Whether you are just learning to dive or thinking of becoming an instructor, Berry Scuba can deliver for you. They are the authorized dealers of U.S. Divers, Tusa, Sherwood, Beuchat, U.S. Tech, Dacor, Bayside, Mares, and more than 70 other manufacturers. Savings go up to 50%, with some specials featuring 75% off.

Bike Nashbar
4111 Simon Rd., Dept. BRS
Youngstown, OH 44512
800/NASHBAR (627-4227)

Cost: Free

Gearing up for summer is always a pleasure: warm weather, quiet rides, lazy days, and the excitement of bicycling. Whether you're cycling for pleasure or racing, Bike Nashbar will equip you with everything you need—and you'll look fantastic too! In their 80-page catalog you'll find cycling apparel, hardgoods, tools, accessories, bikes, and much more with a guaranteed-lowest-price policy.

Cabela's
9PD-603rd
Sidney, NE 69160
800/237-4444

Cost: Free

The staff at Cabela's is committed to bringing you hunting, fishing, and outdoor gear products that you can trust and rely on. They always listen to your comments and ideas with an eye toward bringing you the best merchandise at the best prices. Their free 250-page catalog is exploding with everything you can possibly want for fishing, camping, and boating trips.

Defender Industries, Inc.
42 Great Neck Rd.
Waterford, CT 06385
800/NAU-T-CAL (628-8225)

Cost: Free

Defender Industries has been quietly outfitting boats and boat owners across North America for 57 years. Not advertising enables them to keep their prices low. They also offer a guarantee: If you find a lower quote from a legitimate domestic source that has the same merchandise available for delivery, they will gladly honor the lower price. You'll find everything needed to outfit your boat, such as anchors, compasses, dinghies, fishing products, heaters, ladders, life jackets, and pumps as well as much more in their 375-page catalog.

E & B Discount Marine
201 Meadow Rd.
Edison, NJ 08818
800/533-5007

Cost: Free

Boating enthusiasts will find this 388-page catalog to be an ocean of values. Whether you're into boats powered by sails or high-performance engines, you'll find all that you need from barbecues, fishing reels, water skis, and nautical clothing to bilge pumps, anchors, and engines. Helms alee!

Golfsmith International
11000 North IH-35
Austin, TX 78753
800/456-3344

Cost: Free

As any do-it-yourselfer knows, you can save hundreds of dollars when you provide the labor. Golf clubs are no exception. With the products found in the Golfsmith International catalog, you can build your own set of clubs with your choice of heads, shafts, and grips. In fact, you can even carve your own set of woods. If you think you're out of bounds tackling such a project, their knowledgeable and friendly sales staff can provide accurate information. There are no minimum orders—so if you need only a golf grip, you can purchase just that for as low as $1.45 plus shipping. You'll enjoy looking through their 228-page catalog.

Holabird Sports
9220 Pulaski Hwy.
Baltimore, MD 21220
410/687-6400

Cost: Free

There are hundreds of items to choose from at guaranteed lowest prices on tennis, squash, and racquetball rackets. And don't forget the balls to go with each sport, as well as the proper attire from shoes to clothing. You can buy stringing machines, ball machines, tennis nets, ball hoppers, court equipment, grips, vibration dampeners, eyeguards, and even sports medical supplies. We found many of their everyday prices to be lower than sale prices at sporting goods stores. Brand names include Head, Prince, Wilson, Fila, Ektelon, Adidas, Etonic, K-Swiss, Nike, New Balance, Dunlop, Reebok, and Saucony. Their 48-hour shipping policy can come in handy if you need something fast.

Mueller Sporting Goods, Inc.
4825 S. 16th St.
Lincoln, NE 68512
800/925-7665

Cost: Free

Since 1957, Mueller Sporting Goods, Inc. has put together an incredible catalog filled with equipment and supplies for billiards and darts and other indoor sporting goods. Their typical savings range from 30 to 40%. Orders are accepted 24 hours, seven days a week, and unused items may be returned within 30 days.

Overton's Water Sports and Boating Accessories
111 Red Banks Rd., P.O. Box 8228
Greenville, NC 27835
800/334-6541

Cost: Free

Overton's catalog is filled with everything, and we mean everything, you can think of related to water sports. Products such as boat skis, skis and accessories, vests, running lights, electronics, and navigation equipment are all available at discounted prices. With their no-squabble guarantee, they will gladly refund your money, make an exchange, or give you credit for any unused merchandise minus the original shipping, handling, or C.O.D. charges. Orders are shipped within 24 hours.

Racer Wholesale
1020 Sun Valley Dr.
Roswell, GA 30076
800/886-7223

Cost: Free

With Racer Wholesale's guaranteed lowest prices on racing gear and race car equipment, you'll find yourself in the car a lot. The 59-page catalog is filled with racing helmets, suits, shoes, gloves, and accessories, as well as race car fuel cells, brake pads, gauges, scales, seats, and much more. Returns or exchanges are gladly accepted within 30 days of purchase.

The Sportsman's Guide
411 Farwell Ave.
South St. Paul, MN 55075
800/888-3006

Cost: Free

What we like most about The Sportsman's Guide is their golden rule from the owner, which goes like this: "If I wouldn't use it myself, I won't sell it. If I wouldn't recommend it to my friends, I won't sell it. And, if I can't sell it for less than everybody else, I won't sell it." So, if you enjoy hunting, shooting, and the outdoors, then order this free catalog for big savings on close-outs, military surplus, and much more.

State Line Tack
Route 121, P.O. Box 1217
Plaistow, NH 02158
800/228-9208

Cost: Free

State Line Tack has everything for the horse and rider from tack to apparel. They offer more than 12,000 products for the English or Western rider discounted at 20 to 40% off retail. Their Western Catalog (180 pages) features Circle Y, Tex Tan, Reinsman, Wrangler, Justin, Big D, Tory, and more, while their English catalog (212 pages) lists brands such as Devon-Aire, Schumacher, Kentucky, Crosby, and Professional's Choice, just to name a few. State Line Tack is committed to providing riders with high-quality products at the best possible prices and works with top riders and trainers to develop new and better products. Orders are taken 24 hours a day, seven days a week, and all products have a 100%-satisfaction guarantee. For additional savings, look for their monthly coupon flyer sales.

See Also: (refer to index)
Bikecology–Santa Monica
Crown Billiards & Bar Stools
Eldorado Games
Shamrock Golf Shops

Manufacturers pay a premium to have their products at eye level; always look at shelves above and below for better deals.

Oriental Trading Company, Inc.
P.O. Box 3407
Omaha, NE 68103
800/228-2269

Cost: Free

Oriental Trading Company can help you decorate for the holidays with wrappings, craft accessories, ornaments, stocking stuffers, and dolls at savings 10 to 60% below retail. They also have an entire selection of fun activities and learning games for children. Items include cuddly plush animals, wooden toys, digital watches, magnetic sculptures, baseball stationery sets, stickers, nylon sport wrist wallets, mini turkey erasers, and much more at ridiculously low prices. Orders are taken seven days a week and are ground shipped within the continental U.S. Occasionally there is a promotion offering free delivery with a minimum purchase.

See Also: (refer to index)
LEC World Traders

> Beware of end-of-aisle displays; manufacturers pay extra for this location to focus the consumer's attention on an item that they want you to buy.

A to Z Luggage
4627 New Ultrecht Ave.
Brooklyn, NY 11219
800/342-5011

Cost: Free

A to Z Luggage has famous-maker luggage, briefcases, and leather accessories at up to 50% off retail. Brand names to look for are Hartmann, Boyt, Samsonite, and more. Their discount policies include guaranteed lowest prices on the entire Hartmann line and 30% off Boyt. Happy traveling!

B & J Publications/Budget Lodging Guide
P.O. Box 5486
Fullerton, CA 92635
800/525-6633

Cost: $16.95

This is the most expensive catalog in our book, but it will probably save you the most money if you like to travel. B & J Publications puts out a 490-page directory featuring travel accommodations in the United States and the world, with costs of $20 to $35 per day. How do they do it? All rooms are located at more than 700 university campuses. You'll find uncrowded sports facilities—tennis, swimming, golf, hiking, fishing, boating, theater, film festivals, arts and craft shows, and much more—at some of the most beautiful locations in the world. The catalog has the phone numbers of the universities, prices for single and double rooms, dates available, food service offered, and activities in the area.

On Campus—USA and Canada
2414 Rose Dr.
Glenshaw, PA 15116
412/492-0989

Cost: $9.95

Vacation time is just around the corner, and the purchase of On Campus—USA and Canada, a 102-page book, will save you lots of money on lodging. Instead of paying hundreds of dollars for hotels, you can stay at some of the most beautiful campuses with prices starting at $10 a night for one person or $16 a night for two people. This is a must for travelers on a budget. The cost of the book includes shipping and handling.

See Also: (refer to index)
Trading Homes International

Along with a shopping list, set up a budget and do your best to stick with it.

5

DIRECTORY OF CONSUMER RESOURCES

BARGAIN HUNTER'S
REFERENCE LIBRARY

DIRECTORY OF CONSUMER RESOURCES

Becoming a "smart shopper" involves rational (rather than emotional) decision making. Whether you're purchasing a product or seeking services, there are a number of questions to be asked. How do I get the best value for my money? What do I need to know about the contemplated purchase to make an informed decision? What pitfalls do I need to avoid? What recourse do I have when I am dissatisfied?

Fortunately, an increasing number of excellent publications are available to assist you in answering these questions. The smart shopper will create a home consumer library of pertinent books, periodicals, catalogs, pamphlets, and articles. For a nominal cost (in many cases free), these publications can help you become a knowledgeable shopper, one who is more likely to make sound decisions, avoid mistakes, and save thousands of dollars.

This Directory of Consumer Resources contains brief descriptions of more than 35 such publications, including *Consumer Reports*, a monthly magazine reporting results of comparative field tests of a wide variety of products; the Better Business Bureau's *A to Z Buying Guide*, and *The Frugal Shopper* by Ralph Nader and Wesley J. Smith (both provide consumers with essential information to make sound, economical purchasing decisions on hundreds of products and services); U.S. Government catalogs containing hundreds of printed materials to assist with living more wisely, effectively, economically, and healthily (most of these are free or inexpensive); *Consumer Action*, a guide that details resources available for dissatisfied consumers; and *The AAA Auto/Graph Book*, containing information about getting the most for your money in buying a new or used car.

Of special interest in this chapter are several books that tell you how to obtain a wide variety of goods and services free. You may want to start your home reference library by writing for both free publications and those available at minimal cost (usually government publications), as well as those that discuss ways of acquiring things free.

425

Upon obtaining any of the materials described in this chapter, become familiar with them by glancing through the table of contents and skimming the texts. You are certain to find some interesting and intriguing information. Even this casual reading will make you a more knowledgeable consumer and will enable you to know where to look for more specific information before buying. Over the course of a year, you will probably refer to these resources often and will find them invaluable.

Books with older publication dates are here because the material has remained pertinent. Some may be out of print and no longer available in bookstores; however, your local library may have them. The library may be your source of first choice anyway—the price is right—and you may gradually acquire publications for home use to which you would expect to refer more frequently.

CONSUMER RESOURCE REFERENCES

A to Z Buying Guide—The Better Business Bureau

Publisher: Council of Better Business Bureaus
4200 Wilson Blvd., Arlington, VA 22203

Latest Edition: 1990 ($9.95)

This guide's 300 pages provide essential information for making sound, economical purchasing decisions on hundreds of products and services. It can be obtained at local Better Business Bureaus and bookstores, or by writing directly to the Council. Also includes information about Better Business Bureau's consumer edition books, pamphlets, and other publications and services designed to help you make informed buying decisions.

The AAA 1996 Auto/Graph Book

Publisher: American Automobile Association
1000 AAA Dr., Heathrow, FL 32746

Call your local AAA office

Latest Edition: 1996 ($12.95)

The AAA Auto/Graph Book provides you with the facts you need to walk into a dealer's showroom with the confidence of a wise and prudent shopper. It will help you make the right decision with less confusion and more piece of mind. You will be privy to the test results of 112 of the most popular foreign and domestic car models. Each vehicle's performance, comfort, convenience, workmanship, and value are reported. Lists of each vehicle's best and worst features are provided along with pictures of each car's exterior, interior, dashboard, and cargo area. Price lists are also included. Introductory chapters deal with analyzing your needs, test driving, understanding your warranty, negotiating, maintaining your vehicle, and resolving disputes. You can obtain the book at any local AAA office. It's well worth the investment.

Absolutely Free!
Publisher: Prima Publishing
P.O. Box 1260BK, Rocklin, CA 95677
916/632-4400
Latest Edition: 1995 ($9.95)

This book gives inside information on a wealth of free products and services in the areas of crafts, clothes and jewelry, food, beauty and health, toys and games, and much more. *Absolutely Free!* tells you where to find nearly 300 top-quality products that you and your entire family will want. As a bonus, most of the products and resource guides promote the kind of safe, natural lifestyle that enhances your famly's well-being and our environment. The value of the free products you will receive far outweighs the cost of the book!

Automobile Club—Southern California
Automotive Information Center
Publisher: American Automobile Association
P.O. Box 2890, Terminal Annex
Los Angeles, CA 90051-0890
213/741-4487
Latest Edition: 1995 (Free)

If you're in the market for a new car or you want to sell one, you can order informational brochures from the Auto Club. Choose from "Buying A New Car," "Buying A Used Car," "Financing A Car," "Leasing vs. Buying," and "Selling Your Vehicle." The brochures are well written, contain much useful information, and can save you time and money. Auto Club members need only call, and they will send you any of these free, easy-to-understand brochures as long as supplies last.

Baby Bargains
Publisher: Windsor Peak Press
1223 Peakview Circle, Suite 7000, Boulder, CO 80302
800/888-0385
Latest Edition: 1996 ($11.95)

A big question about having a baby is how to afford it. The average cost of caring for a baby has been estimated at $5,000 for the first year. Economy-minded parents or parents-to-be will be interested in the many ways to save money described in *Baby Bargains*. Denise and Alan Fields, authors of the popular *Bridal Bargains*, provide information on how and where to save 20 to 50% on baby furniture, equipment, clothes, toys, maternity wear, and much more. A no-questions-asked, money-back guarantee is offered to anyone who doesn't save at least $250 on baby expenses by using this book.

The Best Bargain Family Vacations in the U.S.A.

Publisher: St. Martin's Press
175 Fifth Ave., New York, NY 10010
800/288-2131, 212/674-5151

Latest Edition: 1993 ($13.95)

Time to load mom and the kids into the Winnebago and head for some fun in the sun? Imagine going face-to-face with the mild-mannered manatee in Florida's Homosassa Springs State Wildlife Park, or help professional archaeologists uncover a prehistoric pueblo in Arizona's White Mountain Archaeological Center. *The Best Bargain Family Vacations in the U.S.A.* offers over 250 affordable, kid-friendly, nationwide vacation spots, with accommodation prices ranging from around $6 to $75 a night. Everything from resorts to dude ranches to family camps is covered in the book, which provides vacation spot descriptions and cost and accommodation information. A two-part appendix offers information on budget hotels and U.S. Tourist Offices.

Bridal Bargains

Publisher: Windsor Peak Press
1223 Peakview Circle, Suite 7000, Boulder, CO 80302
800/888-0385

Latest Edition: 1996 ($11.95)

According to *Bridal Bargains*, the average U.S. wedding costs over $19,000. In this book, Denise and Alan Fields describe creative and innovative solutions for planning a wedding on a realistic budget. They tell you how to save 20 to 50% off brand-new, nationally advertised bridal gowns. In addition, information and strategies are provided that can save you hundreds of dollars on wedding pictures, catering, flowers, invitations, rings, entertainment, the wedding site, and more. The authors offer the following money-back guarantee: "If *Bridal Bargains* doesn't save you at least $500 on your wedding, we will give you a complete refund on the cost of this book! No questions asked!"

Consumer Action Guide

Publisher: Consumer Action
116 New Montgomery St., San Francisco, CA 94105
415/777-9635 (Complaint Hotline)

Latest Edition: 1993 ($3)

The *Consumer Action Guide* is a useful reference when you run into problems. It includes the addresses and telephone numbers of regulatory and law enforcement government agencies, business-sponsored complaint resolution offices, nonprofit information and referral organizations, and agencies that offer free or low-cost legal assistance.

The Consumer Bible

Publisher: Workman Publishing Company
708 Broadway, New York, NY 10003
212/254-5900

Latest Edition: 1995 ($14.95)

This book supplies consumers with the knowledge they need to shop smart—from how to get the edge on buying essential goods and services, to avoiding scams and schemes. Used for every purchase, *The Consumer Bible* is like giving yourself and your family a 20% pay raise—effective immediately. It includes everything you need to know to get the best value on food, health care, home, clothing, repairs, lawyers, phones, vacations, banks, pets, and more. The author, Mark Green, served as the highly effective Consumer Affairs Commissioner of New York City (1990-93) and became the city's first Public Advocate. This comprehensive book will save you both time and money on a daily basis.

Consumer Information Catalog

Publisher: Consumer Information Center
P.O. Box 100-6A, Pueblo, CO 81002
719/948-4000

Latest Edition: 1996 (Free)

This 13-page catalog lists free and low-cost publications of consumer interest. Topics include car care, children and parenting, employment, federal program benefits, food and nutrition, medicine and health, money and finance, small business, travel, hobbies, and much more. The publications described in this U.S. Government catalog are packed with valuable information and can improve anyone's personal or business lifestyle.

Consumer Reports **1996 Buying Guide**
Publisher: Consumers Union
P.O. Box 51166, Boulder, CO 80321
800/500-9760
Latest Edition: 1996 ($8.99)

Providing up-to-date buying advice and evaluations on hundreds of brand-name products, this yearly guide gives the consumer ready access to information on topics such as automobiles, audio and video gear, home workplace equipment, and yard and garden machines. Featuring a "Better to Worse" rating system, Frequency-of-Repair charts, and additional information on product recalls and reliability, the *1996 Buying Guide* also includes a one-year index to *Consumer Reports* magazine at the back of the book, following the guide index. A new edition is published yearly.

Consumer Resource Handbook
Publisher: Consumer Information Center
Pueblo, CO 81009
719/948-4000
Latest Edition: 1996 (Free)

This is a U.S. Government publication of nearly 100 pages listing many consumer affairs contact names; also lists addresses and phone numbers of hundreds of manufacturers, and county, state, and federal agencies handling a wide variety of consumer problems. A worthwhile addition to your consumer information library.

A Consumer's Guide to Renting a Car
Publisher: Alamo Rent-A-Car, Public Affairs Department
McCool Communications, P.O. Box 13005, Atlanta, GA 30324
404/768-4161
Latest Edition: 1995 (Free)

This 24-page guide provides information that will help you rent a car less expensively and more conveniently. It will facilitate your asking the right questions and making the correct decisions regarding topics such as reserving your vehicle, club discounts, fuel policies, mileage charges, special equipment, one-way rentals, other potential surcharges, additional charges, responsibility for rental vehicles, car rental protection options, loss of use, liability insurance, where to pick up your car, returning your car, mechanical problems, accidents, and travel safety. Enclose a stamped (55¢ postage), self-addressed business-size envelope when requesting this free publication.

Cut Your Bills in Half
Publisher: Smithmark Publishers
16 E. 32nd St., New York, NY 10016
212/532-6600
Latest Edition: 1994 ($8)

The editors of *Cut Your Bills in Half* offer many cash-saving tips, including "First Aid for Gardening Tools" and "Avoiding Flashy Accessories." This guide covers a wide range of topics: travel bargains, affordable furniture, and lower insurance rates, to name only a few. Did you know that your car will last longer if you don't follow your owner's manual timetable for an oil change, or that your canvas shoes will last a lot longer with a spray of silicone?

Don Wright's Guide to Free Campgrounds
Publisher: Cottage Publications
420 S. 4th St., Elkhart, IN 46516
800/303-7833, 219/293-7553
Latest Edition: 1994 ($16.95)

Before you pack the family station wagon and roll off for the Rockies, or plan that yearly excursion to Yellowstone, you'll definitely want to look at *Don Wright's Guide to Free Campgrounds*. Written for experienced campers and rookies alike, the guide lists thousands of campgrounds across the U.S. where you can stay absolutely free, or almost free. National forests, county and state parks, and long-term visitor areas are just some of the vacation sites providing that perfect, fun, and economical getaway.

Don't Go to the Cosmetics Counter Without Me
Publisher: Beginning Press/Publishers Group West
4065 Hollis St., Emeryville, CA 94608
415/658-3453
Latest Edition: 1994 ($13.95)

Designed to prove that the female consumer doesn't have to spend a fortune on skin care and makeup, *Don't Go to the Cosmetics Counter Without Me* sets out to demystify the inflated claims and price tags on the 300 cosmetic lines available in the U.S. and Canada. In addition to taking aim at such brand-name companies as Revlon and Cover Girl, the book covers everything from shopping techniques and an overview of ingredients, to sifting through celebrity model double-talk. The book differentiates between companies and manufacturers that use animal testing and those that don't.

Free Food . . . & More
Publisher: Probus Publishing Co.
1925 N. Clybourn Ave., Chicago, IL 60614
800/PROBUS-1 (776-2871)
Latest Edition: 1992 ($9.95)

Did you know that every year the American family throws away almost $2,000 worth of cash refunds and rebates for products they use every day? An ideal guide for bargain hunters and coupon-clippers alike, *Free Food . . . & More* alerts you to discounts and freebies on food and entertainment, as well as health and household goods. From slashing the monthly energy bill to video rental savings, this book teaches you how to turn daily budget-busting headaches into major savings.

The Frugal Shopper
Publisher: Center for Study of Responsive Law
P.O. Box 19367, Washington, DC 20036
Latest Edition: 1992 ($10)

Coauthored by long-time crusading consumer advocate Ralph Nader, *The Frugal Shopper* helps you win the consumer game. It enables you to make smart decisions on major expenses, professional services, utilities, credit, and marketplace negotiations. You'll learn to discern between credit cards and "credit checks," or how the "fair plan" can help you overcome the restrictions that insurance companies place on "hazardous areas." In coping with difficult times, *The Frugal Shopper* is a valuable consumer companion.

Goodridge's Guide to Flea Markets
Publisher: Adams Media Corporation
Jim Goodridge, P.O. Box 510085, St. Louis, MO 63129
314/296-0990
Latest Edition: 1995 ($9.95 each)

What do a deserted airplane hangar, a parking lot at a major university, and the world-famous Rose Bowl stadium have in common? All are sites of one of America's favorite venues–the flea market. In his four-book series, author Jim Goodridge presents a comprehensive directory of flea markets. Each edition is packed with all the "need-to-know" information, including sizes of markets, directions, average daily attendance, types of merchandise, hours of operation, booth rates, and advice on how to get the best bargains. Four regional editions are available covering the Southeast, Northeast/Mid Atlantic, West/Southwest, and Midwest.

Guide to Free Tax Services—Publication #910
Publisher: Internal Revenue Service
Department of the Treasury, Washington, DC 20224
800/829-1040
Latest Edition: 1994 (Free)

This guide describes numerous IRS tax services, publications, tax tips, and information about many IRS programs. Materials and information programs are free, and most are available year-round. Additionally, *Guide to Free Tax Services* lists toll-free IRS telephone numbers and IRS mailing addresses.

How to Clean Practically Anything
Publisher: Consumers Union
101 Truman Ave., Yonkers, NY 10703
Latest Edition: 1993 ($11.95)

How to Clean Practically Anything tells you how to remove more than 54 common stains, and get the best value from hundreds of cleaning products and appliances. Rating products on a "Better" or "Worse" scale, the pocket-size guide provides the consumer with money-saving and safety tips on every imaginable cleaning agent.

How to Keep Your Car Looking Young
Publisher: Car Care Council
One Grand Lake Drive, Port Clinton, OH 43452
419/734-5343
Latest Edition: 1995 (Free)

Many of us spend as much time in our cars as we do in our living rooms. Keeping your car looking young improves driving pleasure and safety and increases the value of your vehicle. This eight-page pamphlet has numerous valuable tips for getting the job done.

How to Protect Yourself Against Ripoffs
Publisher: Retirement Living Publishing Co.
28 W. 23rd St., New York, NY 10010
212/366-8850
Latest Edition: 1991 ($4)

This 27-page booklet discusses many of the most common ripoffs and provides information on how to protect yourself against them. Topics include: Real Estate Fraud, Free Vacation Offers, Insurance Come-Ons, Health Quacks, Door-To-Door Con Artists, Car Repair Ripoffs, Check

Tampering, Cash Register Cheats, Telemarketing Frauds, Credit Cons, Mortgage Scalpers, and the Newest Scams.

Motorist's Tire Care and Safety Guide
Publisher: Tire Industry Safety Council
P.O. Box 3147, Medina, OH 44258
Latest Edition: 1995 (Free)

This 17-page pamphlet provides information you need to know about auto and light truck tire care and safety. Included are sections on inflation pressure, tire inspection, good driving habits, vehicle conditions affecting tires, the sidewall story, replacement tire selection, cold-weather driving, service assistance, and storage tips.

1996 AT&T Toll-Free National 800 Directory (Consumer Edition)
Publisher: AT&T
Five Century Dr., Parsippany, NJ 07054
800/562-2255
Latest Edition: 1996 ($14.99)

Reach out and save some money! A comprehensive phone guide to consumer savings, the *AT&T Toll-Free National 800 Directory* includes a Consumer White Pages section containing alphabetical listings by name of businesses, organizations, and government agencies that provide toll-free 800 numbers to the public; also includes section numbers that indicate under what product or service heading a listing may be found in the Consumer Yellow Pages. A new edition is published yearly.

The Official Freebies for Families
Publisher: Lowell House Juvenile
2029 Century Park East, Suite 3290, Dept. VH
Los Angeles, CA 90067
310/552-7555
Latest Edition: 1995 ($4.95)

The Official Freebies for Families lists more than 250 "freebie" mail offers, ranging from carry-alls for the kids to tips on horseshoe rules. Filled with concise, readable catalog descriptions, the handbook can easily slide into your glove compartment or knapsack. Catalog descriptions, costs, and company addresses are listed at the bottom of each entry.

The Official Freebies for Kids
Publisher: Lowell House Juvenile
2029 Century Park East, Suite 3290, Dept. VH
Los Angeles, CA 90067
310/552-7555
Latest Edition: 1996 ($5.95)

Keeping the kids busy and happy doesn't have to be a costly Nintendo nightmare. In *The Official Freebies for Kids* you can choose from more than 130 freebie mail offers designed for your children. Crafts, games, toys, and magazines are just some of the items to be found in this slim, handy book. Treat your kids to "Dinosaur Fourus wooden craft plans" or "Spifey Spider and Belfry Bat pins." Entertaining your children needn't be a burden to the budget.

The Official Freebies for Teachers
Publisher: Lowell House Juvenile
2029 Century Park East, Suite 3290, Dept. VH
Los Angeles, CA 90067
310/552-7555
Latest Edition: 1996 ($4.95)

The latest edition of *The Official Freebies for Teachers* describes clever classroom crafts, activities, games, and educational items available to teachers, including more than 100 "freebies" that cost nothing or next to nothing. Most of the selections are fun items to share with students. Some of the "freebies" are ideas for science fair projects, rubber stamps, maps, challenging puzzles, stickers, and personalized award certificates.

The Official Guide to Buying, Connecting and Using Consumer Electronics Products
Publisher: Electronics Industries Association Consumer Electronics Group/CE Books
2500 Wilson Blvd., Arlington, VA 22201
Latest Edition: 1995 ($9 plus $6.95 shipping and handling)

This 172-page book covers every aspect of consumer electronics products—from pre- to post-purchase. It answers questions such as: What do I look for when purchasing a personal computer? How do I hook up my VCR to watch one TV program and record another while connected to cable? Are large and small speakers really the same? What type of alarm system should I buy for my car? Product categories covered are computers, audio, video, home theater, auto sound, mobile electronics, telecommunications, home office, and home control.

The Official Guide to Government Auctions
Publisher: Crown Publishers
210 E. 50th St., New York, NY 10022
Latest Edition: 1992 ($25)

This 494-page book tells you everything you've ever wanted to know, or might want to know, about auctions. In great detail, it explains where and how to find out about auctions and how to participate effectively in them. It indicates the possibilities of finding great deals (up to 80% off) on cars, office equipment, televisions, and almost every type of merchandise imaginable. It also describes pitfalls to avoid. It is a basic reference for anyone who is interested in auctions—both beginners and seasoned auction goers.

1,001 Free Goodies & Cheapies
Publisher: Information USA
P.O. Box E, Kensington, MD 20895
301/924-0556
Latest Edition: 1994 ($19.95)

Who doesn't love a freebie? This book contains all the neat stuff you can get your hands on and put to use for gifts, self-help, teaching aids, toys, investment decisions, and more. The offers are either free or priced less than $10. Take note, though: these freebies are not really free—you have already paid for them with your tax dollars. Just another reason for you to take full advantage of the opportunities described in this book.

1001 Ways to Cut Your Expenses
Publisher: Bantam Doubleday Dell Publishing
2451 S. Wolf Rd., Des Plaines, IL 60018
800/323-9872
Latest Edition: 1992 ($9.95)

There's no doubt these days that saving money across-the-board is a high priority on everyone's agenda, and financial planning guru Jonathan D. Pond has written the sort of dollar-slashing guide that most shoppers want to use. Filled with savvy, step-by-step tips on saving on everything from utilities to courtships, the book includes self-tests, case studies, and budget tables that will help you cut expenses on every front. Did you know you might be able to get a college degree under your employer's tuition program, or that you can save by taking your own bags to the grocery store? Some of the subchapters have a commonsense ring to them ("Don't Lend Money to a Thief," "Buy Artificial Plants Instead of Live Ones").

Phil Lempert's Supermarket Shopping and Value Guide
Publisher: Contemporary Books
Two Prudential Plaza, Suite 1200
Chicago, IL 60601-6790
800/540-9440

Latest Edition: 1996 ($9.95)

Phil Lempert, nationally known as the "Supermarket Guru," has created this unique handbook to help shoppers make their way through the maze of the modern supermarkets while getting the absolute best deals on each and every item. Readers will learn thousands of invaluable insider tips and helpful hints, including how to tell if a product is really on sale, how to get in and out of a store fast, how to get freebies from stores and manufacturers, how to dicipher food labels, which products a shopper should never buy, and many more. Each chapter contains a concise top-10 list of values as well as the answers to the most commonly asked consumer questions. Also featured are hints from supermarket managers and an appendix of food information. No cost-conscious consumer can afford to do without this book.

The Practical Guide to Practically Everything
Publisher: Random House, Inc.
New York, NY 10022
800/733-3000

Latest Edition: 1995 ($13.95)

This is an expert, no-nonsense guide to the most important developments in everything from health and nutrition to money management, education, career planning, travel, entertainment, and consumer technology. Expert Picks, Tips, Lists, Q & As, and Sources will help to clear the fog and give you the truth about what you, the consumer, need to know.

The Safe Shopper's Bible
Publisher: Macmillan/Simon & Schuster
1633 Broadway, New York, NY 10019
800/223-2348

Latest Edition: 1995 ($14.95)

Can coloring your hair cause cancer? Which apple juice is safest for your baby? Is furniture polish making your asthma worse? Where can you find meat without hormones and additives? Here, at last, is a comprehensive guide to answer all your questions about thousands of brand-name household products, personal care products, foods, and beverages. Because many items you buy every day contain ingredients that can cause allergic reactions, breathing difficulty, dizziness, cancer, birth defects, and other problems, *The Safe Shopper's Bible* is a must for those who care about their health.

Shopping for a Better World
Publisher: Ballantine Books
201 E. 50th St., New York, NY 10022
800/733-3000, 212/751-2600
Latest Edition: 1994 ($14)

A shop-smart text with a social conscience, *Shopping for a Better World* rates companies on their performances on such vital issues as animal testing and the environment, to name only two. A bracing clarion call for the consumer activist, the pocket-size paperback grades each company's social awareness and responsibility with a demanding, issue-conscious, 12-column checklist. In keeping with this spirit, the volume also lists the addresses, phone numbers, and names of chief company executives, encouraging consumers to exercise their duty to defend our "endangered ecosystem" by writing to the companies directly.

Shopping for a Safer Car
Publisher: Insurance Institute for Highway Safety
Publications, P.O. Box 1420, Arlington, VA 22210
703/247-1500
Latest Edition: 1995 (Free)

Safety should rank high on the list of considerations when you're purchasing a car. In simply written and jargon-free language, this 14-page booklet answers questions regarding what to look for in safety features. Anyone interested in safety will find useful information here. Include a self-addressed, stamped business-size envelope.

The Super Coupon Shopping System
Publisher: Hyperion
114 Fifth Ave., New York, NY 10011
Latest Edition: 1994 ($5.95)

Shop smart by turning coupon-clipping into bonafide cash clout! *The Super Coupon Shopping System* shows you how to cut your supermarket bills up to 80% by earning hundreds, even thousands, of dollars annually using manufacturers' refunds. A valuable guide to such shopper-friendly information as coupon organization, shoppers' trading networks, and the retail structure, this book provides easy, step-by-step methods to reducing your cost on product prices.

Trash or Treasure
Publisher: Treasure Hunt Publications
P.O. Box 3028, Pismo Beach, CA 93448
800/549-7500

Latest Edition: 1995 ($29.95)

You can make major bucks from unwanted items gathering dust in your basement, garage, or attic. Subtitled "How to find the best buyers of antiques, collectibles and other undiscovered treasures," *Trash or Treasure* is to selling what *Buying Retail Is Stupid!* is to buying. The nation's oldest and most reliable guide to locating honest and knowledgeable buyers of everything from stuffed aardvarks to zeppelin parts worth $1,500, lace worth $50 an inch, or Hot Wheels you can sell for $1,000. Includes names, addresses, and phone numbers of top expert buyers in 3,500 categories of antiques and collectibles, plus a simple, four-step process for getting fair prices for anything you own.

Unbelievably Good Deals and Great Adventures That You Absolutely Can't Get Unless You're Over 50
Publisher: Contemporary Books
Two Prudential Plaza, Chicago, IL 60601-6790
800/540-9440

Latest Edition: 1996 ($9.95)

If you are over 50, you qualify for hundreds of money-saving offers, from vacation adventures to everyday benefits. Now in its eighth edition, this bestselling guide has been revised, expanded, and packed with up-to-date information about trips, clubs, programs, and special deals. The latter include travel adventures; price breaks on airfares; up to 50% off at hotels, motels, and restaurants; exclusive tours; big discounts on trains, buses, and car rentals; tax and insurance breaks; and much more.

SMART SHOPPER'S QUIZ

FIND OUT HOW SMART YOU ARE OR COULD BE AT "BUYING MORE FOR LESS"

PART I
How to Shop

Mark each statement below by checking either the <u>yes</u> or <u>no</u> column.

If your behavior "more often than not" (or often enough in your view) matches the statement, check <u>yes</u>. Otherwise, check <u>no</u>.

		YES	NO
1.	Before buying a high-priced product, I check the ratings of several models in a magazine such as *Consumer Reports*.	___	___
2.	Before buying a high-priced product, I avoid pitfalls by checking books such as the Better Business Bureau's *A to Z Buying Guide*.	___	___
3.	I comparison-shop by calling retail stores for prices and checking newspaper ads.	___	___
4.	I check on a store's return policy before buying.	___	___
5.	I buy items I don't need because they're a bargain.	___	___
6.	I buy items after holidays for next year's holidays to take advantage of sizeable discounts.	___	___
7.	I spend too much time shopping for low-priced items.	___	___
8.	I take enough time when shopping for high-priced items.	___	___
9.	I do a major grocery shopping once weekly to save time and energy.	___	___
10.	I use a pocket calculator when grocery shopping to determine which size of product is the best buy.	___	___
11.	I check the grocery store receipt to make sure the scanned prices coincide with the shelf prices.	___	___

441

<u>YES</u> <u>NO</u>

12. When buying small appliances, I test them before
    leaving the store to make sure they work.

13. I grocery shop from a list to cut down on impulse
    buying.

14. I use discount coupons to save money.

15. I buy generic or store brands for some products.

16. Before buying clothes, I plan a basic wardrobe to
    ensure having a minimum of all essentials.

17. When buying clothes, to ensure they are well made,
    I check seams, zippers, stitching, buttons, jacket
    lapels, and the comfort of skirts and pants when
    sitting and walking.

18. When I buy shoes, they must fit in the store.
    (I don't buy tight shoes, expecting them to
    stretch later.)

19. Before buying a high-priced item, I do some
    research on it.

20. If I need a clothing article for a special event—to
    be worn only once or twice—I consider renting
    instead of buying.

21. I generally inform myself of return policies of
    businesses from which I buy.

22. I keep receipts to make returning purchases easier.

23. I complete and return warranty cards promptly and
    file them for easy access if needed.

24. Before going on a big shopping trip, I make a list
    and a budget to avoid impulse buying.

25. I frequently have my spouse accompany me when
    shopping for high-priced products.

26. As a woman, when shopping for clothing, I wear a
    leotard and tights to save the time and trouble of
    changing clothes frequently.

PART II
What I Know About Discount Shopping

Mark each statement below by checking either the <u>true</u> or <u>false</u> column.

If you believe the statement is for the most part true, check the true column; otherwise, check the false column.

	TRUE	FALSE
27. There are hundreds of discount mail-order businesses throughout the U.S.	___	___
28. Most discount mail-order purchases cannot be returned.	___	___
29. Almost all products—everything from A to Z—can be purchased at a discount from mail-order houses.	___	___
30. Manufacturer outlet malls have many name-brand stores offering goods at discounts from approximately 10 to 80%.	___	___
31. Only a few states have manufacturer outlet malls.	___	___
32. It may not pay to visit a manufacturer outlet mall to make only one purchase.	___	___
33. It's wise to visit garage sales early in the day.	___	___
34. You can negotiate price with the seller at a garage sale.	___	___
35. Near the end of a garage sale, prices will be reduced greatly.	___	___
36. You can sometimes get a great buy at a garage sale.	___	___
37. You can find out where and when garage sales will take place by consulting newspaper classified sections.	___	___

	TRUE	FALSE

38. Some swapmeets and flea markets offer a tremendous variety of merchandise.

39. You should not assume that everything for sale at a garage sale, flea market, or swapmeet is a bargain.

40. Most resale stores take clothing from individuals on consignment and keep a percentage of the sale price for themselves.

41. You sometimes can buy high-end clothes—worn once or not at all—at bargain-basement prices.

42. Shopping resale for children's clothes is an excellent way to save money.

43. Almost always, clothes for sale at resale stores have been laundered or dry-cleaned.

44. Only business owners may participate in government auctions.

45. Government auctions offer only military equipment for sale.

46. Pre-auction inspection is an important means of not overpaying for an item.

47. Police auctions of unclaimed stolen goods are available in many cities.

48. The '90s has sometimes been called the "decade of discount shopping."

Smart Shopper's Quiz Scoring

Instructions
Following are the correct answers for each item in the quiz. Circle each item you answered correctly. You get 1 point for each correct answer. Add them up, and record your total score. Then read the interpretation of your score below.

Correct answers:

1 - Y	2 - Y	3 - Y	4 - Y	5 - N	6 - Y
7 - N	8 - Y	9 - Y	10 - Y	11 - Y	12 - Y
13 - Y	14 - Y	15 - Y	16 - Y	17 - Y	18 - Y
19 - Y	20 - Y	21 - Y	22 - Y	23 - Y	24 - Y
25 - Y	26 - Y	27 - T	28 - F	29 - T	30 - T
31 - F	32 - T	33 - T	34 - T	35 - T	36 - T
37 - T	38 - T	39 - T	40 - T	41 - T	42 - T
43 - T	44 - F	45 - F	46 - T	47 - T	48 - T

Total Correct Answers: _____

Interpretation of Scores
Total
Score

45–48   You could write your own book, but don't compete with us.

35–44   You could probably be a shopping consultant. Think about it.

24–34   Always review the Smart Shopping section of this book before shopping.

11–23   Never shop alone.

1–10   We hope you have more money than you know what to do with. Have someone else in your family do the shopping. If you don't change your shopping habits, you may eventually have to consider declaring bankruptcy.

INDEXES

DISCOUNT STORES & OUTLETS

447

DISCOUNT MAIL-ORDER COMPANIES

COMPANIES OFFERING DISCOUNT COUPONS

CONSUMER RESOURCES BY PUBLICATION TITLE

BUYING RETAIL IS STUPID! DISCOUNT COUPONS

Bring book or page (photocopy not accepted) to any of the stores listed below for discount. The store will initial the coupon and return page to you.

**Discount may not be valid on certain items
or with any other offers.**

Valid for one purchase per store.

Expires 12/31/98

❏ **A & M BOOK CELLARS**   Redeemed:
10% Off Purchase & Free Paperback to New Customers

❏ **A 'N B STATIONERY**   Redeemed:
10% Off Purchase

❏ **A NITE ON THE TOWN**   Redeemed:
10% Off on Dress Rental

❏ **A-1 FOAM & FABRICS**   Redeemed:
10% Off Purchase

❏ **A-1 SHOWER DOOR CO.**   Redeemed:
10% Off Will-Call Orders

❏ **A.A. BAKER'S HARDWARE & PAINT**   Redeemed:
10% Off $50 Purchase

❏ **AAA ETERNAL STAINLESS STEEL CORP.**   Redeemed:
10% Off Purchase

❏ **ABC POOL & PATIO**   Redeemed:
5% Off Purchase

❏ **THE ADDRESS BOUTIQUE, INC.**   Redeemed:
10% Off—First-Time Customers

❏ **AFFORDABLE BOOKS & COLLECTIBLES**   Redeemed:
20% Off Books Only

Buying Retail Is Stupid! Discount Coupons

Bring book or page (photocopy not accepted) to any of the stores listed below for discount. The store will initial the coupon and return page to you.

**Discount may not be valid on certain items
or with any other offers.**

Valid for one purchase per store.

Expires 12/31/98

❑ **AFFORDABLE USED OFFICE FURNITURE** Redeemed:
10% Off Purchase

❑ **AIR CONDITIONING EXCHANGE**   Redeemed:
10% + Free Tape Measure

❑ **AL'S DISCOUNT FURNITURE**   Redeemed:
5% Off Purchase

❑ **ALAN GRAHAM MOTORING ACCESSORIES** Redeemed:
Free Steering Wheel Lock w/Purchase of Alarm

❑ **ALIN PARTY SUPPLY**   Redeemed:
10% Off Purchase

❑ **ALL IN 1 HOME FURNISHINGS**   Redeemed:
5% Off Cash or Check Purchase

❑ **ALL PRO BICYCLES**   Redeemed:
10% Off Purchase

❑ **ALL STAR GLASS**   Redeemed:
10% Off Windshields/5% Off Other Parts

❑ **ALL SYSTEMS GO**   Redeemed:
20% Off Purchase

❑ **ALL VALLEY SHOWER DOOR CO.**   Redeemed:
5% Off Purchase

Buying Retail Is Stupid! Discount Coupons

Bring book or page (photocopy not accepted) to any of the stores listed below for discount. The store will initial the coupon and return page to you.

**Discount may not be valid on certain items
or with any other offers.**

Valid for one purchase per store.

Expires 12/31/98

❑ **ALLAN JEFFRIES' FRAMING**   Redeemed:
10% Off Purchase

❑ **ALMOST & PERFECT ENGLISH CHINA**   Redeemed:
5% Off Purchase

❑ **ALPERT'S BEDROOM & WATERBED WAREHOUSE**   Redeemed:
5% Off Purchase

❑ **AMENDOLA MUSIC, INC.**   Redeemed:
20% Off Purchase

❑ **AMERICAN SURPLUS**   Redeemed:
10% Off Purchase

❑ **AMETRON**   Redeemed:
Gift w/$75 Purchase

❑ **ANGELUS HOME CENTER**   Redeemed:
5% Off Purchase

❑ **ANNA QUEEN**   Redeemed:
5% Off $300 Purchase

❑ **ANTELOPE**   Redeemed:
10% Off Purchase

❑ **THE ANTIQUE HOUSE**   Redeemed:
$25 Gift Certificate w/$100 Purchase

Bring book or page (photocopy not accepted) to any of the stores listed below for discount. The store will initial the coupon and return page to you.

**Discount may not be valid on certain items
or with any other offers.**

Valid for one purchase per store.

Expires 12/31/98

❑ **ANTIQUE WAY**   Redeemed:
10% Off Purchase

❑ **APPLIANCE SERVICENTER**   Redeemed:
10% Off Purchase

❑ **ARMANI WELLS**   Redeemed:
10% Off Purchase

❑ **AROUND THE WORLD TRAVEL**   Redeemed:
5% Off Purchase of Cruise

❑ **ART SUPPLY WAREHOUSE**   Redeemed:
10% Off Purchase

❑ **ARTTYPE BUSINESS MACHINES**   Redeemed:
10% Off Supplies Only

❑ **ASSOCIATED AUTO BODY**   Redeemed:
5% Off Labor

❑ **BABY DEJA-VU**   Redeemed:
10% Off Purchase

❑ **BABY ON A BUDGET**   Redeemed:
5% Off $10 Purchase

❑ **BABYLAND & KIDS FURNITURE**   Redeemed:
Free Mattress w/Purchase of 3-Piece Room Set

Buying Retail Is Stupid! Discount Coupons

Bring book or page (photocopy not accepted) to any of the stores listed below for discount. The store will initial the coupon and return page to you.

**Discount may not be valid on certain items
or with any other offers.**

Valid for one purchase per store.

Expires 12/31/98

❏ **BACK ON THE RACK**   Redeemed:
10% Off Purchase

❏ **BAILEY'S BACKSTREET**   Redeemed:
10% Off Purchase

❏ **BAILEY'S**   Redeemed:
10% Off Purchase

❏ **BALLOONS & FLOWERS BY JOSEPH**   Redeemed:
Free Balloon Sculpture w/$200 Purchase

❏ **BARGAIN FAIR**   Redeemed:
10% Off Purchase

❏ **BARGAINS GALORE**   Redeemed:
10% Off $10 Purchase

❏ **BARON BROTHERS NURSERY**   Redeemed:
10% Off O.H. Kruse Feed

❏ **BAVARIAN AUTO PARTS**   Redeemed:
5% Off Purchase

❏ **BAY CITY APPLIANCES**   Redeemed:
Free Delivery & Installation w/Purchase

❏ **BED BROKER**   Redeemed:
5% Off Purchase

BUYING RETAIL IS STUPID! DISCOUNT COUPONS

Bring book or page (photocopy not accepted) to any of the stores listed below for discount. The store will initial the coupon and return page to you.

Discount may not be valid on certain items or with any other offers.

Valid for one purchase per store.

Expires 12/31/98

❑ **BEDROOM & WINDOW CREATIONS**   Redeemed:
5% Off Purchase

❑ **BEV'S CRAFTS & LACE**   Redeemed:
10% Off Purchase

❑ **BEVERLY HILLS BIKE SHOP**   Redeemed:
10% Off Purchase

❑ **THE BIG, THE BAD & THE BEAUTIFUL**   Redeemed:
10% Off Purchase

❑ **BILLIARDS & BARSTOOLS**   Redeemed:
10% Off Accessories

❑ **BOB MIRMAN'S WESTCOAST TIRE AND BRAKE**   Redeemed:
10% Off Labor

❑ **THE BOOK BARON**   Redeemed:
10% Off Purchase

❑ **BOOK CITY**   Redeemed:
10% Off Purchase

❑ **BOOKMAN**   Redeemed:
10% Off Purchase

Buying Retail Is Stupid! Discount Coupons

Bring book or page (photocopy not accepted) to any of the stores listed below for discount. The store will initial the coupon and return page to you.

**Discount may not be valid on certain items
or with any other offers.**

Valid for one purchase per store.

Expires 12/31/98

❏ **BOOT HILL**   Redeemed:
  5% Off Purchase

❏ **BORN 2 SHOPPE**   Redeemed:
  20% Off $10 Purchase

❏ **BOULEVARD WEST FLOREST**   Redeemed:
  15% Off Purchase

❏ **BOX CITY**   Redeemed:
  10% Off Purchase

❏ **BRASS BEDS DIRECT**   Redeemed:
  5% Off Purchase

❏ **BRITE AND SHINE, INC.**   Redeemed:
  10% Off Cleaning 5 Blinds

❏ **BUNK BED CENTER & VALLEY MATTRESS** Redeemed:
  10% Off Purchase

❏ **BYRNE HOME FURNISHINGS**   Redeemed:
  10% Off Framed Art or Sofa Sample

❏ **CALIFORNIA CACTUS CENTER**   Redeemed:
  Free Bag of Cactus Mix w/Purchase

❏ **CALIFORNIA JEANS**   Redeemed:
  5% Off $50 Purchase—10% Off $100 Purchase

Bring book or page (photocopy not accepted) to any of the stores listed below for discount. The store will initial the coupon and return page to you.

**Discount may not be valid on certain items
or with any other offers.**

Valid for one purchase per store.

Expires 12/31/98

❑ **CAMERA CITY**
10% Off Purchase

Redeemed:

❑ **THE CANDY FACTORY**
10% Off Purchase

Redeemed:

❑ **CANYON BEACHWEAR'S
SWIMWEAR OUTLET**
10% Off $50 Purchase

Redeemed:

❑ **CARB CARE USA**
$20 Off Purchase

Redeemed:

❑ **CARLSON'S T.V. & APPLIANCES**
$10 Off Purchase

Redeemed:

❑ **CAROL'S COUNTRY CORNER**
10% Off Purchase

Redeemed:

❑ **CARPET COLLECTION**
5% Off Purchase

Redeemed:

❑ **CARPET MANOR**
5% Off Purchase

Redeemed:

❑ **THE CARPET STORE**
10% Off Purchase

Redeemed:

Buying Retail Is Stupid! Discount Coupons

Bring book or page (photocopy not accepted) to any of the stores listed below for discount. The store will initial the coupon and return page to you.

**Discount may not be valid on certain items
or with any other offers.**

Valid for one purchase per store.

Expires 12/31/98

❑ **CASTLE CHANDELIERS & LIGHTING CO.** Redeemed:
10% Off Purchase

❑ **CASTON'S T.V. & APPLIANCE**   Redeemed:
Free 35mm Camera w/Purchase

❑ **CFOS FACTORY OUTLET**   Redeemed:
10% Off Fabrics

❑ **CHIC LINGERIE OUTLET**   Redeemed:
10% Off Purchase

❑ **CLARICE'S CAKE DECORATING
AND CANDY MAKING SUPPLIES**   Redeemed:
15% Off Purchase

❑ **COLLATERAL LOANS, INC.**   Redeemed:
20% Cash Discount

❑ **COLLECTIONS '85 INC.**   Redeemed:
5% Off $250 Purchase

❑ **COMPUTER GAMES PLUS**   Redeemed:
10% Off Purchase

❑ **COMPUTER PALACE**   Redeemed:
$25 Off Any Service of $50 or More

BUYING RETAIL IS STUPID! DISCOUNT COUPONS

Bring book or page (photocopy not accepted) to any of the stores listed below for discount. The store will initial the coupon and return page to you.

**Discount may not be valid on certain items
or with any other offers.**

Valid for one purchase per store.

Expires 12/31/98

❑ **COMPUTER RECYCLER**   Redeemed:
   $25 Off Computer

❑ **CONSOLIDATED PET FOODS**   Redeemed:
   15% Off Purchase

❑ **CONSUMERS GUILD, INC.**   Redeemed:
   5% Off Purchase

❑ **COOPER & KRAMER, INC.**   Redeemed:
   10% Off Purchase

❑ **CORAL REEF DIVE & SURF
   & WET SUIT FACTORY**   Redeemed:
   10% Off Purchase

❑ **CORT FURNITURE RENTAL
   CLEARANCE CENTER**   Redeemed:
   10% Off Purchase

❑ **COTTAGE SHOPS**   Redeemed:
   10% Off Purchase

❑ **CRITERIUM CYCLE SPORT**   Redeemed:
   10% Off Purchase

❑ **CRYSTAL'S LACES & GIFTS**   Redeemed:
   40% Off $25 Purchase

Buying Retail Is Stupid! Discount Coupons

Bring book or page (photocopy not accepted) to any of the stores listed below for discount. The store will initial the coupon and return page to you.

**Discount may not be valid on certain items
or with any other offers.**

Valid for one purchase per store.

Expires 12/31/98

❑ **D/M YARDAGE OUTLET**
10% Off In-Stock Fabrics

Redeemed:

❑ **DAN HOWARD'S MATERNITY FACTORY**
10% Off Purchase

Redeemed:

❑ **DAVID APPEL—THE FUR SHOP**
Free Storage & Cleaning w/Purchase

Redeemed:

❑ **DAWN'S DISCOUNT LACE/RUBAN
ET FLEUR**
10% Off $25 Purchase

Redeemed:

❑ **DB COOPER'S WHOLESALE
MUSIC EXCHANGE**
Buy 3 CDs and Get 1 Free

Redeemed:

❑ **DECOR ART GALLERY**
10% Off Purchase

Redeemed:

❑ **DEJA VU BRIDAL BOUTIQUE**
10% Off Headpiece

Redeemed:

❑ **DENNY LESSER FINE JEWELRY**
Sales Tax Paid by Store

Redeemed:

❑ **DESIGNER FABRIC SHOWCASE**
10% Off Purchase

Redeemed:

Buying Retail Is Stupid! Discount Coupons

Bring book or page (photocopy not accepted) to any of the stores listed below for discount. The store will initial the coupon and return page to you.

**Discount may not be valid on certain items
or with any other offers.**

Valid for one purchase per store.

Expires 12/31/98

❑ **DESIGNER INTERIORS**   Redeemed:
  5% Off Purchase

❑ **DESIGNERS FURNITURE MART**   Redeemed:
  10% Off Purchase

❑ **DESIGNERS' BLOOPERS**   Redeemed:
  5% Off Purchase

❑ **DIRT CHEAP PLANT CO.**   Redeemed:
  20% Off Purchase

❑ **DISC-CONNECTION COMPACT DISCS,**   Redeemed:
  RECORDS & TAPES
  10% Off Used CDs & LPs

❑ **DISCOUNT BILLIARDS, INC.**   Redeemed:
  10% Off Purchase

❑ **DISCOUNT FRAMES**   Redeemed:
  10% Off Purchase

❑ **DISCOUNT PET FOOD**   Redeemed:
  10% Off $20 Purchase

❑ **DISCOUNT TROPICAL FISH**   Redeemed:
  10% Off Purchase

BUYING RETAIL IS STUPID! DISCOUNT COUPONS

Bring book or page (photocopy not accepted) to any of the stores listed below for discount. The store will initial the coupon and return page to you.

**Discount may not be valid on certain items
or with any other offers.**

Valid for one purchase per store.

Expires 12/31/98

❏ **DISHES A LA CARTE**
10% Off Purchase

Redeemed:

❏ **DIVERS' DISCOUNT SUPPLY**
Free Plush Slap Strap or T-Shirt

Redeemed:

❏ **DOIN' DISHES**
10% Off Purchase

Redeemed:

❏ **DONNA'S BIRD HOUSE**
15% Off Purchase (excluding live stock)

Redeemed:

❏ **DUTTON'S BOOKS**
10% Off Purchase

Redeemed:

❏ **E.V.S. PRODUCTIONS**
10% Off Purchase

Redeemed:

❏ **EDDIE GOLD FURNITURE, INC.**
10% Off Purchase

Redeemed:

❏ **ELECTROPEDIC ADJUSTABLE BEDS**
$100 Off Purchase

Redeemed:

❏ **ELLIOT'S PET EMPORIUM**
10% Off Purchase

Redeemed:

❏ **ESTATE HOME FURNISHINGS**
10% Off Purchase

Redeemed:

Buying Retail Is Stupid! Discount Coupons

Bring book or page (photocopy not accepted) to any of the stores listed below for discount. The store will initial the coupon and return page to you.

**Discount may not be valid on certain items
or with any other offers.**

Valid for one purchase per store.

Expires 12/31/98

❏ **FABRIC GALLERY**   Redeemed:
  10% Off $100 Purchase

❏ **FACES N' PLACES PHOTOS**   Redeemed:
  Free 8 × 10 + 12 Wallet Photos

❏ **FERGUSON'S MARINE SPECIALTIES**   Redeemed:
  10% + Free Cowrie Shell

❏ **FINDERS KEEPERS FURNITURE OUTLET** Redeemed:
  10% Off Purchase

❏ **THE FITNESS STORE OUTLET STORE**   Redeemed:
  5% Off Purchase

❏ **FLOOR COVERING UNLIMITED**   Redeemed:
  $10 Off $250 Purchase

❏ **FOAM MART**   Redeemed:
  10% Off Purchase

❏ **FOOT MART SPORTS**   Redeemed:
  5% Off Purchase

❏ **FOR KIDS ONLY**   Redeemed:
  10% Off Purchase

❏ **FOR PET'S SAKE PET SHOP**   Redeemed:
  10% Off Purchase

BUYING RETAIL IS STUPID! DISCOUNT COUPONS

Bring book or page (photocopy not accepted) to any of the stores listed below for discount. The store will initial the coupon and return page to you.

**Discount may not be valid on certain items
or with any other offers.**

Valid for one purchase per store.

Expires 12/31/98

❏ **FOREVER TREASURED**   Redeemed:
   25% Off Any Service

❏ **FOREVER YOUNG**   Redeemed:
   $35 Free Merchandise w/$100 Purchase

❏ **FRONTIER SHOP**   Redeemed:
   10% Off Purchase

❏ **FURNITURE LIQUIDATORS**   Redeemed:
   5% Off Purchase

❏ **FURNITURE TRENDS**   Redeemed:
   5% Off Purchase

❏ **GENERAL WAX WHOLESALE
   OUTLET STORE**   Redeemed:
   10% Off Purchase

❏ **GLAMOUR UNIFORM SHOP**   Redeemed:
   10% Off Purchase

❏ **GOLDEN FLEECE DESIGNS INC.**   Redeemed:
   15% Off Purchase

❏ **GOLDEN WEST POOL TABLES**   Redeemed:
   5% Off Purchase

BUYING RETAIL IS STUPID! DISCOUNT COUPONS

Bring book or page (photocopy not accepted) to any of the stores listed below for discount. The store will initial the coupon and return page to you.

**Discount may not be valid on certain items
or with any other offers.**
Valid for one purchase per store.
Expires 12/31/98

❑ **GOLF FAIRE**   Redeemed: _____
10% Off Purchase

❑ **THE GREAT GATSBY**   Redeemed: _____
10% Off Purchase

❑ **THE GREAT NAME**   Redeemed: _____
10% Off Purchase

❑ **GREEN GINGER BOOKSHOP**   Redeemed: _____
10% Off Purchase

❑ **GREY GOOSE CUSTOM FRAMING**   Redeemed: _____
10% Off Purchase

❑ **THE GUITAR STORE**   Redeemed: _____
Guitar Strings/Buy 1 Set, Get 1 Free

❑ **H & M APPLIANCES**   Redeemed: _____
10% Off Appliance + 50% Off Service Call

❑ **H. SAVINAR LUGGAGE**   Redeemed: _____
Free Travel Neck Cushion w/$50 Purchase

❑ **HAIR 4 MEN**   Redeemed: _____
20% Off Purchase

❑ **HARPER'S LADIES WHOLESALE CLOTHING** Redeemed: _____
10% Off Purchase

Buying Retail Is Stupid! Discount Coupons

Bring book or page (photocopy not accepted) to any of the stores listed below for discount. The store will initial the coupon and return page to you.

**Discount may not be valid on certain items
or with any other offers.**

Valid for one purchase per store.

Expires 12/31/98

❏ **HENRY'S SHOE EXPERIENCE**   Redeemed:
10% Off Purchase

❏ **HIAWATHA HOMES**   Redeemed:
15% Off Purchase

❏ **HIGHAM'S VACUUM AND SEWING CENTER** Redeemed:
10% Off Notions & Supplies

❏ **HOME COMFORT CENTER**   Redeemed:
5% Off Purchase

❏ **HOOPER CAMERA AND VIDEO CENTERS** Redeemed:
5% Off Purchase

❏ **HOW & WEN? THE 2NDS SHOP**   Redeemed:
15% Off Purchase

❏ **HOWARD & PHIL'S WESTERN WEAR
OUTLET STORE**   Redeemed:
10% Off Purchase

❏ **IN-A-FLOOR SAFE COMPANY**   Redeemed:
10% Off Purchase

❏ **INDUSTRIAL SHOE WAREHOUSE**   Redeemed:
5% Off Purchase

BUYING RETAIL IS STUPID! DISCOUNT COUPONS

Bring book or page (photocopy not accepted) to any of the stores listed below for discount. The store will initial the coupon and return page to you.

**Discount may not be valid on certain items
or with any other offers.**

Valid for one purchase per store.

Expires 12/31/98

❑ **J. B. SEBRELL CO.**
10% Off Purchase

Redeemed:

❑ **J. ROTHSTEIN & CO.**
Free Watch Battery

Redeemed:

❑ **J. WHITT INTIMATES**
5% Off Purchase

Redeemed:

❑ **THE J.R. COLLECTION**
10% Off $30 Purchase

Redeemed:

❑ **JASMAK AUTO PARTS & ACCESSORIES**
15% Off Purchase

Redeemed:

❑ **JAZZY'S WORLD**
10% Off $50 Purchase

Redeemed:

❑ **JEAN'S STARS' APPAREL/PAST PERFECT★**
10% Off Purchase

Redeemed:

❑ **JET APPAREL OUTLET**
10% Off $10 Purchase

Redeemed:

❑ **JILMOND PERFUMES &
COSMETICS COMPANY**
10% Off Purchase

Redeemed:

BUYING RETAIL IS STUPID! DISCOUNT COUPONS

Bring book or page (photocopy not accepted) to any of the stores listed below for discount. The store will initial the coupon and return page to you.

**Discount may not be valid on certain items
or with any other offers.**

Valid for one purchase per store.

Expires 12/31/98

❏ **JIM'S ONE STOP PARTY SHOP**
10% Off Purchase

Redeemed:

❏ **JOHN MOYEN'S JEWELLERY
CONNECTION**
10% Off Purchase

Redeemed:

❏ **JUKEBOXES 4 RENT**
5% Off Rental

Redeemed:

❏ **JUKEBOXES UNLIMITED**
5% Off Purchase

Redeemed:

❏ **JUNE TRAVOLTA'S ROSEBUD**
10% Off Purchase

Redeemed:

❏ **KAGAN SURPLUS SALES**
5% Off Purchase Under $100—10% Off Purchase
of $100 or More

Redeemed:

❏ **KEYBOARD COUNTRY INC.**
Free Lifetime Lessons + Delivery w/Organ Purchase

Redeemed:

❏ **KIDS OUTLET**
10% Off Purchase

Redeemed:

❏ **KIDS' ART SPACE**
10% Off Purchase

Redeemed:

BUYING RETAIL IS STUPID! DISCOUNT COUPONS

Bring book or page (photocopy not accepted) to any of the stores listed below for discount. The store will initial the coupon and return page to you.

**Discount may not be valid on certain items
or with any other offers.**

Valid for one purchase per store.

Expires 12/31/98

❑ **THE KITCHEN STORE**   Redeemed:
5% Off Purchase

❑ **THE KITCHEN WAREHOUSE**   Redeemed:
5% Off Purchase

❑ **KLEIN'S BEAD BOX**   Redeemed:
10% Off Purchase

❑ **KOWBOYZ**   Redeemed:
10% Off Purchase

❑ **KRYSTAL GARDENS**   Redeemed:
10% Off Purchase

❑ **L.A. GYM EQUIPMENT**   Redeemed:
10% Off Purchase

❑ **LAMPMART**   Redeemed:
5% Off Purchase

❑ **LARCHMONT SHIRTS**   Redeemed:
5% Off $100 Purchase

❑ **LASERS UNLIMITED**   Redeemed:
Free Lifetime Membership

❑ **LE CLUB HANDBAG CO.**   Redeemed:
10% Off Purchase

Buying Retail Is Stupid! Discount Coupons

Bring book or page (photocopy not accepted) to any of the stores listed below for discount. The store will initial the coupon and return page to you.

**Discount may not be valid on certain items
or with any other offers.**

Valid for one purchase per store.
Expires 12/31/98

❑ **LEC WORLD TRADERS**   Redeemed:
   Free Membership

❑ **LEE LAWNMOWER**   Redeemed:
   10% Off Purchase

❑ **LEONORE'S FUR OUTLET**   Redeemed:
   5% Off Purchase

❑ **LESTER CARPET CO., INC.**   Redeemed:
   10% Off Purchase

❑ **LINCOLN FABRICS**   Redeemed:
   20% Off Purchase

❑ **LINDA BERTOZZI**   Redeemed:
   10% Off Purchase

❑ **LORA BEAUTY CENTER**   Redeemed:
   10% Off Purchase

❑ **LORD OF THE RINGS**   Redeemed:
   5% Off Purchase

❑ **LOS ANGELES WASHINGTON   Redeemed:
   GOLF CENTER**
   5% Off Purchase

Buying Retail Is Stupid! Discount Coupons

Bring book or page (photocopy not accepted) to any of the stores listed below for discount. The store will initial the coupon and return page to you.

**Discount may not be valid on certain items
or with any other offers.**

Valid for one purchase per store.

Expires 12/31/98

❑ **LOVELAND COTTON CONNECTION**   Redeemed:
20% Off Purchase

❑ **LUGGAGE 4 LESS**   Redeemed:
5% Off Purchase

❑ **LUNA GARCIA**   Redeemed:
10% Off Purchase

❑ **MAGIC WORLD**   Redeemed:
5% Off Purchase

❑ **MAJOR SURPLUS & SURVIVAL**   Redeemed:
10% Off $5 Purchase

❑ **MARBLE PRODUCTS OF FULLERTON**   Redeemed:
5% Off Purchase

❑ **MARLENE GAINES HANDBAGS**   Redeemed:
10% Off Purchase

❑ **MARTIN'S GUIDE TO WINE BARGAINS**   Redeemed:
10% Off 1-Year Subscription

❑ **MAYA SHOES**   Redeemed:
5% Off Purchase

❑ **MELAMED & CO.**   Redeemed:
15% Off Purchase

BUYING RETAIL IS STUPID! DISCOUNT COUPONS

Bring book or page (photocopy not accepted) to any of the stores listed below for discount. The store will initial the coupon and return page to you.

**Discount may not be valid on certain items
or with any other offers.**

Valid for one purchase per store.

Expires 12/31/98

❑ **MELROSE DISCOUNT CARPET**   Redeemed:
  10% Off Purchase

❑ **MELROSE DRAPERIES**   Redeemed:
  10% Off Purchase

❑ **MERRILL'S MUSIC**   Redeemed:
  10% Off Purchase

❑ **MH DESIGNS**   Redeemed:
  10% Off Purchase

❑ **MICHAEL LEVINE, INC.**   Redeemed:
  10% Off Purchase

❑ **MIMI'S FLOWERS**   Redeemed:
  10% Off Purchase

❑ **MOBY DISC**   Redeemed:
  10% Off Purchase

❑ **MOM'S THE WORD**   Redeemed:
  10% Off Purchase

❑ **MONOPOLY**   Redeemed:
  15% Off $150 Purchase

❑ **MONTERREY FOOD PRODUCTS**   Redeemed:
  5% Off Purchase

BUYING RETAIL IS STUPID! DISCOUNT COUPONS

Bring book or page (photocopy not accepted) to any of the stores listed below for discount. The store will initial the coupon and return page to you.

**Discount may not be valid on certain items
or with any other offers.**

Valid for one purchase per store.

Expires 12/31/98

❑ **MONTROSE TRAVEL**
5% Off Purchase

Redeemed:

❑ **MS. FASHIONS**
20% Off Purchase

Redeemed:

❑ **MUDPIES ... A CHILDREN'S STORE**
10% Off New Merchandise

Redeemed:

❑ **MUSIC EXCHANGE**
20% Off Used CDs

Redeemed:

❑ **MY FAIR LADY**
10% Off Purchase

Redeemed:

❑ **MY SECRET PLACE**
20% Off $10 Purchase

Redeemed:

❑ **NEBRASKA BEAD CO.**
10% Off Purchase

Redeemed:

❑ **NEW & USED COMPUTER STORE**
5% Off Used Equipment

Redeemed:

❑ **"NEW II YOU" BOUTIQUE**
10% Off $25 Purchase

Redeemed:

❑ **NEW METRO TILE COMPANY**
5% Off Purchase

Redeemed:

Buying Retail Is Stupid! Discount Coupons

Bring book or page (photocopy not accepted) to any of the stores listed below for discount. The store will initial the coupon and return page to you.

**Discount may not be valid on certain items
or with any other offers.**

Valid for one purchase per store.

Expires 12/31/98

❑ **NINE MONTHS AND MORE**   Redeemed:
5% Off 1 Item

❑ **NUTS TO YOU**   Redeemed:
10% Off Purchase

❑ **OFF MELROSE**   Redeemed:
15% Off Purchase

❑ **OFF THE BOLT**   Redeemed:
Free 14- to 16-Inch Pillow Form w/$10 Purchase

❑ **OLD WORLD IRONMONGERS
FACTORY OUTLET**   Redeemed:
5% Off Purchase

❑ **OLYMPIC ELECTRONICS**   Redeemed:
Free Walkman Radio w/$50 Purchase

❑ **"ON THE HOUSE"**   Redeemed:
Free Pair of Tickets or 10% Off Membership

❑ **ON THE WALL FRAMES**   Redeemed:
15% Off Purchase

❑ **ONE NIGHT AFFAIR GOWN RENTALS**   Redeemed:
5% Off Rental

BUYING RETAIL IS STUPID! DISCOUNT COUPONS

Bring book or page (photocopy not accepted) to any of the stores listed below for discount. The store will initial the coupon and return page to you.

Discount may not be valid on certain items or with any other offers.

Valid for one purchase per store.

Expires 12/31/98

❑ **ORANGE APPLIANCE & VACUUM**   Redeemed:
5% Off Purchase

❑ **THE ORCHID MAN**   Redeemed:
10% Off Purchase

❑ **P X DRUGS NO. 2**   Redeemed:
10% Off Purchase

❑ **P.J. LONDON**   Redeemed:
10% Off Purchase

❑ **PACIFIC AUDIO & ALARM**   Redeemed:
20% Off Labor

❑ **PACIFIC BODY PARTS**   Redeemed:
10% Off Purchase

❑ **PAR PAINT COMPANY**   Redeemed:
5% Off Purchase

❑ **PARTY CORNER DISCOUNT CENTER**   Redeemed:
10% Off Purchase

❑ **PATSY COMER'S JEWELRY & COINS**   Redeemed:
10% Off Purchase

❑ **PERFUME CITY**   Redeemed:
$2 Off $20 Purchase

Buying Retail Is Stupid! Discount Coupons

Bring book or page (photocopy not accepted) to any of the stores listed below for discount. The store will initial the coupon and return page to you.

**Discount may not be valid on certain items
or with any other offers.**

Valid for one purchase per store.

Expires 12/31/98

❑ **PIER 1 IMPORTS CLEARANCE STORE**   Redeemed:
   10% Off Purchase

❑ **PILLER'S OF EAGLE ROCK**   Redeemed:
   10% Off Purchase

❑ **PLAYMATES**   Redeemed:
   15% Off $25 Purchase

❑ **POTTERY AND FLORAL WORLD**   Redeemed:
   10% Off Purchase

❑ **POTTERY ETC.**   Redeemed:
   10% Off Purchase + 2-Inch Clay Pot

❑ **PRETTY WOMAN**   Redeemed:
   10% Off $25 Purchase

❑ **PRO GOLF DISCOUNT**   Redeemed:
   10% Off Purchase

❑ **PS OPTICAL**   Redeemed:
   Free 2nd Pair of Frames w/Same Prescription

❑ **RAINBOW VACUUM CENTER**   Redeemed:
   10% Off Purchase

❑ **RECYCLEPEDIA**   Redeemed:
   10% Off Purchase

BUYING RETAIL IS STUPID! DISCOUNT COUPONS

Bring book or page (photocopy not accepted) to any of the stores listed below for discount. The store will initial the coupon and return page to you.

**Discount may not be valid on certain items
or with any other offers.**

Valid for one purchase per store.

Expires 12/31/98

❑ **RED BARN FEED & SADDLERY INC.**   Redeemed:
5% Off Purchase

❑ **REGENERATION**   Redeemed:
10% Off Purchase

❑ **RHODA KELLYS FLORAL FACTORY**   Redeemed:
Free Bride & Groom Teddy Bears w/$200 Purchase

❑ **RICH DOOR & WINDOW**   Redeemed:
10% Off $100 Purchase

❑ **RICHARD PRATT'S
MATTRESS WAREHOUSE**   Redeemed:
10% Off Any Mattress Set

❑ **RION SASH & DOOR CO.**   Redeemed:
5% Off Purchase

❑ **RIVERSIDE PHARMACY**   Redeemed:
40% Off Greeting Cards or 20% Off Gift Items

❑ **ROBERTO'S FLORIST**   Redeemed:
10% Off Wedding Flowers

❑ **ROBERTSON'S**   Redeemed:
10% Off Purchase

Buying Retail Is Stupid! Discount Coupons

Bring book or page (photocopy not accepted) to any of the stores listed below for discount. The store will initial the coupon and return page to you.

**Discount may not be valid on certain items
or with any other offers.**

Valid for one purchase per store.

Expires 12/31/98

❏ **ROLLEZE, INC.**   Redeemed:
5% Off Purchase

❏ **ROSEMAN'S MENSWEAR**   Redeemed:
10% Off Purchase for First-Time Customer

❏ **ROTEY'S BOUTIQUE**   Redeemed:
5% Off Purchase

❏ **THE ROUNDHOUSE TRAIN STORE**   Redeemed:
10% Off Purchase

❏ **RTC MATTRESS WAREHOUSE**   Redeemed:
Free Bed Frame w/$250 Purchase

❏ **SAM'S BOOK CITY**   Redeemed:
10% Off Purchase

❏ **SAMPLES ONLY**   Redeemed:
10% Off Purchase

❏ **SANTI'S FOUNTAINS**   Redeemed:
10% Off Purchase

❏ **SARA DESIGNERS OUTLET**   Redeemed:
10% Off Purchase

❏ **SCHOOL UNIFORM CO.**   Redeemed:
5% Off Purchase

Buying Retail Is Stupid! Discount Coupons

Bring book or page (photocopy not accepted) to any of the stores listed below for discount. The store will initial the coupon and return page to you.

**Discount may not be valid on certain items
or with any other offers.**

Valid for one purchase per store.

Expires 12/31/98

❏ **SECOND NATURE**   Redeemed:
15% Off $25 Purchase

❏ **SECOND TIME AROUND**   Redeemed:
20% Off Purchase

❏ **SECOND TIME AROUND RECORDS**   Redeemed:
10% Off Purchase

❏ **SEE ME NOW**   Redeemed:
10% Off Purchase

❏ **SELCO BATTERY CO.**   Redeemed:
10% Off Purchase

❏ **SERENDIPITY BOUTIQUE**   Redeemed:
25% Off Purchase

❏ **SEYMOUR FASHIONS**   Redeemed:
10% Off Purchase

❏ **SFO KIDS**   Redeemed:
15% Off Purchase

❏ **SHAKY WIGS OF HOLLYWOOD**   Redeemed:
15% Off Purchase

❏ **SHELLEY'S STEREO HI-FI CENTER**   Redeemed:
10% Off Purchase

BUYING RETAIL IS STUPID! DISCOUNT COUPONS

Bring book or page (photocopy not accepted) to any of the stores listed below for discount. The store will initial the coupon and return page to you.

**Discount may not be valid on certain items
or with any other offers.**

Valid for one purchase per store.

Expires 12/31/98

❑ **SHELLY'S DISCOUNT AEROBIC
& DANCE WEAR**
20% Off Purchase

Redeemed:

❑ **SHELLY'S DISCOUNT COSTUMES
AND ACCESSORIES**
20% Off Purchase

Redeemed:

❑ **SHOE EXPLOSION**
10% Off Purchase

Redeemed:

❑ **SHOETERIA**
15% Off Purchase

Redeemed:

❑ **SID & ME**
$10 Off $100 Purchase

Redeemed:

❑ **SIDELINE SALES**
5% Off Purchase

Redeemed:

❑ **SIG'S POTTERY & NURSERY**
5% Off Purchase

Redeemed:

❑ **SIMON**
10% Off Purchase

Redeemed:

❑ **SIMON'S CAMERA DISCOUNT STORE**
20% Off 1-Hour Film Developing

Redeemed:

Buying Retail Is Stupid! Discount Coupons

Bring book or page (photocopy not accepted) to any of the stores listed below for discount. The store will initial the coupon and return page to you.

**Discount may not be valid on certain items
or with any other offers.**

Valid for one purchase per store.

Expires 12/31/98

❏ **SIR MICHAEL'S LIMOUSINE SERVICE**   Redeemed:
10% Off Rental of 2 Limos

❏ **SIT'N SLEEP**   Redeemed:
5% Off Purchase

❏ **SNEAKER WAREHOUSE**   Redeemed:
5% Off Purchase

❏ **SONNY'S RADIATOR EXCHANGE**   Redeemed:
10% Off Radiator

❏ **SOUNDS GOOD STEREO**   Redeemed:
50% Off Cost of Installation

❏ **SPENCER'S MATTRESS FACTORY OUTLET** Redeemed:
10% Off Purchase

❏ **SPORT CHALET WAREHOUSE OUTLET**   Redeemed:
10% Off $50 Purchase

❏ **STAR DRAPERIES MFG.**   Redeemed:
10% Off Purchase

❏ **STERN'S DISCOUNT DRAPERY CENTER**   Redeemed:
10% Off Purchase

❏ **THE STORK SHOP**   Redeemed:
$5 Off $45 Purchase

Buying Retail Is Stupid! Discount Coupons

Bring book or page (photocopy not accepted) to any of the stores listed below for discount. The store will initial the coupon and return page to you.

**Discount may not be valid on certain items
or with any other offers.**

Valid for one purchase per store.

Expires 12/31/98

❑ **STRIPPER WALLPAPER SERVICE**   Redeemed:
10% Cash Discount

❑ **STUART FELMAN'S (HONG KONG)**   Redeemed:
CUSTOM TAILORS
Free Custom Shirt w/Each Suit Purchased

❑ **STUDIO WARDROBE/REEL CLOTHES**   Redeemed:
5% Off Purchase

❑ **SUPER POPS RECORD DETECTIVE**   Redeemed:
10% Off Purchase

❑ **SUPER PRO IMAGE OUTLET STORE**   Redeemed:
10% Off Purchase

❑ **SUPER-RITE DRUGS INC.**   Redeemed:
5% Off First Prescription

❑ **SUPERGO**   Redeemed:
10% Off Purchase

❑ **SUPERIOR WINDOW COVERINGS**   Redeemed:
10% Off Purchase

❑ **SURFAS, INC.**   Redeemed:
5% Off Food Items

Buying Retail Is Stupid! Discount Coupons

Bring book or page (photocopy not accepted) to any of the stores listed below for discount. The store will initial the coupon and return page to you.

**Discount may not be valid on certain items
or with any other offers.**

Valid for one purchase per store.

Expires 12/31/98

❑ **SUSIE'S DEALS**   Redeemed:
10% Off Purchase

❑ **TARZANA BEAUTY SUPPLY**   Redeemed:
10% Off Purchase

❑ **THIRD MARKET, INC.**   Redeemed:
10% Off $50 Purchase

❑ **TILE, MARBLE & GRANITE WAREHOUSE** Redeemed:
10% Off Purchase

❑ **TILECLUB**   Redeemed:
10% Off Purchase

❑ **TOP TO TOP**   Redeemed:
Free Socks w/Purchase

❑ **TRADING HOMES INTERNATIONAL**   Redeemed:
$10 Off Membership

❑ **TUAZON'S BIKE SHOP**   Redeemed:
10% Off Purchase

❑ **TWICE THE STYLE**   Redeemed:
10% Off Purchase

❑ **U-FRAME-IT, INC.**   Redeemed:
25% Off Materials

BUYING RETAIL IS STUPID! DISCOUNT COUPONS

Bring book or page (photocopy not accepted) to any of the stores listed below for discount. The store will initial the coupon and return page to you.

**Discount may not be valid on certain items
or with any other offers.**

Valid for one purchase per store.

Expires 12/31/98

❑ **U.S. SEW-N-VAC**
10% Off Purchase

Redeemed:

❑ **UNITED DISCOUNT CENTER**
10% Off Purchase

Redeemed:

❑ **VACATION EXCHANGE CLUB**
10% Off Membership Fee

Redeemed:

❑ **VACUUM & SEWING CENTER**
20% Off Purchase

Redeemed:

❑ **VALLEY INDOOR SWAPMEET**
Free Admission

Redeemed:

❑ **VALLEY RADIATOR**
10% Off New Radiator

Redeemed:

❑ **VALLEY SPA WAREHOUSE**
Free Extra Jets w/Purchase

Redeemed:

❑ **VALLEY UPHOLSTERING**
2 Free Accent Pillows w/Reupholster of Sofa

Redeemed:

❑ **VAN NUYS ARMY & NAVY STORE**
10% Off Purchase

Redeemed:

Buying Retail Is Stupid! Discount Coupons

Bring book or page (photocopy not accepted) to any of the stores listed below for discount. The store will initial the coupon and return page to you.

Discount may not be valid on certain items or with any other offers.

Valid for one purchase per store.

Expires 12/31/98

❑ **WALLY'S DISCOUNT WORKSHOES AND BOOTS**
5% Off Purchase

Redeemed:

❑ **WAREHOUSE DISCOUNT CENTER**
5% Off Purchase

Redeemed:

❑ **WATCH CONNECTION**
10% Off Purchase

Redeemed:

❑ **WEARAGAINS FOR KIDS**
10% Off $10 Purchase

Redeemed:

❑ **WICKER MART**
10% Off Purchase

Redeemed:

❑ **WINE AND LIQUOR DEPOT**
5% Off Purchase

Redeemed:

❑ **WOODEN SHIPS WATERBEDS AND FUTONS**
15% Off Purchase

Redeemed:

❑ **WOODLAND CASUAL**
5% Off Purchase

Redeemed:

❑ **WOODLAND HILLS DISCOUNT GOLF**
10% Off Purchase

Redeemed:

BUYING RETAIL IS STUPID! DISCOUNT COUPONS

Bring book or page (photocopy not accepted) to any of the stores listed below for discount. The store will initial the coupon and return page to you.

**Discount may not be valid on certain items
or with any other offers.**

Valid for one purchase per store.

Expires 12/31/98

❏ **WOODLAND HILLS FIREPLACE SHOP**   Redeemed:
10% Off Purchase

❏ **WORK BOOT WAREHOUSE**   Redeemed:
$10 Off Boots

❏ **YE OLDE FASHIONED CANDY SHOPPE**   Redeemed:
10% Off Purchase

❏ **YOGANICS**   Redeemed:
$10 Off Registration Fee

ABOUT THE AUTHORS

Trisha King and **Deborah Newmark**, two of America's leading bargain shopping experts, are coauthors of *Buying Retail Is Stupid!—Southern California*, called "the shoppers bible" by *Orange Coast* magazine, a bestseller since 1989.

Trisha and Deborah write a highly popular bargain column, which has appeared weekly in the *Los Angeles Daily News* since 1990. Their column has developed a wide and loyal readership. They have been frequent guests on major TV and radio shows such as *Fox News, KABC Talk Radio, KNX/CBS, Live in L.A., The Vicki Lawrence Show, The Susan Powter Show, The Wave,* and many others. Trisha was the weekly *Fox News* bargain reporter for two years.

Known for their energetic, entrepreneurial, and engaging personalities, Trisha and Deborah are dedicated to providing consumers with information about where and how to buy more for less, stretch their paychecks, and get true value for every dollar spent. They are also the coauthors of *Buying Retail Is Stupid!—USA*, which allows a wider consumer public to profit from the work of these two bargain experts.